THE BEARDED LADY

THE BEARDED LADY

Going on the Commune Trip and Beyond

RICHARD ATCHESON

The John Day Company · New York

The John Day Company, 257 Park Avenue South, New York, N.Y. 10010
An Intext Publisher

Published on the same day in Canada by Longman Canada Limited.

Library of Congress Catalogue Card Number: 74-143413
Printed in the United States of America
Designed by The Etheredges

FOR JEAN

ACKNOWLEDGMENTS

My old friend and antagonist Alfie Bester, who is the most grace-ful and accomplished visionary novelist in the language, has many times told me that the writing of books is the hardest and loneliest work in the world. "Sure, Alfie," I would say, lusting prematurely after the laurels, little counting the cost. Now I know, and I can hear him saying, "A-Ha! A-Ha! A-Ha!," shame-lessly savoring this acknowledgment. So okay, Alfie, you were right, goddamit, and only you will know how it hurts me to admit it.

Still, I have to hold out on Alfie a little bit, because the kind-ness of friends in these trying times has been extraordinary. Wit-ness dear old Margaret Gale at the British Information Service in New York, for two years faithfully casting her third eye over the flood of periodicals pouring through her library in order to cadge every communal snippet fit to print, keeping me up to date. Or look what happened when I staggered back from the West with about a hundred miles of taped notes and conversations that had to be transcribed. Who sat up nights and weekends struggling with typewriters and tape recorders to get all that stuff down? Old friends Una Ellis and Fred Young, that's who; and when I shuffled my feet and mumbled something about paying them for that back-breaking work, who said, "Aw, don't worry about that," with a casual wave of permanently cramped fingers? Same parties, of course.

And in the struggle to produce the prose, which I now take to be not unlike the rigors of a patient passing the stone, who was it who most faithfully flogged me to the finish? My darling daughters, who else? Who never failed to break into my study every afternoon and say, "Okay, Daddy, how many chapters today?" With children like that, who needs an editor?

But let's have a kind word for the editor anyway. Al Tucker rarely bought my lunch during the course of writing this book. He did, however, frequently dine at my house on periodic visits he made to the country to reassure himself that the author was still safely handcuffed to the typewriter table. For that and other characteristics of his stewardship too complicated to mention here, he has my gratitude for his guidance, his counsel, and his good friendship. And a patience with my problems and a confidence in this book that will stand, in this household anyway, as a legend.

Of course, there are the many people whose names are disguised here—old personal friends and new communal friends alike—who during my wanderings *expected* to be counted on to provide free sacks and a freeload, a free ear, and free advice whenever I showed up. For their sustained interest and unfailing support, for their many assurances and demonstrations of love and caring, I thank them most sincerely. I cannot name them here but, as my Puerto Rican sergeant used to say to the troops in basic training, "They know who are they."

Finally and most profoundly, I thank my wife Jean. She absorbed blow-by-blow reports of my adventures by long distance, and never hung up. At home during the writing of this book, she endured all my moods, from high to very low, without ever throwing anything at me; in a spirit of professional detachment, she read page upon page of manuscript and made many useful suggestions, never praising when praise was not warranted; she struggled with me through the entire process, and still loves me. This book is about communes—about love and sharing and self-lessness—but nowhere, in any commune, did I find those qualities in any greater abundance than in her. At the end of *The Wizard of Oz,* Dorothy gets back to Kansas by saying over and over, "There's no place like home." Jean is my Kansas, because home really is where the heart is. And truly, there is no place like it.

CONTENTS

ITHAKA

When you set out for Ithaka, ask that your way be long, full of adventure, full of instruction. The Laistrygonians and the Cyclops, angry Poseidon—do not fear them: such as these you will never find as long as your thought is lofty, as long as a rare emotion touch your spirit and your body. The Laistrygonians and the Cyclops, angry Poseidon—you will not meet them unless you carry them in your soul, unless your soul raise them up before you.

Ask that your way be long. At many a summer dawn to enter—with what gratitude, what joy—ports seen for the first time; to stop at Phoenician trading centers, and to buy good merchandise, mother of pearl and coral, amber and ebony, and sensuous perfumes of every kind, sensuous perfumes as lavishly as you can; to visit many Egyptian cities, to gather stores of knowledge from the learned. Have Ithaka always in your mind. Your arrival there is what you are destined for. But do not in the least hurry the journey. Better that it last for years, so that when you reach the island you are old, rich with all you have gained on the way, not expecting Ithaka to give you wealth. Ithaka gave you the splendid journey. Without her you would not have set out. She hasn't anything else to give you.

And if you find her poor, Ithaka has not deceived you. So wise have you become, of such experience, that already you will have understood what these Ithakas mean.

CAVAFY

THE BEARDED LADY

INTRODUCTION

Two years ago, when I started to work on this book, I anticipated a pretty happy time. I liked almost everything that I had read about contemporary communes—the simplicity of the life, the sharing of work and family pleasures, the mutual respect and caring, the human-centeredness of the exercise. This alternative to the aridity of the nuclear family seemed a uniquely American answer to an American problem—a pioneer life, given over to the raising of crops and children, deep in an unspoiled natural wilderness—what could be more integral to the American myth, or a more natural extension of American history? Before the first explorer set foot on the new continent, it had provided the substance for Europe's Utopian dream. Okay, that didn't go especially well, what with massacres and power struggles and fresh battlegrounds for old armies, and the rape of virgin forests, and all that stuff. But the pastoral quality of early American life was a fact that (apart from all that other bloodier activity) did accommodate itself nicely to myth. And then there were two periods in the nineteenth century—just before, and well after, the Civil War—when communes flourished very widely and numerously in the young country, and names nobody can now explain without a reference book, like Brook Farm and the Oneida Colony, entered the vocabulary. The Shakers, remember them? Two periods when writers tramped around the northeastern part of the continent and unearthed hundreds of small communities, dedicated to all kinds of innovations and deviations, from sexual sharing to sexual prohibition, dedicated to practical communism of every stripe, fired by economic and/or religious fanaticism of a high order.

These communal manifestations of the nineteenth century had little or no shaping influence upon the forming society of America. They were individually separate, one from another as much as from the general populace; they never constituted a recognizable "movement" but were simply isolated phenomena, something for historians to take momentary notice of in their chronicles of the rise of an industrializing society. Nevertheless, as H. Rap Brown once remarked about violence, they were as American as apple pie. And now, at the end of the seventh decade of the twentieth century, they were back again, revived because of the need of certain people to escape from the nightmare, as they saw it, of the technological society.

It was not, of course, a dream devoid of twentieth-century embellishments. It was revived first among the young, and not because the young are students of history; they are not. But the young are users of marijuana—a very twentieth-century sort of catalyst—and on marijuana (herein mostly referred to as dope, a popular usage), many dreams are spun. The dream of communality was almost inevitable, because the use or possession of marijuana, already ubiquitous among the young, made criminals of all our children, and there is nothing like the implied conspiracy of mass criminality to make a community of willing conspirators. So the common enjoyment of dope in semi-secret, coupled with opposition to the Vietnam war in public, forged the first bonds of a counterculture, which took to community and communality readily as its form and its style. Us against the rest of them—it was inevitable. Freaks together; obviously in this society people who demanded peace, freedom, justice, and commonweal were freaks per se.

Communes did not long remain the exclusive province of the young. For that matter, a very few small communal efforts, mostly Christian and evangelical, had struggled unnoticed through generations before communal fever hit the kids. And the new communes might have formed in tranquility just as the old ones did, except for the perfervid interest of the media. After 1965, when anything to do with the counterculture became, automatically, news, writers and reporters and TV and movie cameramen hit the communal trail, and clearly they were ravished by what they found.

The pictures in magazines were particularly seductive: vision upon vision of the pastoral idyll, with ranks of hip peasants scratching in the fields, and a caption that usually read something like, "The peace of the soil envelops them." I am not very hip, and I have never aspired to be a peasant, but like many of my generation, and other people even older, I was obliged to impose that image of quiet and gentle people, working together to recapture the root human joys, upon the concrete sight before my day-to-day eyes: the ugly, abrasive, dehumanizing and soul-destroying existence of most conventional city dwellers in this last half of the twentieth century. The superimposition made a mockery of the technological society, wherein the individual seemed to have sold his human birthright for a mess of emotional pestilence and ecological pollution. Surely it was not in this spirit of mendacious desperation that we were meant to grind our lives away. Surely in the mind's eye of every man and woman in this society was some version of a spectral vision: he, gazing bitterly upon the gold watch for which he has spent all the juices of his youth and manhood; she, trudging endlessly from boutique to boutique in search of the nonexistent costume that will make her look loved and cherished, though neither in fact; they, staring stuporously toward their golden, twilight years, side by side and separate, bored with each other and dishonored by their children. The commune hinted of a viable alternative to that overdrawn—but face it, all too common—future.

I had no idea what my inquiries would mean for me personally. I knew that people of my own age were dropping out of what can only be called, by most people, the rat race, emboldened, by the reported successes of the young, to try a communal life for themselves. At the age of thirty-five, with a wife and children and an established if not precisely entrenched pattern of nuclear family life, the likelihood of radical change seemed remote. But I was willing to learn what I could from the communal movement, and to apply those parts of it that might promise to broaden our family's rapport with the larger family of man. I was feeling quite romantic about it, precisely as tutored by magazines and as was my usual inclination anyway. I cry in movies, I cherish happy endings, and I have been sentimental all my life about the paradise that men could build on this earth if they could only conspire to live and work together.

So I set off very cheerfully on a long trip through the communal counterculture of America. My route criss-crossed the country, leading me into the centers of great cities, far into the backwoods and wildernesses, and up a great many mountains. It also took me—sometimes to my great surprise and distress—off the external roadmap into uncharted areas of my own consciousness, where I negotiated for the first time a bewildering tangle of fears, prejudices, and longings. I did that part pretty badly, being unequipped with the ropes, grappling hooks, and climbing boots that are necessary for that kind of terrain. I feel as if I functioned more or less as a straight man to Satan's comedian, and wound up taking all the pratfalls and custard pies head on, all the comic plunges. And if I were inclined to become a cheap tragedian, I could probably do a guru number out of the experience; unfortunately for such aspirations, I have no stomach for it.

Nor, as it turns out, do I have much stomach for most of the communes I met on my way. In very few was I able to remain for more than a few hours at a time without having to get up and go, to overcome an almost claustrophobic unease. Other people's communes—or tribes, or families, or whatever they choose to call them—belong, of course, to other people, and I almost always felt this most sharply. Part of the problem was that I was a writer, labeled as such in advance of my coming, and liable everywhere to charges of parasitism, whoring, and worse. It was a fair charge, considering; but I sure did get tired of defending myself. Visiting communes is very much like visiting foreign countries where you aren't competent with the language or the customs, and a thousand pitfalls lurk just ahead of you at all times. The straight, middle-class society has worked out easements for this sort of thing, a set of social devices for putting the stranger at his ease while guaranteeing that nothing threatening will happen to either host or visitor. Most communards live more candidly than that, and have deliberately eliminated those devices. So there are no mutually safe rituals whereby strangers can co-exist, not touching, for long periods of time. Between stranger and communard no common ground exists, and the stranger better measure up, or he's out.

Perhaps this is as it should be. I am as sick of the phony relationships feigned in the straight society as is any communard, and I have spent too many evenings lying to friends and strangers who are lying to me, all of us as bored as we can be, to want to do any more of that. But if we were all to follow the communal pattern of honesty, we would have to reapportion our time drastically, and be real and spontaneous and present all the time, and I know a lot of people who wouldn't want to do that. The art of society is now, as it has always been, to simulate animation and interest where one feels none, and there are people so habituated to the art, and so skilled at it, that they have lost track of what they might *really* want of their day, or evening, or life. Clearly, communes would not be for them.

In fact, communes are not for very many people I can think of; it is too much trouble for most of us. Apart from the honesty, there is this sharing business, and we are so carefully trained up to possessions, individual ownership, jealousy, all that stuff, that sharing comes very hard. Even in the face of the moral force of one's friends, concepts such as *my* money, *my* tractor, *my* woman, die slowly if at all. We are all emotional money-lenders, and I do not look soon for the purification of the temple.

But I was talking of the difficulty of getting on in other people's communes. Apart from the liability of my profession and professional interest, there was the difficulty that every commune functions so vividly within itself as to screen out, automatically, anybody not attuned to the inner vitality of the group. Groups are groups—something of the same exclusivity doubtless operates in PTAs and Elks Lodges too. But keep in mind that a commune is not a PTA—it is, for all its members, *the* social and familial organization of their lives, and one to which they give not two nights a week and a semi-annual bazaar, but day and night attention, service, and participation, day after day after day. And say you were a participant in such an enterprise, and I came up on your front porch and said, in effect, Hi, there. I'd like to come in, take notes on your life, scrutinize all you do, eat at your table and drink your booze. By the way, how much do you make in business and how often do you screw your wife? You'd kick my ass off the porch, right? And nobody would blame you.

So, although I do not feel of any commune I know that it is home to me or the place where I'd like to spend the rest of my life, I am very grateful to the communards who did not kick my ass. In deference to them, I have very carefully changed all the names in this book, and scrambled many of the locations. They are having a hard enough time of it, making the arduous business of communality work, without more people like me hanging around. As a girl said to me on one occasion, "We are very fragile people, doing a very fragile thing. We are not a place for people *from* somewhere, who have two weeks to spend camping and day-tripping on our trip."

I must admit that it is not only for this reason that I've changed names and locations. In a few cases, I've done it because I'd like to live a little longer, and die a natural death unless I personally decide on some other option. And there are communal groups who, imbued with the conviction that life and death are illusory states, would think nothing of recycling me via kitchen knife, mallet, or pistol shot if they disliked what I have to say about them. In their view I would simply reenter the cosmic ecological system to my vast advantage and their own, which is the same. As Susan Atkins remarked in court on her recycling of

Sharon Tate, "I was coming from love . . . It was like, when I would stab, I was stabbing myself. The touching of a flower, looking at the sun, whatever I do and I know is right when I am doing it, feels good."

In general, I would have to agree with Miss Atkins and any communards who might take a notion to dispatch me and mine, that everything they do is right, and that I am They and They are Me and We are One Together. It's all part of a religious experience that zapped me absolutely in the course of the summer of 1970, and is examined in some detail in Part Two of this book. But unlike them, I do not conclude that because we are all One, I have any right to lop *them* off, as part of our Self. To do so would be to get in the way of their karma. Any other attitude would be worse than spiritual capitalism, which is engaged in by such disparate figures as the Pope, the Aga Khan, and Billy James Hargis. It would be spiritual fascism, of the sort alleged to be practiced by Charles Manson—and a variety of other communal gurus who are *not* in jail. Their trip seems to be that we are all God, but they are just a little bit more avatarish than the rest of us. Do my thing, they say to their followers— who, by the way, are numerous—and on alternate Thursday afternoons, I'll levitate for you a little bit. It's a shuck on the grossest level, and bravado, not bravery, enables me to say so; I'm still scared of them and I'm not giving any names.

Okay, this is the long way to say that life is not invariably simple, pastoral, or innocent in the communes; but please don't suppose that everybody who lives communally would as soon cut your heart out as look at you. On balance, there is infinitely more violence en route to a commune than inside it, and I'm still angry with those romantically besotted magazines for giving so absurdly pretty a picture of communal life to tens of thousands of innocent and vulnerable adolescents. They're all out there on the highways still, prone to God knows what abuse from the straight citizenry, dazzled with visions of love, freedom, abundant dope, and the goddamed enveloping peace of the soil. Hell, even if they do get to a commune and stay, that's only the beginning of their troubles. Communal life can be a very fine thing, but it takes hard work and dedication and gut-wrenching self-examination to do it right, and for many people is nothing less than a Last Judgment, an apocalyptic event after which no fire burns. Peace, bullshit; peace has nothing to do with it.

So what's it for? Self-realization, of course, a hard trip. And many times in the last two years I have wished that I was a simple, stay-at-home dude fully occupied with my family and the cloak and suit business, with nothing more pressing on my mind than how to get home to Queens on the subway without being mugged. And in writing about it these many months since the end of my trip, I have often thought of downing tools altogether and going into something I'm more suited for, like pumping gas or clerking in a store, or selling home burglar alarms door to door. Not that those guys are not vitally interested in the quality of their lives, but if my observations are correct they are not fretting about such large matters in every moment of their day. Whereas for the last couple of years I have been possessed by the subject—and worse, in the course of the research I had this extremely inconvenient religious experience which convinced me that I am God. I admit that I come a little late to apotheosis, but I had an extraordinarily detached catechism teacher and some highly uninspired preaching in my childhood, and never got the point. Until right around my thirty-sixth birthday, and who needs it then? Believe me, being God is no picnic. Like so many communards, I now have to be responsible for my life and can no longer blame everybody else for my failures and fuck-ups. Please don't tell me that the life of a customer's man at a broker-age firm, who has a wife and 3.2 children in Mamaroneck and goes sailing on Sundays in the polluted Sound, isn't a hell of a lot easier. No apotheosis for him, the lucky son-of-a-bitch.

Here's the thing—if you are going to take up the question of your own life, and examine such profoundly affecting areas as whether it has any meaning, and whether there are ways in which to live it so that you can respect the doing and the being, and sleep at night in something like the security of virtue; if you are going to live as a man rather than exist as an automaton, your conscience is going to plague the hell out of you until, stiff and rusty from disuse, you begin to act on the dictates of your inner voice. You don't need me to tell you how tough that is; you make waves and suddenly everybody you love and cherish is going up and down, up and down, you included, and there is hell to pay. Do you then, in this stormy sea, find home port in a commune? Not, I think, unless it is a commune of your own making. In short, other people's communes are not for you. If equity and community and real family are important to you, then don't go running down the world's highways in search of instant nirvana; start at home. Where *you* live.

All this summer, particularly when I was, with three other people, caught in a brief myth we called the hour and a half commune, we talked endlessly about who we were, and where home was, and said profoundly boring things like, Home is where the heart is, and found ourselves automatically touching our breasts when we said it. Well, that's banal but that's true; nothing starts except with you, right where you are. If anything does start, you can confidently count on wishing, many times over, that it never had. At the same time, you may be embarked on the most thrilling adventure of your life.

So as it turned out, I did not have "a pretty happy time" while trying to learn about contemporary communes. In some ways, I had an awful time, and if you have the patience and forbearance to read on, you will learn all about it. The book is divided into three parts—for my convenience as a writer and yours, I trust, as a reader. The first is a collage of short essays and vignettes which are intended to provide a sort of cumulative insight into other people's communes, from the point of view of a man who is rarely allowed, among communards, to function as anything more real than a journalist. These are, then, outside reports by an outsider, and are to be distrusted slightly. For all that you and the journalist know, those people were just putting him on.

The second part is intensely personal; it begins as a flirtation with the idea of communality, and ends in a certain amount of tasteless squealing, grunting, and fleeing in all directions, as if in alert evasion of a speeding freight train. But I won't apologize here or elsewhere for the personal squalor of our responses; the song says that freedom is when there's nothing left to lose, and for a little while that's where we got to. Many have been there before us and stayed longer.

The third part is the aftermath, when all my metaphors were communal ones, and I finally knew more or less what I was seeing and what I was talking about. There are bits and pieces here, excerpts of taped dialogues, another collage. About those dialogues, and scattered items in Parts One and Two signed S.B.: obviously, I wasn't talking to myself. For the last year of this project, I was joined by a friend named Steve Bornstein. He began as a research assistant on a three-week trial and ended as colleague, companion, alter ego, and occasionally, keeper. Steve is twenty-seven, single, a graduate of MIT, and a drop-out from the profitable world of management consulting. He was interested to work with me on the book because, as he once put it, "communes are craziness on many levels—social, sexual, economic—and I'm into craziness." Also, because, having dropped his flourishing business career in mid-hustle, he was considering becoming a writer, and it seemed to him that close collaboration with me might bring out the "lyrical" in his prose, me being, of course, supremely lyrical and giving it off by osmosis twenty-four hours a day. I wanted to work with him because he has a brilliance, a fineness and tidiness of mind, that lends itself effortlessly to the analytical, the encapsulating. I guess I hoped that some of his natural clarity would rub off on me.

In the spring of 1970, we rented Steve's brother's MGB for the life of the project (or the start of the fall term at Yale, whichever came sooner); Steve drove the car to the West Coast, visiting a few communes en route, while I did research for various magazine pieces in the hinterlands. We met in San Francisco, where the pivotal events of Part Two took place to our equal astonishment, fear, and excitement.

Now that the collaboration is over, I do not know that Steve is any more lyrical than he used to be, or that I am any clearer in my thinking. Probably not. But the book is beneficiary of the mix, if we individually are not, and where there is precision and clear thinking on these pages, the swift, analytical mind of Steve Bornstein must be credited. If we did not exchange professional skills and virtues in any permanent way, that is not to say that nothing at all rubbed off. In the intensity of the collaboration, we found ourselves very eventful people together for an extended period of time and developed a candid rapport that was unprecedented in the experience of either of us. Together we evolved what was for us a new definition of friendship; if nothing else at all had come from the efforts of the last year, that alone would be more than enough.

Some people who read parts of the manuscript were cross with me because I don't try harder to sell my point of view. But that's precisely the point. The most important thing I learned on my communal trip was for crissake to leave other people's heads alone, to the extent I'm able. We are all good people just as we are, and it would be fine if we would all finally cop to that and stop fiddling with each other's destinies. This infernal, devilish drive we all have to put the other guy straight is part of the infection that kills villagers in Indochina and stabs socialites, movie stars, and retired grocers in Los Angeles. We would all do better to keep our moral imperatives to ourselves. As they say in the communes with annoying frequency, Do Your Thing. And that does not mean somebody else's Thing. You want to sit in a room by yourself for the rest of your life? Do it. You want to go out and get in trouble like me? Do that. The commune is not a universal panacea, and it is not a Soviet plot, and it is not a happy, pastoral trip. For many, it is meaningless, however long they sit in one, hugging everybody up. For some, it may be a fiery crucible; for others, a crematorium.

All the options are yours.

PROLOGUE: THE AUTHOR WEARS A BEARD

For some years I was the travel editor of *Holiday* magazine, a designation likened, by some of my waggish friends, to the condition of being dog editor of *Dog World*. But never mind semantics—the title and the job meant that I spent a lot of my time traveling very widely in the world, fairly often right around the globe. It was a job that merged beautifully with my inclination to see everything I could, at whatever disadvantage or inconvenience to myself, and I have been in some silly crises in some very silly places where—it usually doesn't occur to me until the instant of danger—I have no serious business to be. For example, I have been up the Zambesi without a paddle; I have flapped through the sky in a disabled helicopter over the Great Barrier Reef; I have been menaced by slitty-eyed pimps in the back alleys (almost indistinguishable from the avenues) of Tijuana. In these unlikely fixes (I mean, do I *really* want to die by hurtling over Victoria Falls in a canoe?) I have been pretty scared. But I have never been as scared in distant places as I was while traveling in my own country, in the summer of 1970, while wearing long hair and a beard. Nor did I ever feel, in any exotic place, as alienated as I did at home.

Let's establish quite quickly that I am thirty-six years old, a product of parochial schools, private schools, and Princeton University, a veteran of corporations and their politics, nine years a husband and three times a father. I should also underline that I am a very clean man ("cleaner than an Englishman," says my wife, who is English) and, while indisputably hairy, widely known to shampoo both hair and beard daily, and scrub the entire corpus in the shower. I go on at length about these credentials of cleanliness because the people of the hip world are constantly charged with being dirty, with having no fondness for the washcloth. Failure to wash constantly, indeed frantically, seems to have become the ultimate American crime. I do not share this view; sometimes I wish I *could* be a little less fastidious, and maybe I'll get there someday; meanwhile, I have to argue that most of the hip people I know are at least as hung up on scrubbing as I am—some even more so. Even the residents of a commune called Hesperus, who live in adobe huts atop a dusty mesa near Taos, daily make a long and hard trek to water, and daily wash.

I am reminded of the adventure of a New York colleague of mine, a distinguished novelist in his fifties who wears an impeccable gray-black beard and comports himself after the manner of Monty Wooley. This paragon of American letters came out the door of his Manhattan brownstone one morning to find a woman and a dog on his doorstep. The woman was encouraging the dog, a poodle, to enjoy a bowel movement at the author's very portal. "Madam," said my friend (he says that sort of thing). "Madam," said he, "may I ask you to find some other place for your dog's toilet?" The woman struck back like a Manhattanite. Taking in, in a instant, the fact of his beard, she shrieked: "You filthy thing! Why don't you take a bath?"

This sort of attack is mounted most frequently by that breed of hardy traveler that I have come to call The Blue-haired Ladies. While traveling in line of duty for *Holiday*, I have come to know this lot very well. They seem always to be a group of twenty-nine retired spinster schoolteachers from Sandusky, Ohio, and they go everywhere with me. I have always admired them for their energy but never for their manners; however, I was never precisely their victim until early this summer, when it was my misfortune to tour with them extensively in Alaska.

Never have I been cold-shouldered by so many so often, and at first I was truly surprised. Nothing about me had changed except that my hair was longer and my beard was hanging out, and I was not going around hyperconscious of my hair. In fact, I sort of forgot about it—but The Blue-haired Ladies constantly reminded me that I was being judged on my hair alone. Usually, when you climb onto a tour bus in the morning to join people you've been touring with for days, there's a kind of ease, a light banter, a casual familiarity. I was utterly excluded from this. I'd come aboard in the mornings and say good morning to folks and be rewarded with a stony and general silence, and a great deal of looking away out windows. I used to be pretty good with old ladies, or so I had thought—a kid who grows up in the South just automatically learns how to get on with them—but not any more. At first it hurt my feelings that they refused to respond to my most innocent overtures, or were rude to me. As for example on the day I was seated well away from the mass, smoking a ciga-rette. All the windows were open and a breeze was blowing; others older and less hairy than I were also smoking. But a woman sitting three seats away from me, an older woman with a pinched face, took the occasion to turn right around in her seat and say to me, "Put that thing out!" in the most arrogant fashion, waving the back of her hand at me. That made me mad; I mean, who the hell was she to speak to me like that? My first inclination was to move up to the seat directly behind her and blow smoke over her shoulder, or perhaps to "push the Princeton button," as my friends say I can do in tight situations, and offer elevated verbal insolence. But then I noticed that she was shift-ing in her seat a lot, and squirming around with her bottom, and it hit me suddenly that she probably was suffering from a bad case of piles. This realization cheered me up at once, and relaxed me. I didn't have to take personal revenge on the old harpie; God (as my grandmother had always assured me He would) was punishing her.

I am sure that God will ultimately punish all of them for their meannesses; He's probably doing it all along. And I stopped feeling any great rancor. Once, at a gold mine outside Nome, all the old biddies were gathered around an antique organ, and one of them was playing singable old tunes like "Let Me Call You Sweetheart," and they were all singing away and having a sweet time. I was feeling benevolent and wistful (I used to sing a lot when I was young, and I love to harmonize, however horribly), and enjoying the scene, and looking out on a crisp Alaskan morning, with a silvery stream gurgling by just below the house. And then a young girl, the only young person in the crowd, worked her way out of the warbling throng of oldies and came over to me and said, raising her eyebrows: "Can you imagine having to get your kicks that way?"

We walked out of the house into the morning, and she told me that she was a sophomore at the University of Oklahoma, that she had come on a month-long tour with her widowed mother, that she had been trapped for three weeks with these old folks, and that she was going out of her mind. Later, on the bus, she took bold action; leaving her seat with her mother, she strode to the back of the bus and sat beside me. "I hope you don't mind," she said, "but I have just *got* to talk to somebody young. You're my fountain of youth this morning." I said I didn't mind, but I noticed that everybody else on the bus most certainly did, looking daggers at us both as we jounced along. At the next stop I attempted to chat politely with the girl's mother, remarking that I was also from Oklahoma. The mother refused to address me; she simply ordered her daughter to Go Stand Over There Out of The Sun.

Well, I let it be. If she wanted to be rude, she was welcome. Anyway, I was beginning to realize that what set me apart from The Blue-haired Ladies was beginning to make me acceptable to the Emotional Underground. And there is such an underground—sparse in Alaska, perhaps, where everybody is pretty damned independent anyway and where judgments of persons are never made on appearance, and an underground scarcely needs to exist, but rampant everywhere else. It's a kind of Youth-Peace-Marijuana Underground, though all members do not necessarily embrace all three categories, and copious hair is not necessarily its giveaway. As I traveled, I got peace signs from all sorts of unlikely people, suggesting that—though they didn't look like it—they were in on My Conspiracy.

The peace sign is the basic signal of this underground, usually followed by a grin if nobody is watching. It is also flashed by frankly hairy people and then the grin is not cautious—it suggests the emotional link among the members of an oppressed minority, and I got to be glad to be a member of it. The oppression is not simply a matter of being harassed and insulted in restaurants and other public places, made to wait endlessly for service, in some cases to be refused service or to be thrown out. There is something very sick happening in the minds of the straight majority; there is some kind of ugly sexual envy animating their hatred. Grow a little hair and you'll see what I mean.

For example, not long after the Oklahoma coed had sat with me on the bus, one of the male companions of the Blue-haired Ladies, presumably a blue-haired lady himself in spirit (and I lump all their males together with them), one of these elderly gents with a chicken-neck sidled up to me and addressed me for the first time. "Well," says he, "I see you're making time with the little blond girlie. Think you're gonna score?"

Now I may be a little slow, or a little deficient in lust or something, but "scoring" with that little nineteen-year-old girl had really not been in my mind. This may sound corny, but she reminded me of my sister, who like me is also from Oklahoma. She looked rather like my sister, and she sounded like her. And *that* had been on my mind. But here's this old buzzard breathing a little too hard and working up some masturbatory, raunchy scene in his elderly brains, and projecting it onto me. "You can probably make her," he went on to my astonishment. "Listen, you can really put it to her. She's a hot one, I've been watching . . ." It was my turn to walk away without answering.

My travels with a beard began to remind me of a book published some years ago called *Black Like Me*. A Louisiana journalist dyed his skin black and hitchhiked through the South, accepting rides from white men, and wrote about the obsessive sexuality of their remarks to him, their vulgarity and obscenity with respect to sex generally and particularly with respect to the supposed hyper-lubricity of black men. I began to imagine that I was living a book that might be called *Hairy Like Me*. Men of my own age, dressed as I am perfectly capable of dressing, in Brooks Brothers suits, with heavy brogans, attaché cases and short hair, would approach me in bus stations or rail terminals or hotel lobbies, pick up conversations with me, and start almost at once to inquire into my sexual habits: did I get much, did I give it to them in the mouth, how many inches did I have. These were not homosexual approaches, at least not so far as I could tell, because I didn't usually hang around to hear the whole number. These guys just seemed to assume that because I was hairy I was some kind of incredible stud, getting laid constantly, and they wanted a little vicarious buzz. It made me feel pretty sorry for whatever their sexual lives must be, but it also helped me to understand at least one very important source of the hatred and violence that are visited constantly upon the long-haired young. They are presumed to be sexually free, and they have to be hated for that.

Unlike the Blue-haired Ladies (and their consorts of whatever age), younger women did not usually project hatred toward me. They are, like longhairs, the victims of the sort of men who whispered to me in waiting rooms; they are the women of those men, I take it. When traveling alone, they too often fell into conversation with me. One charming and lovely woman of my own age, who sat next to me on a plane, told me that she had been watching me in the airport for forty-five minutes, spying on me at the magazine counter to see what I would buy, studying my clothes and my manner, trying to figure out how old I was, what I did for a living. Another woman, equally charming, got into terrible trouble in a train on my account. She had determined that I was an aging hippie and had provoked a conversation; we had chatted idly about things that were on her mind— racial unrest in the country, welfare reform, the education of her children, the war and pacifism, and her admiration for conscientious objectors. "I feel the way they do," she said. "I'm just a housewife with four little kids, and nobody is ever going to ask me my opinion; in fact, my friends wouldn't *like* my

opinion. But I feel that I just don't want to kill anybody. I don't
want to kill people, I want to understand them."

Suddenly the portly man sitting in front of us got up and
loomed over the lady. "And what about The Communist?" he
boomed at her. "What will he be doing while you are 'understanding' him? The Communist is not interested in 'understanding' you. The Communist only wants to kill you and take your
wealth—and he will do so, if you do not kill him *first*."

"I'm sorry," said the lady. "I just don't want to kill anybody."

The man was very angry. "I don't care *what* you want. You
must want to be dead. The Communist will kill us all; he only
wants what we have. This is the Greatest Country on Earth, and
the Richest. If we did not kill The Communist, he would take
all that we have."

This guy was beginning to sound as if he were doing a radio
show for H. L. Hunt; his stentorian tones traveled up and down
the railway carriage, attracting the interest of others. His wife,
and some children I took to be his grandchildren, had turned to
witness his performance. I knew there was no use in talking to
him, so sat silent. But the poor housewife sitting next to me
still thought she was in a conversation, albeit a conversation she
had not solicited.

"Sir," she said, "I simply said that I don't want to kill, and I
won't kill. I think there have to be better ways to settle arguments than taking other people's lives."

The man was outraged. "This kind of talk is national suicide,"
he thundered at her. "We must kill to live. This has always
been so, and it is still so. The Communist is an animal and we
must hunt him down and kill him."

This militant address went on and on, the poor lady protesting weakly time after time. After forty-five minutes or so, the fat
man shouted this line to us—and I say "us" because, although I
kept staring out the window, I knew it was hairy Me that the
fat man was trying to reach. "Let me tell you something," he
said, as if he had not already told us plenty. "The men who bear
arms are all that stands between you and your certain death. Let
me tell you: you better get down on your knees every night and
YOU THANK GOD for the men who bear arms."

At that moment I created a diversion by shouting some indorsement of the beautiful mountain pass we were going through; everybody turned to look out at the scenery, and after a while the fat man went away and sat down. Then the lady and I sat in silence for a long time, before daring to continue our conversation; even when we dared, we spoke in whispers.

"I'm sorry I got you into that," the lady said. "With my friends I've just learned to keep my mouth shut and I don't get into trouble. But I've never known how to get out of things like that when strangers intrude."

At that time I thought I did, and that to turn conversations from politics to scenery or music or anything else was an effective technique. But that was before Taos, where the conflict between longhairs and chicanos (Mexican-Americans, they used to be called) is particularly sharp. I was traveling with Steve Bornstein at the time; he wore as great a sufficiency of hair and beard as I did, and in tandem I suppose we were compounding the outrage. Our early ignorance of the extent of local tension served us well, because having arrived in the Taos plaza at dinnertime, tired from a long drive, we walked blithely into the best restaurant in town. There was initially a certain sullenness from the staff, but my order of a martini must have calmed the natives just as our casual entrance must have astonished them; it was a good restaurant, and we ate there often during our stay. But when we told local longhairs that we often ate there, they were stunned to know we had been admitted at all.

More difficult problems arose when we went anywhere frequented by chicanos. In the lunchrooms and greasy spoons of the town the food was deliberately slung at us, if we got it at all. And in the bar of the hotel on the plaza, which appears to be a local chicano watering place, we found it impossible to drink in peace. There are a few sound reasons for this, which I'll discuss in a later chapter. But the reasons had nothing to do with us personally, and we were at first slow in understanding that.

As I mentioned earlier, we were not walking around in constant awareness of How We Looked. We just walked into that bar one night to hear the rock band (not bad) and have a couple of drinks. Service was not refused, but we were joined almost at once by a chicano who sat down (with a smile but without an invitation) and came on to us like one of those banditos from a sequence on *The Rifleman*. "Eh, gringitos, where you from, eh?"

There was no talking to this fellow at all. At one point he asked why we came to Taos, and I remarked that the country was very beautiful. "You don't know *nothing* about this country, goddamit," he replied, and when I amiably agreed, he found fault with the way Steve was tapping his swizzle stick in time with the music. "You don't do that at *my* table, bastid," he said to Steve. Steve stopped tapping, but reminded him that it wasn't his table, it was ours. The chicano said we didn't know where we was at, did we, and gestured significantly at the bar, crowded with his buddies. We said we knew very well that we were drinking in a bar in Taos, New Mexico, USA, and had every right to do so. But he said we didn't. He went into a long thing about how he'd *fought* for this country, he'd worn the *uniform* of this country, he was a better American than we were. And I found myself involved in an absurd argument about which of us had been the better *soldier,* for God's sake. In the first place I put no store whatsoever by my army service, but I was bugged that he took it for granted that I had not served in the army, and refused to believe that I had. And there I was practically quoting General Orders at him to prove something I don't care about in the least. So finally we just split and went home. We would have ended in a bar brawl if we hadn't, and I think I would have started it. And all we'd gone in there for was to hear the music.

It didn't seem to matter much where we went in the country; we were never more than one or two words away from a fight. In Arizona it was: *"You can't come in here like that!"* In a restaurant outside Indianapolis the waitresses plastered themselves against the walls and shrieked: *"We're closed! We're closed!"* It was doubly amazing because the two of us together scarcely weigh two hundred pounds, we're just skinny little guys and not in the least dangerous. But we spent the whole summer obviously scaring people to death—and I must admit that it became sort of fun, some of the time. After all, if you started life with empathy for those Charles Atlas ads about bullies kicking sand in your face, and if you were always the smart kid in the class instead of a classy athlete, it's delightfully refreshing to find yourself frightening the multitudes. But it can cause you to miss a few meals.

There was only one time when I really thought I was going to be missing a few teeth too. We were passing through Gallup, New Mexico, one night and stopped at a very big motel so that Steve could make a phone call. We'd been driving all day and I repaired to the bar at once, because all I had in my head at the time was the vision of a nice, icy, dry martini on the rocks. The bar was a big room, full of cowboys, or anyway guys dressed as cowboys; there was a band playing western music, and these cowboys were dancing up a storm with girls and women who tended to wear flouncy skirts, frilly blouses, and plastic-rimmed glasses shaped like bat's wings. It was a jolly scene, everybody drinking beer and talking loud and all this wonderful, 1950's style dancing going on, with the girls passing under the armpits of the cowboys, and doing all those jitterbug steps I remember from the eighth grade. It really took me back.

Meanwhile, I was minding my business at the bar, and it was a fine business: just the ice cold martini I had wanted; delicious. I really didn't think anybody had paid me the least mind until a cowboy came up and started talking to the two cowboys on the other side of me, who had been leaning together in close conversation all the while that I had been standing there. So this cowboy came up and interrupted them, and I heard him say, "Are you boys gonna *stand* for this?" And then they all three craned their necks around and stared at me, and then turned back into a huddle, and I stood there sipping on my good martini and pretending not to notice. But my ears went out like trumpets, just in case I'd be able to hear the first fist coming, and maybe dodge out of the way, and I heard some of their conversation.

The one fellow, the troublemaker, said it was a disgrace to the place for the likes of me to be in there, and he guessed the other two would just about drink with Anybody. The oldest one of them said hell, it wasn't any of his business who drank in the bar. "Hell," says he, "he's *drinkin'*, ain't he? Hell, I'll *drink* with any man." Well, the trouble-making cowboy was very upset by this. He said it was the Principle of the thing, and it went against all they stood for, and he argued every which way but he didn't budge the older cowboy or his friend. And finally he said he never thought he'd see the day when a thing like this would happen, and he said again and again, "You mean you're going to *stand* for this, Verne?" And Verne finally said, a little testily, that Hell, Yes, he was going to stand for it, he *had* to stand for it, it was a free country, wasn't it? And that angry cowboy just said, "Sheee-*it!*" and took himself off into the throng again, and I later saw him dancing with a fat girl, as calm as you please. And maybe all of this means that the Old West is truly dead, and a lynching would have been preferable, and what have we come to. But if we've come to the point where a cowboy can say it's a free country, and make it stick in a crowd of drunks, then I say we've come a fur piece, and Yippee.

In my home town it was a different story. I never was afraid of getting beat up in Tulsa. I did grow up there, and still feel I know the town. But Steve was quite prepared to believe he could get beat up there, and I don't blame him. We were there to see my mother, who is the only member of the family still living there, and it happened that my sister and her husband, who live in California and were on vacation, were in Tulsa at the time. That made for a nice family reunion, which was fine with those of us who were kin to each other, but it was hard enough on my sister's poor husband, who after all is only an in-law, and not all that interested in what Aunt Maggie said to Granddaddy that day in 1913 when Lila Hadley, that was Uncle Arthur's friend from Conroe, came to Houston to see Cousin Caddy and ride a streetcar. So you can imagine how interested Steve Bornstein from Boston, Massachusetts, was in all of this. And I whispered to him at a point, "Steve, if you want to get out of here, you take the car and we'll go in my sister's car." But he said no, he would stick through dinner, but maybe later he'd take off and see a movie.

So the day wore on and then we decided to go to dinner at a Chinese restaurant in Brookside, which is a part of town that was there even when I was a kid, but in those days it was the New Part. And in my time there certainly was no such thing as a Chinese restaurant in all of Tulsa, Oklahoma, and I was intrigued to know that there was one now. And that's more or less why we decided to go there, because in case you don't know it Tulsa is probably not the most sophisticated or cosmopolitan city in the United States.

Now I'm not telling this story in order to report that that Chinese restaurant is possibly the only one in the world that doesn't have chopsticks and has only one kind of tea—iced. I'm telling it because of the strange events that followed our trip over to Brookside in two cars so that Steve could take off later and see a movie. I should tell you that my sister is a very pretty girl who has blond hair that is *not* all the way down to her backside, but fashionably long, and that she was that night wearing a very atttractive mini-skirt. Her husband, who is by any standard a good-looking, tall, blond fellow, wears his hair in a sort of WASP-Afro corona, and he also has a handsome blond zapata moustache. Then there were Steve and me, and I concede that we looked a bit like the Smith Brothers, but Very Clean. And finally there was my mother, who looks like . . . well, she looks like a mother.

So we walked in the door of this Chinese restaurant and honest to God, all hell broke loose. There were four couples at the table nearest the door, and I suppose they were drunk (though I doubt they were drinking, because you can't drink in a restaurant in Tulsa unless you bring your booze in a paper sack and stick it under the table), and all those grown-up people erupted with catcalls and hollering and carrying-on as if the circus had come to town, and we were the elephants and they were the kids. My poor old mother was purely mortified, and I was embarrassed for her, and for all of us too, and embarrassed in front of Steve that he should see how the town was, and even embarrassed for the goddam yokels that were carrying on. It just seemed terribly pathetic and hopeless of them; and I thought, my lord, I grew up in this town, and I learned all my first lessons here, and I never remember anybody telling me that you poke fun at other people in any circumstance, nor most particularly if they are different from you. And I wondered what those folks are teaching their children, if they behave like that in a public place.

We sat down at our table, as nice as you please. We put our napkins in our laps and made our dinner order as politely as you please, despite the inconvenience of no chopsticks and iced tea only. And we ate as well as we could, and it wasn't bad. The front table kept on making remarks but my mother and the rest of us, frozen into dignity, pretended not to hear. And when dinner was over, Steve took our car and left, and I didn't see him until much later that night, when my sister and brother-in-law drove me back to our motel. "Well," says I, on coming in, "what movie did you see, Steve?" And he said, "Dick, I didn't go to the movies. I just came straight back here. I was sort of afraid to go anywhere else in this town."

All these events led us to the conclusion that there are only three cities in the country, and if you haven't already guessed I'll tell you that they are San Francisco, Los Angeles, and New York. For people who hear the beat of their own drums, there is only wilderness and danger in between the coasts, and if your hair is long you better look out. Of course, you'd be somewhat better off if you don't drink; sometimes I think liquor is half the trouble. Because God knows there's no more sophisticated city than New York, and yet the strangest thing happened in the bar of Penn Station, just after I returned from my long travels. My wife and I had missed the six P.M. train to Princeton and had to wait an hour for the next one, so we went into the Iron Horse to have a drink. We were having it, very quietly and respectably, talking of family matters, the children and dogs and cats, such dowdy and unremarkable things. And this businessman walks in and surveys the scene, and that presumably included me. I don't understand his behavior and perhaps I never shall, but I know that he walked up behind us at the bar, and he breathed very heavily over our shoulders and stared at us both with great anger and hostility, and there came over me the now-familiar anticipation that this guy was about to punch up on me. I don't know why he didn't; I only know that he stared at us, practically breathing fire from his nostrils, for about thirty seconds, looking to my wife, then to me, then back again to her. And then he whirled and stalked angrily out of the bar.

This was a novel experience for my wife. "Darling," she said with amazement, "I thought that man was going to hit you." I said that I had been sure of it. "What an extraordinary thing," she said, then paused, then went on, "Well, if he had, he'd have had *me* to contend with." And she brandished her hefty pocket-book above the bar in what will always be for me a darling gesture.

Poor old wife, called on in her middle years to protect her shaggy husband with her purse. I don't know what that guy thought he was accomplishing, but it appears that he initiated the radicalization of one more housewife. I suppose he was try-ing to indicate that he felt outraged at the sight of a respectable woman speaking to a filthy hippie like me in a public place. I don't know. But above all I wonder why he felt he had to make it any of his business.

So I say to anybody who thinks of growing long hair or a beard, or who wears contemporary clothing—okay, do as you please, but remember to stay in the three cities, and stay out of barrooms, or expect to be hassled constantly for no reason what-soever. That's the way it is in this country, these days.

PART ONE: JUST LOOKING AROUND

What lies before you in this first section is a grab-bag of communes, a whole Heinz-57 varieties of efforts people are making these days to Get It Together. There is no general rule; curiously, the passion for community is highly individual, and you will find here completely disparate sorts of efforts, side by side. These people have, perhaps, just two things in common: a horror of nuclear marriage, and the sense of isolation it brings; and wellsprings of enormous energy, which serve them to buck the tide, wherever they are, and to struggle endlessly to build the kinds of lives for themselves that they have long dreamed of. Some groups have had a relatively easy time of it; others have known little but hard work and paranoia since the start. But all in all they're a tough lot of people, and not so much iconoclastic as heart-breakingly visionary. Some picture of an attainable utopia dances in every pair of eyes; they are full of hope. And even if you think some of them are wrong-headed, or crazy, or immoral, or dangerous, you must also muster up some admiration for the bold and courageous way in which they have seized upon their own lives, to make of them what they want.

The form of the telling is a little odd, I'll concede. I made my first communal visits more or less coincidentally with work I was doing for Holiday, and occasionally you'll catch me running off at the mouth about a group or a place, exactly as if I were evoking Mozambique or Java or something of the sort. For the scenic excesses of the Mendocino item, I especially beg pardon; the problem is that I think that whole area is one of the loveliest in the world, and I justify dwelling on it by telling myself that descriptions of natural settings have every right to be in this book. If I fail to wax quite so eloquent about such settings as Boston or Cleveland, it is because there is, from the scenic point of view, very little poetry to evoke, and the worst has already been said elsewhere.

Almost every kind of contemporary commune is represented here, at length or briefly, with the exception of the ashram or other cult forms, such as the Hari Krishna group, and the radical political communes such as are operated by the Weatherpeople. I've made a little list of some of the types represented here: affluent; rural; acid consciousness; student; drop-out; urban professional; creative; gay; independent global; therapeutic; apocalyptic; naked, free love; academic; rural religious; corporate; satanic. If the list alone does not boggle the mind, please read on; you can decide for yourselves which are which.

One brief comment about style: my stuff flows on with a certain *sameness which may be lulling; prepare yourself for an abrupt change of mood near the end, when Steve takes over for a few concluding numbers. He hit several communes on his own, on his long drive west, and though he aspired to a lyrical style, the consciousness of a drop-out management consultant came to the fore when the chips were down. So you will find some quite terse management-consultant-type evaluations here, which I think provide a refreshing break from lyricism.*

NEW YORK IS FINISHED

Just a few years ago a group of very talented magazine people—
editors, art directors, illustrators—downed tools, sold all that they
had, boarded an ocean liner, and set sail for the south of France.
For those of us who did not know them very well, or not at all
except by reputation, this mass defection from our tormented
business was quite a shock. Not that their various magazines and
ours would not stumble on for a few years more without them; that
was not the point. It was the renunciation implicit in their group
action, a renunciation not only of New York publishing, but of
New York, indeed of the country itself, that was breathtaking.
That, and the sheer weight of their numbers—a total of seventeen
people, including wives, constant companions, children, heirs,
and assigns. Lock. Stock. And Barrel.

Their destination was an obscure village in the Var, so obscure that it does not appear on maps, where Angus Black (not his name), the acknowledged leader of this group, had bought a tumble-down vineyard and its buildings. It was Angus who had had the vision and the persuasiveness to turn everybody else on, the money to finance the entire venture, and the courage to renounce his editorship with a powerful but, admittedly, internally-riven magazine. It was Angus who was most sorely disenchanted—his despair had fed the disenchantment of all the others. They were not going to build a commune in France; they refused to call it that. They were just going to live a simple life with the soil, and live it together. That was all.

About a year after their departure, I found myself in Europe, en route ultimately to the south of France, and I wrote Angus to ask if I could come to see them. When I got to Berlin I found a letter of welcome and a hand-drawn map awaiting me; as soon as I could I flew to Nice, where I rented a car and, after an hour or so of fully justifiable paranoia on Route Nationale Number Seven, turned north into the mountains. Angus's little village is not so terribly far from the Côte d'Azur, as the crow flies, but back roads in the French countryside adhere more to the rugged terrain than to the inclinations of crows. They also accommodate to the locations of the tiniest villages, no matter how inconveniently these villages were established several centuries ago. So I was on the narrow, twisting roads for several hours, constantly losing my way and having to retrace my course, never absolutely certain what town or village I was in, trying to accept directions from café loungers in a language of which I understand scarcely one word.

Nevertheless, I finally found my destination—just a cluster of ancient stone buildings by a rushing stream, with fat old trees in a row, hanging their branches out over the water and the narrow village street. I found at the inn that Angus had reserved a room for me, as promised. "I won't ask you to stay here with us," he had written. "I know well the devotion of New Yorkers to their comforts, and we haven't any. You'll be happier at the inn." I'd been a little bit put off by Angus's assumption that I was a pure sybarite who couldn't take a night of country privations—but the inn was charming, small and dim and cool, and I was satisfied. At one side was an open courtyard with tables on gravel under tall fruit trees; the crowded, stone-floored dining room was also the lobby; my cavernous room was on the first floor front, with louvered windows to the floor, tiny, wrought-iron balconies and a gigantic bedstead. The bath was down the hall.

I scrubbed up, took the innkeeper's advice about how to find *les Américains,* and drove up a steep road into the country again. After many steep turns on muddy lanes, I came at last to the place marked X on my map. This had to be the place; yet there was nothing much to see. A gate; several acres of scrubby vineyard; far across the fields, a mound of stones under a nest of willows. The countryside was vivid under the hot, firm press of the midafternoon sun; the surrounding hills, uncultivated and wild, were intensely green with thick summer foliage. The air was dense and faintly sweet with the scent of turned earth, and I heard the low, heavy buzz of insects at large in the clumps of weeds along the road. Pleased but slightly disbelieving that a clutch of New Yorkers could be camping here, I drove slowly through the gate and across the fields, coming up to the mound of stones, which turned out to be two very ancient farm buildings of weathered stone, each of them partially in ruins. Several naked blond children were playing in the dirt yard as I pulled up beside a muddy Land Rover. Angus's wife Lucy emerged from the more residential-looking of the buildings, wearing a shirt and jeans and carrying an immense pot, just as Angus materialized nearby, straightening up, stripped to the waist and sweating, from the far side of a partially-assembled stone wall. I had arrived.

After greetings all around, and accounts of the journey, Angus took a squint at the sun, proclaimed day's work at an end, and suggested that we all go for a bath in the river, where he had rented a few yards of the bank for hygienic purposes. "We don't have any water," he explained. "Not even a well; the water is trucked in and we'd rather use it for cooking than washing. So we wash in the river." Lucy declined to come—she had to get dinner—but Angus and the children and I piled into the Land Rover and set off for the bathing place.

The river was not visible from the road at Angus's bathing

place; all we could see was an open field, slanting downhill, and an endless row of thick trees at the bottom. It turned out that the river was hiding completely in shelter of the trees, so that when we came to the riverbank, we were entirely obscured from public view. It was a good, cold stream dashing over broad rocks, and there was a nice pool at that point too, splashed with peeping sunlight, and we and the children spent the rest of the afternoon washing and swimming there. As we lay in the grass, drying off, I finally asked Angus where everybody else was. "Left," he said. "All gone. All except the Waggoners; they're vacationing in Italy right now, but I'm not sure they're coming back. There's just us."

Why? What happened? What went wrong?

"Nothing went wrong," Angus said, annoyed with my question. "Everything was open, there was no contract that people had to stay. We tried it, that's all. Look, it's a pretty primitive life, you know. No water, no electricity, those tumbled-down houses which I happen to love. Some of them said I was a fascist in the end. Maybe so—but at first we hung around smoking dope and talking about the work we were going to do on the place, get the vineyard going again. But then the dope ran out. So then we hung around drinking wine and talking about all the work we were going to do. And finally I said, 'Look, talk is cheap but we're just sitting on our asses. Let's get to work.' And that started right away to break things up. It's okay with me; I still know what I want to do. I want to work with my hands, you know? I want to sweat. I want to be in touch with nature, with the soil. And I'm doing that. And if it has to be just us, that's fine with me.

"Lucy loves this life. The kids love this life. They're all speaking pretty good French now; we're in the village a lot. Of course they all think I'm crazy, the crazy American. But I can make this place work again, I know it. And even if I can't, I like to try. The problems we've got here are all real. Do you understand what I mean?"

I did.

That night Lucy gave us a dinner of stew, served in earthenware bowls at a big trestle table in the stone kitchen of the house. She served it out of a big iron pot up on the wood stove that dominated the room. We ate by candlelight, and drank the local wine from juice glasses. The kids drank imported Kool-aid and ate peanut-butter sandwiches. Some things, apparently, do not change too fast. They asked me about Esalen, where I had recently been, and we did a few sensitivity experiences—modest, nonthreatening things like "coming to standing," a process wherein you just take some trouble to notice whether you are standing on the floor or the floor is supporting you. Angus, eyes shut, threw himself into this experience, knees flexed, breathing stilled. In this, as in everything he does, he was utterly passionate, greedy for contact with the experience.

Later we went outside to enjoy the night. First just Angus and I, later joined by Lucy, who had put the children to bed, we sat in the lotus for over an hour, silently noticing the night sounds and the shifting nonlight around us. The wild hills turned to a gauzy blue film before our eyes; fireflies dotted our vision. The odd breeze curled under our chins; there were chirps and croaks and creakings on all sides. When we stirred to go, Angus said, as if in a temper, "You don't need dope in country like this. Something is always happening. I could spend hours watching a chrysalis become a butterfly. In fact, I have."

Neither Angus nor Lucy had any regrets about their escape from New York, from the publishing world or, in Lucy's case, from the world of the dance, in which she had been a pretty, graceful, and talented soldier for many years. Her dancer's body now was used for hauling the water, breaking up the firewood, hand-washing the clothes, physically making possible the decent daily life of her family. She did not look tired, she looked ecstatic. Angus looked rugged—something he had always longed to be, though city-raised, city-styled, finally—city-choked. He showed me his calluses, proudly. "When that stone wall is finished," he said, "and I look at it, I will know that I lifted every one of those goddam stones and put it in place. I am *building* that fucking stone wall." And a big smile, nothing very usual for Angus, spread across his face.

They were no more than politely sorry about the defection of their friends. "It would have been nice if they had stayed," Lucy said. "But really, things get so very practical in a situation like this. I was doing all the work for everybody, and it wasn't fair. And Angus really wants to make a go of this vineyard. So the basic thing was dramatized—it was our thing, we had the commitment. It was probably a mistake for Angus to underwrite everybody else. They didn't have the same stake in things. Anyway, now we know."

The next day I spent the morning with Angus and Lucy and the lovely, naked kids; then drove out of their lives down to the coast again, and got on with my business. I was heading for the Île du Levant, a nudist island in the Mediterranean, to do a piece for *Holiday*. And I had tried to persuade them to join me. Angus said he would like that, sometime, but right now it was time to work on the vineyard. "There's an old ruined abbey over the next hill that we like to visit sometimes," he said. "That's about as far as we get these days."

Our leave-taking was not very fervent. Angus is prone to changeable moods; he seemed distant and aloof when I said goodbye. I don't think it was anything I said or did; I'm sure I didn't give offense. His last words were, "You're a better man than I thought. So next time will be better." I didn't think, really, that that time had been so bad.

THE NAME OF THE PLACE WAS LOST

The name of the place was Lost, and it was for anybody who was. I heard about it for the first time four years ago, while visiting Mendocino, a rather magical little town in northern California. And I would have gone looking for the place, but everybody told me that Lost did not receive idle visitors. It existed "somewhere up in the woods." If you were running from a world you couldn't live in, and your route of flight had brought you into northern California and along the sandy fringe of the continent; if you had looked into the cold and turbulent Pacific Ocean and could not bring yourself to jump into it, you might backtrack a few steps, wander up a forested mountainside, and find shelter—perhaps even a home—at Lost.

The founder of the place had been lost, once upon a time. But he had stopped running, somewhere in those woods, and he took his stand for survival right where he stood. He survived for a long time, too, at least in part because other people fled to him and joined him; together they built primitive comforts into the wilderness with primitive tools, and the reports were that they were hacking a good life for themselves out of the forest. They must have got very hopeful, because at one point they tried to raise enough money to buy the land they were living on. Here they failed, because they couldn't raise the necessary cash. The courts were patient, but in the end the people were ordered off the land; finally driven off it. I heard that the houses were bulldozed; nobody lives up there anymore but the deer and the chipmunks.

That's too bad; so many more people are lost these days than were four years ago, and there should be no shortage of havens awaiting them. Sometimes it seems that half the country is on the roads, looking for something, and the other half stir fitfully in their beds and gaze with gathering perplexity into their bathroom mirrors in the mornings.

Some portion of these unsettled people find their way, in long and twisting drives north from San Francisco, past the gorges of the Russian River country, to Mendocino. You may have heard of the place: movie production units sometimes use it as a location when they want to suggest Maine, or a fishing village, or just an ambiance that is both charmingly antique and a little creepy at the same time. If you saw *East of Eden* you will recall scenes of James Dean skulking along on board sidewalks past vaguely Victorian storefronts; a funny, misty light always suffuses the outdoor action. I used to think that the light had been simulated by some clever cinematographer, but then I went to Mendocino and saw the light for myself, courtesy of nobody but God.

Mendocino is an almost gratuitously beautiful place, and it is a long, long way from most other places; inevitably, it has become a hip retreat. When people feel extremely isolated from the society, when they have been beat up or run off for what they feel must be the last time, they light out for somewhere. Out in the West, they often head for the Big Sur, which has been the spiritual capital of the hip world for a long time because it is very beautiful, relatively empty, and reasonably at peace with itself. Mendocino is, I suppose, the penultimate destination, after the Big Sur; it is rather more populated, a significant percentage of the population is hostile to freaks, and nature is a little bit more accessible to everybody. It is not so rugged as the Big Sur; therefore a dedicated freak cannot be sure that he will meet only kindred souls.

However, despite the risk that you may be hassled in Mendocino, it is a good place to go. Here is the faraway, improbable-looking little town on the high bluffs of a barren peninsula jutting well out into the ocean; mountains, shrouded in dark-green forest, rise steadily away from the fourth side of the town, a second-growth wilderness penetrated by logging trails and ocean mists. The fringes of the town, toward sea or mountains, do not conclude urbanity so much as they simply give it up, in a helpless shrug of tangled picket fences, aborted sidewalks, the remains of abandoned houses, and the inexorable reclamation of beach grasses and wildflowers. The smell of brine mingles deliciously with the scent of sap; good people live there; Mendocino draws the wanderer.

The ordinary tourist spends the day there idling in the dirt streets, shopping in the crazy little stores that now dot Main Street. He buys, for his amusement, a floppy hat or a sand candle or perhaps a hash pipe of phallic intent; he lunches at a little shingled restaurant where he can see a blue-haired grandmother entertaining her freaky, hairy grandson to pompano steaks— granny picking delicately at hers with knife and fork, sonny shoveling his mouthwards with his fingers, family gossip occupying the attention of both. If he is lucky and the whales are passing, he can go out to the edge of the bluff and see them pounding, grinding past, blowing plumes of white water above their heads.

There is the endless drama of the crashing surf, of course, and its savage punishment of the rocky outcrops above the edge of the sea, and the birds and seals that live in that violent vortex. And there are quiet, secluded beaches under the bluffs where you can lie naked and undisturbed all day long, simply taking the sun and watching the sea. North of the town, there is a fenced beach, part of an old dump, where a hundred years of crushed glass is worked endlessly by the waves; when the sea recedes, the whole beach sparkles in the sunlight like Aladdin's treasure, and you do not know which bright blue or golden bauble to scoop up first. In retreat, pockets bulging, you pass fields of spreading beach daisies, each blossom more opulently golden than a sun-flower, and think seriously about breaking the law by picking some.

So people come. And a few stay.

The last time I was there, I wandered into a little shop on Main Street and found myself in a paradise of hand-crafted things: leatherwork, pottery, glass, paper—every kind of useful or fanciful object, displayed with no particular intent, every piece signed. Also for sale were spices and condiments of every kind, and grains in great variety, but the most impressive aspect of the store was the profusion of handwork. I asked the lady in charge if this were a retail outlet for a crafts cooperative, or something of the sort.

The lady told me that there was no cooperative or commune of hand-craftsmen in or around the town; that everybody repre-sented in her shop was an independent worker. But that some workers did, in fact, live in communes or expanded families. I asked how many communes there were in the neighborhood.

"It would depend on what you mean by commune," she said. "I live in a sort of commune, I guess . . . my child and I in one house, and a couple and their three children in another, and we share all the major expenses—rent, food, share the cars. Is that a commune?"

I said I didn't know; she replied that she thought not. "There's a lot of sharing up here," she said. "It's rugged country; with this wind and dampness, you don't know how cold it can get sometimes. People tend to group together.

"But if you mean a regular, organized commune, there are some of those too. In fact, my ex-husband runs one. If you want to talk to him, why don't you stick around? He's supposed to come in this afternoon to pick up a check."

Before long a tall, rangy, bearded guy, about forty, strode

into the shop, chatted briefly with the lady, then went swinging suddenly out again, the screen door whanging and banging on his exit. "Uh . . . was that your husband?" I asked the lady. "Oh, yeah, I'm sorry I forgot," she said. "Name's Ralph. Go on . . . you'll catch him."

I swung myself through the screen door onto the board sidewalk. "Mister . . . uh . . . Ralph!" I called after him. And when he stopped, puzzled, I spilled out that I was interested in communes and would like to talk to him.

He seemed a little bemused as he heard me out. "Sure, you can talk to me," he said, as if it were the easiest thing in the world. "I'm just trying to get to the bank before it closes. I've got a commune over in Caspar and you can visit if you want to. You can visit this afternoon. I mean, if you want to. Look, I don't make appointments; but I'll be back there after four, and if you come after four, I'll be there." And then he gave me instructions, and strode off down the street to the bank.

By four o'clock I had driven north on Highway One the three or four miles to the Caspar turnoff, had passed through the nearly abandoned and effectively defunct town of Caspar, and was headed down a narrow paved road toward the sea. On my right, as forecast, I saw a 1920s sort of large cottage, with widespreading eaves, behind heavy foliage, and beyond it along the roadside a high, redwood fence, nearly obscured behind climbing vines. The road seemed to carry on to a point of land above the ocean, where I could see a few very conventional, ranch-style houses clustered. I pulled off at the old cottage, and tried to find an entrance, but there didn't seem to be any natural ways in. It was obvious that the house had undergone a lot of reconstruction that wasn't completed yet; finally I just hammered on a pair of French doors that I got to by teetering up a leaning plank. Inside there was a stir, and then Ralph came through an empty room and, after some difficulty, unfastened the doors.

When Ralph admitted me, I saw at once that all the interior partitions of the house had been removed, and new spaces suggested by placement of plants or shelves; there were hangings on the walls of Indian fabrics, there was a bed in a far corner with a dark red coverlet on it; however, it was clear that the work was still in progress.

Ralph took me through to a warm kitchen, where it seemed to me there had been no reforms. It looked like the kitchen my grandmother once kept, quite in the period, but the pretty, longhaired girl at the stove was not in my grandmother's tradition. "This is Sally," Ralph said. Sally nodded; she was getting a meal, she was very busy, and there were good smells in her kitchen, of baking bread and other delicious cookery.

"Look," said Ralph. "I'm just about to eat some food. Why don't you go out in the garden and look around? I'll come out when I'm finished." I said okay, and he let me out a back door into the garden behind the kitchen. I was in a strange, Alice-in-Wonderland sort of outdoor space, surrounded by high redwood fences from which a strange variety of pots and decorations were suspended. In the pots, most of which hung from hooks on leather thongs, herbs or flowers were growing. The decorations seemed no more than that; assemblages of spools and cones and other bits of wood. It was like a garden by Louise Nevelson, and there were chickens pecking the ground around my feet. It had rained that afternoon, and every hanging thing was adrip; the ground was damp under me.

I let myself through the nearest high gate, and a long construction of vari-colored spools clattered my passage. I found that I was in the center of a compound of unpainted redwood houses, and that vegetable gardens fenced by chickenwire joined the houses and framed the compound on three sides. On the fourth, a line of towering eucalyptus defined the edge of the property, which was also the edge of a cliff over the sea. The center of the compound was in weeds, weeds higher than my head, but there were paths trod through the high grasses, and I wandered in them, coming finally to the center, where a rowboat, improbably equipped with oars, sat primly in a muddy wallow. I was tempted to climb in and row away to nowhere; instead I made my way back through the maze, coming out on the wrong side of the compound. From inside a shingled building, I heard a violin; on the door was a hand-lettered sign: DON'T YOU DARE COME IN WHILE I'M WORKING. Intimidated, I reentered the maze, and by a series of abortive tries, found my way back to Ralph's gate.

I sat, rather disconsolately, on a huge blue-painted wooden

spool, kicking alternately at the chickens and stones on the ground, until Ralph came out of the house. "Well," he said. "What did you want to talk to me about?"

I explained that I was just starting to do a book on communes, that I was not just idly interested but also hoping to learn something about how to answer the needs in my own life, and that in general I would just like to know what he was up to.

"Would you like to drink some wine?" he asked. It was the first and only hospitable thing I'd heard in an hour, and I said I'd be glad to. We reentered the kitchen, Sally poured red wine out of a jug into hand-turned, handleless pottery cups, and we sat on cushions on the floor of the warm kitchen to talk.

"I used to be an advertising man," he volunteered. "In San Francisco." Then suddenly, "How old are you?"

I said I was thirty-five.

"I was thirty-one when I knew I'd had enough," he said. "My wife . . . you met her at the store . . . she was an illustrator in the agency. We'd had enough. And we had a little money, so we quit and came up here, and I bought this house. We both started to paint, and I opened a gallery in town, but I didn't make any money at it.

"For the last five years I've done all kinds of jobs, short-term and long-term, indoors and out. The gallery turned into a store with paintings, not just ours; and I've started sculpting now too. A year and a half ago, she moved out . . . and I went down to Mexico for three months and just sat still in one place and tried to piece my life together.

"This is what I figured out—that I wanted a community here, not just a landlord-tenant thing, which is what we've always had on this property, in order to pay the mortgage. It was one of the things that separated us, the idea of a larger community. It wasn't what she wanted; in three months, I was sure it was what I wanted.

"So when I came back, I got all my tenants together and I put it to them. We were all friends—that's the only kind of landlord I could ever manage to be anyway—and there were a couple of people who didn't want a community so they left, no hard feelings. The rest of us agreed to share economically, to develop this place as a home for all of us . . . to be a family, really. We figure that, out of our own gardens, and by fishing, and with very careful community buying, the place can support twenty-eight adults. We're only twenty-three at the moment, but everybody has some kind of part-time job and everybody puts in enough cash every month to keep the mortgage up to date.

"It's still my property and my responsibility, and by general agreement I'm the chief honcho around here. For good or bad, I seem to be the guy who can maintain good relations with the Man; I've lived in this area for a long time now, I've worked around here for all those years, I have a reputation as a reliable person. There are some beautiful people here who can function just fine within our community but they can't handle the outside. That's okay with me—I can remember to renew the truck registration, to make the mortgage payments, to *relate*. So that's my job; that's what I'm good at. Other people are good at cooking, or fishing, or gardening, or carpentry—and as we go on living together we'll learn all that stuff from each other by sharing. Meanwhile, I'm getting pretty good at carpentry and I'm still holding down the administrative stuff. You can see we're into a pretty big architecture and environment trip here at the moment."

Just as I agreed that I could see that, the door swung open and a very big, very rugged man entered the room. He was introduced as Jerry; he looked me over with glittering blue eyes, shot me a toothless grin, and settled on his haunches in a far corner, where he rocked back and forth on the soles of his boots, silently. Sally, who had been puttering at the stove and sink, brought him a cup of wine and held it in front of him, but he didn't look up. She set it beside him on the floor and returned to her chores.

Ralph and I talked on about his community, and the numbers of people who came looking to become a part of it. "I look them over very carefully," he said, "and nine out of ten aren't right for us. Some young guys, and girls, are just looking to crash; they want some easy dope and sex, or they literally just want to rent a room—there aren't many places to rent around here—or sometimes they're small-time hustlers just out of jail and trying to get lost up here while they think up a fresh hustle. That's why we're still short a few people; the right ones haven't shown up yet."

Suddenly there was a booming, shattering shout in the room and Jerry was on his feet, blue eyes staring straight ahead in some awful vision. "OH WOW" is what he had said, causing me to leap right out of my carefully cultivated lotus. And "OH WOW" he said again; then very slowly, he settled down on his haunches again, and slowly dropped his head into his arms, and subsided utterly. Ralph continued talking as if nothing had happened; Sally continued to putter at the sink. I sat there electrified, trying to attend politely to Ralph's discourse while I waited for a further comment from Jerry. But after a while it was clear to me that Jerry had nothing more to say. Ralph talked about the architecture of the place, the reasons for erecting the high redwood fence ("We have to get along with the community, and when those straight ranch houses went in down the road, and the builders sort of objected to our being here, I put up the fence to avoid any kind of harassment. It didn't bother me—I was planning on a fence anyway.") And plans for the weedy center of the compound. "I kind of love it as it is," he said, "just a maze of weeds. But we *do* have plans—I have an idea for a sort of Japanese fantasy, with a lily pond and little bridges and swans. We put the rowboat out there to remind us of what we'd like to have sometime. And . . ."

"OH WOW!" It was Jerry again, on his feet again staring, and I was about half dead again from shock and trying hard not to show it. But Ralph's voice continued, after only the briefest pause.

". . . and I wonder if you saw that building at the north corner of the compound? That's going to be our Japanese bath. We're going to fix it up so we can all bathe in there together. If there's any ritual we are all into, it's bathing together; it's our 'sacrament.' Right now we have to heat water for a portable tub . . . not the kind of thing we want always. And we want to get the bath-house fixed up real soon. But first things first—roofs, walls. You come back in a year and this place will really be Together."

That night I was in the old-fashioned, Matt Dillon-style saloon of the Mendocino Hotel, listening to the owner deliver a diatribe against the filthy hippies, when an extraordinary apparition walked through the door. To all appearances he was an Indian scout misplaced from a John Wayne movie, a hairy, lanky youth dressed all in fringed deerskins, with a pack on his back and a floppy, wide-brimmed hat on his head. Chestnut hair framed his face and flowed luxuriously over his buckskin shoulders. Around his neck on a leather thong he wore a tiny silver bell, and as he clumped down the barroom to where the owner stood, he went tinkle-tinkle-tinkle.

As the owner stood behind the bar, mesmerized and furious, the Indian scout addressed him. "Good evening, sir," he said. "I wonder if you would oblige me by bringing forth a case of that good Genesee beer that you keep in your cooler. I would be pleased to purchase it from you."

There was no hint of condesension in the scout's tone, but the other two patrons and I were aware that the owner might nevertheless fabricate an offense. He had just broken off a series of remarks condemning "the goddam hippie longhairs that are ruining the whole goddam town," when one of them walks in off the street and uses college talk on him. That's a dangerous tactic. But we perceived that the Indian scout was holding a ten-dollar bill ostentatiously between thumb and forefinger of the hand resting on the bar, and the owner perceived this also. Angry, red-faced but silent, the owner went to the back, returned with a case of beer, threw it on the bar, and accepted the ten-spot. With a cheery shout of thanks, the scout pocketed his change, hefted the case onto his shoulder, and left the bar, going tinkle-tinkle-tinkle.

I was so charmed by the performance that I polished off my own beer and followed the young man into the street. I caught up with him and started right in with encomia. "Man," I said, "that was the greatest performance I've seen in years. That guy hates longhairs. He just got finished saying that he thinks they all ought to be hanged, drawn, and quartered. And given haircuts. And in you came . . . what style . . . out of sight!" The young man took the praise with a slight, modest smile. "It was nothing," he said. "Anyway, it was ordained that I should be in this place at this time, and that he should be here too." I observed that a strange, not entirely sane gleam leapt from the boy's eyes. "He has heard me coming . . . he has heard my bell ringing in the mountains . . . coming closer and closer . . . I have been coming over the mountains for a long time . . . he has heard my bell. . . ."

Ralph had suggested that I visit two other communes in the area: Roberta Bean's place, and the Sleepy Valley Ranch.

The trip up to Roberta Bean's place would make a pretty good purgatory for dedicated ecologists. The gravel road is the most developed part of a logging trail that leads deep into the mountains; long before you get to Roberta's gate, you've seen a thousand giant redwood stumps, as big around as boulders, cut off at a height of about twenty feet. They line the road and stand like tombstones in a desecrated churchyard, all over the foothills—stumps, maybe, but huge enough to memorialize forever the magnificence of the forests that once were here. And even the second-growth is pretty impressive; big and thick enough to constitute a virgin forest in the effete East.

I had been told to watch for the sign of a sunburst on a farm gate. "There isn't anything else to look out for," Ralph had explained. "You can't see any buildings from the road." I had not been encouraged to expect a welcome at Roberta's. "There are about fifteen people living in the barn," Ralph told me. "They spend as much of the time as possible in the nude, and live completely communally. Roberta is not part of the commune; she's a middle-aged woman with a little money, and she bought the place and lets everybody else live there with the understanding that they will build her a house of her own. If Roberta comes to the gate, and you use my name, she *might* let you in. If she's not there, you don't stand a chance."

When I drew up in front of the sunburst sign, I read a sign below it which said: PARK CAR, BLOW HORN, AND WAIT. So I did those things, and in course of time a figure emerged from a distant woods and walked slowly toward me. As he drew nearer I could see that he was a bearded man, dressed in coveralls; Al Capp has been making fun of people who dress like this for years. "Good morning," he said, when he came abreast of me on the far side of the gate. I greeted him back, and he wanted to know how he could help me.

"Well," I said, somewhat ill at ease, "I'm doing a book on communes and . . . uh . . ."

"This is not a commune," he said sternly. "This is a Family."

"Ah, well, I'm very sorry," I said, "Families, then."

"A commune is a political institution," he said. "We are not political here. We are just a group of people who chose to live together as a Family."

I said fine. I said I had not formed the proper terminology for my research as yet, and I wondered aloud if Roberta Bean might be at home. He said that she was away, and that he did not know how to reach her. "We're very busy working on her house right now," he said, "and we're also getting ready for a wedding on Saturday." Taking no hints, I bluntly asked if I could come in to visit.

"No," he said. "There wouldn't be any point. There's hardly anyone here now. People are away visiting in other parts of the country; it's very quiet right now. Anyway, we don't want any publicity."

I said I didn't mind if it was quiet, and that I wasn't planning any sort of "publicity," that a book at the research stage could scarcely be called "publicity." The man, who said his name was John, was very patient but quite unmoved. He did, however, chat on awhile at the gate. He said that the family had not yet been able to grow enough food for themselves, that the ground was not very fertile and the weather very harsh. No, he said, the members had never fished in the sea; it was a good idea, though, for another year. He said again that what they were doing at Roberta Bean's was not political. He said it was religious. John said he was an ordained minister but not a practicing one, not anymore. "Community, you know, is itself a religious act," he said.

Another morning, another logging trail—but no gravel this time, and much steeper, harder going. The little car bounced in and out of muddy ruts and seemed to lose power as the air got thinner. I was watching for a broken wagon wheel and a small hand-lettered sign that said SLEEPY VALLEY RANCH. When I saw the markers I turned off to the left, on a road hardly worthy of the name, and jounced along deeper into the forest.

Finally I came to a clearing, where a blackened quonset hut and an old jalopy stood disintegrating, side by side. A sign said,

Francisco, so when I came back from Europe last year, I came out to San Francisco, and met some people . . . and about then Samantha was one year old, and I started wanting to have her grow up with other children, and some people were coming up here, so . . . there *were* some other children then, but those people split, and now Samantha is the only child. So I'm not exactly Working with Children, which is what I'd wanted to do."

I asked about the others, who they were, and why they weren't together. "Well, there are twelve of us now, seven men, five women. We were twenty all through the winter, all huddled in that house— it isn't insulated, you know, and we just about froze to death. The winter was hard on us; we were together too much, we couldn't get away from each other. So now we can and we do."

I asked about rituals, techniques for being together. "Well, we did all eat dinner in the nude once . . . without any utensils . . . but we never did that again. And this one guy and I were doing yoga together every morning, but he stopped doing it a few weeks ago. I don't know why.

"We don't have anything like plans right now. We don't have any expectations. We're just waiting to see what's going to happen. One guy here, used to be a divinity student, he told me he came with all kinds of projections and programs, and now he doesn't even want to try for that kind of thing. He wants to let community happen when and if it happens, not forcing anything. And that's kind of what we're doing."

Janie did not seem to be getting very far with her gardening, and the gardens looked so hopeless that I asked if they had any plans in *that* department. "Well, that is a hard one to take," she said. "There is a guy here . . . and old Iowa farm boy. He could tell us a lot about how to raise vegetables. But he won't. He won't say a word about farming. See, he's just not on a farm trip right now."

Janie did not know when the others would be back; she didn't think there would be much point in my waiting. I said I hoped it wouldn't disturb her too much to have talked to me without some general consensus, first of all, from the group. "No," she said. "Don't worry about that. It was kind of nice to talk to an outsider. I sort of enjoyed it."

We embraced briefly, and I left her and started the slow climb back up the path toward the rise. When I reached it, I looked back and she was still standing where I left her, head cocked a little bit to one side, grinning and squinting into the sun at the same time, and waving goodbye, while tiny Samantha tugged at her trouser leg, drawing her back to the empty garden.

SHANGHAI-ED BY GANDHI

It was a Methodist minister in San Francisco who told me about Sam Atkins. "If you're interested in group marriage," he said, "you ought to go see Sam Atkins. He's a sort of religious leader out here, he has a huge following; he's a hip prophet, if you know what I mean. And he claims to be married to three other people. I think he'd talk to you about it; why don't I give him a call?"

Some days later it got back to me that Sam Atkins would be glad to see me; when I called his number to confirm, I got not the voice of a prophet (Cecil B. deMille genre) but the voice of an All-American boy: youthful, vigorous, articulate, and hip. "Oh, yeah," he said. "Listen: if Skip says you're okay, then you're okay with me. Have you got a car?" I said I had, and he gave me directions to his house, and suggested that I show up around three in the afternoon.

I could have found Sam's house even if I hadn't had the number; it was in a row of identical, bay-fronted houses in the Western Addition, and nobody could miss it. It was the only one, for example, painted lavender, or heliotrope, or whatever you might call that slightly acid shade of purple; against the white trim, painted psychedelic vines climbed toward the eaves. A white VW bus, parked in front of the garage door, was decorated with mandalas in bright colors. I had read that Sam Atkins preached that LSD was a sacrament and marijuana a daily necessity, like vitamin D; I knew I had the right house without double-checking.

When I rang the bell, the door was opened by a tall, thin, blond youth. I introduced myself, and he said, "I'm Paul," and led me up a flight of stairs and into a conventional San Francisco house (they must have built a lot of them after the earthquake) with a long hallway and a series of rooms leading off it. "Sam's in there," Paul said, indicating the door to the front parlor; he headed toward the back of the house as I entered the room, noting that every inch of wall was covered by Indian hangings, mandalas, every kind of busy, active pattern. Seated in the bay window was a bearded young man with long hair. He wore a tartan shirt and jeans; his legs were folded under him in an easy lotus, and his elbows rested on the arms of his chair. He was alone.

"Hi," he said. "You're the writer."

"I guess I am," I said, and he gestured me toward a wooden swivel chair that stood on the far side of the bay. As my glance took in the long sofa beside him, the routine furniture in the room, the rather dim afternoon light, I explained what I was up to, and said that I'd recently read a piece about him in *Look* that didn't make much sense to me.

"I couldn't get together with that dude," he told me. "He came around here a couple of times, and I talked to him straight, but I never could figure out where his head was." He smiled engagingly. "Maybe I'll have better luck with you."

I said I hoped so, and the thought flashed through my mind that perhaps I *would* be able to pick up on Sam Atkins, straight as I was; God knows he seemed warm, easy, friendly. "I told him that all the wisdom in the world comes down to one thing," Sam went on. "I said it comes down to recognizing God in yourself, and anything that helps you get that recognition is a good thing. I'm not so hard to figure out: I just feel that you should be stoned all the time, and you should drop acid for real enlightenment, about once a week. It's not accidental that these drugs have come upon us when they have, you know; it may be too late for everybody to go sit on a mountain for the next twenty years. I don't think enlightenment can wait."

Meanwhile, I was startled at the approach, just to the left of my vision, of a wheelchair. I turned to see, in it, the same young man who, recently perfectly ambulatory, had let me in the door.

He drew the wheelchair up beside me, and I was just assimilating that he simply preferred to sit in a wheelchair when two girls floated into the room from the same direction, dressed in long flowing robes, and settled themselves silently on the sofa, looking at me.

"This is my family," Sam said. "My husband, Paul, you've met." Paul nodded. "My wives . . . Lucia [she nodded solemnly, a dark-haired, dark-eyed girl] and Polly [nodding also, as blond as Lucia was dark]. The children aren't here right now."

"You say you are married . . . all of you?" I asked Sam.

"Yeah," he said. "We've been married for a year now. We'd talked about doing something like that for a long time, but a year ago we were all four of us in different parts of the country, and it hit each of us at the same time, by telepathy, that we were really the same person, that we were married. So we came together here, naturally, no written appointments. We just all came together."

"How do you live?" I asked. "I mean, where does the money come from?"

"We have friends who help us," Sam said. "I preach regularly, you know, and take up a collection. And the dealers help us a lot. It's a sort of tithe with them, you see; I mean, I preach LSD as a sacrament—we drop acid once a week, when we have our family meeting. This is when we take up all the troubles of the week, the petty disputes and arguments, and settle them under acid. And of course we try to stay stoned the rest of the time. By the way . . . uh . . . would you like a little dope?"

I am aware that my wits function at something less than optimum on marijuana, but I felt it would be churlish to refuse; anyway, the offer of a trip is always a generous gesture, and if the dope is any good it often relaxes both friends and strangers, and makes for better conversation. So I said a little dope would be dandy, and Paul swung his wheelchair around and sped off to the adjoining room. He returned with a cigar box on his knees; out of it he produced about half a lid of grass in a baggie, a book of papers, and an elaborate and fanciful roach clip. While he rolled a few joints, the conversation covered the details of family living, and I realized that I was in the presence of four people who completed one another's thoughts.

LUCIA: "At first Paul did a lot of the cooking because . . ."

POLLY: ". . . Lucia and I were working, but when . . ."

PAUL: ". . . Polly gave up her secretary-thing and really . . ."

SAM: ". . . concentrated on the house, she got very . . ."

POLLY: ". . . interested in food. It's wild, you know, what, we . . ."

PAUL: ". . . can do with simple things. We're definitely into . . ."

SAM: ". . . simplicity in all things, food especially. Just lately . . ."

LUCIA: ". . . we gave up meat altogether; we're trying a vegetarian . . ."

POLLY: ". . . trip. And natural grains, and honey, stuff like that . . ."

SAM: ". . . because it brings its own high. If you eat the foods that are right for you, you can stay stoned indefinitely, and . . ."

LUCIA: ". . . anyway, we don't *have* to be natural carnivores. If . . ."

POLLY: ". . . we cleanse the system of all poisons, and rid . . ."

SAM: ". . . ourselves of sick dependencies on what we do not need, we are in a better condition for acknowledging the sanctity of ourselves—literally, temples of the Holy Ghost. Of course . . ."

LUCIA: ". . . we gave up cigarettes months ago, and liquor."

"I think you'll like this dope," said Sam, as Paul passed me a lighted joint. "The pushers always see to it that we get the best, and this is pretty good—Vietnamese stuff."

I was glad to keep my head still long enough to take a toke; I'd felt as if my neck were a swivel, trying to keep up with the alternating sources of the conversation. And I was glad to smoke that dope—one drag and I knew it was the best I'd ever had. Instantly a little buzz was working inside me, and the physical relaxation of tired muscles in my arms and legs felt like the most exquisite sensual thrill. Ordinarily it takes pretty good grass to do that at all, and certainly a good many more tokes before it happens. Here I was, suddenly very calm and deliciously comfortable in my wooden chair.

The conversation continued in the same vein of food and purity, but as the joints passed, I was concentrating less on what was said and more on the terrifically fine feelings in my body, which was so at ease, so agreeably heavy, that I felt as if I were bolted into the chair.

Bolted into the chair!?! I *was* bolted into the chair; there was no possibility that I could move at all—and then it seemed that all four people were staring at me in such a strange, almost menacing way. I sensed that they were waiting for me to answer some question, but I didn't know what question; I hadn't heard the question, and there was no time to ask what it was, or try to remember what it was. What *was* the question?

Lucia's eyes seemed to bore into me as Sam's voice droned on. "We are all One in the Spirit," he was saying. "There is a golden flow of energy that does not just connect all mankind; it *is* all mankind . . ."

But I thought he was asking a question, I said to myself, and at once identified the question: it wasn't verbal, it was a sort of spiritual demand, and I had to comply. I didn't know what I was wanted to comply to, I didn't know what they wanted me to do. Lucia and Polly exchanged glances, then gazed back at me.

I *understand,* I thought. They want me. Physically. They want to use me in some way—there's going to be an orgy—we're all one—they want to use me, make me one of them, initiate me. It's weird, I want out . . . and suddenly the room started to glow, the walls came alive, all the mandalas and figured draperies and wall decorations started to move, to writhe. The light was golden, as warm as a hearthside, I felt wonderfully light-headed, physically light. And I was soaring upwards like a rocket, chair and all, whizzing straight up in the air and there were showers of sparkling blue embers cascading from my shoulders, I could scarcely catch my breath, I was moving so fast, I was exploding across the ceiling in spectacular bursts of fireworks, I was a brilliant fireball, I was beautiful, I was an orgasm, and the best orgasm in the world. It was total.

And then I was just sitting there, bolted to the chair, and Sam and the others were looking at me and smiling, and Sam said, "That was pretty psychedelic, wasn't it?" At once I was terrified again; it's my head and my trip, How Does He Know It Was

Psychedelic? I must be calm, I must be sneaky. They want me to be One of them.

"That was pretty scary," was all I could say. My mouth didn't move well. It seemed numb.

"Scary?" said Sam. "It wasn't meant to be scary. Nobody is going to hurt you here; this is just for the good, this is just to feel God in us . . ."

But I couldn't listen to him. His voice was sweet, calm, gentle; he seemed to be saying perfectly ordinary, helpful things. But the golden light was coming back again, it seemed to be coming from a fishbowl on a table in the bay window, where the setting sun was striking the glass, only the fishbowl turned to neon, to orange neon, it was an orange neon globe . . . no, it was a ball of orange fire, and it lit up Sam's face, it set his head to glowing with the same orange light, so everything disappeared but his features, burning in this orange fire. And he kept on talking but I couldn't understand anything but "God" and "One" and "Love." And, oh shit, his face was melting and distorting itself . . . no, not melting, more as if transparencies were sliding over one another so that his features constantly changed, and he wasn't Sam Atkins, he was Gandhi, as sure as I'm sitting here that's Gandhi, little wizened head and spectacles . . . no, it's Jesus, Jesus Christ, absolutely complete, it's Jesus . . . no, it's some bearded guru, I've seen the pictures, somebody from India . . . no, oh, dear God, it's a lion, this man is a lion, and every time he stops talking he snarls at me, just like a jungle cat at an enemy, a victim—he's human but he's animal and he lifts his lip, just so, and hisses at me, the most feline, feminine gesture in the world. Like Yvonne de Carlo taking herself off in a bad movie, but like a lion, goddam, it *is* a lion.

While this went on I couldn't dare to look away from Sam Atkins. No power on earth could have forced my gaze away from him, and it seemed we sat like that for days, face to face, while he took on the aspects of prophets, and then of a lion, alternately purring religiously at me, and then snarling at me like a beast. In the background I thought I heard somebody say, "Here come the children," and then I think there were children in the room, but I still don't know if there were, or if so how many, or of what sexes, or what they looked like. I think they were there;

I'm sure the others were there; but for me there was only Sam Atkins and this incredible series of transformations he was going through before my very eyes, and every now and then we would soar up to the heavens again . . . I was always unprepared, we'd just zoom up and up and burst all over the sky and be back again. And his voice went on. What *was* he saying? Still about "God" and "the One."

And then at a point I noticed that everybody was up, and stirring about the room, and leaving it. Sam Atkins came over to me and he said, "Are you thirsty? Would you like some tea? Let's go in the kitchen and have some tea."

From very far away from my mind, I directed my lips to slur out that, yes, I was very thirsty, and I'd like to go to the kitchen for tea. "But I can't get out of this chair," I said, rather sorry for myself.

"Sure you can," said Sam. "Come on. Just get up and come on back to the kitchen with us." And the bolts fell off my limbs, and I *could* stand, and we walked very slowly down the hall to the kitchen, where the girls were preparing a light snack of tea and bread and honey.

I remember asking if I could smoke, and very sweetly they all said they wished I wouldn't; that they had given it up and would like to keep the house free of tobacco smoke. But after that I lapsed again into a sort of semi-coma; nothing like before, but still too strong for me to remember much else, except that Sam kept talking, and telling me all kinds of interesting stuff, and I kept struggling to take it in but just couldn't file a single word. I remember that I wouldn't have a sandwich, but I did drink the tea. And then it seemed to me that I ought to leave; it seemed I had been there so very, very long, days on end, what would they think.

We stood in the hall, and I embraced them all, and thanked them profusely for the most extraordinary trip in my life. So I did, by then, have some perspective, did recognize that I *had* been on a trip, and a trip that was slipping into the past tense. They all smiled at me indulgently, and said, so far as I know, perfectly kind things to me, and saw me to the door, which I passed through quite jauntily.

On the street I put together in my mind that I had come in a car, a rented car. Now where had I parked? Let's see—and my eyes ranged up and down the street until I found the right car. I got in, and the radio came on, and the announcer was saying that it was seven o'clock—and I was so shocked that I had to pause before putting the car in gear. Seven o'clock: that meant that I had been in the house of Sam Atkins only four hours, not days at all as I had thought, not a lifetime. For some reason the news cheered me; in fact, I felt wonderful, cheerful, absolutely elated, practically giggling with joy. And the nicest thing of all was that here I was in this lovely car, about to drive off into the streets of San Francisco, and nobody but me knew that I was absolutely the finest, the best, the most daring and superb driver in the entire world. Now Richard Atcheson, famous driver, puts ever so dainty a pressure from his toe upon the accelerator, and his sleek and shiny Batmobile slithers from its parked position into the street; intrepidly Richard Atcheson maneuvers the powerful, snarling behemoth through heavy traffic—witless, indolent, stupid traffic—and onto the Bayshore Freeway, whizzing along at high speeds in perfect, utter control of the brute machine. And in this fantasy I continued all the way to Palo Alto. I have no idea whether I was ever in my own lane, or whether I made the entire trip in someone else's.

I reached the house of friends; I had been expected, we had been planning to go out to a party, and obviously I had remembered that. But I was very late, and my friends were disposed to be very cross with me, until they detected (it didn't take them long) that I was very, very stoned. I was so stoned I was practically floating a foot above the parquetry, and I *stayed* stoned for two full days. Then, abruptly, it was over. There was no crash when I came down; I was just right back at home in the ordinary, workaday world at last, and was able to hear about my exploits with reasonable perspective. My friends were full of news and curiosity. "What *was* it?" they demanded to know. And, "Can we get some?"

I never knew what it was. It seems likely that Sam Atkins and his family laced strong Vietnamese grass with something: opium, perhaps, or LSD. It was a fine trip in many ways, the only psychedelic trip I've ever had (you don't get psychedelics from plain old marijuana), and I'd be delighted to go on a trip like that again sometime. My only reservation is that I would prefer to be invited on trips, not shanghai-ed aboard. It is rotten to take people to places they don't know they are departing for, and I will always hold it somewhat against Sam Atkins that he didn't warn me. That basic decency would, at least, have prevented the heavy paranoia I experienced when the trip got, for me, unconventional.

Of course, I had brought a lot of paranoia with me to that meeting, and the paranoia of the drug trip helped me to realize that. I had arrived suspicious of Sam and family, a little hostile, and vaguely afraid of them and their manner and their dope. There was also a lot of sexual anxiety slithering about in my head, unexpressed and unacknowledged, even to myself, until the drug brought it out in fantasies of sexual threat. God knows I was afraid of those constant allusions to how we are all One, how God Is Us; I wasn't ready to go on any real Christian trip, however pious my background. I mean, after all, I didn't *know* those people, I didn't even know where they were *from*.

In fact, I had arrived there as a pretty up-tight little creep, and I didn't leave much improved, except perhaps temporarily. But I did learn a little something about myself, if not very much about Sam Atkins and his group marriage. And everything I learned was not the work of the dope; some of it was the work of Sam Atkins. He had received me openly and honestly, and I had repaid him with guile, snobbery and paranoia. Somehow, if I were going to dwell for any time in the counterculture, I would just have to grow up.

A QUESTION OF COMMUNICATION

Ruthie was a senior at San Francisco State, a friend of my sister and, like her, an English major. They took only one class together—a workshop entitled "Communications." My sister took me once—it was the day I met Ruthie—and I found that the class was designed as an encounter, with fifty or so students breaking up into small groups of six or seven for the two-hour lab. My sister had introduced me to Ruthie before we went in; when the class was over, we met again in the corridor.

"Ahem," says I, feeling portly and superior and acutely supernumerary, "did we all communicate properly during these exciting two hours?"

"Communicate, shit," said Ruthie, scowling. "I do more communicating in five minutes at home than we've done in a whole quarter in this course."

Ruthie lived in a commune, a student commune—not, perhaps, as intensely dedicated to social change as many communes are, but formed largely by the dictates of economics. That, and love.

"I really like it," she said. "It's real. Not like these stupid communications labs where everybody spends weeks working up the nerve to say, 'I don't like your dress today, Sharon.' Jesus, what Mickey Mouse. If Sharon lived in our house we wouldn't be talking about her *dress*."

Ruthie was living in a commune (1) because her boyfriend, whom she loved, wanted to; (2) because neither of them had enough money to afford an apartment for themselves; (3) because they both thought it was the only decent thing to do. "If you consider," said Ruthie, "the waste that's all around us. It's obscene that one person could be living in eighteen rooms and eighteen persons could be living in one room. It's just not fair. Wayne thinks that it's a noble experiment, and that we can learn to share. I think it's terrific."

There were seven students living in Ruthie's commune and they shared a five-room flat, all the groceries and all the dope. "Not that we can afford much dope," she said, "but just enough. One of the guys is dealing now, that's how we get by. Because a lid of Panamanian Red is up to $25, when you can get it. Otto— that's his name, Otto, isn't that a gas, he's a humanities major— always cops a couple of lids for the family and we chip in a few dollars. So at least we always have some dope. And we eat okay too—Pamela, this other girl and I, do the cooking, and we do all right. The other night we had veal parmigiana, Pam's mother taught her."

The girls do all the cooking and all the cleaning in Ruthie's commune; everybody joins in studying and smoking dope. Ruthie did not complain of any imbalance. "There's only one thing wrong," she said, "and that is that when Wayne and I would like to be together, somebody is always there. There is absolutely no privacy. And there is maybe one other thing wrong, which is that Wayne feels we should expand our sexual horizons, as he calls it, and I should ball Lewis, who is the only guy there who does not have a chick. But Lewis does not turn me on. And I think that if I would ball Lewis, this would give Wayne the green light to ball Pamela, whom he secretly covets."

"Secretly covets?" I parroted. "I thought you were having a lot of communication in your commune."

"Well," she said, "he won't admit it straight out. But that's what he'd like to do. I know it. And Pam wouldn't mind it either, and her boyfriend Carl is for it. Because he's into Sarah, who is Nelson's chick. And Nelson is into Wayne!"

I asked if anybody was doing anything about all this tension to get a Round Robin going, inasmuch as everybody was so into everybody.

"Oh, Christ," said Ruthie, "it's all talk-talk-talk. We talk so much that sometimes I could scream. The truth of the matter is that the problem isn't sex at all, it's mayonnaise."

"I beg your pardon," I said, certain I had misheard.

"Mayonnaise," she said, most distinctly. "Whenever anybody has any extra bread, they may buy something special for themselves—a little mustard, some anchovies, a jar of mayonnaise. And what I hear around the house, more than anything else, is when somebody goes to the refrigerator at midnight, after studying for hours, to get a special kind of sandwich made out of their own stuff, and they're rooting around in there for an hour and a half, and you hear this voice from the kitchen, really angry: "Okay, you guys, who took my goddam mayonnaise?""

DESPERADOES OF THE DESERT

I don't know if you know the mountains just outside Palm Springs. They are Dalmatian mountains, if you stretch the point a little—bleak, sere, tan peaks, dotted all over with desert foliage. Very beautiful to look upon but hard to live among, I would imagine, if you didn't have any water. Of course, there are canyons, formed by streams and rivers, and alongside these watery courses, more like cataracts than rivers in their steep drops from desert plateau to desert plateau, there is an uncommon greenery, a happy shade, for anybody who chances to come there. The Indians hold the land, making no use of it, but indeed how could they? It is utterly desolate and of interest to nobody—except for anybody who is trying very hard to get away.

In the old days, Tahquitz Canyon would have been a really good place for outlaws or renegade Indians to hide out in. The canyon is a deep cut in the mountains, rising from the desert floor in a series of three plateaus, wedded by steep, sometimes sheer cliffs. The river is mostly vertical in there, falling by degrees and at angles and at a very great speed, so that here and there are crashing curtains of white water and deep green rock pools.

It used to be that nobody would go into Tahquitz Canyon except occasional hikers and butterfly-collecting schoolboys on class projects. But a couple of years ago, Tahquitz became a retreat for increasing numbers of longhaired kids, who would park their cars and vans on the empty and unpopulated last paved street of Palm Springs and hike in across the desert. They would stay for, sometimes, weeks at a stretch, hiking out sporadically to replenish their food supplies, and it became common knowledge that a sort of transient hippie commune existed back in there.

I doubt that any harm would have come to this casual retreat except for two factors. First was the development of that last paved street, the one nearest the mouth of the canyon. A builder put up a row of very expensive ranch houses, and several very expensive families moved in. These families objected to the fact that cars and vans, most of them bearing psychedelic decorations or peace symbols, were parked in their street for long periods of time. The police began to take an interest in the matter, and commenced to ticket and tow the cars. They also placed NO PARKING signs on all the streets in the area, even the ones with no houses on them. It is a curious sight to see now—all those empty streets in the desert, with NO PARKING signs every twenty feet, like the cartoon home of B. O. Plenty and Gravel Gertie. A very wistful vista indeed.

The second factor of change was the aftermath of a heavily promoted local rock and roll concert in the town, when several thousand kids were turned away from the event for lack of space. There was indignation, there were hippies in the streets, there were police confrontations, and even a killing, when an over-excited service station owner fired his rifle into a crowd. Ultimately, many of the young people retreated into Tahquitz Canyon—the mouth of which is a two-hour desert hike from the Palm Springs city limits—and there they did as they pleased.

Notwithstanding the remoteness of the canyon from the city, the authorities retained a lively curiosity about the activities of these young people, sending planes and helicopters over the canyon to see what they might be doing. The reports were distressing—the kids were swimming naked in the rock pools. They were probably even ingesting psychedelic drugs and copulating. This was clearly a case for Dick Tracy.

Nobody produced a verifiable count of how many kids were in the canyon. Some said twenty thousand, though that figure is improbable, however exciting it may be. The figure was closer to several hundred, though, and you cannot have several hundred people in a canyon with little food and no facilities without creating a health hazard. Of course, it did not occur to the authorities to carry in "facilities" such as food, bedding, chemical toilets, and litter baskets. Authorities do not facilitate Love-Ins. Nor did the authorities think of biding their time until the great masses of longhairs would undoubtedly come out again and disperse to their urban homes. The situation demanded Action; it was determined that the kids should be driven out.

Driven out they were, at rifle point, by deputies delivered to the canyonsides by helicopter. These arms of the law descended upon the campers from either face of the canyon like a wedge, forcing all before them, driving the kids like cattle to the canyon's mouth, where their colleagues stood ready to arrest everybody on a variety of charges, principally Public Lewdness. Few saw the humor in pressing such a charge against people who had been miles from the public gaze at the time of the alleged offense; few saw the absurdity of the fact that the offended parties were none other than policemen flying past in airplanes. Nor did any of the kids secure clever attorneys to beat the rap. Fines were levied, jail sentences dealt. The issue was closed and the town and canyon cleansed.

Sort of. By the time I came to Palm Springs all these events were concluded, but the original communards were still somewhere in the canyon, and so were varieties of stray groups and individuals, some of whom had trekked back in to the scene of the original crime immediately upon release from jail. My outdoorsman friend Frank and his wife had hiked into the canyon only a few days before, taking along a basket of food for anyone who might need it, and had learned that the commune had removed itself from the first valley to the second—much higher and more difficult to storm, almost an impregnable fortress, a hippie Masada. Frank invited me to hike in with him at the next dawn. "We have to go in early," he explained. "The heat on the desert floor gets up to well over 110 degrees by midmorning and we don't want to be out in the open in heat like that."

So when the first slivers of light were peeking over the mountains, Frank and I were setting out on foot across the boulder-strewn desert, keeping a sharp watch for rattlesnakes. It is often at times like this when I ask myself what in God's name I am doing. I'm a city kid, I hate to hike, I hate rattlesnakes, and especially I hate to get up before dawn. But I'm curious, I hate to miss anything, so I find myself in preposterous situations like this one, inadequately equipped, tearing holes in my fruit boots on sharp rocks, snagging my chemise Lacoste on cactus and brambles, a handkerchief tied around my head to keep the sweat from running down my spectacles.

Frank's wife had put together a large package of rolls and cheese, in case we ran into anybody who was hungry; apart from that, we hadn't anything to carry. Water wasn't necessary. "The canyon water is very cold and very pure," Frank said, "and when we get there, we'll be glad to see it."

By seven-thirty (I'm a little slow crossing deserts) we were at the mouth of the canyon. The water was running out wide and flat over glistening stones, and the canyon walls rose in deep reds and pinks on either side of us. I hadn't expected the scene to be so beautiful, so dramatic, as we advanced over boulders and through crevices alongside the rushing stream. We ascended to the first plateau without any difficulty. Sometimes there were even paths, and here and there beside the water were gnarled trees that gave a little shade. There were many signs of recent occupancy—stones blackened by campfires, out in the open or in caves. But no spectacular trash, and no people—until we climbed into hearing distance of the first waterfall. The rock pools were becoming more frequent now, and in one of them we saw two boys swimming—both wearing cut-off blue jeans. The boys gave us a wave and we climbed on toward the booming sound of dropping water, coming at length into a little open space. Through a cluster of overhanging trees we could now see the waterfall—a mighty sight—and the deep pool beneath it.

We stopped for a while to mop our brows and bathe our hot feet in the stream, and talked a little with the handful or so of young people who were encamped all around the pool. They seemed to be having a delightful time, lazing in the sun. They said nothing much was happening, they were taking it easy, and there had been no pigs in the neighborhood for several days. "But we don't take our clothes off until nighttime," one boy said. "Bare-ass really freaks the pigs." When we asked about the semi-permanent commune, they pointed vaguely upwards. "We've never been up there," said one. "It's a rough climb. But they come down sometimes, a few at a time, to go for supplies." This lot seemed to have all the food they needed, so we put our shoes back on and started to climb again, this time up a loose rock slide.

I guess I have never had a worse time in my life. Frank is an experienced rock climber, a dignitary of the Sierra Club, a true mountaineer for whom the next couple of hours were sheer child's play. I get dizzy at six feet above sea level; I get notions in high places that I want to jump, need to jump; but also, I'm stubborn. Frank pulled out well above and ahead of me, but I clambered on, never looking back or down, because I'd heard once that looking back is disastrous. And after a while I got quite pleased with myself, as we negotiated the slide and came into steeper but more solid terrain, where the problem was to pull ourselves up from ledge to ledge. The thing to do is to grope above your head with your hands, feeling for an outcrop to pull up on. I had forgotten all about rattlesnakes that like to snooze on outcrops; if I had remembered them I would have had a heart attack on the spot.

So things went well, in a desperate kind of way. My sweatband was soaked and my glasses were streaming, but there wasn't anything to see anyway except the stones and pebbles in front of my nose. And then I panicked—at least, I assume that's what I did. Because at a point I couldn't find any more ledges to grip, though my hands went up and out as far as they could. And when I tried to go down again I couldn't find the toehold I had just left. Also, I looked over my shoulder and I saw that I had climbed a long way up, maybe a couple of hundred feet from the first plateau, and far in the distance I could see the shimmering desert, and it was out and down, far down. And I croaked out, "Frank! I'm stuck."

Frank's voice came from above and slightly to the right of me, and without loosening my grip on the rock face I craned my neck around and gazed in that direction, and he was standing straight up against the sky with two other people. So sheer did the cliff seem to me that I imagined they were leaning slightly outwards, and I wondered how they were able to do a thing like that. Frank said, calmly, conversationally, "No, Dick, you're not stuck. There's a good path just to your left. If you look closely you'll see that everything flattens out just fine."

He was right. There was a way sideways, and I inched toward it, and finally got my feet and came along very obliquely, moving upwards all the while, until I reached Frank and his two companions. "Isn't that lucky," Frank said, as I moved up on them in a kind of crouch. "Finding that nice flat path. I wish I'd seen it myself." And then he introduced me to the young couple with him. Janis and Jim. "Dick, this is Janis and Jim," he said, just as if we were not tettering out on the edge of space.

Janis and Jim looked to be in their early twenties, and they looked very healthy, like Sabras. They were deeply tanned and their tan had a silver sheen on it, the kind you get from being in bright sunshine most of the time. They said they'd been up on the second plateau ever since the bust, and it was fine up there, but it was a nuisance to have to climb down and up so far to fetch supplies. "There are twenty of us," Janis said. "We have plenty of water, but not much food, and absolutely no dope at all."

"I think the pigs think we've got some big stockpile of grass up there," Jim said. "I don't know where they think we'd get it. We haven't had any dope in here for weeks."

I asked what they did with themselves. "We just live," Janis said. "We've living right with nature up there, very simply. We're learning how little we need. We do lots of meditation, swim a lot, sleep under the stars. It's beautiful. You guys can go on up if you want to—the only way up is over to the left and you'll see a steep rock face. You can make it if you're barefooted." Frank gave Janis the bag of goodies, and she was grateful, because they hadn't had any breakfast that morning. And then, with a wave, they were on their way down, and we started trudging upwards.

We came at length to the sheer rock face that Janis had told us of—about twenty-five feet of vertical stone, and it looked to me as smooth as glass. "No," said Frank, "there'd be lots of little crevices; you just can't see them from here. Janis was right. A good, barefooted mountain climber could do that." I could see that Frank wanted to do it. He was fascinated that the communards hadn't rigged a rope tow or anything of the sort. "Young bodies and bare feet," he said, shaking his head.

"Frank," I said, "you go on up if you want to. I'll wait here. I'd never be able to climb that face. I can take off my shoes and socks, but I don't have a young body, and I'm scared to death as it is." But Frank refused to leave me alone there, clinging to my perch, and said he would just as soon go on down again with me. I think the going down was more spine-chilling than the climbing up, because the vastness of open space was always before my eyes, and there were long, stretching descents between ledges that seemed harder and steeper than I remembered. But I kept in mind Frank's only advice to me, "Just be absolutely certain of every step you take," and I made out all right.

We were both a soggy mess when we came finally to the first waterfall again, and we tore off our clothes and fell straight into the icy pool. Some of the kids were sitting on rocks above the pool and they looked on sort of sadly. They didn't dare undress and dive in, and rock pools with your clothes on are not what they are otherwise. "I hope there aren't any pigs up here," one boy said, "or they'll bust your ass." I wouldn't have much minded if they had. With Frank in his late fifties and me in my late thirties, we'd have made an amusing catch. Anyway, that beautiful swim would have made any hassle worth the trouble.

Later, we lay out on wide, flat rocks below the pool and sunbathed, while the water rushed past us with the agreeable gurgles and gargles that a rock stream makes. Occasionally, the stream would rise slightly and sheet over the flat rocks, backing and spilling around our bodies and dashing downwards with the light of the sun dancing on it. And finally, when we had swum and sunbathed all the kinks out of our bodies, we dressed and headed down again, and did not encounter anyone coming up. As we descended toward civilization, I thought of the baking streets of Palm Springs, and of how lovely and peaceful the waterfall pool had been, and how nice to spend a few days there, doing nothing. And of the grim climb to the second plateau, and the lengths to which our children have to go to get away from us.

The police made another raid on the first plateau that same afternoon, arresting all the kids we had met there on some charge or other. The communards continued for several more months in their Masada—picked off by ones and twos when they came out for supplies—but mostly holding their own. However Frank told me, last time I was in Palm Springs, that the story was completely over, that even the communards had been arrested, and the mouth of the canyon blocked, and the three plateaus of Tahquitz forbidden to everyone.

So nobody can go there now. Not even the butterfly collectors. Isn't that wonderful?

SATIE AND SATORI ON A DAIQUIRI TRIP

"I know lots of people who live in communes," Corinne said, astonishing me. Corinne is not a member of the New Society. She is about forty, twice-divorced, an encyclopedia editor in San Francisco. A warm, vivacious woman but a martini-drinker, a practitioner of serial monogamy. Nobody's "chick." However, encyclopedia editors not being what they once were, she had colleagues at work whose life styles differed radically from her own.

"There's Fred," she said. "He's gay, but not flagrant. His lover left him with a huge apartment and he was feeling down on the gay thing after that and asked around at the office for room-mates. Well, Fred's really very likable and it's a stunning apart-ment with four bedrooms and considering the salaries we get . . . anyway there are now eight people living there and all of them except for Fred's new lover work for us. They call it the en-cyclopedia commune."

I said it sounded more like a boarding house to me, or a share-the-facilities kind of thing that young people often arrange when they start out in business.

"Oh, no," said Corinne, "they're completely serious about the commune thing. It evolved after the fact but now they're all very much into it. Not into sexual sharing, I believe, but everything else. Especially the work. There are five men and three women and everybody takes fair turns at all the housework and cook-ing. They have all their meals together, and do all their home socializing together. And these are not kids, by the way—they're all editors or production people in our firm and they're in their late thirties, early forties. I think Fred is probably the oldest."

"Isn't it sort of peculiar for Fred to be gay and everybody except his lover be straight?" I asked.

"Why do you assume they're straight?" she asked, laughing. "No, really, nowadays only your hairdresser knows for sure, but the other people *are* straight, so far as I know. And it's a matter of principle with them, that everybody's sexual preferences are their own business and everybody's sexual preferences ought to be represented. If you read the *Berkeley Barb* or the *Tribe* you'll see ads from straight communes soliciting gays to membership. In this case they didn't have to do it, obviously, because as Fred says, he was already the resident faggot.

"They do have great parties," she added, wistfully. "And don't forget, this is a cosmopolitan town. This is San Francisco."

"Okay, Corinne," I said, "you are now an official Unexpected Source. You got any more?"

"Well, there's Margaret. I don't know her very well yet but she did tell me she lives in a commune. I also happen to know that she teaches belly dancing at Heliotrope, the free university."

"Corinne," says I, "you are putting me on."

"I am not. She's an editor with us full-time but in her spare time she teaches belly dancing and I hear she's very good. If you don't believe me, I'll ask her if we can come over."

Corinne spoke to Margaret and later called to say we had an invitation for Sunday afternoon daiquiris. "Daiquiris in a commune?" I said. "Served by a belly-dancing text editor? You must be crazy."

"Wait and see," said Corinne.

On Sunday afternoon we drove up Telegraph Hill to the highest streets, parked practically upside-down alongside a tilted sidewalk, and stumbled crazily along to find Margaret's address. We had to climb up a couple of insubstantial-looking outdoor wooden staircases to find the right door, and when we rang, a beautiful dark-haired girl came to the door. This was Margaret, and she invited us in and up another interior flight of stairs into a large apartment that seemed to be carpeted in people. We may have been in a commune, but it seemed to me indistinguishable from a huge cocktail party. And sure enough, the promise of daiquiris was instantly made good.

Not everybody in the house was part of the commune, and I confess I never did get sorted out just who was in and who was not. What I saw was a very jolly crowd of people, mostly in their twenties and thirties, dressed in hip clothes—but not in the fashion of weekend hippies, who wear coats and ties during the week to work; these people were more at ease than that, in the manner of professionals who wear what they please all the time. A blond girl told me that all the flats in the building were part of the commune, which numbered on and off some fifteen people, and that the group's affairs were more or less administered by Ernest, Margaret's old man, a certified public accountant. Ernest, a balding sprite in a psychedelic vest and granny glasses, looked too hairy in the face to be an accountant, but he assured me that he was while he filled up my glass. He was just about to launch into details of his communal administration when a tall, red-haired young man (Ernest whispered that he was an all-night disk jockey) began to spellbind the group in a loud voice with tales about getting laid on duty, on account of the many carloads of groupies who, unable to reach the Rolling Stones personally, were willing to drive out to the studio and settle for him. The disk jockey was just as enchanted with his stories as everybody else—perhaps even more so—and he went on at great length and in baroque detail. I passed part of the time gazing out from the huge picture window over a classic view of San Francisco Bay, which swept from the Golden Gate and the hills of Marin all the way past Alcatraz. It was twilight, a million tiny lights were winking on around the shadowed bay, and the fieriest traces of the sun still lit up the sky in irregular patterns. It was one advantage to living in this commune that nobody had mentioned; they wouldn't need to, having it gratis every day.

Still the disk jockey talked, and most people were getting up to go and waving farewells to Margaret. Corinne and I thought we ought to split as well, but Margaret whispered that we should stay for supper, which would be forthcoming as soon as the disk jockey concluded his rambling discourse. Finally he did. It was late, he said, implying that it was our fault, and he had to get to the studio. With many prolonged goodbyes, and scooping up with him a dazzled, lingering girl, he took himself off, still talking.

That left about ten of us for supper, and while Margaret bustled about getting it ready, the rest of us sat in a circle on the floor near the picture window. As Ernest explained the economics of the house (he was the tenant of record, selected the people who would live there, and collected their shares of the rent) Margaret set out plates, and in the center of the circle a large roast of beef and several cheeses. She also lit candles in colored-came and sat beside me, and during dinner she showed me glass holders, because it had become very dark. Then Margaret brochures of Heliotrope, the free university, and explained about her belly dancing.

"It's terribly good for you," she said. "Better than yoga, I think. I learned it in Schenectady while I was in college, and

I've used it a lot to pick up some bread when I was flat. Showbiz-wise, my name is Muna, same as Hussein's wife. Then when Heliotrope got started, and a lot of our friends were in it, and they started looking for people that had some skill who would teach it to others, I volunteered. I didn't know what kind of turnout to expect and I got twenty-five students in the first class. Their husbands and boyfriends think it's a gas. But it's more than a gas, it's an art."

About then, Ernest signaled for another round of mountain red, reached into a nearby cabinet, and produced a hash pipe and a little ball of hashish. He and Margaret had a brief alter-cation about what kind of sounds would be best, finally settling on Satie's "Trois Gymnopédies," which is fine, clean music to smoke hash by. Very quiet and crystalline. That, and the hash, three or four tokes, and I found myself in a stoned reverie, watching the music dance in colors before my mind's eye, with each note disintegrating in a tiny explosion as it was struck. And for a long time I was utterly with the music, and only vaguely aware that people came in, and joined the smoking, and went out again.

As I emerged from this very fine high, I noticed that Ernest seemed very deeply into the music. His eyes were shut, his head thrown back; I considered that he was having a visionary trip— until a single snore rasped through the room, and I realized that Ernest was sound asleep. My manners overwhelming me, and wondering for God's sake what time it was, I signaled in the silence that we should go. Corinne, who had been sitting across from me, almost motionless, all this while, nodded assent, and Margaret showed us, tippy-toe, to the door.

As we drove back to Corinne's house, she thanked me for providing her with an opportunity to visit the commune. "I've been dying to go," she said, "but Margaret never suggested it." I asked Corinne if she had ever considered a commune for her-self, instead of ladling out all that dough every month on her own apartment. "Oh, not really," she said. "I'm too old for that sort of thing."

"Bullshit," I said, "there were people there older than you."

"Oh, I know," she replied, "but I don't mean chronologically.

I mean my style. I'm just not right for it. I like my privacy. And I'm old-fashioned. I like my martinis. Dope doesn't do a thing for me. I've tried it several times and I never have a trip."

"Never?" I asked, amazed, because that had been very fine hash.

"No," she said, sadly. "Like tonight. I could see you were far gone. Everybody was far gone but me. I just sat there. I was looking at Margaret, sitting next to you, so still. Just like a cat. In fact, it crossed my mind that she *was* a cat."

"Corinne," I cried, swerving the car. "*That* was your trip."

"Oh," she said.

KEEPING MUM ABOUT THE BASKET

As everybody surely knows by now, San Francisco is a very gay city in both senses of that word; because it is so beautiful, so tolerant, so cosmopolitan, and also the silliest goddam city on the continent, it has long been a mecca for homosexuals from all over the country and from very far parts too. So it is not surprising that, while in the city to do a piece for *Holiday* on the hip society there, I should have run across a homosexual commune without even having to look for it.

San Francisco's hip community is large, noisy, flamboyant, and very radical. There is room in it for almost every political and sexual persuasion; probably the only thing it's prejudiced against is the John Birch Society. For the last few years the Gay Liberation Front has been picking up a lot of headlines for demonstrating in behalf of homosexual/human rights; in Baghdad on the Bay, people are no longer willing to apologize for deviating from the norm. Last year, when Macy's started making trouble for people who they said were loitering in their men's room (by all counts the most famous homosexual watering place in the country), homosexuals did not slink away under cover of straight clothing. No, sir. They picketed the store.

And as it happens, the hippest bar in San Francisco is also a gay bar, located on the wrong side of Market Street and called The Basket. (No, it's not, but I'm pledged not to give the real name.) The Basket draws the funkiest crowd in town because its taped music is wilder and its denizens freakier than you can find anyplace else. But the sustaining patronage comes, of course, from the gay world. Never mind that there is not a limp wrist or a soprano voice in the whole leather-trimmed, hirsute throng. Faggotry is no longer in fashion, but according to plenty of purple bumper stickers in the bay area, Gay is (still) Good.

I was taken there one night by a radical activist friend of mine, and I dug the phantasmagorical scene, with bouncing lights, shrieking music, and a clientele by Diaghilev out of Heironymus Bosch. I danced with anybody who asked me, and a lot of people did. If you know anything about gay bars, you know that they tend to be very boring places where everybody stands around preening and waiting to be spoken to. Not so The Basket; it's the only friendly gay bar I've ever been into. After a while of dancing and sweating and rapping idly with a lot of people, my radical friend suggested that we go next door to the Universal Life Corral, an all-night coffee house, to visit his gay radical friend John, who he said would be on duty there that night.

The Universal Life Corral turned out to be a store-front establishment fitted out to be a pool parlor with lounging space and a coffee bar at the rear; tending that bar was John, a big blond guy who (after the radical fashion of the place and period) wore work clothes and a Tonto haircut with headband. He was amiable, he slipped us a couple of free coffees, and when he had time he chatted with us about what was going on at the Corral.

"We have a gay commune upstairs," he said. "About thirty guys, and most of us work in gay bars around the city. We run this place as a service to the gay community: we're open all night, we charge minimum for doughnuts and coffee, we keep a nice, dark place with groovy music; after the bars close, it's a good place to come. And it's also a fine place for coming down from a trip; we designed it with that in mind.

"Everybody in our commune is a mail-order minister of the Universal Life Church, and that's why we have our name. This place really is for service: if somebody doesn't have the price of a cup of coffee, we don't demand it. Everything is by donation only, anyway. Listen, there are a lot of street people and night people in the gay community, and after two A.M. there has never been anyplace for them to go. Now there's us, and we get a good crowd every night."

John was telling it straight. After two, the Corral filled up fast. The pool table, glowing greenly in the dark room, was constantly busy, and all the chairs and sofas were filled. It was a kind of homosexual USO, and it provided one last chance to make a contact for the night. In the largely promiscuous world of homosexuality, that one last chance is a special break.

While I was still there, the manager of The Basket came in and joined us at the coffee bar. John introduced us, and I explained to this man that I was doing a piece on the radical community in San Francisco.

"Oh, Jesus," he said, "will you please leave us out of it? No kidding, please promise me you won't write anything about us in your magazine. Look—have you noticed the groovy atmosphere at The Basket? Friends, getting together in a friendly way, no hassle, no tourists, a cooled-out scene. Well, we had that once before, a few years ago, and then *Life* magazine came to town and we allowed them to photograph the place and they ran it very big. And the next thing, the place was filled up with tourists and the regulars stopped coming. I mean, there wasn't any point. It wasn't their place anymore.

"We're a community here, and we are not looking for publicity. We are looking to do our thing among ourselves in our own way. Please don't write anything; we couldn't stand it. Please."

So I promised, and I did not write anything about The Basket or the Universal Life Corral in *Holiday*, or the gay commune composed of gay bartenders upstairs. After all, I expect to be back in San Francisco, and back at The Basket, many another time in the future. And I don't want to find the place jammed with tourists, do I?

A HIP GYPSY IN THE GLOBAL COMMUNE

He is a tall, strikingly handsome young man with long blond hair, a full blond beard, and pale blue eyes. When he speaks— in a soft and somewhat glottal tone of voice which never varies —his eyes sometimes seem to fix on far-distant points that are not visible to the naked eye. I do not mean to suggest that he is fey or in any way addled. He has a sharp mind, a pleasing sense of humor, a readiness to be delighted—in all, an air of innocence that is charming in a twenty-two-year-old army veteran and college student. And a little disconcerting too.

In many ways he is like a character from Hesse, a wanderer in the world's garden, carefully and selectively sampling everything, chewing very thoughtfully, meticulously preserving recollections of flavor and texture but unwilling to pronounce on anything until, out of cumulative experience, wisdom comes. Maybe it is wisdom, somewhere in the far distance, that his eyes are focused on.

The last time I saw him, he was calling himself Ian. For some months before that he said his name was Brian. I don't know if Ian has stuck, or if he has reduced that further to An or initial N, or if perhaps his fancy has taken him further afield, to Irving, perhaps, or Sigismund. There being no pressing need that he can see to bear the name his parents gave him (he will not tell it), he prefers to pick his own, according to the seasons, his moods, or a whim. The popular farewell of the younger generation is "stay loose." Nobody is any looser than Ian and he doesn't need to be reminded to stay that way—his life is a constant flow.

Ian lives in a little wooden house that he built for himself on the flatbed of an old truck. The truck is his mobile home and he's very comfortable in it, taking it wherever he goes, and it suits him just as much as an Airstream Silverliner Trailer suits its middle-aged owners. Of course, Ian lacks water, but while he's still in college he can always wash in the gym, or park his truck in the driveway of a friend's house and use the house's facilities; if he's roaming, there are gas stations and campgrounds. He has a Coleman lantern, candles, and a Coleman stove to cook by. He makes all his own meals, can even entertain to dinner in his truck, and has had as many as four overnight guests on a rainy night, in crowded but cozy and dry circumstances. He designed his house for maximum efficiency, with shelves and drawers and compartments of all shapes and sizes in likely and unlikely places. He knows where everything is and I have seen him demonstrate that, while remaining seated at his tiny desk or lying full-length on his bunk, he can reach out and touch everything he owns.

For all of last year Ian parked his truck every night in the driveway of a student commune in Palo Alto. He was not a member of the commune but a sort of paying nonresident. He slept and ate in his truck but washed and cooked and took his recreation inside, and for the parking and other privileges he paid five dollars a week into the kitty. He was invited several times to become more fully a part of the household but, warily, he refused, and at the end of term he severed his connection with the commune altogether.

"They are nice people," he said. "Especially the girls—and one girl I was really into. But the girls were first and foremost into having a commune. I think they worked too hard at it. After a while they got mad when the guys wouldn't work as hard, would, you know, forget to do stuff, miss their jobs, or leave a mess. They were into fair sharing but the guys were undependable and the girls couldn't stand it. They got angry all the time—or anyway at least one girl was angry at any given moment. Not at me—I wasn't really in it, I was like an observer. But I stopped enjoying being there, you know, with all the fighting and hassling. I really hate angry women, boy—they just can't leave anything alone. I don't need that. So I split."

I asked Ian if he thought he would keep roaming for a long time, or would settle in somewhere one day soon. "Well, there's a bunch of people I met through the Mid-Peninsula Free University, and they want to start a commune as a learning experience and everybody teach each other—Zen, yoga, macrobiotic diet, transcendental meditation. They're good people and I'd kinda like to do it . . . I *may* do it. But I'll hold on to my truck."

EVEN IN PRINCETON

For the past three years we have been living in an old farmhouse near enough to the town of Princeton that, from our attic windows on clear days, we can see the Gothic towers of the university floating above the green elms and the long, flat meadows that sweep five miles from our village to the town's main drag, Nassau Street. We very much enjoy living there, though I confess to wry misgivings when we took the house: I was a student at Princeton, where the college song is entitled "Going Back," and I once swore in adolescent insolence that they would never catch *me* going back. And of course, when I did, it was a matter of absolutely no moment to anyone but ourselves.

Princeton is an old town; it beautifully preserves traces of its pre-Revolutionary past; its shops preserve an almost English tradition of service and courtesy; the grandeur of its residential districts rivals anything on the Main Line; the university's campus is of such historical interest and patrician elegance that many lines of bad poetry and many beautiful picture books have been dedicated to it. However bolshy I am about both town and gown (and that is pretty bolshy at times), I do not kid myself: I love the place. The university was stuffy, unbearably stuffy, when I was an undergraduate. It had been stuffy for many years before that, too, and in many ways we were educated, between 1952 and 1956, in the habits and manners that would suit us for admission to some very exclusive gentleman's club, nobody noticing, of course, that the club was already in the process of being dismantled. Many Princeton alumni, including a great many of my own classmates, do not yet know that the all-powerful cabal of aristocratic privilege has vanished. I was not surprised to find, on attending my tenth class reunion, that many of my classmates had not had a fresh thought since June of 1956, and what's more, did not expect to. And to a considerable extent, the minds (if any) of alumni influenced the life of the university, which is private and has existed for many years on the generosity of Old School Tie. The town, dominated by and always reflecting the sleepy, aristocratic manners of the university, has never been a very exciting center of intellect. Cambridge and, to a lesser extent, New Haven, are college towns in the best sense. Princeton has never been so vulgar; no political coffee shops, no crowded little bookstores, no bearded anarchists. An increasing number of New York and Philadelphia commuters, of course; a good, lazy, exurban life; and more often than not, more somnolent than peaceful.

So I have never expected much of Princeton town or gown—it has gone on dreaming so prettily in its magic green enclave, for so very long, that I do not look for it to become a center for radical activism in the near future. Yet, since we've lived there, there have been some changes that have, given the circumstances, startled us. After much soul-searching, the university admitted women. Oh, such groans and threatened suicides and snatching away of bequests and contributions from the alumni you never saw. And such epistolary Blimp-ism in the alumni weekly: How *dare* you, sir! Then, after Kent State and the invasion of Cambodia, the student strike: chapel undergraduate deacons wearing red armbands at Sunday service; radical rhetoric under the elms in front of Nassau Hall. The Princeton Plan—a scheme for suspending the university calendar during election campaigns, to facilitate undergraduate political activity. A new coeducational residential college, with men and women living On The Same Corridors, possibly smoking dope and copulating. Egad, sir, indeed! So the hoary old joint has come a distance, after all. Nassau Street hasn't changed much, though, except for more pretty girls on the sidewalks and student couples sitting on the lawn in front of Nassau Hall. The Old Guard is deeply distressed by this show of anarchy—in two hundred years nobody has dared to sit on that grass until now—as for me, I find the scene rather refreshing.

Despite my awareness that the town reflects the university, I was stunned one day last winter when my wife called me in New York to say we'd had an invitation, out of the blue, to attend a meeting to discuss a Princeton commune. This was a development I had never expected, and sometimes I wonder whether it's Princeton that's behind the times, or simply my assumptions about it. That night I took an early train, Jean met me at the station, and after a quick supper in town, we followed complicated directions over icy roads to a farmhouse on the far outskirts of Princeton. There we found ourselves sitting in a circle on the floor with about twenty other people—a very mixed bag indeed, in age ranging from childhood to about fifty-five or sixty. There were a few Princeton undergraduates, but most of the people were married couples in their late thirties and early forties.

As we went around the room, identifying ourselves, I heard various people describe themselves as theologian, sociologist, librarian (not unusual in a college town), and also salesman, realtor, social worker, teacher, corporation vice-president. Housewives, too, though it was clear that none of the women cared much for that designation. Students. Children. We sat there for almost four hours, ourselves contributing very little, fascinated to hear a conversation in Princeton, among these clearly middle-class people, about their need to establish a commune. The conversation was open, leaderless, shapeless—a combination of tribal powwow and Quaker meeting—and the corporate vision thus evoked was staggering. These people wanted to establish nothing less than a sort of expanded East Coast Esalen, probably on a very large farm property near Princeton. It would incorporate working farm acreage, a free school, a seminar and therapy center, individual housing for all families, and a full sharing of tasks without respect to stereotyped sexual roles. A local doctor, whose brainchild this commune idea initially was, added the unexpected provision of sanctuary—some means of caring for people who, for one reason or another, might be temporarily unfit psychologically for coping with the outside world.

As it turned out, the doctor and his wife and several other couples in the room had been in gestalt encounters; it was this impetus, more than any other single factor, that had started them thinking seriously about communality. There was a great deal of talk about the commune being of a "one-to-one, male-female orientation," and heavy emphasis upon shared work. Yet most of the men were professionals and clearly intended to go on with their outside activities. It was never clear to me how they imagined that they could do that and at the same time run such an extensive operation as they were planning. Or how, if the husbands continued to be the ones bringing home the bacon, the wives were going to achieve the strict equality everyone was insisting on. The general gist, however, was explained in a pamphlet produced by the Princeton Gestalt Center, and passed around at the meeting. Because it explains something of the motivations of most of the people we were with that night, and because I endorse it myself 100 per cent, I reproduce it here.

SEX ROLES AND SELF-ALIENATION

One of the aims of each workshop at the Princeton Gestalt Center is to explore the stereotyped male and female images, and to illumine and express the crippling effects of these sex roles on our spiritual as well as sexual life. Unlike most therapy and growth centers, we feel that accepting one's sexual "identity" usually means acquiring a more profound degree of self-alienation. We examine evidence from science and from personal testimony in the "rap session" to examine whether psychological maleness and femaleness is the result of culture or nature. We thus acknowledge an important social dimension in the quest for selfhood.

The Center pays special attention therefore to the problem of woman, and to the exceptionally strong and dehumanizing image furnished her. We do not believe it possible for woman to find and become her *self* within the woman's imposed world of passivity, sexual ornamentation and repetitive tasks. Her alleged destiny merely to "be" ignores the wisdom that one must *do* to *be*, and that if one chooses nothing, one becomes nothing. Thus one session of each workshop treats this and the male's parallel bind of excessive action, competition and production. From this view we inspect the alleged failure of sexual romance and love ever to give what they promise. Finally, we consider whether romance and marriage may not be a radically different lasting ecstasy, when the partners are truly equal, sharing with each other two independent worlds.

This statement explains, I think, the source of the group's dedication to equal sharing of tasks, something that is certainly easier to achieve in a reasonably large group of people than in a nuclear family. But I was concerned to ask how this elaborate scheme could be carried out financially. There seemed to be no problem about that. Though no details had been worked out, several people had already pledged a total of very nearly $100,000 as seed money. A scheme would be devised for all members to pay equal shares, or to buy property jointly, or something of the sort. And it was thought that the free school could probably not, at first anyway, be entirely free, except for ghetto children who would be sought and found to make the enrollment less WASP, more socially conscious. Freedom, in any case, lay more in the area of educational innovation than in terms of money. The corporate demand was for an unstructured teaching and learning process, on the abundant evidence that children are natural learning machines anyway, and learn at their own pace, eagerly, until conventional methods turn them off. As one woman put it, there would be no labels of "teacher" and "student" in the school. A child entered the conversation at that point to ask a question. "Mommy," she said, "if we don't call the teacher 'teacher,' what do we call her?"

"I don't know," Mommy replied. "Call her anything you like. Call her Harold. The point is that we will all be teachers and we will all be students, and we will grow together." Judging by the excited babble of junior voices, and the half-suppressed giggles that animated it, this was the best idea the kids had heard all night.

When the question of housing came up, one of the Princeton undergraduates had a lot to say. For over a year, he explained, he had been in correspondence with a large rubber company in Ohio. The rubber company had developed an air-supported bubble house suitable as a dwelling for many people, or for any sort of domestic use; he knew well enough because he and his wife had twice journeyed to Ohio to live in the thing on a trial basis. What he proposed was that, if the adult commune got off the ground, certain communally-oriented undergraduates be permitted to live on the premises during their college years, utilizing the bubble house, which the rubber company was prepared to donate to a student commune if university permission and a suitable location could be secured.

This young man, whose name was Charles, really interested me. Here he was, a Princeton senior and the very image of the Princeton gentleman—tall, handsome, well-groomed (no abundance of hair, no hip clothes), articulate, persuasive. Just the kind of undergraduate superstar that college deans used to take along to address alumni meetings, a flattering reassurance that, even with the passage of time, Princeton was still turning out gentlemen as handsome as F. Scott Fitzgerald, as wealthy as Pierre duPont, and as conservative in their thinking as Calvin Coolidge. But Charles assured me that college deans were not inviting him *any*place, mostly because he was constantly badgering them to allow the establishment of an off-campus coeducational commune in the town. The administration was dead-set against such a scandalous proposal so, in the summer before the first freshman women arrived on campus, Charles took matters into his own hands. He sent a form letter to all the incoming girls, proposing the scheme to them independently, guaranteeing a nucleus of interested, not to say enthusiastic, undergraduate males. Charles received two theoretical acceptances, a flood of hate mail from the girls' parents, and a summons to Nassau Hall for a recitation of the administration's displeasure. Apoplexy, though, would be more like it—parents of incoming freshmen girls were demanding to know if Princeton was running a bordello, and all this while the virtuous administration was feverishly installing double locks on the doors of the dormitories set aside for women. Rarely has an institution so dedicated to Olympian caution been subjected to so much social embarrassment.

But the excitement died down very quickly—not because there was anything prankish about Charles's scheme; he was in deadly earnest, which was the most disconcerting thing for the administration to deal with—but because Charles was in his senior year, up to his ears in work, and no longer liable to benefit from efforts of his own to establish a student commune. Also, he was married, automatically entitled to live off the campus, and perhaps somewhat less personally indignant than formerly. Charles's younger cohorts in this scheme assumed the leadership, however, and did what they could to keep the issue alive. When the university opened the new coeducational residential college in the fall of 1970, the administration was making manifest its recognition that the times have greatly changed. It has not licensed a coeducational commune in a bubble house yet, but I don't think the day is far away. Just last fall students erected a sample model on a university playing field, as a demonstration, with administration sanction. There was even a picture of it in the alumni weekly. Time marches on.

As for Charles, he and his wife live in the state of Washington now, far from the ramparts of Princeton undergraduate freedom, detached from the continuing efforts of the Princeton commune to get itself established. If a student commune ever becomes a reality, and if an adult, family commune in Princeton comes into existence, I hope the two can be arranged to function jointly. It would fulfill the aspirations of one couple who were invited to that first communal meeting, but couldn't come. They are old friends of ours and we spent an evening with them some weeks later, telling what we knew, hearing their thinking.

Andy is a public official in the state; before their baby was born, his wife was a social worker. He has done a lot of independent reading in the history of American communes, more or less as a corollary of his professional interest in developing community consciousness at local levels in New Jersey. Increasingly, the idea intrigued him. "I started to think very seriously about it when the baby came," he said, "and I began to consider what kind of life he would have, what kind of influences there would be on him, how he would be different from me. And I thought about my own raising—we were a great big family, lots of aunts and uncles, people of all ages very much into things together. For example, my grandfather was a very old man when I was a kid, and we were *friends*. My grandfather was one of my closest buddies, my confidant, when I was eight, nine years old. That was really a privilege, you know, to have friends, people you loved, of all ages, living with you and around you. And it just doesn't exist anymore. Here we sit in this house, and as Danny grows up we'll probably be the oldest people he knows.

There won't be that rich mix of people and emotions and human politics that made my growing-up really exciting and educational. And—somehow—secure. Any commune we ever considered would have to have an age range from eight to eighty, the whole gamut. Anything else is just too lonely."

It is strange how we have arranged things for loneliness in our lives: children as distinct from teenagers as distinct from college kids as distinct from young adults as distinct from young marrieds as distinct from middle-aged couples as distinct from their sad, withering elders, who go to "homes" and die without honor and no child nearby to hold by the hand.

I suppose it is not efficient for the generations to know and love one another, and live intimately with one another's joys and problems. I suppose the gaps are there to maintain order and neatness, and a strict sense of categories. But the idea that somebody might someday call me a Golden Ager or a Senior Citizen, and send me away to sit in the Senior Citizen box, fills me with dread. I would prefer the goulash of the Princeton commune, with people of all ages in close contact, pulling together as they are equipped to pull. And surely it would be a fine thing if adolescents and college kids could actually fraternize with adults again. How pretty to think that it might actually happen in a stuffy old place like Princeton.

And for my money, the sooner the better. There are a lot of candidates for community, right in our community, and nobody is soliciting them yet. We were at a semi-academic dinner party recently, and I met the widow of one of my former professors. She's doing social work now in Trenton, and she will have seen the last of her three sons through college by the end of next year. "I wish there were a commune for me," she said, surprising me somewhat. "Well," she said, "it would make a lot of sense. I'm about to be all alone now, and I'm a long way from finished. If I belonged to a whole community of people, I wouldn't be facing this awful loneliness that I *know* is coming. As it is, I feel as if my life is over, and I'm not even sixty years old yet. If there was only a commune, or a family . . . I don't know what, but anyway, people who cared for me, that I cared for, a life going on . . . ."

THE CLASSIFIED CHOO-CHOO

If you are revolted by a world gone mad, stay calm and take the D Train to Prospect Pk. 1530 Stuyvesant Ave. Apt. 2C Locomotive Family Commune

All through last year, this ad, or one very similarly phrased, ran weekly in the *Village Voice*. Most communes do not advertise, though it is a rising phenomenon in the classified sections of hip and underground papers nowadays, and we thought it would be interesting to call upon the pioneer advertiser in the field. So one dismal, rainy Sunday afternoon, Steve took the D train from the Village to lower Brooklyn, Locomotive's ad in hand. His report follows.

"When I got off at Prospect Park I was expecting a park—you know, trees and grass. But there was no park, and it wasn't exactly a neighborhood either, or a downtown sort of section. It was just drab, undistinguished. Gray-brown buildings on a wide, empty street. There was only one store open—a fast-food operation called Wetson's, with a few black youngsters milling around inside—but that was the only sign of life.

"Stuyvesant Avenue turned out to be four blocks away, and 1530 was right on the corner—a big old apartment building, dark and dingy. I climbed the stairs to the second floor, found 2C, and knocked on the door. A tall, thin man answered. His graying hair was cut short, he wore several days' growth of beard, and his face looked drawn, almost tired. He just looked at me.

" 'I read your ad in the *Village Voice*,' I said. 'I'm working on a book on communal living and I'd like to come in and talk with you. May I?' I said all that very softly and politely; the guy was staring at me with such intensity that I thought low gear would be best.

" 'Why have you come here?' he said, after a pause.

"I thought I had explained all that, but I guess my low gear wasn't low enough. So I said, 'I really want to find out what you people have going here.'

"He hesitated for a moment, then motioned me through the doorway and led me along a narrow, unlighted hall into a small room on the left. The room was furnished with a double mattress on the floor, covered with an Indian print; there were two small chairs, and a couple of end tables stacked with old magazines, newspapers, and soiled clothes. The room was dusty and the house was quiet. I thought perhaps there was nobody else there.

"I asked my host, who hadn't told me his name when I gave him mine, how many people lived in the commune. He replied brusquely that he would tell me all of that when he got to know me better. Meanwhile, just talking to him would be sufficient. I am always going wrong by asking communards for objective, concrete information; they don't like it. They always start by pushing me to talk about myself, about how I feel, about what I want, about what they are and feel. And never, never about what I *think* about anything. Thinking and communes do not mix well. And this guy's next question was, typically, a feeling question.

" 'How would you feel,' he began, 'if I told you that I had the answer to it all?'

"I said I would be pretty excited.

"He went on to explain that Locomotive is an evolutionary commune, an organization that is not compromising with the system in any way but is taking a developmental step beyond it. He described people on the outside, gesturing toward the window, as 'emotional zombies' living in 'economic insanity' on a 'planet about to explode.' People out there, he went on, are bound by a set of insane Western traditions which render them helpless, frustrated human beings. Instead of looking for future possibilities, they are 'looking at life through a rear-view mirror,' realizing all the self-destructive results the Capitalist-Judaeo-Christian system was designed to achieve. People out there are lying to themselves about themselves. This is true not only of the Right but of the Left. 'Abbie Hoffman and Julius Hoffman are equally insane,' he said. His voice was soft, his manner mild but firm, and so far his thinking was solid enough to bring me along with him.

" 'Locomotive is a way out of that mess,' he said. 'As you speak to me you are speaking to all of us. Combined awareness. Whatever I say is said by all of us, whatever I feel is felt by all of us. You see, I am a kind of Messiah. But my message is different from some of those other self-proclaimed messiahs who need disciples to exist. All disciples will ever do is get you nailed to a cross. My thing is communication, honesty. I turn others on to what I know, I don't demand that they follow me. These other so-called messiahs are compromising with tradition, with traditional structures, with that whole fucking system. They're not stepping out of it any more than the rest. Those traditions are a waste of energy, they're inefficient. If everybody knew how to live, and lived together, there would be a powerful force for change. A thousand people, just a thousand, could control everything that's happening out there. Did you know that?'

"That question stopped me. I was beginning to get all kinds of satanic vibrations from this dude and I must have squirmed in my seat. He may have thought I was afraid of what I was about to hear—actually I was just as interested as awed by his arrogance. He stopped, flattered me by saying I was 'different from most,' and invited me into the next room, where I would meet The Others.

"We had to pass through the kitchen, where he pointed to a basket on the floor and said, 'That's what it's all about.' Inside the basket were five spotted kittens and a sixth black one, all sleeping. 'The five spotted ones are from one litter,' he said. 'The black one was brought in to breed a new species. The mother of the five is rearing them all.'

"As I understood it, my host was implying that Locomotive was the beginning of a new species. He went on to explain that eventually he would bring all forms of life into the commune, to breed a whole new world. Sort of a latter-day Noah's Ark, I stupidly suggested. He merely nodded acknowledgment as we entered the living room.

"The doorway was shrouded with another hand-blocked print. We pushed the curtain aside and entered a large room with two stuffed chairs, a makeshift mattress-sofa, a coffee table, and a stereo set. A sweet incense filled the air. Two girls in their early twenties were lying on the sofa. One wore dungarees and a shirt, the other a floor-length shift.

"I said hello and gave my name and finally the man volunteered his, which was Joe. However he said that they didn't use names there.

"Joe then proceeded to fill me in on all my speculations. Yes, he was cohabiting with the girls. Yes, many guys had responded to the ad just to get laid. Yes, the ad was designed to find a fourth, a man to breed with the ladies. No, it didn't seem that the lucky stud had yet been found.

"I never found out why. The conversation abruptly switched to me.

" 'Who are you?' Joe asked, quite seriously.

"I said again that I was a writer doing a book on communes. This reply made everybody very angry. Joe turned on me and said they didn't know a thing about me. Since I'd arrived I hadn't expressed one feeling or given an ounce of my ego away. I was concerned only with what I could get out of something. I was lying to myself just like 'all the zombies out there.'

"Earlier, Joe had suggested an exchange—an exchange of information about Locomotive for some kind of payment. I thought I had convinced him that my contribution would be some explication of Locomotive in the book. But that conversation was forgotten. Joe explained that there are doers and sayers. Those who *do* haven't the time 'to scratch it down on a piece of paper.' It's like sitting beside a pool observing other people swimming. The swimmers are doing the changing, not the observers. 'Reality is what you do, not what you say.'

"I tried to make an argument but Joe took my response as further evidence of my inability to feel or be honest. He accused me of lack of committment, and the girls loudly agreed. I wasn't committed to myself and I couldn't be committed to anything greater than myself.

"Coolness is impossible for me to maintain in any of these environments. The communards are serious people, they don't usually crack smiles, and they seem to get right to the heart of the matter. And the matter always seems to be me. It's weird, and every experience is turning out to be an emotional one with me.

"My conversation with Joe was degenerating. He was becoming more personal, more accusatory, and I was getting angry. His language was getting vague and I couldn't follow him. Patience was growing short on both sides. Joe accused me of expressing only what was of value to me. He said I was there only because I wanted to ball his chicks. This charge I politely denied, saying that I really didn't want to. Which pissed him off even more. I was getting arrogant and defensive, Joe the same. About the girls, I asked Joe if he loved them. He said that if I tried to hurt them I'd find out. I then asked, 'Don't you *value* them?' At which point Joe declared, 'Mister, with that question this interview is ended.'

"And it was."

AND THAT MAN IS A DOCTOR

One night last spring, when Steve and I were in Boston, we went to call on Justin Reed, who lives with his tiny band of communal lovers in a lower middle-class district of Cambridge, about a mile from Harvard Square. Following directions, we found ourselves not far off Brattle Street in a neighborhood of chaste, nicely kept McKinley-era houses—fat, comfortable, and respectable. Justin's house was no different. It was a big, gray-frame house with a generous front porch, sitting ponderously behind a trim garden and a white picket fence. Alongside the door was a neat plaque inscribed JUSTIN REED M.D. What could be more discreet?

Justin is a psychiatrist, or rather, was. He calls himself an anti-psychiatrist now, perhaps rather self-consciously, because he has given up on psychiatry to solve the monumental problems of cohabitation at the mass level. He is a man who has thrown out all conventional techniques and scholarly proposals; he believes that solutions lie at home, and because he is courageous and maybe something of an exhibitionist too, he has cast aside the muscle that his doctorate might assure him, and has gone, literally, naked into the world. Or, if not into the world precisely—and that *is* his goal—at least naked into his own living room. Penelope Stone, who has lived with him for seven years, has done the same, jettisoning an equally impressive professional degree. She is a lawyer, qualified to practice before the New York bar, but she does not practice. She says she is more interested in legal concepts; for her, law is more an intellectual exercise than a job of work. Justin and Penelope believe that the world is in a terrible mess; privately, on their own terms, they refuse to participate in the general squalor. They are glib, persuasive, extremely attractive, and very warm, and in that warmth—and in the articulate militancy that underlies it—they have attracted a few others to share their chancy life, and have won a few timid but excited supporters in their struggles against the Commonwealth of Massachusetts. Let it be said at once that Justin and Penelope have no present quarrel with the Commonwealth, or at least would not have chosen this time and place to pick one. The quarrel was picked with them, based on an anonymous complaint that they were running naked on the semi-enclosed (upper half glazed) rear porch of their Cambridge house. They were; they often do, because the refrigerator is out there. But the charge is rather more elaborate than just that; under a Commonwealth statute passed in 1783, the specification is that they engage in open and gross lewdness and lewd and lascivious cohabitation. They rather love the language of the eighteenth century and are delighted to find themselves so described; so much so that they and their friends at once formed a "Lewd Defense Fund" to raise money in support of their defense. This is all no joke, really; they face penalties of up to six years apiece in prison.

The night that Steve and I went there, we had no idea what to expect. I suppose we were suspicious and therefore startled to meet people so attractive, so charming, and so hospitable—though I confess that their style of life is, initially at least, difficult to adapt to. They were just finishing supper when we rang their doorbell; a pleasant young man wearing just a tee shirt received us and showed us to the kitchen, where several naked people were just getting up from the table. They greeted us affably and took us into an adjoining parlor, where we sat down to chat.

We found that a social visit to naked people is not easy—even for such reasonably liberated souls as ourselves. The charge of exhibitionism creeps inevitably to the fore as male and female persons sprawl unselfconsciously before you, genitals rampant (all I really mean is "showing," but rampant was a word I couldn't resist), as comfortable in their pelts as a clutch of kittens. I had constantly to remind myself to cut out such conclusions; after all, I was in *their* house and I had invited myself. Where did I get off calling them exhibitionist on their own turf, where, by the way, all the windowshades were firmly drawn.

In their publicity releases (related to their defense fund), they call themselves a commune of "four, sometimes five people." Nothing very ponderous in terms of numbers, obviously—but their education, their easy ability to deal with complicated legal and psycho-sexual matters from a professional platform, and especially, I think, their good looks and personal charm, make them a more threatening manifestation in their community than if they were a thousand stoned freaks.

The basic four are Justin (dark good looks, snapping eyes, shoulder-length black hair and a black beard, muscular body, moderately hairy); Penelope (a pert face, pale skin, lightly dusted with freckles; luxurious red hair on head and pubis, lovely breasts and legs); James (a handsome but kind and gentle face, sandy hair at the Prince Valiant length, and a fuzzy beard; relatively smooth-skinned body with opulent pubic hair and fuzzy legs); Art (tall, broad-shouldered, dark black hair, smooth-shaven; the face of a riverboat gambler; as for the rest, he was wearing a pair of green slacks so I couldn't comment). Another girl, Angela, was about to move in but was not on the premises that night; Helen, formerly a member, had left for single-blessedness in Cambridge, but remained a friend of the family.

We were in a pleasant parlor, much like any other, nicely and conventionally furnished. Justin lay on his back on the floor, supported by his elbows; James sat or lay near the arm of the chair where I was sitting; Art sat in an armchair on the far side of the room, and a girl from outside the family perched all evening on the edge of his chair. She was fully dressed, and in a rather virginal style; perhaps it was for her sake that he had his pants on. Steve was on the sofa, fidgeting most of the evening because they don't allow smoking in the house; with the same problem, I fidgeted in my own chair, in my own way. Penelope, utterly at ease, moved casually from Justin to James and back again, snuggling, purring, cuddling; she would nuzzle Justin's crotch for a while, then roll across to John, blow into his ear, and lick his inner thigh. The room was warm, almost humid, there was something slightly moist, tropical, and sweet in the air —the result, I realized with a ridiculous inner blush, of exposed genitals in a small, steam-heated space. And for a while it seemed that genitals were everywhere I looked, until I forced myself to stop looking. Through it all Steve and I sat there in our little suits, dutifully asking sensible questions, pretending that everything was Perfectly All Right. Of course it was—but they must have had a royal laugh on us after we left.

Justin does not so much converse as lecture. There is no question that this is his commune and he provides the rationale for everything done in it. On more than one occasion during the evening, he would pick up on what he considered an inadequate statement by somebody else and enlarge upon it while everybody else nodded and said, "Oh, gee, we never thought of it that way." But let me quote from Justin's publicity release to put you basically in the picture.

"The Crime: we live in an Urban Commune. Four and sometimes five. We love. Each other. Ourselves. Our bodies. Our hopes. Our senses—the sounds of voices, music, touch, the smell and feel of each other, the clean air, the bright sun, the cool water, the fresh earth. We are Unashamed."

And that they are—unashamed, by golly. But still middle-class. Justin said it himself. "Of course we're middle-class. For instance, we have private rooms here. Each of us needs private space. That's certainly middle-class." And they have problems that are not brought on by the Commonwealth, problems of personality. "We live together," said Justin, "and we love together. But we're not a smoothly oiled machine. And we're not revolutionary, in that we're not going anywhere." He explained that proper revolutionaries would be constantly expanding, proselytizing, gathering the hordes. "No—we just want to live peaceably right here in Cambridge.

"Of course, I do look for the time when I can walk naked down the street if I feel like it, without getting into the life space of someone walking, dressed, down the other side of the street. I think that ought to be. I don't tell him whether or how to dress, he ought to allow me the same freedom. And I certainly ought to have the freedom to live as I please in my own house."

"The problem," said Penelope, in mid-roll between Justin and James, "is that too many neighborhood kids were dropping by here or talking with us in the park. The people in this neighborhood are mostly lower middle, they worked a long time to get what they have, and they are first worried about what our presence here will do to their property values, and second that we will corrupt their children. So right now we are just not having any kids in; especially since the big bust, it's not worth the hassle."

The family was busted by the Cambridge vice squad on April 10, 1970. They arrested Penelope on the premises, and later found Justin out shopping, fully dressed. The group talked animatedly about that bust, the most exciting event in their lives, with cops creeping in through the back garden, and surrounding the house. It seemed to them very funny, and of course it is, but I don't know if I would be laughing if charged with lewdness. Of course, they didn't expect to win in any lower court; their only hope was in appeals. Curiously, James and Art were not charged.

During the evening Art said very little; his fully-dressed lady companion said nothing whatever. But he did reveal that he is a jewelry store salesman, that his father owns the store, and that he is a drop-out electrical engineer. His salary, and James's as a hospital aide, go toward the groceries. Justin's and Penelope's savings help, along with odd psychiatric consultancies Justin does; the parents of the pivotal pair kicked in cash for the downpayment on the house. It is a modest existence—no champagne and caviar—but they're comfortable.

Art seemed to be less erotically involved in the ménage than the other three; witness his outside girlfriend. But he's known

Justin and Penelope for three years, and he says he greatly values the intensity of the relationship. Justin holds that the measure of success, for them, isn't time—it's the quality of relationship. They all set to praising relationship.

James alleges that his feelings are very uncomplicated. "I came to a party here in October and I never left. I reacted not at all to the ideas or the philosophy—I didn't even hear any at first. I just felt comfortable and happy and I wanted to stay." In an ambiance of open affection, James felt himself deeply drawn to Penelope; the feeling was mutual. "I felt he was somebody I could help," she said. James said he'd been interested in nudity from the age of eight or nine; raised in a liberal Quaker household, he was nevertheless obliged to feel guilty about many things, including his body.

James (who is now twenty-four; Justin and Penelope are both thirty; Art is twenty-five) grew up in Connecticut, took a bachelor's degree at Northwestern, and came east for graduate work. He wanted to do social work, but after falling into Justin's ménage, he gave up school and took the hospital job. "I felt very happy, very settled," he said, "and I wanted to share this with my parents, whom I really love. So I wrote and asked them to come and visit."

His mother reportedly fell into an instant swoon and declined to come. But his father, a college professor, agreed to make the journey. "They're nice people, they're really fine people, my parents," James said. "I love them very much. I wanted them to be happy for me." James's father arrived; the ménage, true to its principles, made no concessions for him. "We just behaved as we always do," Justin remarked, caressing Penelope's breasts as she lay back on his chest.

I asked how James's father had taken it. "Well," said James with a sad smile, "he threw up. He got physically sick to his stomach."

It seems that James's father made it bravely through the afternoon and evening, until everybody fell asleep in whatever assortment they happened to be in at the time. "I thought he'd gone to bed too," said James. "But the next morning he was gone, and there was a note taped to the refrigerator door. He said he hoped I was happy, that he still wished I'd go back to graduate school, and that he was sorry but the whole thing made him sick."

I find it a tragic story, but I don't know how it could have had any better ending. However liberal James's parents are, they are stuck with the mores of their own time, and personal guilts they've probably never looked into. Justin's ménage is not defiant off its own terrain, but their refusal to make the least concessions to age and timidity, even out of sentiment, not compromise, creates a cultural gap that very few older persons can bridge. Hell, it was hard enough for Steve and me, and we are contemporaries. In theory, I endorse the kinds of personal freedoms that Justin is lobbying, indeed going to jail for; my practical mind, however, whispers to me that his insistence is impractical; my sentiment tells me that I would not be able to make my father endure (and for him it would be just that) the spectacle of social nakedness.

What is best? The mores of the past are outmoded, and served but poorly even in their best times. They are full of cant and hypocrisy, and I abhor them. The statute under which Justin and Penelope are charged is an absurd anachronism, of course, and ought to be struck down. In the public sphere, Justin's intransigence may well have a salutary effect upon law and upon the attitudes of others. But the story of James's father continues to sadden me. It seems to me that they sure were tough on the old man—but I guess revolutions are like that.

THE POWER OF THE WRITTEN WORD

When Larry Jansen was a junior at Harvard, he was ravished by a book—namely, *The Harrad Experiment,* a novel by Robert Rimmer. It postulated a fictional college in the Boston area where coeducational cohabitation of undergraduates was a feature of the by-laws, and boys and girls were not only paired in their dormitory rooms but thrust together in compulsory naked gym classes, to underline the institution's policy of support of a healthy heterosexual orientation for all young people. You have to be a monkish relic of the Ivy League chastity of the 1950s to understand how intensely this notion struck Larry Jansen. Nobody, by the way, is here or elsewhere suggesting that Larry and others might have been captured by the sheer lyric strength of Rimmer's prose; Rimmer himself makes jokes about his style, which is abysmal. It was the ideas that got into Larry's head, and he never got them out again.

Before his senior year began, Larry married a pretty and petite nurse from Massachusetts General Hospital. "You know the jokes about nurses," Sarah says now. "Well, in my case, they were true." But when she met Larry, she fell in love, and her love was shored by his earnestness and great sense of purpose. And while he finished his undergraduate work, they lived in a small flat just off Harvard Square. All was not bliss—Sarah was pretty soon pregnant, then delivered of a child. Larry had to take night jobs after school to supplement his scholarship and help from home; Sarah, who was used to working and in other circumstances would have done so, was suddenly stuck at home and feeling very useless. "Finally I invited a girlfriend of mine to come rent our spare room," Sarah says. "We needed the money, and frankly, I needed the company."

By now, Larry had read Rimmer's first (and, according to Rimmer, roughly and vaguely autobiographical) novel, *The Rebellion of Yale Marat*. In it, we find tweedily educated Yale inadvertently married to two indescribably lovely girls; they all three decide to set up housekeeping together in a staid New England town, and though their neighbors are scandalized and some ugly incidents must be borne, they are convinced of the good logic of their efforts, and live happily ever after. When Larry had finished the book he passed it on to Sarah and her boarding friend. No girl, they say, was ever ruined by a book; as that may be, Larry was soon in the middle of a ménage à trois, which was lovely for all participants.

"I wasn't at all jealous," Sarah says. "What we had, sexually and otherwise, was very beautiful, and we had it together. My problem was that, if we were going to be at all serious about this thing, then there had to be some sharing of work responsibilities. The baby was my commitment always; I couldn't ever walk away from that. But Grace, our friend, was free to do as she pleased, with nothing to tie her down. Don't get me wrong; she did share and do her part as much as she could see it was her part. But basically she was still alone and on her own, a free agent. And I was stuck. Frankly, I resented it."

For this reason, and other aspects of passion, jealousy, and resentment that never seem to arise in Rimmer's books, the ménage disintegrated and finally, in a friendly but terminal spirit, Grace moved out. After Larry got his degree, he found a corporation job in Boston, and he and Sarah were able to rent a large, not very expensive house in a near-suburb of the city. Meanwhile, Larry had read *Proposition 31,* still another Rimmer book, in which the author provides a sort of sequel to *The Harrad Experiment.* Group or corporate marriage eventuates for several couples in the course of this work; Larry and Sarah began to discuss corporate marriage.

There is one thing that must be said of all Rimmer characters —they are one-dimensional, message-bearing figures, and they all turn out to have vast sums of money. They sometimes seem to be nice, believable, bourgeois people of ordinary means, but when trouble comes, as it inevitably does, several of them will come up with bequests and secret stashes that finance all legal and other disputes. Also, they know everybody that matters, and often succeed with influence and reputation where vulgar money would never dent the body politic. Of course, Rimmer is not to be blamed for this; he is out to make a point, and he endows his characters with whatever they need to make it. But Larry and Sarah— not to mention the many other middle-class couples who have been fired by Rimmer's ideas—usually have no secret stashes and influential friends. And it does make a difference.

But first, about those interested couples. Larry was so keen on Rimmer's oeuvre that he wrote him, asking for a meeting. Rimmer, who is a business executive in downtown Boston, wrote back promptly, proposing drinks. When the men met, they experienced an instant rapport. There was in it something, perhaps, of the master-disciple relationship; but also, Bob Rimmer is an altogether genial, personable gentleman, and Larry a bright, eager young man. Suffice it to say that they hit it off at once. It was Larry's suspicion that many more couples than he and Sarah had responded enthusiastically to Rimmer's notions; Rimmer said that was true. He had at home many thousands of letters from enthusiasts; he'd answered them all and also kept them, feeling that at some point he would want to do something with them. (By now he has, having collected them in two published volumes.)

Larry proposed that they compose a letter of invitation to all correspondents in the greater New England area and hold an open meeting or discussion group or something of the sort, in Boston on a weekend, to see what would happen. Rimmer agreed to this, a conference room in a Boston hotel was rented, and the invitations went out. Both men were thunderstruck when several hundred people showed up—couples in the main, but many single people as well, and a wonderful time was had by all. Though Bob Rimmer is himself monogamous (a condition he attributes to his wife's preference), he is, according to Larry, "an inveterate match-maker of couples," and it pleased him very much to see that so many people viewed corporate marriage not only as desirable but feasible. The first Boston gathering was followed by two more—on popular request—and out of this early nucleus came strong support for a "nonorganization" to be called "Harrad." Subscribing nonmembers receive a bi-monthly newsletter, containing reports on communes, group marriages and other alternative family structures, and articles and book reviews pertinent to the subject. The letters column is, generally, the liveliest section. In one issue, for example, one correspondent takes issue with what he describes as a "put-down" of homosexuality by Rimmer and the newsletter.

If we members of the "Liberated Generation" put down any group of people because their sexual desires are different, we negate the whole sexual revolution . . . To quote Gautama, "Wise is he who does not name things Male and Female." Homosexuality is needed to fully understand oneself. As a member of the Gay Liberation Front, a group of both gay and straight people who are striving for the total elimination of Society's damnation of any Free Love, I have learned more about myself than through any other means . . . Until you show support for the most ignored minority group I will not become a subscriber to what is probably the best anthology of new ideas I've read in a long time. That probably doesn't mean shit to

you but it is important to me. It is only by living our lives that we
will be able to create that change which we all know must be made.
It is for the same reason that I disagree with Tim Leary. Acid (LSD)
does have its educational benefits but it is not a way of life. Also I
disagree with *your* little blurb about anonymity on the other side.
For their own sakes, people must have the balls to stand up for what
they believe in and accept the effects which they have caused.

The editor's answer:

We believe homosexual expression of love can be a very important
facet of group marriage—*definitely not* something that is to be swept
under the rug. It is a part of everyone's sexuality that is all too
often avoided or denied. We envision that in a close group marriage,
if physical homosexual love does not become a practice, it at least
has been considered and discussed and is *not* feared.

Later in the same column, a correspondent signing herself CW
writes about the isolation of women, and feminine doubts which
she believes may be quite common:

It has become clear to me that the average woman has few if any
people to talk to. How many women can sit down with their next-
door neighbors and talk about feelings that can arise when one is
contemplating a group marriage? Or talk about how it really feels
on the gut, irrational level to "share" one's husband? How does one
cope with these feelings? What good does it do to lose control? How
does one find out whether she wants to be involved in such a venture? How does a person set about discovering her limitations? We
all have them. How do you cope with the feeling of being left behind
—is it my imagination or is it easier for men to get closer to others
(turned on) than for women?

At the end of her letter, CW asks for other women to address
themselves to these and other questions, and create a women's
forum in Harrad. "I do hope the men will read it too," she adds.
"I daresay they could probably learn a lot!"

Larry and Sarah Jansen do a great deal of the production
work on the newsletter themselves; also, in the past couple of
years, Larry has taken increasing amounts of his free time to
attend communal meetings in many parts of the country. They
still live in their big suburban house, and have two children

now, and the last disintegrating shards of a cooperative communal arrangement that began in the fall, a year ago. The group, all in the Jansens' house, consisted of one other couple in their thirties, childless; two senior students at Harvard; one Radcliffe junior; and two girls from Boston University. Once again, the parting of these people (the other married couple had already left by the time of my visit) was amicable. "It was not a question of bad vibes," said Larry. "These were all good people, but in many ways we lacked common ground. The other couple found, through us, an Episcopal priest and his wife with whom they preferred to share their lives. Those things happen. The college students were not, in the end, as committed as they thought they were last fall. They're still in the formative stage; they have careers they want to get on with—it just wasn't going to work out."

"I feel most definitely," said Sarah, "that married couples with children should not try to establish a group marriage with young single people. The commitment simply isn't there yet. It really takes mothers to understand mothers. There is a degree of bonding to principles of family that cannot be escaped—ever. I really don't think most men understand that either. If we are ever going to do this again—and I'm not so sure—then one of *my* conditions is that it must be with another couple or couples with children."

When I left Larry and Sarah, I had the impression that, though somewhat worn down by this latest failed experience with corporate marriage, they intended to go right on searching, and learning by doing, in the full confidence that one day they will hit the jackpot and live as happily ever after as any characters invented by Robert Rimmer. And I hope they do.

A THERAPEUTIC LITTLE ENCOUNTER

Last winter eight quite prominent university professors and/or administrators, and their wives, went out to Esalen for a two-week couples encounter. It was the culmination of long months of planning, by meeting and letter and long distance, among the eight professionals and their wives. The idea was based on their mutual recognition that there was plenty wrong with the process of education as they found themselves and others practicing it; they wondered whether humanity had not got lost somewhere in the process, and whether it might not be—to some extent anyway—their own fault. This they knew: that students were not protesting for nothing, that there were many evils in the system and that one of them might be an adherence to systems in the first place. What kind of people, they wondered, are we? Shall we not go into the hotbox at Esalen and find out something about ourselves? And will that not serve at least to brighten the various corners where we are, light a few little candles here and there? Many possible outcomes of the experience were contemplated: if real union and growth were achieved, and if it seemed right, they could abandon their institutions and band together in a communal college of their own creating; or if at the end of the experience physical grouping seemed wrong, they could at least establish a firmer bond than simple friendship, and have a sort of educational commune by long distance, sharing themselves and their information. Whatever else happened, the two-week marathon would determine better than anything else whether they really were friends, really were colleagues, and whether they were living honestly with their wives and might stand a chance of living honestly with one another. A couple we know, old friends, were one of the eight pairs; they left for California in great excitement, full of hope.

When they came back, it was not with good news—not, at least, for our friends. Their group leader, whom I know slightly, is a fine person and a fine group leader; I met her at Esalen when she was in training there, and admired her then for the tough lady she is. In subsequent years, she has gained a certain amount of fame within the growth movement for her effective work with couples; I was surprised and sorry that a couple I cherish could have had such a bad time with her.

"*I* didn't have a bad time," Harriet said. "It was hard . . . I think encounter must always be hell . . . but it was very good for me. For Louis, though, it was bad."

"Harriet," Louis said, "I'd really rather not talk about it."

But in the end they did talk, mostly because I'm pushy. The trouble turned out to be that Louis would not be provoked into playing games, anybody's games. He would not confess guilts or inadequacies of any kind, and he refused to be moved by the tearful breakthroughs of anybody else. Even when fifteen people were gathered around him, shouting "You're up-tight!" and "Tight-assed!" and "Let Go!" and similar exhortations, Louis kept his dignity. He kept it partly by pulling out his Kodak and taking snapshots of group sessions and partly by flatly refusing to participate when asked to say what he felt about others. He wouldn't wrestle with anybody or try to push himself out of a circle or anything of that degrading sort. He just kept smiling through, consciously an interested but detached observer, even when all his friends were calling him names, even when they wept and begged him to open up. And in the end all his old friends decided they really didn't like Louis very much and he certainly wouldn't be a part of *their* commune. One other couple wouldn't be in it either; *they* took a look at their marriage, under the pressure of encounter, and decided to get a divorce. But Harriet, despite her distress with Louis's rigidity, is sticking.

Louis said that the major problem for him was the degree to which encounter reminded him of the evangelical Christian action he had once so avidly engaged in, during high school and the early years of college. That particular process had failed him in so profound a way that he determined that he would never be suckered into any such thing again. Confession, fellowship, action—if it all boiled down to malarkey once, it would surely do so again. But he wished it had been otherwise; he hated to lose his friends. And though he felt he had been right to be stubborn, his stubbornness had cost him much loneliness.

"I just couldn't do it," he said. "Not verbally. It was just too threatening to me. Maybe if it had been nonverbal—touching, feeling, gently. I might have made it then. At least, touching would not have got to my intellect."

Louis is wrong there, in my opinion, born of my own experience. But it's certainly true that after spending a long, hard time climbing upward in the intellectual establishment, Louis is extremely protective of the device that got him to the top of his profession. Obviously, it would take more than Esalen encounter and all his professional friends to persuade him to come down out of his precious head for so much as a ten-minute break. So long as this is so, Louis will remain a dear but difficult friend to those who understand his barrier, an extremely difficult husband to his wife, and a member of no commune. For one thing, Louis never cries.

But Harriet loves him, and she's a sticker. Also, she learned a lot about herself at Esalen, and a lot about their friends too. And the situation made her sort of mad. "Listen," she said, "Louis is Louis. He's a good man but he couldn't break through and weep and hug everybody within a two-week period. Does that make him a leper? By the end of that two weeks nobody was even speaking to him and it's not fair. Louis is not the only up-tight person in the world. What's going to happen? Is the New Society going to shoot everybody that won't cry?"

PLUTO IS/ISN'T THE NAME OF A DOG

One of the largest communes in the country occupies one entire block at the heart of a black ghetto in a sprawling Midwestern city. The commune is nameless; it has over one hundred adult members, and more than thirty children of those members; and it is entirely controlled by—and is, in fact, the manifest superego of—a forty-five-year-old former stage carpenter from Maumee, Ohio, name of Morty Wells.

Who, you may ask, is Morty Wells, that a hundred people should follow him and obey him in all things? For they do obey him; indeed, exist only for him. Morty Wells is Jesus Christ, come to earth again, just as he promised, to judge the living and the dead. And just as has been forecast by many writers in this century, Christ's return—to our kind of society, anyway—has proved to be very inconvenient for everybody. Except, of course, for Morty and his disciples, who have evolved a very decent and organized and agreeable life together for these years preceding the apocalypse—and a happy one, unquestionably, so long as everybody does exactly as he is told.

Morty's people, who range in age from the late teens to late middle age, could not be a more attractive, wholesome-looking group. They are also heavily weighted with academic degrees, bachelor's and master's, from some of the nation's finest universities, and to a man are polite, self-contained, and impressively articulate. In order to join Morty they have had to give up all outside relationships and all their possessions, notably their right to self-determination. In return Morty tells them exactly what to do, which is exactly the way they want it.

Not a very desirable situation, you say? But wait a while—what if Morty Wells really *is* Jesus? If he were not a thin, dark little guy with jug ears, wearing a tee shirt and jeans on his bony, boy's body, but were a conventional Jesus with long hair and a beard and a robe and sandals and incredibly expressive eyes, *then* would you give up all you have, and follow him? People go to church every Sunday and say they would, but I wonder.

Morty's position is, as advertised anyway, severe enough to suit an Old Testament patriarch. He has condemned the use of drugs as blessed sacraments. He has accused the mindless, anarchic flower children of missing the whole point of the Aquarian Age. He believes that the country is on the verge of a spiritual rebirth, a rebirth being retarded by helter-skelter hippie efforts to turn on, tune in, and drop out. To achieve this shimmering goal, Morty Wells demands that people transcend the use of drugs and embark on an emotional struggle to become Themselves, now. The proposed formula for achieving Selfhood calls for giving up everything you want and accepting everything you are. So far, neither Old Testament nor Esalen and Gestalt patriarchs could disagree. But he gets more specific, demanding that magic and the supernatural be abandoned. He preaches that there is only One Power and only One Way to it. The One Power is Morty Wells himself, and the way to total merger is through (are you listening, Middle America?) Hard Work.

Morty believes that he is more than mere man because he speaks The Truth. He writes (Morty never speaks to outsiders) of himself as the Reincarnation of Christ and he deeply believes that. He describes the tragic condition of mankind, and the many useless attempts man has made to build a decent society, all without good result. He repudiates sacraments of all types and insists that Utopia is within reach if we could only give up lying, both individually and as a society. The embodiment of The Truth is, of course, himself—a man who has been through all suffering and who has made the ultimate sacrifice of giving up his material reality in order to take on the problems of the world. He feels, perhaps with some justice, given the isolated life he lives, that he is the only man in the world who has accepted that he is God.

Among Morty's people there is no room for doubt or speculation. They say to you straight that Morty is God, that they are there "to serve Morty Wells." Or, "Don't misunderstand," they'll say. "I'm not here for myself, I'm here for Morty." You get the same kind of acceptance and conviction from them that you would get from a cloistered Carmelite if you could ask her why she's in the convent. But these statements are delivered entirely in the modern, hip idiom, and are all the more disconcerting when you hear them for the first time.

The first time I heard them, I was already on Morty's turf. I'd heard a lot about his commune, which has occasionally been mentioned in underground papers, and I'd seen pictures of the most uninspiring face and form of Morty Wells, but I had never met him and his people before Steve and I hit the Midwest and called to see if we could visit. The call was taken by a girl who said her name was Linda Libra; she said it would be fine for us to spend a day at the commune, but she wouldn't guarantee that Morty would be free to see us. She gave us careful directions for finding the place. "We have the whole block," she said, "but come and knock at number 68; that's the switchboard and reception."

We drove deep into the black ghetto—as depressing a sight as Harlem, perhaps more so—and finally found our block. It was clearly different from all the blocks around it. The buildings, old, six-story tenements, had been carefully and handsomely restored and were freshly painted. Low hedges and flowerbeds framed the identical entrances all along the street. The contrast with the houses on the opposite side of the street—half-ruined, with windowpanes vacant, ragged curtains fluttering, and paper blowing down the sidewalk—was stark. An intercom and buzzer system operated at number 68; an attractive blonde of about thirty, dressed in a jumper and long-sleeved blouse, welcomed us at the inner door into a kind of combined office and reception area. "Hi. I'm Linda Libra," she said, smiling. "Now let's see," she went on, scanning our faces, checking out our vibes. "You're Steve, and you're Dick." She was right.

Linda was alone that moment. "I've got the phone duty right now," she explained, "but I'll be relieved soon." About then two girls came in, to pick up their mail as it turned out. And then a young man, and then another. We were all introduced and received warm welcomes from everybody. "Hey, you guys," said one of the men. "What are your signs?" We admitted that we are both Leos, me a triple Leo in fact, Steve with his sun in Leo but Scorpio both in his moon and his ascendant. "Heavy," they all cried, but not disagreeably. There then followed at least an hour of light banter, and ten or more additional people wandered in and wandered out. The switchboard kept lighting up meanwhile, and Linda kept conducting quick, inaudible conversations. At least twice, turning from the board, she announced, "That was Morty," but that was all she said about it. Finally a tall young man came in, introduced himself as Ron Hebert, "a sort of majordomo around here," and volunteered to take us on a tour of the establishment. I was enormously relieved to have a chance to get up and get out of the small, crowded room; Steve and I had been conducting, not to say fending off, a nonstop conversation cum interview for a long time, and I badly wanted some fresh air. Linda Libra said she had been going to show us around, but that Morty had felt Ron would be better at it.

"By the way," I said to Linda not long before we left, after she had showed me many stacks of his printed Thoughts, "does Morty ever speak in public, to groups, in lectures, that sort of thing?" She looked at me solemnly for a moment and then cast her eyes to one side. "Not in any way *you'd* understand," she replied.

The rest of the day we participated on the fringe of the communal life. First Ron showed us the large and elaborate reconstruction work that had been done on the entire block, not all of it finished. And we skirted Morty's house, a small, almost suburban dwelling, completely surrounded by a fanciful stone wall, in the center of the block. Wherever we went, the phone would ring and it would be Morty, but when I asked whether we were going to meet him, people always looked very doubtful and never gave definitive replies. For part of the morning we joined several men working on an interior construction job, the revamped entire second floor of a tenement. Just before lunch, somebody suggested that the whole place be cleaned up, and Steve and I had brooms in our hands before we had a chance to ask for them. With everybody falling to at once, the place was spotless in minutes, and we walked together to a nearby building, where lunch was being served.

Leaving our shoes at the door (a rule of the house), we entered a huge kitchen with a big round table in the corner. A couple of girls were busy serving out great platters of sizzling lasagna and bowls of salad, pouring glasses of milk or tea for the men. A lot of good-natured kidding was going on; everyone seemed to be of very good cheer. The style was as gross as I've ever seen, the guys tearing into the food like loggers—presumably the work ethic which is holy among Morty's people extends to workmen's table manners. But the girls appeared not to find any of this caveman dining at all disagreeable.

We remarked to Ron that we had not seen any blacks in the communal work projects or around the place. He explained that Morty feels that the blacks have their own problem and will have to work it out for themselves. He cannot be God for everybody. A color line is most strictly kept, and the commune is somewhat at war with its neighbors. "We even have to keep a standing patrol," Ron said. "Everybody takes guard duty here, the men I mean, round the clock. This is a black area and the blacks would like to see us out. They've tried to block-bust on us—we had a problem with the house next door. When it came up for sale the blacks knew it was the last house on this block, and they tried to buy it. Ran the price way up. It was a clear conspiracy against us—they knew what they were doing. But we beat the bastards and we'll go right on beating them as long as they try to divert us from our work. Morty respects their cause but it can't be allowed to interfere with the cause of a World Savior."

Ron sort of giggled at this title for Morty; so did others at the table. They know it sounds pretentious, however deeply they believe the truth of it. Ron remarked that Morty himself gets a laugh out of the designation. For the commune, the assertion is on the order of Christ's own mind-blowing announcement that he, an obscure carpenter's son (and Morty, by the way, is also a carpenter's son), was in fact the Son of God.

Though all-white, the community consists of a wide variety of individuals from all walks of life. There are writers, artists, filmmakers, photographers, poets, musicians, engineers, graphic designers, manual tradesmen, and a few high school and college drop-outs with varying levels of skills. Very few are presently able to pursue their professions. "We have all the construction problems," said Ron, "as you see. And we do the work that needs to be done. I'm a writer myself, but we don't need writers in the community right now, so I'm sort of a construction foreman. And we'll all do anything we have to do for Morty's sake."

As I surveyed the cheerful table and the hearty enthusiasm of everyone present, not only for their lunch but for one another, I remarked to Ron that they seemed to have worked out a happy plan for living. "Oh, don't be deceived by appearances," he said. "It's not all sweetness and light by a long shot. I don't like everybody in this commune myself—in fact, I have only a few real friends here, and there are some members that nobody can get along with very well. But we do have group strength. One, we're embattled by the blacks, surrounded by them. That helps to solidify and strengthen us. Then, all the personal problems of living together actually serve to strengthen us, because we don't lie to each other or sweep that stuff under the rug, we talk it out and fight it out as we go. And of course we have only one common purpose in being here in the first place, that's to serve Morty. And this purpose transcends all personal preferences or differences. What we have here is communication—between ourselves first, and then with the outside world. We talk all the time about how we feel, how we're working out our problems, and how Morty has helped us to get our heads together in order to resolve community problems. See, it's important that we do this, so that our communication outside can be strong and consistent. What this community is about is feelings—Morty taught us that. And Morty reveals his divine spirit through us, the people who live with him. It's the spirit of divine love, of course; it's the One Real Truth. For that Truth, we've all given up everything. For example, Harry here gave up his wife."

Ron was gesturing down the table to a pleasant, balding young man we had met on the work project, a man who had gone out of his way to make us feel at home. "Yeah," said Harry, cheerfully. "And to *him*." He pointed right back to Ron. But before we could pursue this, a general conversation at the table turned to an orgy which, we gathered, had been scheduled and staged, but had come to nothing. It appeared to have happened just a couple of nights before. People commented on why they felt others could not get into orgy that night, or any night, why they themselves couldn't get into it, and what it all meant to them personally. At first I was sure that this was a put-on for the benefit of gullible strangers, and I took it all with a large grain of salt. But after a while, the earnestness of the conversation could not be held in doubt. Ron lectured a couple of the guys at the table on their failure of spirit. "When we're doing a thing, we have to do it wholeheartedly," he said. "These hang-ups—social, sexual, whatever—we're just going to have to overcome them." Everybody solemnly agreed.Then some guy accused the girls present of having been too scared to get into it. "Aw," said one, "who'd want to ball with a bunch of creeps like you." It was all delivered in high good humor; there were plenty of disagreements among them about this event and about many others, but the discussion remained at a level of caring and affection that I found remarkable.

Before we left the commune, we arranged with Ron and Linda Libra that Steve would return to spend several days living and working there. I had to be off on another assignment; he would remain in town, get a more thorough sense of the place, and then continue to the West Coast, where I would hear all the details. When we drove off, Ron, Linda, and several other members were out on the street to wave us away. Though Steve and I had many reservations about the community, we had been deeply impressed with the sincerity and dedication on all sides. It seemed clear that Morty Wells had an enormous power over everybody; it would take a person of remarkable parts to win so much fealty, and we hoped that Steve would have a chance to meet him during his stay. "Remember," said Ron as our car left the curb. "We have what you want."

When Steve returned alone, he was again treated as a friend, automatically and instantly, by everyone. Ron at once put him to work on a construction project, where everybody already knew his name and his astrological signs. Whenever community member talk about themselves or others, they always give the pertinent sun signs and often refer to other planetary aspects, as appropriate. They believe that the planets influence the seasons, and the seasons influence our behavior, and that it is obvious that the planets must influence our entire lives. They consider astrology to be their language—this is handed down by Morty, who is thought of as the structure in which that language is used. Morty, it seems, has four planets in Aries. Aries has been described as "energy looking for a place to happen." Aries is what is known as the ruler of the first house, the house of creation, the house that is also ruled by the planet Mars—the male principle—and the house that rules the head. An Aries is usually an assertive person, full of energy and drive, and full of self. In its capacity as the first sign of the zodiac, Aries is what astrologers refer to as "cardinal," by which they mean that it is a source, rather than an object or receptacle, of active energy. Aries is also a fire sign, which underlines the energy principle still further. Morty, having four planets in Aries, is for believers in astrology a very heavy person, per se. (By way of comparison, Charles Manson has four planets in Scorpio, an equally heavy but far more insidious sign than Aries.)

Before Steve started work on his first day, Ron told him that a member of the community was busy preparing his astrological chart, an absolute necessity if he were to stay there. Steve worked the day out, helping to clear an entire tenement floor of rubbish and scrap wood. That evening, Ron took him to dinner in a different house—Morty's own. His hopes to meet Morty were dashed when he learned that the Son of God had had to go to Chicago on business. But Morty's first wife, a beautiful woman of about thirty-five, was present. Her name was Laura, and she and Steve were just beginning a conversation when Ron announced excitedly that it was 7:25, and almost time for *Gunsmoke*. "*Gunsmoke*?" said Steve, thinking he had to be kidding. "Oh, yes," said Ron. "Morty wants us to watch it every week. It has more humanity than any other program on the tube." At once, everyone present turned his attention avidly to the show, a segment in which Matt Dillon outwits bandits by pulling down the curtains of a stage coach so they will not see that he is concealed within. After the bandits stop the coach and start the robbery, Matt Dillon throws up the curtain, gets the drop on them and commands, "All right. Drop your guns." This absolutely wowed everybody in the room but Steve, who felt a slight pain over his right eye.

Later, Laura spoke at length with Steve about the community. She explained that the community and all in it are synonymous with Morty Wells. Morty is the ultimate responsibility and the ultimate strength. You start out in the commune as a weak and flawed person, not much use to Morty. But you grow by accepting the rigid discipline of the chain of command, doing everything you are told. As your own response to discipline becomes automatic, you rise in the hierarchy, becoming more responsible for others when you grow in strength—in fact, when your personality merges more completely with the source of all strength, Morty himself. Laura said that all this strength and discipline were absolutely imperative if the purpose of the community were to be realized, to transmit Morty's message—The Truth through Hard Work and Self-sacrifice—to the world. Though many members were working at tasks below their level of competence, it was all part of a plan combining self-sufficiency and cohesion. They had learned that their individual and varied creative efforts together constituted more than the sum of the individual parts. "We are open and honest here," she said. "We do things when they need doing. We don't waste our energies, and we don't rely on others to help us. We are not a place, we are an idea." An idea, she might have added, whose time had come.

Laura reported that everybody in the community could not necessarily be a complete part of Morty. There was the problem of the influence of the planet Pluto; in fact, it was for this reason that Morty had had to go to Chicago, where the community maintained a large apartment for its Plutonians. Plutonians are people whose sun sign is strongly in conjunction with the planet Pluto at the time of birth. Since Pluto is a planet of relatively recent discovery, astrologers know little about it, but assume, from its placement so far from the sun, that its scope of influence is universal. In fact, they call it the planet of universal conscience. Pluto is also referred to as a powerful planet, and its powers are, at the moment, associated with the underworld. According to Laura, Plutonians exist on the periphery of the world rather than in it; they tend to be unfeeling individuals, whose only touch with reality is a casual stroll through the complexities of human relationships, followed customarily by immediate retreat into separateness and disdain. It seems that all the members living in Chicago were Plutonians, utterly incompatible with the larger community, "androids," Laura called them. They were all extremely talented in a variety of fields, all held excellent jobs in advertising, publishing, and the arts which provided a healthy source of income for the community, but were personally intolerable to the membership and were better off together in their urban exile. Morty occasionally had to go and reorganize their life and work patterns; it was a chore, and as distasteful to him as to everyone else, but in his capacity as God, unavoidable.

Later that night, as Steve was crossing the compound to his new quarters in a dormitory set aside for neophytes, he ran into a group of members who were chatting in the dark. It was only about 10:30 and he thought something might be going on—some music or some dancing, good times of some sort. So he asked the group what was happening. "Well," said one young man, most earnestly, "I think there's some work going on over at number 74." Floored, Steve trudged on to the dormitory, where he found his male roommates fast asleep.

His sleep was disturbed regularly from about 4 A.M. onwards, by roommates rising to do two-hour stints of guard duty. In a comradely spirit they always shook him awake to invite him along, but there was no implied obligation. Everyone in the community must do as he is told; but in areas for which no directions have been given, everyone is free to do as he pleases.

Steve slept on until 10 A.M., chatted for a while with one of his roommates, who was in a state of distress because he'd been told to go out and get an outside job (this is seen as a terrible deprivation by members), then got some breakfast and had a long conversation with still another young member. This one, who was twenty-two and a college drop-out, had come to the community originally because his elder brother had become a member. "I figured my brother knew what he was doing," the boy said. "Not me. I was messed up at the time, flunked out of Wesleyan, no job, no chick, and I really needed something to bring me together. I came up here and I met Morty. Let me tell you I was scared to meet the cat. I had read his stuff, you know, my brother sent it to me. And man, that cat had something to say. Who the fuck was *I* to meet him? What was I going to say to the cat? I stood outside his room for fifteen minutes before I dared to go in. Just hearing his voice gave me the chills. But I could hear what he was saying and it was beautiful, man. When I got the courage to walk in, I was scared shitless. But Morty, man, he was beautiful. He saw I was scared, he felt it the moment I walked in. But by the time I walked out, I knew I had spoken to God, because that's what Morty is, man. God. The cat is unbelievably powerful. It's hard to handle, because you know, all the people here are strong too, man. This is a unique place—but then I guess you couldn't have the world savior around and not have a unique place, right?"

Back on the same work project, Steve found things going along vigorously, "organically," as Ron Hebert puts it. You do the work you know needs doing, at the time you're ready to do it, and this practice, faithfully performed, prevents Ron or some other heavy from having to come up to you and tell you to do it. In practice, people simply show up and do, quite agreeably, whatever work is needful for the community. That morning, the conversation had to do with the nature of commitment to Morty. Present mostly were neophytes, locally called "kids." They all acknowledged that there was no social life to speak of, and practically no sexual life at all. But they all thought that was as it had to be; hard work and service were the routes to strength, and they had to be strong before a thorough integration into the life of the community would be possible for them. Steve reports:

"It would be presumptuous of me to make any judgments about the sexual life of the community, but I daresay it is no obsession with these hearty, hard-working guys. They don't think of the girls as sexual objects and they rarely, if ever, treat them that way in public. I didn't see one sign of tactile affection in my time there. There was much affection shown, but in much more subtle ways. Sex is by no means unsuitable for conversation, either. It's brought up, suggested, discussed in a light-hearted way. You just don't see any going on. Women are treated in an unusual and deferential way. The men think of them, in astrological terms, as moons reflecting the light of their suns, as the emotional half of an emotional-intellectual personality, as suppliers for the male producers. They are loved for their quality of heart and used for their quality of mind; men, on the other hand, are loved for their quality of mind, and used for their quality of heart. The two fit perfectly together, and the men respect their women's subservient role—completely traditional in a pioneer sense—as much as they respect their own."

Late in the afternoon, Steve was informed that his horoscope had been cast, and he was summoned to the nursery for his reading. He entered a large complex of rooms, where Laura and several other women were looking after the children. A pretty girl in her mid-twenties was sitting behind a table in the far corner, waiting for him. Steve writes: "I was a Leo, double Scorpio. My sun was in Leo, but both my moon and ascendant were in Scorpio. Leo was in Midheaven so my sun and moon were square. My sun and Part of Fortune ('where it's all going') were in opposition and Mars was in Taurus, opposite my Scorpio rising. I was just a bundle of conflict. Squares, I am told, are obstacles you have to overcome within yourself, and oppositions are obstacles that you must overcome with others. When two planets are square one another, that is when they rule over houses 90 degrees apart on the circular zodiac; and when they are in opposition, that is, when they are 180 degrees apart, they compete with one another. When sun and moon are square, your outer self is in competition with your inner self. And so on, for at least an hour.

"The most startling finding, however, and one which Laura claimed she had suspected from the start, was that the planet

Pluto was strongly conjunct my sun in Leo. I was a Plutonian. Heaven help me, I thought, more conscious of my surroundings now than ever before. The girl who did my chart stood up without a word and left the room. Laura, after saying, I thought so, left also. The children went on playing, and the other women kept on tending them, and nobody spoke to me again. I just sat there in a daze."

By late afternoon, one hundred and more people knew that Steve was a Plutonian, and Steve knew it was only a matter of time before someone called him on it. During dinner, which he took in still another house, his companions were perfectly polite; after the meal, they retired to an adjoining room to listen to a record made by some members of the community. "I realized," Steve reports, "that at no time during my stay had I, before this minute, heard any music. And I thought how unusual that is in the hip world, where everybody has his stereo. But of course I simultaneously realized that I was not in some hip pad. This was about the straightest place I'd ever been in in my life. There wasn't a male there wearing long hair. There wasn't a soul not wearing funky, down-home clothes—sweatshirts, workshirts, and jeans for the men; cotton blouses, long woolen skirts or jeans for the women. No beads, no bangles, no music, no hair— they talked the language of the hip society, but there it stopped."

While the group was listening to the record, Steve asked where it had been produced. One of the young men looked at him very closely and said, "You know something? You're a pisshead." What he might just as well have said was that Steve was an unmasked Plutonian, and instantly repellent to the community. His stay there was just about over.

"You're a creep," the young man continued. "Everybody here thinks so. Ever since you came into this house, you've been giving us creepy feelings. I want you out of this room and I want you out now, or I'll take you out on the street myself."

Steve was abruptly overwhelmed with an awareness that he sat in the middle of a commune of a hundred people who despised him, in the middle of a black ghetto where he could be cut four ways on any avenue, at the center of a city where he was a complete stranger. It occurred to him to square off with his attacker, but how would it profit him? There were ninety-nine more lined up to take a punch at him. Steve left and sought out Laura at her house, where he also found Ron. They were mildly sympathetic. "I told you," Ron said, "that not everybody likes everybody here; this is a closed society, and in it, people say what they feel, whenever they feel it. This was bound to happen. Anyway, you know how we feel about Plutonians." Very quickly, Laura summoned a number of members to her house, and Steve was asked to explain recent events. But before he spoke, Ron inserted the observation that the community was very close, that "there are no visitors here. Anyone who comes here lives here, works here, like the rest of us. He's one of us. He's never a writer, or a reporter, he's here. We have no *time* for visitors." In short, the community *was* the communal Self; there was no other. And the Self was Morty Wells. He didn't have to be physically present; in the cumulative energy of the members, he *was*. And Morty Wells can't abide Plutonians. They cannot give themselves; their detachment precludes community.

The group settled back to hear Steve's statement, and he ran through it once again, though without much hope of gaining advocates. Everybody listened intently, and then Ron suggested that Steve's attacker be asked over to state his case. Laura asked Steve how he felt about the incident and he replied, "I'm confused. I really don't understand why this happened."

He was lying, of course; he understood very well why this had happened; and everyone present *knew* he was lying, and that he understood. In a very few minutes, Steve Bornstein was out on the night streets, little suitcase in hand, walking rapidly down an empty avenue in a strange city, and wondering how he ever got out in one piece.

STEVE'S TURN

ENERGIA

HISTORY. Heard about Energia from David Shirey, art critic for *Newsweek*. Shirey reviewed their shows in Boston and at the

Museum of Modern Art. At the MOMA show, Energia artists created a dazzling sound and light environment that covered the entire garden area. Beams of light and streams of sound were programmed by computer to bolt out at passers-by from all heights and angles, thus engaging the viewer in a direct, subjective experience with the work of art. *Vogue* carried a short piece about these way-out, electronic environmentalists this spring.

ACCESS. Energia lives in a big, white farmhouse in the Connecticut countryside, about a forty-five minute drive northwest of New Haven. Their place is reached by a paved, two-lane road that winds for ten miles or so from the main highway through some very beautiful and lush countryside. The farms that straddle the road on both sides are of the quaint, well-kept New England variety. The grass is very green, the trees tall and sturdy.

PHYSICAL LAYOUT. A sprawling two- or three-story white farmhouse with perhaps as many as ten rooms. House is set back from the road some fifty feet and is reached by a private, gravel driveway to the left. Lawn to right of the house is green and manicured. Just off the two-lane road, to the left of the driveway, is a huge, weathered red barn across the face of which is written ENERGIA RANCH in bizarrely shaped and colored letters. Further up the driveway beyond the house is another barn, larger even than the first. Around the house and barns is green pasture. A horse is grazing in a fenced patch to the left of the second barn. The grass is high and uncut beyond the barns as far as the eye can see. Like the rest of the area around it, the land rises and rolls.

PEOPLE. I drive up the gravel path and park behind the house next to two other cars. There is no noise in the house and no one seems to be around. I wander past the house toward the lawn on the right. There I see four longhaired men seated cross-legged on a blanket. The lawn spreads out around them in all directions, bounded on the far side by a grove of trees. I walk closer and begin to hear a weird thumping sound. The men have earphones strapped around their heads and what appear to be stethoscopes pressed against their chests with their hands. About twenty feet from each corner of the blanket stands a speaker pouring forth the harmony of their collective heartbeat. I feel a little bit like Gulliver.

I cannot disturb the four, who appear to be in deep concentration. I look elsewhere for faces and find two, one of a man and one of a woman, peering out of the hayloft window in the farther of the two barns. I walk up to the barn and begin a conversation from the ground up. They invite me inside and the three of us get to talking about Energia's art and the composition of the commune.

Energia, I learn, is made up of ten people, six men and four women. The six men have known one another for five years. They all used to live in New Haven and were all somehow associated with Yale University. The men have been collaborating for several years. They bring together the skills of computer science, electrical engineering, sounds, lights, and painting. The four girls are not part of the original group of artists but, in living with four of the men, contribute to the overall life style of the place.

After a few years of working separately out of dingy New Haven apartments, the men decided to bring their work and their lives closer together in a commune. The Energia artists make no distinction between their work and their lives and so they consider the ladies as much a part of their art as themselves. Two years ago, they bought the house and land they now live on and moved in en masse to merge their living and working environments.

The Energia artists have some very strong opinions about the world of art. First of all, they believe that the individual artist is becoming obsolete, soon to be replaced by the group working in concert. They also believe that the museum is an obsolete form. The Energia artists feel that a single imagination expressing itself in a confined space is an unnecessary limitation on the immense artistic possibilities of the environment itself. They want to combine their many talents and bring art to the people where they are. They want their art to speak to the people, to reach out to them, to engage them in experience rather than just sit there on the wall or pedestal. The Energia artists believe in interactive art, art with which one can have a sensual dialogue, a relationship.

After about a half hour's conversation with these two, I noticed the heartbeat group break up and I wandered back to the house. One of the ladies of the house had returned by that time and the two of us got to talking about social life in the commune. Members of the household spend almost all of their time together on the farm. The girl I am talking to, Marie, is the only person in the house with an outside job. She works at Yale. The rest of the group is supported by the proceeds from exhibitions and by a small grant the group had this spring to give a series of seminars at Yale. The commune lives from hand to mouth, but they don't mind and prefer their freedom to economic dependence on the system. The group has planted a garden in which they grow some—though not all—of their vegetables. The women, it seems, do most of the housework.

I asked about sexual sharing and Marie assured me that the commune is essentially monogamous, although she herself was having sexual fantasies about some of the men other than her lover. The two single men have been known to invite visitors to stay with them on the farm but that did not appear to be a regular thing. The impression I got was that the Energia people spend the lion's share of their time with one another, practicing what they preach, so to speak.

I stayed for dinner that evening and got a feeling for the mood of the place. The house, though commodious, is modestly, almost scantily furnished. It is not, by any means, the way-out electronic environment suggested in the *Vogue* piece. Except for the kitchen, the downstairs has almost no furniture. Most possessions are placed on bookcases or are simply strewn around the various rooms. This holds true for the few bedrooms downstairs as well as the living room. The television room downstairs is an exception. In it are two or three chairs and an old, beat-up couch. The point is that Energia has really made no attempt to outfit their home in any way-out electronic way. The reasons, I'm sure, are economic.

CONCLUSION. I had a nice few hours at Energia. The people were very gracious to me and to one another. They seem to be sophisticated people who are all capable of making it in the world outside but have chosen, for reasons of their art, to come together and live as a family. They are very much aware and very interested in what is going on in the world outside and are especially keen on communal living. One of the men was leaving the next day to visit the Taos and Colorado artist communes on a kind of fact-finding and contact-making mission.

When I met them, the Energia group was in the middle of two projects. The more pressing of the two was preparing a street exhibit for the New Haven green, a city festival to which they had been invited to contribute. The second project was the conversion of the larger of the two barns into an environmental theater for the rehearsal and presentation of their work. The Energia artists consider possibilities in every artistic medium when they put together an exhibit. David Shirey says that they have gone further with light and sound than anyone else he knows.

Their commune seems to work quite well. They have been living together for about two years and appear to have done so amiably. They show little physical affection for one another in the presence of strangers but that might just be urbanity. They are very much tied up in their work and spend the majority of their time thinking about it. The conversation around the dinner table was light and touched several times on ideas for their work. There was a minimum of conversation about personal feelings toward one another and interpersonal problems that have cropped up. One guy explained to me that such things are worked out naturally, as among adults, and no special or regular meetings are held outside of their work. For Energia, art is really a full-time riff.

S.B.

THE DELL

HISTORY We knew about the Dell from *The Modern Utopian* and from Larry Jansen. Larry described its founder, Jason Cripps, as one of the key figures in the communal movement for the past couple of decades. He also said that Cripps was a fascinating man, an impression that was also stressed by a recent acquaintance, a Harvard grad student in psychology who has been writing a paper on American Utopian communities.

ACCESS. The Dell is located in Whitewater, Ohio, the home of Palestra College. The town is small and the Dell is a community of small farms located on the outskirts. It is reached by passing over a wooden bridge from the last street onto a dirt path which winds its way through the various groves in which the houses lie. Jason Cripps's house is the last of these, about a mile up the road.

PHYSICAL LAYOUT. Cripps's house, like most of the others, is surrounded by a lawn, a garden, and an expanse of farmed land. The trees around the various houses obstruct their views of one another. There is considerable underbrush along the sides of the road and around the houses as well. The houses cannot be more than a few hundred yards from one another along a sort of linear path. The scene is very pastoral. I can see no livestock.

PEOPLE. Cripps and his wife are the only two I really meet. He must be in his sixties or seventies and is wearing a name tag on his shirt pocket when he greets me at the door. She is somewhat younger, but not much. Their home is a small, white wooden affair with a screened porch. We sit down together on a sofa on the porch and chat for the next two hours.

I ask Cripps about himself and about The Communal Guild, an organization he and his father (Dr. William Cripps, who is in his nineties) operate as a kind of clearing-house for communal information. Cripps has been interested and involved in communal living ever since he was sixteen. His father was one of the key organizers of the Community of Whitewater, the first whole town to be established as an intentional community. William, the father, was asked to be the president of Palestra College when it was founded by their local church group. Jason spent several of his early years apprenticing in other communes, in Kentucky and Tennessee, as cook and general communal spirit.

Jason founded the Dell in the forties primarily for economic and nostalgic reasons. He had a close connection with Whitewater because of his father and was also a theoretical communard in the economic sense. Cripps is a Marxist, in that he believes that capitalism is insanity and that the exploitive aspects of that economic system are psychically destructive to the winners as well as the losers. He believes in sharing, in communism in the true sense. He established the Dell as common land which would be worked in common by a group of kindred spirits. Today, the Dell consists of about ten family households, including two Palestra families; they own the real estate in common and are tied together socially and emotionally through common bonds of friendship and self-interest. Cripps believes in the sharing attitude as the only safe and sane way to get along in this world.

The families are all middle-aged and have been a part of the Dell since the beginning (except the Palestra families which are more recent). They are very loosely organized and convene officially once a year, to discuss the business of their corporation. They see one another often in their capacity as friends and neighbors and often share their food, especially when there is a garden excess. They grow some, though not all, of their own vegetables and have some livestock. Their main purpose in being together is to hold the land in common and to work it for their common economic welfare. Otherwise their lives are rather separate, a fact which Cripps underscores as one of their reasons for success. Community must insure privacy as well as togetherness.

Another success factor, according to Cripps, is selectivity. The Dell is an exclusive club and new members are accepted only when one of the houses is vacated, which doesn't happen often. A new family must be acceptable to the group as a whole. It is clear that only close friends are able to penetrate the community, and Cripps sees this as one of the Dell's great strengths.

I asked about the children and whether there was any expectation of their joining the community. Mrs. Cripps explained to me that everyone in the community, including the kids as they grew up, was his own man and would make his own decisions. Sure, they would love it if the kids wanted to carry on, but it was neither expected nor encouraged. Whatever happened was right. (Cripps's eldest son was living in another commune, by the way, the Camphill Village therapeutic community in upstate New York). Community is a voluntary act.

According to Cripps, community is a religious act as well. Though the Dell is nonsectarian, Jason considers the very act of belonging to a community a religious commitment, a commitment of the soul to a reality greater in all respects than one's own self-interests. The members of the Dell are there because they believe in community and have faith in the fact that communal spirit is what ties them all together. They come from many different religious persuasions—perhaps even practice them now—but have community in common.

Several years ago, Mrs. Cripps and the other ladies in the community established a school for their children in an empty barn on the land. The kids went to the school from the kindergarten through the third grade. Anyone in the community could teach and many of them did. Now that most of the kids have grown up, the school has become open to outsiders, kids from families outside the Dell whose parents are friendly with members of the community. The school operates on a much reduced basis now but has become a community service.

Mrs. Cripps cited two cases in which Dell families took in children from Whitewater who had lost their parents through misfortune or whose parents were incapable of bringing them up properly. The Dell thinks of itself as a Whitewater community organization despite its exclusive admission policies.

Where this is most obvious is in the Communal Guild Organization. This is the clearing-house of communal information that the Crippses operate out of Whitewater. After our chat in his house, Jason took me over to CGO, which is located near the college. It is housed in an old, three-story frame Victorian building on a quiet, tree-shaded street. The building contains a small library of communal literature, a good deal of it written by Jason and his father. Together, the two men and the few college volunteers who have associated themselves with the Crippses publish pamphlets, books, and newsletters describing the history, mechanics, and present push toward communal living in America.

As Larry Jansen and my Harvard friend both reported, Jason Cripps is indeed a fascinating man. He was very interested in my communal experiences and made a special point of riffling through the materials I had brought along with me. What excited him most were the sexual experiments going on in group marriages and the like and the use of drugs among younger communards. Jason felt, on the basis of his personal experience, that totally free sexuality (à la Oneida, for example) destroyed the fabric of community, that it ate into the spiritual bond that was created among people who were making a lifelong commitment to an alternate life style. He was interested to see if contemporary young communards were able to free themselves from sexual limitations, either through drugs or otherwise, and still build strong communal spirit. Was free sex just another flash-in-the-pan? Jason had not heard of Larry and Joan Constantine's research on group marriages so I turned him on to two pieces of theirs which I was carrying with me. He was eager to share the literature, and, in general, was a man open to all progressive ideas that had to do with coming together.

Jason's fascination with social psychology approached the academic in intensity. He knew about many biological experiments currently being undertaken that bear on his own theories of human nature and organization. He talked knowledgeably about one isolation experiment with rats and electrodes that led him to the conclusion that human beings are being overstimulated in today's world and that they need to be isolated for a certain part of the time in order to keep their internal mechanisms in proper working order. To investigate this phenomenon still further, Jason had built an isolation chamber, free of external stimuli, on Dell land not too far from his house. The chamber is a one-story makeshift structure built against a dirt hill that admits only scant light through its two small windows. It seems protected from almost all surrounding sounds and natural movement in the area. One of the two college couples now lives in it.

CONCLUSIONS. As far as the Dell itself is concerned, it is a community of families rather than a commune of individuals and supports itself through the common use of land. It works because the families who comprise it are all endeared to that land and to the idea of holding it together. Their personal relationships do not appear to be too close but their community is built on something far more durable than passing emotional interest in one another. They get together at least once a week for a pot-luck dinner in which everyone brings one dish for all to enjoy. Otherwise they meet only for business, emergency, or general neighborliness. There is little tension (though Mrs. Cripps mentioned one family with which they did not get along especially well, but so what) and the idea seems to hold and last. Theirs is a strong community, to use Jason's own term.

Nevertheless, Jason concedes that it could be stronger, and what he thinks is missing is more of a day-to-day emotional connection among the various members. I mentioned a *Psychology Today* article that concluded that communities that feel together stick together. Jason agreed and reminisced about his earlier communal experiences in the southeast. He did feel that more of that would strengthen the Dell still further, but as it was he had no great qualms about the Dell's future.

RESOURCES. As I say, more notes with Jason's community ideas and much literature written by Jason and his father. Also some information about a loan fund which Jason and other communards around the country have organized as a sort of short-term emergency purse for communities either in trouble financially or just trying to get off the ground. Maximum loan is about $3,000. The loan fund is just another of Jason's attempts to materialize his communal America.

S.B.

MOUNT OLIVE

HISTORY. *Modern Utopian* listing only.

ACCESS. Mount Olive is located in the middle of the Ozark Mountains in Missouri, near a town called Hanley. It is reached easily from a two-lane highway that rolls gently over hilly farmland. Its exact location is pinpointed by a series of signs that name the place and then ward off those who will not respect its integrity. (I was to find out later why these warnings were necessary.)

PHYSICAL LAYOUT. The community occupies a huge ranch of some 1,800 acres. The members built all the buildings on the ranch and until recently were manufacturing fence posts as well as raising livestock and growing vegetables.

The access road is dirt and takes you about two miles off the highway to the main house. The main house is a wonderful combination of ramshackle architectural styles that include what looks like an aluminum airplane hangar that serves as dining room, office, and chapel for the community. The living complex consists of several other makeshift buildings to house the people, the animals, the tools, and the automotive equipment. The post factory burned down the week before I arrived and the story behind the burning is the principal substance of Mount Olive's saga. More on that later.

PEOPLE. Mount Olive now consists of about sixty people. Most of them are the sons, daughters, and grandchildren of Zack Jones, patriarch and founder of the community. Jones is huge, a burly man with a grayish-black growth of beard that hangs down from his chin like a square icicle. He organized the commune some thirty years ago to provide a place for his children and for poor people who were not able to fend for themselves. Originally a chiropractor, Jones realized after several years of practice that there were many welfare recipients out there in the world who were being down-trodden by a capitalist economic system in which they were incapable of achieving prosperity. So he decided to open up his doors to these people and provide them with an atmosphere of support in exchange for whatever work they were capable of doing. All he asked in return for food and lodging and comfort was that an able-bodied man put in a good day's work. If he were not able to, that was okay and the commune would carry him.

For years this worked well and the commune grew to over a hundred souls. Then one day a man named Teddy Ledbetter arrived at Zack's doorstep asking to be allowed in. Teddy was a blind man and had been a very famous gymnast in his youth. At this point he was in his fifties. Zack of course admitted him to the commune and for two months supported him without asking anything in return. Then one day Teddy approached Zack and gave him a check for $150,000. Zack knew nothing of Teddy's money and accepted it as a token of gratitude to the community.

Everything was fine for a while and the community prospered

with the help of Teddy's huge endowment. It came to pass, however, that Teddy, blind as he was, took a liking to Zack's youngest unmarried daughter, aged twelve, and after several months of close friendship asked if they could marry. The little girl, as I understand it, did not know what to do, and when Teddy approached Zack to ask for his daughter's hand, Zack suggested that he rethink the idea. Teddy was incensed and vowed to destroy the community. He subsequently left the commune, taking as many as sixty followers with him, including some of Zack's own family (I'm not sure about the little girl). He sued Zack for stealing his money—which Zack returned to him with interest from the profits of the ranch ($220,000). But Teddy was not satisfied with that and accused Zack of manhandling certain of the departed children with a cattle brand, an accusation which Zack roundly denies.

Anyway, the burning of the fence post factory, which Zack and the others claim lost them at least $35,000 in equity, not to mention the income it had been bringing in, has been attributed to Teddy and his followers and is the subject of much controversy in Hanley. Zack and his eldest son are still awaiting trial on the child abuse charges and the whole thing is in one glorious mess.

Through all of this, Zack, who is perfectly prepared to fight this one through to the end and even die if need be, is wonderfully calm and self-assured. He told me the story with a gleam in his eye that made me believe that he was in the right and that God would stand behind him no matter what happens. He is a sweet man and, even though he seems to lord it over the others, does it in a most gracious and loving way, a way to which the others can and do respond. They respect him immensely and he them, and the family that I met was as loving, close, and warm as any I have ever seen.

He took me into his home without a thought, sat me down, served me lunch, and generally occupied my afternoon with interesting and pleasant conversation. He had a good sense of humor and a keen interest in me as a person and I could not help but appreciate his hospitality. He is proud of what he has done, and he has good reason to be. Just to emphasize the good feeling of the place still further—when I left, after being there but a few hours, Zack took motion pictures with his 8mm Kodak of my putting up the top on the MG (by then it was early evening and growing cold) and driving down the road. He also gave me piles of press clippings and other literature about Mount Olive, including some of his own writings on the subject of religion.

Essentially, the commune is a religious order that is devoted to helping others. Zack himself is a missionary of that order and spends a good part of the year in New Mexico converting Navahos to Christianity. Mount Olive has become part of a national order dedicated to the service of Christ. Orders like Zack's are springing up all over the country and Zack is keenly interested in their doings. He has been to visit several communes and is convinced that this alternative is our only hope for fending off the economic disaster that threatens to follow on the heels of capitalism. He is an Apocalyptician.

CONCLUSIONS. What's most impressive to me about these two Christian communes, the Dell and Mount Olive, is their ability to absorb outsiders without the slightest ruffle in their feathers. Sure, they probably get fewer visitors, especially dudes from New York, but they are open people who openly and easily express their inner warmth, and that is what I presume communal living is ultimately about.

Both of these communes were spawned by the apocalyptic visions of their founders and, although their founders differ in their degree of autocracy, both have been warmed over by the essential pleasure of living with people for whom, as Jason said, community is a religious act. The degree of commitment involved in coming together is for these people lifelong, lifewide, all-encompassing, complete, spiritual. They are in it for real and for real it seems to work. There don't seem to be any illusions about why they are there and consequently they have little difficulty in determining how to do it. They really respect what they are into and that respect glows. I knew the moment I entered the room. I was seated and eating before I was even aware of where and with whom. They were completely transparent people and it was their honesty that swept me from the estranged outside right into their hearth.

Of course, the Christian thing is heavy, and toward the end

of my conversation with Zack he got around to asking about my religious persuasion. I felt a little embarrassed to have to admit I didn't have one. All I say is that if it works for you, and it indubitably does for them, then outasite. So I am different, my commune will be different. One has to recognize that group personalities will differ as markedly and as profoundly as individual personalities and that you have to find your group-friend with the same powers of discrimination that you use to seek out individual friends. Since the commune will by definition be multi-faceted (one facet per member, at least), the job of finding contentment should be a lot easier.

S.B.

FREEDOME

HISTORY. Listed in *The Modern Utopian*. Also heard about it from a girl friend who had traveled all over the country visiting communes. She told me she heard about Freedome when she was in Colorado but spent six futile hours trying to find it.

ACCESS. I can well understand why my friend had trouble finding Freedome. *The Modern Utopian* lists it in Spruce, Colorado, which turns out to be a small frontier town about thirty miles off the main highway north from Denver. And Freedome is not really in Spruce; it is located ten miles up a dirt road off even that secondary road about halfway to Spruce. I found it out of sheer luck. I happened to stay at a motel in nearby Saltville and asked the proprietor, a chicano, if he had ever heard of Freedome. Fortunately for me, he had, in fact had delivered milk to them the year before, and he drew me a detailed map. I can assure you that I never would have found it otherwise.

Freedome is at the end of a terrible dirt road that gets worse and worse the closer you get to the commune. Along the road are several large ranches where horses or cattle can be seen grazing. The land is dry and craggy and looks terribly unsuited to farming. My chicano motelier said that Freedome is situated on the worst piece of all.

So it is. By the time you reach Freedome, you have driven at least ten miles across prairieland over gently rolling hills into what is part of the last American frontier. The commune, however, does overlook a beautiful virgin valley surrounded by distant rounded hills. It really gives one the feeling of space.

PHYSICAL LAYOUT. The dirt road is barred by an outstretched wooden gate hitched to a post with a piece of wire. A sign on the fence reads PLEASE CLOSE GATE. Farther up the road, maybe a hundred yards, is another sign slung across two poles high in the air. This sign reads FREEDOME, handpainted in white letters and surrounded by faint psychedelic graphics. A third sign reads VISITORS WELCOME ON SUNDAYS ONLY.

Two trucks and perhaps four cars were parked beside the road which bends and drops as it approaches the first of the Freedome houses. The Freedome real estate is hilly, hillier than any of the area that precedes it on the dirt path. The homes, of which I think there are about seven, are built out of sight of one another by design. Freedome people want to live in isolated areas and build their homes in accordance with the particular piece of terrain they choose as a location. The houses, however, are not far from one another and can be walked to easily.

That is, if you know your way round. The paths between houses are almost indistinct and are obstructed, except under the clearest possible circumstances by the rocks, trees, stubble, and other underbrush covering the area.

Where the road ends, the first house begins. It is a ramshackle affair, as they all are, only this one is built in normal style, wooden, rectangular, like a prospector's shack. You walk farther into the woods and you suddenly come upon another house, this time a geodesic dome in shiny aluminum material reflecting the bright sunlight. The dome is about twenty feet high and is almost a perfect half-sphere. It stands on a flat piece of grassy land surrounded on all sides by trees. A third house, this time a combination A-frame and dome, stands still farther into the woods, somewhat higher up the hill than the first two. This house was one of two I was allowed to enter. As I arrived on a day other than Sunday, I was lucky even to be invited in.

I entered the house through the A-frame, the apex of which was perhaps twenty feet in the air. The room contained a sink, a kitchen table, a few chairs, a portable electric stove, a small refrigerator, and some dry goods. The room was perhaps five feet wide, ten feet long. It opened into the dome room, also twenty or so feet high, which served as bedroom, living room, and studio all combined. A double mattress lay in the middle of the floor, beside it a lamp, some reading material, and clothes. Several canvases were wedged against the dome wall to the side. The room was mostly bare.

The other house I was able to see was a small adobe whose owner had gone to great lengths to depart from the simple spaces of the other houses. His mattress lay in a sunken area near a fireplace and the rest of the room was designed in such a way as to create other interior spaces for living and working areas. The owner of this adobe, however, had by no means completed his environment and, according to the man I spoke to, was at sea as to what was coming next. There was a community garden, and a small lake.

PEOPLE. I spoke to only one guy the afternoon I was there. He told me that most of the other inhabitants are uptight about visitors, especially during weekdays, and that I would do well not to bother them. The Freedome people are all artists. There are twenty-three of them and seven children. They live monogamously in their own separate homes but share food bought in bulk, like flour, and have formed a sort of informal council which meets mainly to discuss new members. Many people have passed through Freedome's gate and many have asked to join. The selection criteria, however, are fairly rigorous (that is, the Freedome people are fairly hip and they expect would-be members to meet their own personal standards), and my informant assured me that the admission sessions last well into the night and often for several days. Along with a peyote ritual, which the members use to usher in each new season, this meeting is the most spirited event of their social lives together. It gives them all an opportunity to run down their feelings about one another as they come out in the appraisal of new members.

Otherwise, the members of the commune live fairly separate emotional existences. They work together, of course, on the garden and clearing the land in general. But each family is expected to do its own building and is expected to come up with whatever money it needs to do so. Some do work on the outside—part-time—some are still selling paintings, sculpture. They do not meet regularly and appear to maintain fairly separate social lives as well. They get up with the sun, work, and go to sleep. The men, except for one about whom I will relate more, all live with women, some have kids. They go into town together, on one or another of the trucks owned in common, to buy supplies, but that seems to be the extent of their communality. They maintain separate economies, except where already noted, and live pretty much their own lives.

The womanless man whom I mentioned just lost his girl a week before I visited. After living with him for three years, she just upped and left him without a word to build her own house and live by herself a few miles away. He says that he was shocked by her leaving, hadn't any inkling of trouble, and was astonished to find her packing one afternoon when he returned from work. He also said that she was Spanish and that her parents were always at war so she grew up in mortal fear of making a scene. She left without uttering so much as a good-bye to him. It blew his mind, as it would have mine.

The Freedome people are all artists, as I say. Eight of them are from New York, some more from Texas, and the rest from California. They got tired of the gallery scenes in the various areas in which they were displaying their work and decided to split for something less commercial, more real, more challenging. They are all in their late twenties, early thirties, hip, urbane, solid citizens. They are all into a survival trip, as evidenced by the piece of land they occupy, and appear to enjoy the communing with nature, the simple life, the getting into the land, the hard work, the natural schedule, the roughness and readiness of it all.

They are not without their problems, however. One that I sort of discovered had to do with one girl, originally living with one guy, turning on to another guy in the commune who eventually left his own wife and baby for this new thing. I do not know what the consequences are of this exchange but I do know that its reverberations are still being felt at Freedome. According to my informant, this was not the only break-up that has occurred in their two years together as a commune.

How it all started is not completely clear to me either. From what I understand, the original members of the commune were originally involved with Drop City in Trinidad, Colorado, about forty miles to the southeast. They left Drop City because of the too frequent visitations from outsiders and bought this land with the help of some money they hustled from a friend. Two couples moved in at first and the others came in slow succession through various friendship patterns that had been set up when they all lived in cities. They hold the original land in common now.

Where it's going is another puzzle. They have a common garden and are planning to buy a herd of goats in the future. They are loosely organized, I would say anarchic, and I do not get the feeling that this aspect of their community is likely to change. My informant told me that it would be hell to try to get all those strong egos together into anything like a hierarchy. I guess the admissions sessions corroborate that.

CONCLUSIONS. Really few. I did not speak to enough of the members to get any feel for their togetherness, if they have any. I never reached an understanding of why these people came together except that they are all sometime friends and all share the nature trip in common. They are all artists, too, painters and sculptors, but my informant specifically told me that they are on their own trips in this regard. (Examples of their work can be seen along various of the communal paths. Along one, I noted some regularly shaped, yellow wooden objects tacked to adjacent trees. I thought they were trail markers; I was told they were the environmental sculptures of one of the members. Along another path I saw a huge canvas lodged up against a distant tree atop a hill. The canvas was covered with decreasing concentric squares that grew darker as they grew smaller and closer to the center of the canvas. The effect was like a tunnel through the neighboring trees; almost mystical).

S.B.

I think it is self-evident, from the foregoing, that the con-temporary communes of America present a rather forbidding field for inquiry. They take all shapes and sizes, pursue all man-ner of philosophies and theologies of greater or lesser obscurity, and come and go with the speed, almost, of light. They are hard to find and hard to get into, and who can blame them for hiding from the likes of us? The acquisitive drives that dominate the culture are, for communards, anathema. To them, we looked very much like messengers from a culture they had already de-cisively renounced and fled. They certainly didn't need us.

Steve and I were aware that we were only scratching the sur-face of the communal experience. We had stood in the doorways of, and taken meals with, a wide variety of sharing groups; but we still didn't have a substantial hint of interior motivations. Why, after all, should a bright young girl tend an unresponsive garden, day after day, in company with a group of people among whom nothing was happening? Why would graduates of MIT renounce all they owned in order to become One with a former carpenter named Morty Wells? And where was all this widely advertised peace and freedom we had heard so much about? Communal metaphor had become our metaphor—we could scarcely speak of anything out of context with the sharing ethic. But we knew that we still didn't know why. Before we parted, we determined that, when we met in San Francisco, we would get under the surface of the drive for community, or die in the attempt. But we didn't know how close we'd have to come to dangers more profound than mere dying, or how deeply we'd have to probe under the surface. Nor did we have a notion that the surface we'd be probing under would be our own.

PART TWO: THE REVELATION

Moods change. Men, exhausted by the accomplishments of reason, whose processes undergo further refinement even as its products are discovered to be elaborately pernicious, realize that something is wrong. *With reason suffering a partial discredit, with science increasingly suspect, there is a turning toward other ways of knowing, the non-rational, the "feminine," feeling-with. Women choose this moment to mobilize. If, as Ortega says, the core of the feminine mind is occupied by an irrational power (he intends this positively), the next three hundred years are going to be wonderfully different from the last, in ways which no one has contemplated.*

DONALD BARTHELME

I wonder if you remember an old joke that has made me chuckle quietly ever since I was a kid. It goes like this: some guy dies and goes to heaven, but meanwhile his doctors are working on him like crazy and somehow they bring him back to life. And the word goes out that he has seen God, so of course the reporters are breaking down the door to his hospital room, and finally he agrees to an interview. And CBS and The New York Times and the Earmuff Gazette, they're all there screaming, "Did you see God? What was He like?"

And the reborn guy is saying, "Yes, I saw God, but I don't want to tell you about it, you'd just get upset."

So they holler and yell, "No! No! You've got to tell us. You're the only dude in the world who knows, you've got to tell."

And finally he says, "Okay, but you won't like it." And they say, "We'll like it, we'll like it. Tell!"

So he says, "Well, first of all, she's colored."

I guess if it were a modern joke you'd have to say "she's black," and I apologize for the absence of uptotheminuteswingingwithitness here but that's the way I heard it from my father. I suppose my father thought it was an absolutely absurd projection and therefore funny; but the funniest thing I found in it, even at a fairly young age, was that I secretly felt it to be true. Or, anyway, as true as any other effort to define God.

I remember that when I was in a freshman philosophy course in college the instructor was talking about "true believers" of various kinds, fundamentalists and such, and he hypothesized this scene where a bunch of fundamentalist shouters are loaded on a rocket ship and shot far up in the sky past the stars and planets and finally somewhere up there they see an old man in a nightgown sitting on a cloud with a sign pinned on him reading, GOD. And he said, "I doubt very much if they'd jump up and shout 'Hooray!'" Well, of course not, but it's a sweet sort of vision and I've never been able to put it out of my head. Mostly, perhaps, because as a little Roman Catholic altar boy I didn't have a much better perception of God, except that my one was disembodied and lounging in a golden box on the altar, secreted in a wafer. We conversed, though, very often and very vividly, in my head; as I recall it, He had a resonant baritone voice despite the absence of corporeal vocal chords, and He was very kindly.

When I grew up I learned, somewhat to my embarrassment, that in the modern church, Catholic or Protestant, God was—if at all—Up There or Out There but, most decidedly, Elsewhere than in me (despite my secret suspicions); and in any case, not the subject for polite conversation since probably nonexistent anyway. By that time I was twenty and reading the Summa until I was confused enough and bored enough to agree. And for fifteen years I dropped the matter altogether, which was socially more acceptable and much less troublesome than worrying about it.

I tell you all this because, once Steve and I settled in San Francisco we found ourselves being overtaken first by a sense of community and second by an ongoing mystical experience, which we had certainly not been expecting. And we came to realize, as have many people, in and out of communes before us, that God does indeed turn out to be a black woman. And a sand castle. And the bearded, hairy Devil. And a child. And all creation, including what is seen and what is unseen. This is, I realize, a spooky way for a proper, sophisticated agnostic to talk—but I only seem to be that these days. That's just the illusory me talking. In fact, really, I'm God.

So is Morty Wells, if you want specifics. And so are you, of course, but let's not any of us get smart about it. Being God imposes very heavy responsibilities; it's very hard to live up to. You have to be a grown-up and that's awful.

What I mean—and I can't be all that precise about what I mean, because I'm not a very articulate mystic and a lousy theologian and cosmologist—is that each of us embodies the whole story, the entire burden, the start and the finish. I could be cute and say the Alpha and Omega. No use writing to Washington or petitioning the Pope. The buck stops right where it starts—here. Male and female, black and

*white, good and evil, inner and outer, self and other, I and Thou—
all those bi-polar concepts are simply two sides of a common coin:
man. Each of us. And corporate us. A realization somewhat compromised by Charles Reich when he calls it Consciousness III. It is, anyway, a realization that animates many young people today, and
pervades communal life like a powerful but invisible gale. This fresh
wind blows mainly through the collective psyche. It's the major reason
why people are out in the woods wearing Indian headbands and
screwing all and sundry and erecting teepees and munching peyote.
They may not, many of them, be God yet, but by God, they're en route.*

*In the communes—particularly in those charged most vividly with
the Holy Spirit, variously called The Power or Grace or Goodstuff—
life is a religious act, community its inevitable form. I am You and
You are Me and We are One Together—they really believe that. And
when the Goodstuff comes, in a pattern of waves, in an ebb and flow,
it comes like the fires of Pentecost, and there is nothing boring about
it, nothing distant or remote or polite or in the least good taste. It's
a total mind-zap, and it feels good, too.*

*We had a very scary time with all this business, as you can imagine,
and, in the end, though we did think we could cope with it and
fancied ourselves, temporarily, as extremely divine, we ran from it.
And a good thing, too, in practical terms, since it was very inconvenient to be Godly just then, and in that precise company. Those
who were with me in this inadvertent experience were Steve, a girl
whose name is not Nora, and a guy whose name is not Oz. The hour-
and-a-half commune would not have happened in precisely the same
way, if at all, with any other company. In terms of this book project
alone, we were very glad it did happen; it opened our understanding
to what had been, prior to that, inexplicable behavior and conversation
in other people's communes. We could observe other people's communes in a detached, interested manner, but until we were touched
ourselves by the experience, the meaning of communal life escaped us.
You will have noticed several signs of that, perhaps, in Part One.*

*Part Two attempts to explain how communality came upon us; it
attempts to describe the physical manifestations of a spiritual experience and lends itself readily to doubt. But it was a powerful and
overwhelming time, and we do not now flinch from calling it an
apotheosis. Our identification with God came about when we recognized ourselves first as androgynous, then as invisibly connected, then*

as, in fact, the same consciousness. And we realized that our utter interchangeability, our ultimate sameness, or Oneness—not only with each other but with all things—was God. And that is essentially why the title of this book is The Bearded Lady. *That is Steve and Nora and Oz and me; that is all of us. In short, the buck stops right where you stand.*

One more thought about the Bearded Lady. We settled on that image one afternoon last summer while driving through the Big Sur, on the coast of California, a part of the world that has always held a lot of magic for me, even when I didn't believe in magic. And it happened this way: Steve and I were talking about the magnitude of our experience together, trying to reduce it to some scale we could deal with. And I found myself rattling on about a modest revelation that had passed unnoticed in the previous spring, when my wife and I took our children to the circus at Madison Square Garden in New York. A friend of mine, who is a former circus clown and now works in the circus administration, had kindly arranged for our family to have a box facing the center ring, and we could see everything, and it was a mighty show. The children were utterly dazzled, and I don't think anything entertained them quite so much as the monumental indiscretion of an elephant, who took an elephantine shit directly in front of our box. The kids were giggling and nudging each other and thoroughly digging it. Kids love stuff like that.

So at mid-point, my circus friend came to visit us in the box. And though he could have walked up the aisle like any grown man in a business suit, he is a circus man, so instead he did his Human Fly number for us, climbing up the grandstand girders and leaping in among us to vociferous family applause. And soon he fell to philos- ophizing about the greatest show on earth. "The circus will always be with us," he told me. "It will never die. Parents bring their children to us year after year; they don't know why, but we do."

"Why?" I asked, sensing a moral.

"Well, look what we've got," he said, gesturing grandly into the glittering arena. "We've got big tits and bulging crotches, death-defying deeds, and the rank sweat of beasts. We're vulgar, and we're real. Where else today can you give your children that?"

At the time I didn't have any answer, not one single alternative to the circus. I guess it was the only gritty, real-life, grossly rapturous thing I could show my children, or safely participate in myself. Now, however, I have an alternative—and as Steve and I looped the loop on the cantilevered coastal highway, we decided that the closest meta- phor for our communal experience was the circus. Life at the brink, and the primal ooze—we had had all of that. Including the rankness. And the magic. I think that's what e. e. cummings was getting at when he wrote, "Damn everything but the circus." You betcha.

But Corita Kent has already stolen that image for a beautiful volume collecting her collages, so it was opted for. Never mind—we sorted through all the circus images we could think of, until we found one much more apt for us. By-passing high-wire artists, trapeze artists, lions and tigers and bears, even the Human Bullet, we settled happily on the Bearded Lady. Yin and yang in one gaudy and astonishing pack- age, the secret, lurking unity in every bi-polar self. The androgyne. Our selves. The Devil. God.

By no means are all communities operating post-apotheosis, but if they intend really to bring about a social revolution, they might try first to whistle up a revelation. It is past time we realized that primary sexual characteristics are purely incidental and need not, indeed must not, any longer dominate and separate us as they have in the past. Even the most extreme anarchic and/or revolutionary communes have lately been rent by inequality of male and female members, with the guys saying to the girls, "Get off my tractor and haul ass back to the kitchen." This attitude has given birth to women's lib communes, where revolution and Lesbianism comfortably co-exist—but I hazard to observe that in neither sort of revolutionary commune has God yet made much of an impact. And until these communards wake up to their androgynous selves, there will be no apotheosis in their com- munities, and no peace either, and damn little meaningful revolution.

In fact, in long months of searching, we found only two stable communities, both described in Part Two, in which everybody's ener- gies, physical and spiritual, were unencumbered by moral fascism, and where open delight in a common apotheosis enabled everybody to sizzle cheerfully in common.

It is, perhaps, for this reason that communes have, by and large, such a short life. Three to six months is about all you can expect of most groups. And after our own brief but profoundly climactic tussle with the communal experience, we think we know why. (1) A group of people decides that the idea of a commune is charming, pretty, and romantic. They come together and hug and kiss and go Auhmmmmm all the time, and at first it's fun. But because they are basically un-serious and disastrously insensitive to one another, dwelling solely on the surface of being, nothing really happens. They might as well be embracing a lot of store dummies for all the vibration that passes between them. In these close quarters, with these frustrations, there finally erupts a festival of jealousy, meanness, and bad smells, a jarring nonharmony. Talk of "vibes" increases, but vibes do not materialize; hardships do. In the end, with or without free and group sex (which they may by now have resorted to), everybody wonders why he came. They split. (2) A group of quite sensitive people comes together with great intensity and an eagerness to love and share. They love not the idea of communality but each other. They find themselves developing a common spiritual consciousness, they throw off all social and sexual taboos, and the vibrations are deeply felt. For a time there is great elation and excitement, but then somebody literally sees the devil, or perhaps they all do, and there then arises the Stepin Fetchit syndrome: "Feets, don't fail me now." They post out of there, follicles still stand-ing to attention all over their bodies, in as many different directions as there are people. (3) Some refugees of the former group try new groups elsewhere, with fresh and innocent personnel. They try again. But up pops Satan, sooner or later, the Stepin Fetchit syndrome comes into effect again, and the new group takes to its heels. This pattern may be repeated any number of times, depending upon how stubborn and/or idealistic the refugees are. As they invariably see it, Satan is nothing to do with them. (4) A group of people gets to the Satan stage. Some may split but others brazen it out. They knew it was coming, or they are wise enough to recognize psycho-sexual eruptions brought on by living closely together in a joint renunciation of taboos, and/or they are wildly excited to come face to face with Satanism, witchcraft, and related forms, and their adrenalin flows. They feel themselves corporately very powerful, like saints, the elect. Psychic phenomena of an extraordinary sort begin to obsess them—the walls vibrate, cats jump, they read each other's minds. They can do any-thing: they are God. However, as God they turn out to be unsatis-factory, more helpless to effect good than in their previous android condition. They feel that they are unsuitable vessels; anyway, it turns out that God is lonely. Their union disintegrates in a variety of wholly acceptable directions, because now all directions are acceptable. Some contemplate suicide, because life is a cosmic joke and it's not *too funny, especially when the joke's on you. Others retreat to mystical or occult sects and begin to play power games with other people's divinity. Some go up to the mountaintop to just be, others wander as holy bums. And some return to straight life, or to straighter sorts of communes. They make sandals out of leather, screw a lot, and pretend the whole thing was just a dream, or a nightmare. (5) Some few go through all these stages many times. Ultimately, in fatigue and cynicism, they build communities along strictly nonemotional, nonpersonal lines, ashrams without gurus. Everyone to his own, solitary satori, physically together but sexually, emotionally, psychically estranged. This is scarcely any different from the first category of commune but, in subtle ways connected to routine and ambiance, superior. Also, because nothing whatever is happening among people, it tends to remain stable. But I don't really get the point; it was the alienation of contemporary society that set them on this cycle of psychic implosions in the first place. However, it remains true that wholeness, happiness, joy, security do not reside in other people. In the end, man is God alone. And there's nothing like a bunch of other people at close quarters to prove the truth of that.*

Our hour-and-a-half commune achieved the fourth category, and though for excellent practical considerations (and a few emotional ones) we are now in different places, we remain connected through our recollections of what we learned together, and our mutual acceptance that nothing happens for no reason. Oz, I know, still searches restlessly for the right people and the right conditions for the establishment of his earthly Nirvana. The rest of us might be said to be in limbo. Or, perhaps, on a spiritual vacation. Apart from other considerations, there have been jobs to do that we could not do except alone. One of those jobs was this book.

If you read on, you will quickly see how bamboozled I have been by all these events. I have not tried to hide my confusion because it was so integral a part of the experience; and I confess that I am more than a little clumsy with theology and metaphysics. It's better, I think, not to pretend to any wisdom I do not have, and then be caught out as a poseur. There is only one thing I can say, after this experience, in confidence:

No commune, no tribe, no nuclear family even, will ever achieve real human freedom until the barrier between male and female in the self is dissolved, and along with it the sexual and spiritual capitalism that thrive on that division. When we are all of us just us, not denying any part of the dual strengths that would, if allowed, make us whole, then we will see real emancipation. If you try to take the commune trip, try not to choose up sexual sides. Try instead to love all the facets, male and female, that constitute you. Only by doing that will we ever be able to really love one another.

This is no new message, I realize, having latterly looked up Norman Brown on the polymorphous perverse, Karl Jung on man and his symbols, R. D. Laing on the divided self, Wilhelm Reich on the murder of Christ. Speaking of whom, by the way, reminds me of a kid I met in an occult Christian sect on the West Coast. He was in a hallway, deeply absorbed in the New Testament. We chatted awhile and he remarked of this ancient book that in reading it, the scales had literally dropped from his eyes. I said, a little cynically, that I thought I'd heard that before, and he said, "No, really. You don't want to read this stuff the old way, the cold way. Don't analyze, don't interpret. Man, just read the words."

It's not bad advice.

THE BIG LEWDNESS BUST AT PYRAMID LAKE

One of northern California's very special attractions for me has always been the existence, here and there along that ravishing coastline, of several beautiful nude beaches, or "free" beaches, as they are sometimes called. These are areas within easy reach of San Francisco where people may run and swim and picnic naked, spend the day naked in nature, if they wish to. There is almost nothing (in fact, I can think of only one thing) that I like better than running naked in nature. Naturally, I prefer the sun to be hot and the ocean bracing, but I have run naked in the rain too, perfectly cheerfully; and once this summer my wife and I spent the entire day naked on a free beach near Santa Cruz, perfectly comfortable though caught in a gauzy cocoon of light sea fog. It was an enchanting experience because the sun's warmth thoroughly suffused the enwrapping fog, which in turn softened our view of the sandstone bluffs and long-stretching beach, the crisp surf, and other naked couples and families in the distance. It was as if we had entered the fuzzy reality of a pointillist painting. We splashed and ran and wandered, but finally settled on a blanket, ate and drank our way through crunchy sourdough bread and fresh Monterey Jack and a bottle of good red wine, then lay back lazily and dreamed our way through the rest of a magic afternoon, while the crash of waves sent a rhythmic shower of light ocean spray over our recumbent bodies. We even got an all-over golden tan out of it, despite the fog or perhaps because of it. And a warming inner glow that lasted us a long, long time.

I also love to go to the free beach at San Gregorio, when I am out on the coast. There, too, you can see whole families playing and picnicking naked together through golden afternoons, or huddling around fires of driftwood if a chilly fog rolls in, everybody hunkering down into the sand for coziness. Children love it especially, of course, because they have no hang-ups about running naked until we teach them to be ashamed, and I always get a boot out of the sight of little kids and their parents running naked into the surf, or dancing in a stair-step row along the tidal edge of the sea.

Don't tell me you can have the same kind of fun in a bathing suit. You can't. Think of all those people jammed onto Jones Beach, sitting around all day in itchy wet bathing suits, sand in their crotches and genitals all wrinkled and shrunken in there. Who in the name of reason would independently *choose* to spend a day in that condition? It just doesn't make any sense, when the world knows that the only way to swim is naked. This whole "beachwear" thing is such a laugh, when it's perfectly clear that the thing to wear on a beach, so long as the weather is right, is nothing.

The laugh is usually on me, of course, as much as anybody, because I am rarely at San Gregorio to do my swimming, and I have to go along with all these people who apparently are so ashamed of their bodies and mine that we all have to cover up. I remember one day in Palm Springs, when I was enjoying a day all by myself in the pool of an apartment complex. There was not another creature around the place but me; the temperature of the pool was 90 degrees but the temperature of the air was over 100, so the water was deliciously cool when you plunged in, and you felt chilly in the air when you came out. I had to keep my bathing suit on all day of course, and I didn't mind it too terribly much, because it's a terrific bathing suit from Paris and I dig it; but it seemed so silly to me to have to wear it solely because somebody else *might* wander to the pool and *might* be scandalized at the sight of my parts hanging out. Oh, I cheated a little bit: now and then I'd slip my suit down to my ankles and, holding to the edge, slip around some in the water to enjoy the feel of it over my entire body, get some reminder of how pleasant it is to move naked in the water. But I didn't dare more, because of the risk of freaking somebody out.

Why do we persist in covering ourselves up when there is no logical reason for it? Presumably because we haven't managed to accept the natural fact, not to mention the beauty, of our genitalia, male and female. We don't know how to deal with our parts. We are ashamed, and so we teach little children to be ashamed too, to regard a part of themselves as frightening, horrifying, disgusting. I don't get it.

Oh, there are a few families at San Gregorio. There are the people of the hip world, at last. But these comprise just a tiny, missionary band, absolutely a drop in the bucket, while the great mass of society are sitting around in slimy nylon, still hiding from themselves and each other, keeping a dirty secret everybody knows anyway but is *sure* is awful. So the girls keep putting their confidence in Crest Toothpaste and Cover Girl Eyeshadow, and the guys keep reaching for their rifles (to use old army parlance) instead of their guns, the sole recourse of the now-famous male chauvinist, who fires rifles and cannons and rockets and God-knows-what when he'd be better off at home expressing himself genitally. Sex crimes—rape, sexual murder—are all too often simply the final shriek of a man in torment because he's not been allowed to accept his genitality, his rightness as an animal human being. And the bathing suit—this final fig leaf that designers keep fiddling with nervously—is the ultimate symbol of society's persistent plague of guilt. Bathing suits are designed to hide, to titillate, to flatter, and to seduce. They are deliberately wanton, right at the flesh level, a brilliant device for focusing obsessive attention directly upon that which they are pretending to obscure. I can be turned on as readily by that kind of coquetry as the next guy; I'm not knocking the coquetry, I'm knocking the hypocrisy that underlies it. Any way you look at it, a bathing suit is a pretty lewd mockery of what we've been taught to regard as God's image, and most of us go right along with it.

Please don't get me wrong. I don't want to outlaw bathing suits, or legislate for beach nakedness by fiat. But I do feel that, on this question as on so many related to our bodies, most of us are harboring aspirations in what we imagine to be lonely isolation, saying to ourselves privately, Wouldn't it be nice if we were more like the Danes? I look for the day when we can all wear or not wear what we please on public beaches, thus rendering all beaches "free." Well—perhaps not all. I don't think it would be fair to those who absolutely could not overcome shock and shame at the sight of genitals. Perhaps a few secluded beaches and swimming pools could be set aside for their exclusive use, where they could continue to play the game of Let's Pretend as long as it suited them, without interference from voyeurs or the police.

It would certainly be a better arrangement than that now obtaining at Muir Beach, an extremely remote crescent below jagged cliffs, most difficult of access, north of San Francisco. People have been climbing down there to swim naked for years and years, but every now and again they are arrested on the complaint of a woman whose house sits high atop the cliffs. With binoculars she is able to keep a pretty close watch on that beach, and tries not to miss a chance to be offended by what she sees. When the police act on her complaints, the arrests always hit the San Francisco papers, and the lady has become quite well known in the Bay area—but not, perhaps, in exactly the way she'd like. She has, in any case, fairly sharply retarded nude swimming at Muir Beach; I wonder that her success can be any great satisfaction to her.

Once people have experienced a certain amount of social nakedness, they don't really enjoy swimming any other way, and they don't like to miss opportunities to do it. And this fact led to a few very sticky moments at the start of our travels in the far west this summer; the sticky moments probably led to some further complications, which in turn make up a significant portion of this book. So I must explain that, shortly after Steve Bornstein and I had met in San Francisco, we were invited by David Allison, a photographer friend of mine, to join what he called "an ecology camping trip" to Pyramid Lake in Nevada. Some fifty or more ecologically and radically chic people from San Francisco were going to safari up there to survey the Latest Outrage, i.e., a plan to tap the lake to provide drinking water on the California side of the mountains. David had a little brochure that explained that Pyramid Lake was part of a Piute Indian Reservation, that the Indians were getting the usual raw deal that is regularly dealt to redskins, and that the earth was going to be the poorer for any sapping of the lake, which lies in very arid, semi-desert country. The whole excursion seemed to be very neatly planned, and the idea was that a naturalist would guide the party all around the lake, calling their attention to natural wonders they would otherwise be too stupid to recognize. He would also lecture the party on wildlife and Indian lore and a great store of additional vital information; plus there would be a big cookout and sleeping under the stars and a wonderful time for all.

I sometimes feel that I am the last of the great indoorsmen. I am a rotten camper, I don't know how to do anything with a knife or an ax or a compass, and what's more I don't much care to. But there was an item down at the bottom of the brochure that caught my interest, to wit: "Bring your skinny for dipping." There was also some reference to Indian hot springs, another of my enthusiasms. Oho, thought I, a little naked swimming in a beautiful desert lake, maybe a hot springs dip—sounds nifty. Steve showed an equal interest, and neither of us wanted to disappoint David, who after all was going to put us up subsequently, so we said yes. I warned David that we were city kids, intellectuals if you will, and unlike him, not up to date on woodsy lore; David, and his steady, live-in old lady named Lenore, are always cumbered about with sleeping rolls and back packs and bowie knives and Italian racing bikes and Chap

Stick and army boots. This is not our style. "Never mind," said David, cheerfully. "You don't have to do a thing. I have all the equipment you'll need (I knew *that*) and all you have to do is come along for the ride."

So it was that on our first Friday morning in San Francisco, we found ourselves scrumming on the street out in front of David's apartment with a great clutch of people we had never met. It seemed like the whole fifty of them, but after counting heads we totaled only ten; the remainder of the party were departing from a variety of other points, and we would all come together with the naturalist on the lake shore on the following day at noon. It is very hard for me to deal with introductions at eight A.M. on any morning, and I did not get personalities sorted out until much later. In any case, nobody was at all interested in saying How Do You Do; the preponderant question seemed to be how to fit camping gear for ten souls into two tiny cars, closely followed by who was going to ride in what car, closely followed by why hadn't anybody thought to make any coffee, closely followed by who has a map.

It turned out that David, when his attention could be drawn from the orgy of tying, snapping, buckling, sheathing, and encasing he was engaged in, had answers to all these questions, and didn't need a map, since only he knew where we were going. It was for the driver of the other car, a very chic and very radical lady of about forty named Connie Grier, to follow David's exhaust pipe until we got there. In the end, we stood not upon the order of our seating, but simply climbed in whichever car we stood nearer to, and roared off into a lovely San Francisco morning, over the Bay Bridge and eastward, across the baking central valley, past Sacramento, finally pulling steeply up into the cool, green Sierras. And in the middle afternoon we finally came to rest beside a lovely mountain lake with a shore of rocks and pebbles and dense forest all around it. "This isn't anything like I expected," said I, a stranger to those parts. "Oh," said David, "this isn't Pyramid Lake. This is just on the way." And then he at once departed for the woods with his faithful Lenore, not to mention the key to the trunk of his car. Connie split in some opposite direction with *her* keys and a great big, blond-bearded fellow who had been in her car. So that left six of us standing at the rear ends of two hot cars, shifting from foot to foot and wondering what to do next.

Fortunately we all had our bathing suits loose in the front of the cars, so after a kind of decision by osmosis we trekked off into the woods to find a place to change, out of sight of the campers and day-tripper family groups clustered along the pebbly beach. Looking furtively from right to left as we changed, I saw that we were two gents—Steve and I—and four ladies, two of whom were changing right alongside Steve and me, jumping like us from one foot to the other, drawers snagged at the ankles. The other two ladies had withdrawn to the cover of some low bushes and were doing their best to hide themselves from my aforementioned furtive gaze.

We worked out identity problems on the beach, where the steep incline toward the water caused us to splay ourselves out like so many butterflies in a case, gripping with fingers and toes just to remain stationary. In this awkward posture, which we called Lying in the Sun, we learned that the two ladies who had changed with us were Tamara, twenty-three, of Hartford, Connecticut, a graduate of Boston University, temporarily unemployed; and Nora, nineteen, of Oak Park, Illinois, an incipient sophomore at the University of Chicago. Both girls were paying houseguests of Connie's; Tamara was in the last days of a four-week stay in San Francisco, a little breathing spell before throwing herself into a film-makers' cooperative in New York, and Nora had only just arrived in San Francisco, had found a job clerking in a bookstore, and meant to stay out the whole summer.

It emerged that the two girls who had been hiding in the bushes were Poppy and Ella, both twenty-five, former classmates at Center College of Lexington, Kentucky, presently both reporters on a small daily newspaper in a small city in southern Indiana, also presently enjoying a three-week driving vacation in California, using Ella's car. I had trouble understanding their connection with this curious safari until Poppy explained that Lenore, David's ole lady, had also been a classmate of theirs and a good friend, and that they were bunking in, for the ensuing week, at David's apartment. Curiouser and curiouser, said I to

myself; I thought that's where *we* were supposed to say.
girls were remarkably stolid and silent, as uncommunic
four girls have ever been since the beginning of time, I
and that's about as far as conversation went that afternc
wrote it off to the fact that we were all hot and tired and thirsty,
all on absolutely foreign and strange turf, and none of us
charmed in the least by the cant of the rocky beach or, for that
matter, by the company. Steve and Tamara seemed to be establishing a certain sluggish rapport, but there wasn't much else
going on.

Soon, there was a lot going on. Three amazingly crummy-
looking males loomed over us, and one fattish sort of girl, and I
saw in a flash that the males wore leather jackets bearing the
escutcheon HELL'S ANGELS, and the girl was tattooed in a variety
of interesting places, most of which I could clearly see, since she
was wearing a bikini. What they *said* they wanted was cigarettes;
what we *knew* they wanted was our four women, if you'll pardon
me for using the possessive. They certainly weren't our women
in any sense, but it was clear to all parties that in any dispute
over exactly whose property they were, it was Steve and I who
would get killed. And this is something I wish women's lib
would look at a little more closely in their dialectics.

We did our male number, coping with these drooling idiots,
handing out cigarettes and trying to find that mythical level
where they dimly imagine sincerity to lie. With the Angels that
means that you do exactly as they say and convince them that
you love it; in fact, your mind is racing at high speed to figure
out how you and your friends are going to emerge from all this
alive. Let's face it: we toadied. We didn't know anything else to
do. Any one of them was bigger than the two of us; one of them,
their principal slob, was bigger than three of us, if we'd had a
third. He was an extraordinary throwback called Tiny; he was
myopic, he needed a shave, he stank, and he weighed in at, I'd
guess, about three hundred pounds, and his intelligence was not
conspicuous. The other two, whose names I did not retain, were
Tiny's lieutenants. One was a hulk, the other a rat-faced little
fellow with sharp teeth. The tattooed girl seemed to belong to
all of them. She didn't do much but smoke our cigarettes while
sitting on a log that extended slightly into the water, occasion-

ally kicking her feet and setting up a splash for everybody.

She was the only one in "beachwear." The guys showed no inclination to go anywhere near the water, nor any sign that their jackets, or their sweat-stained tee shirts and muddy jeans, had ever been off their bodies since the day they were acquired. All the guys wanted to do was smoke cigarettes, and drink beer (their own), and talk loud. And about every fifteen minutes they would engage in a mock-serious wrestling match that left open which one of them was going to be thrown, fully dressed, into the lake. This wrestling was mostly a matter of great tugging and pulling of one another, accompanied by hysterical laughter in which we were expected to join, and a lot of calling each other "mutha-fucka," in which we were not expected to participate. Nobody ever went into the lake, of course. It was the spirit of the thing.

As the late afternoon wore on, I thought to myself that this was surely the longest day of my life. I was stuck with these creeps, I could not think of one effective thing to do to get us out of there, and as dusk approached I began to fantasize that we would have to sit there forever in our bathing suits, all six of us wearing frozen smiles and emitting, on command, the best simulacrum of laughter we could muster. Heh-heh-heh. The other people on the beach were, of course, no use whatever; everybody gave us a wide berth, and had any real violence erupted, they would have grabbed up their kiddies and scurried away as fast as they could, the chicken-hearted bastards.

So, much as I hated him at that moment for the finkery of his unexplained (it never was) disappearance, I welcomed the sight of David loping along the beach toward us, the faithful Lenore straggling in the rear. David has a wonderful way with all manner of people, a special genius for convincing them—on short term, perhaps, but that's good enough—that he is perfectly delighted with them and admires them tremendously. He is also very bright; so, taking in at once what our problem was, he set out at once to delight and divert the slobbering Angels, engaging them in conversation and whipping out his Nikon to take frame after frame of their ugly mugs. This enabled first the girls and then us to make a discreet withdrawal to the cars, where we found to our enormous relief that Connie and her big blond fellow (later identified as Osmond "Oz" Olmstead, thirty-two, former Georgia redneck, graduate of the University of Tennessee, reformed acid and amphetamine freak, drop-out stock broker and aspiring novelist) had returned and were unloading the trunk of her car. Then Lenore approached with the key to David's car, and it became clear that we were intended to camp in this place for the night.

Following a trail into the woods, we saw that several public campsites were laid out under the redwoods in a sort of compound; there was a cold tap in the center, and the sites were marked by stone ovens and concrete tent platforms. We established ourselves on the one vacant site, unrolling our sleeping bags all over the terrain and piling our food on the picnic table by the oven. A warm day was giving way to cool evening, and darkness was coming on fast. A sweet perfume of natural pine filled the air, I put two bottles of wine to cool in the creek alongside the site (congratulating myself on having had the sense to buy and bring them, especially since everybody else had registered some sort of vague disapproval of my having done so), and in anticipation of getting a smidgeon stoned on the wine, which I thought was going to be a necessary state in order to endure this ourdoorsy night, I sort of relaxed a minute.

My next apprehension shattered my baby calm, as I saw Tiny and his friends come up the path, pass us, and enter the very next campside, where a tent and elaborate gear were already set up. Oh Jesus, thought I; our neighbors for the night are going to be Hell's Angels. That's just terrific. Meanwhile, David came over, and while buckling or snapping something, confided that Tiny had wanted to know of him, "Hey, do those girls fuck?" He seemed blithely unconcerned about the query, while I had the deepest foreboding.

Steve had been busy building a fire in the stone oven, and the rest of us ravaged the food packages for something we could eat right away. Oh goodie, somebody brought carrot sticks. So we crackled away on those, and there was even some *celery*, and I kept casting eager glances at my wine bottles in the stream. Hot dogs were also on the menu, and fresh corn, and I thought that would be just fine if Steve could ever get the oven sufficiently revved up. And maybe the Angels would leave us alone, and maybe this ill-assorted group of nature freaks would get some rapport going, and maybe we could even have a sort of good time.

But at this point Tiny strolled massively past, a little dog at his heels, and the adorable Ella trilled, "Oh, what an adorable little puppy." Tiny, more than civil, came over to our little group at once and started bumming cigarettes and laughing insanely. I could have wrung Ella's neck, the simple, stupid girl. We had no sooner established a decent distance than she blows the whole thing and invites the creep and his friends and his dog right back into our midst. I guess if I were good at karate or judo or something, I would not have been so nervous, but I am not good at any of that stuff; and as I remarked before, Tiny weighed three hundred pounds. I was grateful only for the fact that I hadn't pulled the wine out of the creek yet; if I had, Tiny and his friends surely would have consumed it all on the spot. This would have mixed provocatively with the gallons of beer already in their bellies, and we would have been in a particularly bad way.

Fortunately Steve and I were the only smokers, and we didn't mind lying about being out of cigarettes. Even Ella seemed to sense that she had done the wrong thing, and gave out decreasingly receptive vibes, so at last Tiny and his cohorts withdrew. Then I retrieved the wine, and the hot dogs started going into the fire on sticks, and the corn was roasting, every ear in its own casing of aluminum foil, and we gathered slavering around the bright orange glow of food cooking, as night fell with a crash into the woods.

After dinner, which included a variety of honey-and-wheat-germ sorts of gloppy concoctions, and which I didn't much like but ate ravenously anyway, Connie and Oz announced that they were going on a night nature walk to a cliff top, where they had established their sleeping bags, and anyone could walk with them who wished. Well, David and Lenore had already run off into the bushes again, so they were out; and Tamara had revealed that she had a little bit of marijuana to share, and Steve and I had said we'd like to join her in that; which left only Nora and the two southern Indiana girls (who averred that they *never* took marijuana and never would, how dreadful) to tag along with Connie and her woodsman lover (for so Oz was at pains to establish himself) on a stumble-and-crash excursion through the dark forest. Tamara, Steve, and I withdrew to the far, more thickety side of the creek, settled in the dark into a little triangular crouch, and passed a joint or two. I started to feel a little better again, and also sorry that this nice, quiet Tamara would be off and gone at the end of the weekend.

It was tolerably good dope that Tamara had, and pretty soon we were laughing quietly together while telling stories of high school silliness, and making puns that seemed delightful at the time, and encouraging each other to say put-down things about the nature-freak companions of our party, who would rather scrape their skins on tree bark than enjoy a quiet little high together. The fact was that we felt rather hurt at the coldness of the party, professing themselves indifferent to Tamara's friendly overtures and generous offer of dope, and we made a triangular pact that the rest of them could just go to hell, so far as we were concerned. But directly we were joined by David and Lenore, who emerged from the darkness hiking their jeans back into place. And then pretty soon Nora and Poppy and Ella came along, announcing that Connie and Oz had remained on their cliff top, and joined our expanding circle. Everybody had a little marijuana except our southern Indiana contingent, who however did produce a bag of peaches and passed them around. The peaches were wonderfully ripe and juicy, and we noticed their deliciousness all the more for being stoned, and enjoyed the experience of eating them right down to the detail of juice running lavishly down our chins, and laughed incontinently and, for the first time that day, found ourselves having a very good time. Somebody proposed an Om—something I had never done except with my own family around my own dinner table— and we all wrapped our arms over our neighbors' shoulders, leaning our heads toward each other, and in our various timbres began to sound, as resonantly as we could, repeated Ooooommmmmms. Or more, Auhmmmmmmmmmmmms. The leaning of our bodies toward one another, the tightness of our physical embrace, and the vibrations we were producing in a circle set me to the fancy that we were physically describing a little dome, a little igloo of familiar protection against the darkness of the night. It was a nice feeling, and it was pleasant for me to detect nice feelings in myself; I was tired of being such a grouch.

However, when we broke for our sleeping bags, anxiety flowed in on me again. The goddam Angels were just beyond us, whooping it up on still more beer by the light of a Coleman lantern, and I began to feel like the Last Picket, or the point man on patrol. It occurred to me that if those louts drunkenly decided during the night to find out if "those girls fuck," they'd have to get through me before they could get further. And getting through me would be *easy,* boy. It would be a cinch. I worried about it a lot, and I spied on their lantern circle with gimlet eyes, and wished them Mickey Finns, each and every one, until I fell into a troubled but consistent sleep.

I was actually amazed to awake in daylight. The Angels had not attacked our beachhead in the night after all, though there had been a certain amount of movement I hadn't noticed: the southern Indiana girls, formerly established virginally outside our little circle, had in the night got anxious about their exposed position, and had crept right into the midst of us, for safety's sake. I suppose that even a lot of hairy dope fiends like ourselves were preferable to the attentions of the Hell's Angels.

We moved about stiffly for a time, taking turns to wash our faces under the cold tap, doing push-ups and squat-thrusts and the like to limber ourselves after a long night on the unaccustomed ground. And then breakfasted on some cold concoction of Connie's containing beans and peas and wheat germ and blackstrap molasses. Goody, again. Fortunately (and by now you know me for a black-hearted, sybaritic villain) I had stashed away a little instant coffee for the trip, and while everybody else breathed deeply of the morning air and struck yogic postures that are very good for you, I sloshed down Maxwell House and smoked my first Salem of the day.

Connie and Oz showed up in our charmed circle, breakfasted with us, and proposed a long and difficult woodsy walk to a little cove they'd found, where—they assured us—we could take a naked swim without the risk of offending the straight campers and/or inflaming the Angels. I thought this was a terrific idea, and made one with their party at once; we were joined by everybody save the two southern Indiana girls, who cowered together at the very thought, and we set out through brush and woods, and along the lakeside, to find this sequestered spot.

After forty-five sweaty minutes we straggled into the little cove, a long backwards bend of the lake at that spot, with high bluffs and a narrow beach of large boulders. A mass of drifting logs had jammed into the bend, and among them a whole family of water snakes played, dangling vertically in the water. We stoned the poor snakes until they dispersed, then got out of our clothes while balancing awkwardly on the boulders, and plunged in among the logs. Happily, Lenore had brought a cake of soap. I suppose it didn't serve the ecology of that lake particularly well to introduce Camay to its pure water, but we all felt badly in need of a bath, and it was nifty to lather up while teetering on the side of the bluff, and then plunge into the icy water to rinse and frolic. There was a warm morning sun striking the bluff, and just enough variety to the rock face to allow all of us a perch, and we sat about drying for a very long time, chatting and dawdling and having a happy time. Oz and I developed a little nonverbal competition about which of us was more skilled in walking on slippery logs, and which could maneuver them, half-submerged, with what dexterity; so we showed off in that adolescent way for the assembled party, and I felt manly and competent and pleased with myself.

Reluctantly we dressed, and trekked back to the camp. We still had a drive of several hours into Nevada to Pyramid Lake; we had already dawdled so long that we knew we would not make the noontime meeting of the whole group, but agreed that we would be able to catch up with the party without much trouble.

As far as Reno, the drive was pleasant; after that, as we began to cross the desert flats, we found ourselves baking like so many buns in an oven. It was one of those transits in which even the breeze is the breath of Purgatory, and to touch the outside of the car is very Hell. We didn't sweat, we sizzled; and any high spirits remaining from our cool morning dip had been utterly evaporated by the time we crested a desert rise and had our first look at Pyramid Lake. It was like a mirage, sparkling improbably on the sand, and behind it, as if ordained to be set there by some omnipotent pharaoh of a long-forgotten civilization, stood a slate-gray mountain in the shape of a pyramid, its triangular mass reflected upside down in the gleaming lake.

"Water!" we all croaked, and pantomimed the clutching gestures of the dehydrated desert rats that show up so often in cartoons. "Give us water!"

At the inn we learned that the main body of our group were well up the lake in a caravan of cars. "We're supposed to look for two rocks sticking straight up at the edge of the lake," David said, and we set off down the highway, peering far across the sand and sagebrush toward the water. It seemed that every two miles or so there were two rocks sticking straight up; dutifully, we struck out over the dusty access roads each time, but failed to find the people we were looking for. As the light dust settled over our clothes and faces in increasing layers, our dehydration pantomime began to sound like the real thing. So we decided that we would stop and swim at the next pair of straight-up rocks, whether a party of amateur ecologists was present, or not. As it turned out, the ecologists were not on that scene, but at once, we were. There were a few tents clustered by the rocks, and a few swimmers in floppy-legged bathing suits, so we took counsel together and decided to go far down the lake shore, out of sight of these persons we might offend. We strung out in a long line along the beach, walking with difficulty over the uneven terrain, picking up masses of cactus thorns on the soles of our shoes, finally coming to a point from which we could see no one and, presumably, no one could see us. Then, in full view of rattlesnakes and gophers and a cloudless blue sky, we took off our clothes and, heeling down a steep sandbank, struck noisily into the cool, clear water.

As we splashed around with cheerful relief, I wondered how the southern Indiana girls were coping; girls from Center College do not go swimming with naked people every day. But I saw that they were okay—all done up in their bathing suits, of course, which I learned they'd had the foresight to wear under their clothes, but frolicking happily with the rest of us, apparently undisturbed. After a while, Steve and Tamara announced that they were going back up on the bank to sunbathe, and as they paddled away from the group, and then climbed the steep bank again and started to spread their towels, Poppy came paddling over to me and said, "You won't believe this. I know you think I'm just a hick from the country. But in another few minutes I'm pretty sure I'm going to take my suit off."

I was astonished and I must have looked it. "Well . . . don't be so surprised. We're not *dead* in Indiana, we're just a little shy. Anyway, it makes me mad, all of you having so much fun, and you look so beautiful. Look." She pointed to the shore, where Steve and Tamara were just starting to stretch out on their towels. "Did you ever in your life see anything as beautiful as those two bodies against that sand, in this light, with all this *sky*? With those mountains in the background? It's wonderful, it's so natural, it's so *right*."

Poppy got no argument from me. There was a dazzling innocence about the scene, a distinct if dreamlike impression of grown children at play in some desert Arcadia. Naked bodies did look right in this setting, this timeless bush country with its triangular mountains and wide, still lake. Everything we saw was raw, original, untouched by a single man-made "improvement." Until Poppy saw something else.

"Oh, look," she said, squinting. "Isn't that a man up at the top of that hill? No . . . three men. And one of them seems to have a . . . gun!"

As I turned to look to the top of the nearest hill, I had just time enough to see three heavy male figures silhouetted against the sky, arms akimbo, in the instant before one of them drew a pistol and all three started to charge down the sandy bank toward the lake edge, where Steve and Tamara lay unnoticing. David and the others spotted the charge just after we did, and we all started yelling at once. STEVE! TAMARA! Steve and Tamara sat up and gazed uncomprehendingly toward us, way out in the water. NO-NO-NO. BEHIND YOU. LOOK BEHIND YOU, FOR CHRIST'S SAKE!

But the marauders were down upon them in no time, sending up great clouds of dust with their boots. Steve had his trousers at better than half mast when the one with the pistol stopped triumphantly just above him and said, "AHA. You didn't do that quite fast enough did you, kid?" Tamara was covering herself with her towel and, out in the water, the rest of us clustered together, trying to decide what to do. The armed men were now waving their pistols at us in a circular gesture, and ordering us to come out of the water in the name of the law. David counseled that we should stay submerged; all that was showing was our heads, and we could hardly be charged with lewdness for that. But somebody else, Oz I think, remarked that if we stayed in the water, the law might well construe such defiance as resisting arrest, and with perfectly pure consciences plug us where we paddled. So—angry and afraid—we plodded our way toward the shore. The lawmen turned out to be one white sheriff, fat and red-faced, and two deputized Piutes, great big pudgy fellows, all three in Western clothes with tin stars on their chests. "All right, all right," the sheriff kept saying nervously, "you get your clothes on right quick, while my men take your names. All right, hurry up about it."

Sullenly, I pulled my jeans over my wet and sandy legs, furious that I was not allowed to towel myself dry, and was apparently expected to jam my sandy feet into my socks and shoes just as they were. I wasn't used to being a criminal yet, an arrested person without prerogatives of any sort, and I wasn't enjoying the transition. Connie Grier, she of Marin County chic and radical convictions, hadn't been busted before either, and took it even less well. She charged the blushing sheriff, tits flying, eyes blazing. "I demand to know the charge," she demanded righteously. "Miss Civil Rights," Oz calls her. "Book her," said the sheriff.

Stunned, Connie shut up. Until that moment she thought she had something to argue about, and then saw how it was. As with the Hell's Angels, we would do exactly what these pistol-packing fellows told us to do, from then on. "Have you no clothes to put on?" he asked Connie. "A woman of your age! Cover yourself."

Connie did. And so did the rest of us. And as the deputies came around with little blue notebooks, demanding our names and addresses, we all politely gave them. They even took the names of the Center College girls, which seemed to me unjust, since they had been modestly attired in modest mid-Western bathing suits the whole time. But there must have been something about our general manner—after all, we weren't really filthy hippies or thrill-crazed drug addicts, and we weren't children, either, or blacks—which disoriented the sheriff. Police are accustomed to pushing around kids, hippies, addicts, and black-folk without a flicker of concern for their own hides; with us, the sheriff confronted an unfamiliar bag of tricks: Naked. White. Milddle-class. Grown-ups. "Now I'm going to tell you something," the sheriff announced. "You are all in violation of the laws of Washoe County, Nevada, and of the laws of common decency." (He was getting up thunder now, beginning to shake with the effort to control his rage.) "I'm not going to book you. I booked a bunch like you last week and I'm tired of it. I don't want to get my fingers dirty on you. But we have your names and addresses, and it will go on the public record that you are banned from this reservation and from Washoe County for one calendar year from this date.

"Don't any of you show yourselves in this county again or I'll book you. You better believe I'll throw the goddam book at you if *I* see you. And I'd advise you to get in your cars and get right back on to wherever you come from—California, is it? Well, you get your asses over that border again if you know what's good for you. As far as I'm concerned you're nothing but a bunch of filthy pigs, and we don't want your kind around here giving our county a bad name. Get on over to California—maybe they can stand your stink over there, but we can't. Go on, git."

Silently, our little band straggled through the sand and cactus to our cars, each thinking his own thoughts. I felt angry, very angry, but also enormously relieved. I could be fancy about it and sputter that nobody had ever talked to me like that in my life, and that would be true, but so what? People get talked to like that all the time, hundreds of thousands of them, in this country. I had never been on the receiving end of it before, but in my Chicago days, when I was a police reporter, I saw the realities of corrupt police power at first hand, and I've never trusted cops since those days. So my relief was born of the strong suspicion that, if that man had arrested us and taken us to jail, we would have lost a good deal more than our liberty—our teeth, say, or our ribs.

Once in our cars and heading out, loud debates rent the whistle of the driving wind. David felt we should drive around for a while and then return; I thought he was insane. So long as we were still in the sheriff's jurisdiction, there was nothing to prevent him from stopping our cars on any pretext and going through the whole thing again, this time worse. I was amazed that he hadn't searched us, in fact, certain of turning up marijuana on one or another of us. And he would have turned it up, too, on poor Tamara, who already had her plane booked and everything, and had no more interest than the rest of us in going through the toils of a dope bust. "Oh," said David, "he can't do that. He can't search you without a warrant."

"Listen, David," said I, "that little bastard can do anything—bust us now, search us later, fix the books . . . anything. All it means for us is more and more hassle, and Tamara *is* holding. So let us please shag ass out of here." This counsel won consensus, and we sped toward California, hastening to spare Washoe County our bad reputation. Steve thought it was a gas that the sheriff had called us pigs. "Wouldn't it have been right to shake his hand and say something like, 'Oh, hi. What a coincidence.' "

We took a deliberate turn down the main street of Reno on our way back; most of us had never seen it. We gaped at all the neon signs blazing in the light of day, and all the tatty-looking people popping quarters into sidewalk slot machines and jamming themselves into open-fronted gambling dens. How, we wondered, could the likes of us *possibly* give Washoe County a worse name than it already had, or with our naked human bodies be any more obscene than Reno itself. And to myself I repeated over and over the amusing fact that the former travel editor of *Holiday* magazine was banned from Washoe County for a year. Because he is an obscene pig who stinks. Wow—I kind of liked it.

That night we made camp off on a side road in the Sierras, California side of the border, you betcha. It took us a long time on rutty roads to find a decent site, and we were all very tired and feeling ultimately gritty and grungy by the time we settled around the fire with dinner on our paper plates. Most of us spoke out in anger about the sheriff and the bust, or near-bust—because after all, we were not in jail. We were just banned persons. But Oz, not so resolutely middle class as the rest of us, veteran of many a serious bust and easier in the ways of the real world, had some gentler words for the sheriff. "You all have to understand," he said quietly, "that people like that are in pain. They're really suffering. Look at it from the sheriff's point of view: bunch of filthy hippies, naked in *his* lake. You can figure out what his life's probably like—always done what he was told was the right thing, worked hard, been righteous. Now these days, probably his wife isn't sleeping with him and his son won't talk to him and he knows something is really wrong and he's hurting. And then he sees these guys with these good-looking girls, all naked together. It's like, by living our lives, we're laughing at him, all he's done.

"Now the fact is we weren't cool about anything. I didn't think you all should swim naked there, I never did. I felt real bad about it. If you want to swim bare-ass you should hike a day, get far away from straight people. It's not cool to throw things at people that you know they can't handle."

I said yeah, and I admired Oz for his charitable and practical observations. "But, Oz," I said, "how did he possibly find us? We were miles away from anybody else. There wasn't anybody to offend, even if there had been something overtly sexual going on, which there wasn't. I mean, unless he's got spotters in helicopters or up on top of those mountains with binoculars, I don't see how he could even know about it."

"Well," says Oz, "that's what I mean about being cool. I walked all over that area before you all got down there, and I saw that behind that big rise was the highway. I figure we weren't more than fifty yards from it, because it curves toward the water right there but you can't see it from the beach. But anybody up there can see you."

We all screamed at once: "Why Didn't You Tell Us?"

"It wouldn't have done any good. I knew you all were determined to take your clothes off there, and I'd been feeling trouble coming for hours, but there wasn't any use in me fussing about it any more than I did, because you wouldn't listen anyway. So that's why I just took off my clothes and joined you. What's gonna happen is gonna happen, and beyond a certain point you can't do anything to change it."

BREAKING SOME MORE RULES

A week before she died, an interviewer asked Janis Joplin why she preferred to work in California. "I just like the people's attitudes out here better," she said. "They seem a little friendlier, a little less jaded, a little less anxious to be critical, more willing to just accept you and flow with it than back there, where everyone seems to be trying to pick each other apart."

There is nothing like adversity to draw disparate perpetrators together; the Big Lewdness Bust created an instant bond among us. Thanks to the long and agitated arm of The Law, even the southern Indiana girls participated gleefully in the new conspiracy: weren't they just as much banned from Washoe County as the rest of us? Within hours of our escape to California, the Bust had ceased to be a sordid event and had become an adventure, a binding myth that was to hold some of us together for a long time.

Some of the perpetrators were unable to get deeply into the situation: Tamara flew out from San Francisco on Tuesday morning, and the southern Indiana girls meant to set off for home, via Disneyland, within a few days. But with whatever elements were present at the time, we created an ongoing mob scene at David's apartment on Telegraph Hill such as none of us had ever participated in before. Poppy and Ella slept in their sleeping bags, neatly laid out on couch and window seat in the living room; my bag was on the floor alongside the coffee table. Steve and Tamara were in sleeping bags in the hall, creating an obstacle course en route to the bathroom. David and Lenore had their big double bed in the bedroom, and a door to close. David rarely closed it. Lenore always did.

David is one of the kindest people I know. He may not think things through very carefully, but his instincts are inevitably generous, and he was happy to have us all jammed in together under his roof. "I want my house to be open to my friends," he said on Sunday night, and many times thereafter. But of course, a lot more was going on than simple open house. We were break-ing social taboos—a lot of them in a hell of a hurry—without consciously noticing it. There was the business of hanging around naked whenever possible—partly, I think, a reaction to the Bust; partly to jar the prim certainties of the southern In-diana girls; mainly, I hope to confirm that we really were at ease with our bodies in company. About this the girls never complained; they had not driven 1,500 miles to San Francisco to get what they could find readily by the banks of the Wabash. There was also a deliberate effort on everybody's part to say exactly what was in his mind; if we were being honest about our bodies, it follows that we would be honest about our feelings. Also, we started to smoke a lot of dope (Poppy and Ella ex-cepted), which enhanced the truth-telling mood.

One of the major subjects of conversation was David's infatua-tion with Nora. He had taken a great shine to her during the Pyramid Lake excursion. In fact, we all had, because she is a beautiful girl with long, raven hair, sparkling black eyes, and a body that is, as they say, outasite. I had come to like her very much but never considered pressing matters beyond that. I was going to be away from home for several months, I was certainly going to let the sexual chips fall where they might during that period, but it never occurred to me that a nineteen-year-old girl and I might produce the right combination of chips. David had a different view of the matter, referring to what he described as an "energy exchange" rippling, he claimed, between Nora and himself. While we were still in the Sierras, David reported this phenomenon to Steve and me with great excitement. "But what about Lenore?" I'd asked, rather squarely. "That's the whole point," David said. "She feels it too. She's a little scared of it, but turned on. I have this terrific idea that we might all three be able to make it together."

On the drive back from the Sierras, in the car with David, Lenore, Nora, and Poppy, I had watched everything very closely, hoping to observe this energy exchange, but all I saw was David's hand snaking occasionally into the back seat to stroke Nora's knee vigorously. She would smile and he would smile, and

Lenore would look very sour. I didn't assume too much from Lenore's scowling—she was constantly making scenes with David, seemed extremely volatile to me, appeared to enjoy tears and anger. But she always seemed to make it up with David very quickly, whereupon the sun would come out and shine brightly until she elected to make the next scene.

That Sunday night, after we reached civilization again and were reestablished in David's apartment, my single craving was for a shower, a really hot shower with lots of shampoo and soap and deep-crevice scrubbing. I wanted to exorcise the woods as thoroughly as possible, and then go out and drink martinis and eat good food and restore myself to city comforts. But David had a better idea: he thought we should all go have a bath together. Nora agreed enthusiastically, Poppy said no thanks, and Lenore split for the bedroom—in order, I imagined, to ready herself for the group soak. I really just wanted to get clean, but I was turned on by the idea of a four-way bath, having never had one in a conventional tub, and I thought, well . . . okay. I realized that four adult bodies would displace all the water, and that we wouldn't be able to get on with much washing, but I was letting those old chips fall steadily. Good thing, I thought, that Connie's car is not back yet: four is really maximum for that tub.

David drew a bath and Nora and I undressed—it was great to peel off the dusty weekend duds—and Poppy sat with us in the living room, chatting, while we waited for David and Lenore to come out of the bedroom and get with it. And we waited. And waited. Finally, my interest in hygiene overcame my carnal appetites and I said, loud enough to be heard through the living room wall, that I felt too grimy to wait any more, and was going to take a shower. In I went and had one, standing calf-deep in the cooling tub that David had drawn. While I was drying, Lenore came into the bathroom to brush her teeth and get ready for bed. She said she was terribly tired and was going straight into the sheets, and no reference was made to any four-way tub. I thought, well, too bad, but what the hell; and how nice it was to have these unstressful, un-uptight relations between hostess and house guest. Sometimes I don't think things through very deeply myself.

When I emerged from the steaming bathroom I saw Nora

walking around in the hall with a very uncertain air, and David visibly upset, and Poppy looking nervously out the window. It seems that Lenore had Said Something. There was nothing unusual about that—she was always Saying Something—and I felt that, whatever it was, it was David's business and not mine. I dressed and Poppy had her bath and changed (I had invited her out to dinner with me) and we were about to leave when David came out of the bedroom and put his arms around me. "Can I ask you a favor, old buddy?" he whispered. "Would you take Nora along with you to dinner? Lenore is all upset—I don't know what's wrong but she's really pissed off and I think it would be better if Nora is not here." Of course I agreed, and spoke up as if spontaneously to Nora, inviting her. She quickly accepted.

Late that night we drove Nora home to Connie's place, then returned to David's darkened apartment and, stumbling and sshhing each other in the blackness, groped our way to our sleeping bags without kicking anybody else *too* hard en route. As I drifted off to sleep I reflected that during my research I would not have to infiltrate myself artificially into any local crash pad; I was already in one.

The next few days were a process of letting everything finally hang out. There was no structure, no agenda—the consensus seemed to be to let the least tendency take its own course without respect to any of the social rules to which we were acculturated. There were similarities in this to a very long marathon encounter, but an open-ended, leaderless one. The crash pad analogy is probably the most accurate one—the only difference is that most of us were older than typical crashers; we had a cultural orientation to work and structure and linear time, and these habituations were not easily jettisoned.

For example, I had magazine pieces to write. I didn't write, of course: first, the dynamics of the group preoccupied me; second, there was no privacy whatever for working. A crowded pad is not the place to produce the great American novel, much less a reasonably cogent magazine article. Still, I worried about not working. Steve felt he should be out doing footwork on the communes that are so abundant in the San Francisco area; preoccupation with the group made that impossible. But he worried too. David should have been in his darkroom and office, working with transparencies and prints that were to go into a book he was doing. He worried too. Lenore was designing and making dresses for a North Beach boutique, but she could never get to her sewing machine. If she ever forgot to worry about it, a daily call from the boutique would remind her. Poppy and Ella knew they should be finishing up their shopping and sight-seeing before the end of the week, because they were supposed to get organized and get off to Los Angeles. Only Nora, who was not living on the premises, kept straight hours, working in a book-shop in the Fillmore district. Somebody was always expecting her; nobody was expecting us anywhere, in any urgent sense.

The days were very strange. The household usually started to stir when and if the phone rang. Invariably we had talked and listened to music and smoked dope all through the night, so nobody was eager to be up with the birds, and typically the day would be launched about one P.M., everybody strewn naked and gimlet-eyed in the living room, in a welter of sheets and sleeping bags. There would be coffee and, more often than not, a couple of joints, which slowed things down even more. Poppy and Ella were not smoking dope but they seemed to fall into the langor-ous mood nevertheless.

Most of our conversation touched on the special wickedness of living with schedules, of burdening our lives with "shoulds" and "oughts." Consciences stirring just below our new liberation, we had to talk away the old shibboleths, or at least try to. David's eagerness to make a sexual troika with Lenore and Nora was a topic closely related to the question of "shoulds" and "oughts." The general position among us was that people should do, sexually, what they wished to do, so long as everybody wished it. But in purely practical terms, it wasn't at all clear that all three parties to this particular troika wished to engage in it.

Nora professed herself to be a completely free agent, unbound by convention and innocent of prior obligations to others. She said she preferred to operate strictly on her feelings of what was right or wrong in a given situation; if and when a troika was right, it was right. She felt herself completely bi-sexual and capable of responding in both sexual directions, but she needed a lot of confidence in that response before acting out her feelings sexually. David said he realized the implications of wanting to make it sexually with two women; when asked how he would respond if Lenore had wanted them to introduce another guy into their bed, he fell back on situational ethics also, explaining that he had never experienced a homosexual love affair because of his cultural fear of faggotry. Now, however, he felt ready to confront the possibility without terror—*if* the guy was right. Lenore's position was a good bit more complex: despite a lot of experience in homosexual sex, which she liked and wanted, she could not approve of her bi-sexual nature. She was ready to concede that she derived these feelings of disapproval from an uptight Kentucky raising for which she had no respect, but that concession was not of much use to her in dissipating guilt. "I can't help feeling that it's wrong," she said. "Why can't I be just an ordinary girl and live with David and not want something else, or someone else, or some other kind of sex?" Lenore explained that she felt threatened in two ways by David's proposal. Just the fact of admitting that Nora turned her on sexually was threatening. She "shouldn't" feel that way. And the possibility that David might prefer Nora to herself in bed was a terrifying threat. Lenore's sexual ambivalence had always cost her a lot of torment. "Sometimes I feel very aggressive, very masculine. A normal woman shouldn't feel that way."

"Bullshit!" we all cried in unison. "A woman is aggressive when she needs to be, and there is nothing unfeminine about it," I said. "You are who you are, a complex web of feelings and learned responses. Trust your feelings, whenever you can get to them, and you won't go wrong." But this was all just so much rhetoric to Lenore, and rhetoric couldn't help. Never mind that there was no one in the house who had the least inclination to point the fingerbone of scorn at her; Lenore's own fingerbone did all the pointing necessary.

I still don't know exactly what my role was in those days. I was having a good time, enjoying the frankly bohemian ambiance of North Beach and the tentative bohemia of David's apartment; I liked it that we were trying to be open with one another about intimate things, as the intimacy of nakedness and crowded living progressed toward an intimacy of the spirit. Nobody was inviting *me* into a sexual troika but I was apparently reckoned to be useful to these counsels because I was already a bi-sexual of record;

a book of mine, resting even then on David's coffee table, had
made that perfectly clear. I have recognized and remained pretty
cheerful about my catholic sexuality for several years, ever since
facing it head-on in an encounter at Esalen. For me, being bi-
sexual doesn't mean that I want to hit the sack with all and
sundry; it's simply that I *may* respond to people sexually without respect to gender, and when I do I don't go all to pieces
about it. It's okay with me; in fact, I feel that the added dimension has enriched my life. And I would like to think that someday lots of people will accept this duality as natural in themselves and it will no longer be considered a social and sexual
problem. But I am aware that the concept is deeply threatening
to many people, despite the work of Reich and Jung and Laing
and Perls, despite the easements of the hip life styles and the
success of Mick Jagger and unisex fashion. For a long time I
had felt rather lonely and embattled and sorry for myself, because most people I knew or met felt threatened if I were out
front about my bi-sexuality. So it was interesting to me, and
comforting too, to find that our ongoing discussion of alterna-
tives to the man-woman sexual relationship had opened up into
this consideration of social-genital identity.

Long before we decided to work together, Steve and I had
discussed the subject thoroughly, and his views in the group
were consistent with his position months before. Other people's
sexuality was their own business; he thought everybody should
do whatever he liked. He sought the same option for himself.
He had never had the least homosexual or bi-sexual inclinations,
the feelings just weren't there, and that was that. But he was
more than ready to engage in long discussions of the subject, and
to make quite penetrating observations in the manner of a passionate but personally detached social scientist.

And so the days drifted one into the other, until finally Poppy
and Ella *had* to leave. Poppy told me it had been wonderful for
her to be among people who were willing to discuss matters
that, in southern Indiana, are never spoken of, certainly rarely
acted upon. "I can sight-see some other time," she said. "Any
other time. But to live like this, to get a glimpse of this kind of
life, that I'd only read about before . . . it's been fantastic."
Lenore was going with them, as far as LA. There was much

embracing and kissing, in all numbers of combinations, and then the girls piled in the car and gunned off toward the freeway. The next morning David flew to LA on a photographic assignment. He planned to return with Lenore after about three days; meanwhile, he gave Steve and me the complete run of the place; he even took the trouble to chop up a whole bunch of fruit and drown it in kirsch and put it in the refrigerator, just in case we should have a taste for fruit while he was away. In all our talk we had reached no conclusions about the desirability of a troika, but there was no rush: David, Lenore, and Nora were going to be in San Francisco for a long time.

After everybody had left, Steve remarked that he would very much like to see Nora himself. He said he didn't really believe that David wanted a three-way relationship so much as he wanted just a casual roll with Nora. "It's all part of David's usual tit-tickling thing," Steve said. "If he can't think of anything else to do he's tickling Lenore's tit, or Nora's tit. He's just horny for Nora and he's using the troika idea to get around Lenore. But meanwhile he's sort of staked a claim on Nora and I can't very well do anything about it."

Steve was referring to what I usually call the Ancient Code of the Hills, i.e., in matters of courtship, don't fuck your buddy. If some other guy has affixed his brand to a lady's rump, you are not supposed to covet her. Nobody had consulted Nora in this matter, but that isn't necessary in the Ancient Code, which in this case featured Nora as the cow and Steve and David as the contending cowboys. I figured that things were going to get even more interesting when David and Lenore returned from LA; for the moment, the decks were cleared of interpersonal relations and rivalries, and we determined to get down to hard work.

SOMETHING IS BETTER THAN NOTHING

I had been eager to visit one particular San Francisco commune —Something Else. I had had a glimpse of its founding, a year before, had been struck by the earnestness and sincerity of its earliest members, and had hoped for the best for them. This was a group composed largely of seminarians from the ecumenical Graduate Theological Union in Berkeley; with a piece of change and the academic blessings of the seminary, plus the use of a defunct old church in the heart of San Francisco—courtesy of the Glide Memorial Methodist Church—these twenty-five people, mostly young and starry-eyed, idealistic and intellectual and breathtakingly middle-class, had thrown themselves together to see what would happen. Officially, they had no goals and would, like Topsy, just grow; however, each of them had some private end in mind. A few were pursuing scholarly tasks, hoping to complete papers on the experience of building community. All burned to understand urban problems in human terms. Collectively, they were seeking a way to create and radiate community in a lower-middle-class urban environment, to build a real home in the center of the city, for themselves and for those drawn to them.

When I had last seen them, the old church had been a shambles only halfway en route to order, and the same might have been said for the members; then only two weeks together and still strangers, they were only just beginning to shape a family life. So when I discussed the group, a year later, with Connie—whose interest in the radical life of the city extended to very nearly everything that was happening—she said she knew the place very well, and often took her children there for the weekly "celebrations." What were they, I asked.

"Well," she said, "I don't know what they intend them to be, but so far as I'm concerned, they're a way to meet good people, and have a good time, and sort of alert myself to what's going on in the city."

Steve and I attended the next scheduled celebration, at Connie's urging, and my first feelings were very positive. The place had been beautifully fixed up. A trash-strewn basement had been cleaned and wrestled into pristine, white-washed meeting rooms; members' private quarters had emerged from coal-bin status into spare but comfortable rooms. The huge chancel had become a high-ceilinged all-purpose room, and was, on that evening, serving as a rock palace. In a dense throng of dancers in the dark, we managed to locate Connie, her kids, and Nora, and spent a long evening with them, dancing in very free style (sometimes just holding hands in circles, jumping up and down), drinking a little soda pop, and sweating profusely. It was a good night for working out sheer animal exuberance—the band prompted it, and the ambiance permitted it, and we had a very good time. It even provided Steve and Nora with an opportunity to signal each other, discreetly, in the dance; so much so that he determined, later, to see her even if David protested. Ancient Code of the Hills, be damned.

When we left, I picked up a communal leaflet at the door, a sort of weekly program, and found that on every single night of the week, a room or rooms at Something Else was in use for some sort of extra-communal activity. That was very nice, I thought, very activist; but there was no way of telling what was happening within the group itself. So the next day I called the commune, asked for Slade, a guy who had been reasonably friendly to me on my last visit, and got us an invitation to come to dinner that very night.

We arrived for dinner at six (communards eat early); ten or twelve people sat, supping, at a long table in the chancel. Slade, the big, bushy-haired country boy who had said we could come over, rose from his seat, greeted us perfunctorily, and said, "You all help yourselves." There were no personal introductions.

At the bottom of a steel pot I discovered a stew of zucchini, rice, chickpeas, and tomato, and by means of a long dipper lifted a portion into a shallow bowl. A girl sitting nearby said, "You guys want some coffee or Coke or something?" We said yes, over-enthusiastically, I thought, to coffee, and the girl brought us a pair of mugs of it.

The meal was just terrible, practically inedible, but I spooned it down. One, I didn't want to appear rude. Two, I knew that in the New Society, very little notice is taken of the taste of food —while changing contemporary conditions and assisting in the revolution, food is only fuel, and doesn't have to be tasty. Three, a lot of people in the revolution profess really to *like* unseasoned gruels such as I was eating, mostly because the textures are so terrific and the contents so good for you. For these and perhaps some other reasons I've forgotten, I ate as if I liked the hell out of it, hoping meanwhile that Slade might say something to make me feel more at ease. He didn't—what's more, having finished and burped, he left the table and walked across the room to a lounge area, where he threw himself on a sofa and immersed himself in a newspaper. A loud rock record was blaring over there; I figured Slade wasn't into talking just then.

Neither were the people left at the table, except for one large, plump, bespectacled girl. She'd been there only two weeks, she said. I asked about the various people I'd met on my last visit; all gone, she said. Of the people I had met a year before, only Slade and two others remained. Of the life, any life, within— nothing. "This is a very outward-oriented commune," the girl explained. "There really isn't anything happening inside at all. I came because I needed a place to crash, and I'm into folk guitar, and they need some music around here, and I can do my thing. I'd like it a lot better if something was happening, but you can't get into these dudes, and the chicks are just as, like, cold. I mean, I could see a commune, and getting into a dude or a chick or a little group sex and such as that, but it isn't hap- pening and I can't see where it will while I'm here. I'd go back to Connecticut if I had the bread, but for me it's groovy enough here right now, if I can do my folk thing at the celebrations."

I found myself feeling sort of annoyed. It wasn't only that my romantic aspirations for Something Else seemed to have evolved into nothing more than a sort of hip Elks Lodge. It was Slade himself, half-asleep on the sofa in full view of his guests, ignor- ing us. Not caring much whether it was cool, I went over and said, "Well, Slade, we came to talk, but I don't want to interrupt your interest in current events." Slade lowered the funnies and said, with baby-faced innocence, "Oh. You into talking? Well, let's talk."

News of Slade. "I'm not into the ministry anymore at all. All I ever wanted was the chance to build community, and now I've found that I can do it without the whole seminary thing. I'm not sure when I'll leave here, or where I'll go after this. When I feel this thing is really going, that's when *I'll* go. But what I'll do from now on is the same thing, some other place. You all were at the celebration last night, right? Well, you see what I mean."

"No, Slade," says I. "I really don't see what you mean. The celebration was a nice dance, but what happened to the community you were going to have right in this building? According to that big girl over there and some of the other people we met, they're just sort of crashing here, they say there isn't anything happening within, it's all outward-bound. What happened to everybody?"

"Well," said Slade, "I don't really know what you mean. We have something happening here every night, like tonight is our rap session, where people come in from outside to plan the activities of the next week, and the whole idea is to get the community involved in this place as an action center. And that's happening. You all ought to stay and get in on it; it's outasite. And as for the others—everybody had something he had to do— I don't really know exactly—I was doing some drugs this winter and didn't keep up too good, but I got my own head in a good place and I think everybody's doing okay." And he reeled off a list of names, and tied them to vague locations, but it was clear that he didn't much care.

The rap session was supposed to start at eight in one of the meeting rooms downstairs. At quarter to nine Slade and a few other communards decided they'd trickle down to see if anybody had come. By nine-thirty there were about fifteen people strewn around the meeting room on the floor, elbows lifted on pillows. They came in all sexes, ages, shapes, and sizes, seemed not to know or to relate to one another very vividly, and by ten o'clock were still lackadaisically involved in the most rambling and unstructured conversation I've ever been frustrated by. Somebody would dominate the conversation for a while, discoursing apparently without point about X, but meanwhile three other people would begin a side rap about Y, argue, gain precedence, and hold the floor only until two others, loudly disputing Z, would outshout the Y people. X, now an abandoned topic, might or might not later emerge. Although there were endless opportunities for bringing some direction to this aimlessness, neither

Slade nor any of the other resident communards would seize that option. The idea was most specifically to rap, not to organize; therefore the conversation was "free" and could flow anywhere it wanted to. Unfortunately, it didn't want to flow in the direction of planning or problem solving, and that may have been all right with everybody else, but after a couple of hours I was going out of my skull. What used to be called a college bull session was never supposed to go anywhere, and its pleasure was in its aimlessness. This session had been called for reasons of clear and present urgency, it was supposed to be a planning session, and I could see it would be hours before the conversation flowed in any direction that specific. Slade was in the act of saying something like, "Well . . . uh . . . I feel sorta that . . . if you all want to . . . considering all sides of the question . . . uh . . ." when I got up and slipped out of the room. I had heard so many sides covered by then that it was anybody's guess what question he was talking about. I felt that I should rush out to some all-night bookstore and buy the commune a copy of Robert's Rules of Order. But that was, of course, exactly what they didn't want.

As Steve and I drove home, I complained of my disillusionment with Something Else. And at the same time I confessed my confusion. The old church obviously *had* become a gathering place in the community. Local neighbors *had* focused on it as an action center—and if they did no more than meet one another there once a week to dance and have a good time, that was something. Fair enough—not many neighborhoods have even that much to bind neighbors together. Somehow, out of these seemingly aimless rap sessions, the commune extended a sense of community to the community at large. And yet at the core of the thing was disaffection, departure, disinterest, indeed indifference to human bonding. For Slade and a few others, the commune was, perhaps, no more than a platform for working out their particular power trip, the manipulation of large groups in aid of some theoretical social good. In ways I had to applaud, Something Else was bringing people together; yet I knew for sure, and it continues to make me sad, that Something Else will never be a home for anyone.

STEVE'S SECOND INNING

THE PLACE

HISTORY. Discovered The Place from two sources: Oz talked about it in terms of the Social Action agencies involved and Al Rinker said that his San Francisco Switchboard will be located there from now on.

ACCESS. The Place is located in a huge old candy factory at the corner of Tenth and Howard, right in the middle of San Francisco.

PHYSICAL LAYOUT. The building looks like a warehouse and has been freshly painted a dusty mustard color. It is six or seven stories high, each floor supported by a rectangular array of cylindrical pillars that divide the floors into separate bays about twenty-five feet square. Ceilings are high, perhaps twenty feet, and everything has been recently painted white. The top floor has a wide piazza which The Place is considering for an outdoor restaurant. There is a central service core in the building with staircase, elevator, storage, and room for plumbing facilities. The building at present is in a stage of renovation by the new renters and is not expected to be completed until next summer sometime.

Each bay is a rentable space (6 cents or so a square foot, $4,200 per month for the whole riff) and has been taken up by either an artist (painter, sculptor, potter, leatherworker, silversmith, etc.) or by a community-oriented agency (three schools, Fort Help, Alternative Education, for example). Several artists have formed small groups and rented space together. Some of the agencies have rented multiple bays.

PEOPLE. I met a couple of people during the one afternoon I was there. I walked in asking for Jacques Goldman, the Alternative Education man. He was not in so I explained my purpose to an older, bearded, pony-tailed man who looked authoritative, receptive, and available. He got immediately uptight about my being a writer and wanting to pigeonhole him with my questions. I should have just asked him what was happening without all the introduction; it would have saved me the heartache. But I didn't, so my conversation with him ended rather abruptly and I was whisked away by a much more amiable Chinese guy who offered to show me around.

The Chinese guy took me to each and every bay in the place and described who had rented the space, what he was planning to do there, and if the cat was about, working on his thing or whatever, he introduced me to him and we spent a minute chatting. This went on for about half an hour until we finally got back to my friend's bay and found a friend of his working there. The three of us got to talking about how The Place got started, what was happening now, and what these guys wanted for it.

The Place is today a community of about thirty people, in the arts or agencies, who have decided to purchase common space, live there, work there, and merchandise their wares there. A man named Fred Berger, as I understand it, is the inspiration behind the whole thing. By profession, Berger is a civil engineer. He has purposely rejected anything like a final design for the place, just wants it to grow—socially and physically—in an organic way and to become what it turns out to be. Berger is trying to raise money for the whole shebang now and I think is looking mainly at foundation sources.

The people involved in The Place got there through their own initiative and personal contacts. It sort of evolved into being, having been burgeoning in the minds of at least the original crew for two years. Berger made the first part of the dream come true this June when he raised enough money to rent the building and pay for some of its renovation. Now, each of the lessors is being expected—for the time being only, until a grant can be secured—to put up his share of the rent, individually—$32 per bay per month. The guys I spoke with expected to be able to live in the building on a full-time basis once the financial problems have been settled. But city zoning regulations prevent the building being used for residential purposes so, right now, they are living there on the sly and are hoping that someone like Berger will straighten out the zoning problem as well.

If you haven't already guessed it, there is no conspicuous formal organization at The Place but a strong kindred spirit among those involved. As my Chinese friend described it, "Why should we hire plumbers, carpenters, and other contractors to do our work for us when we have the guys right here?" What my friend was saying was that these people have decided to become economically self-sufficient because they have brought together sufficiently diverse talents to form a cooperative in the true sense of the word, everyone working for everyone. There would be no need for outside help if they could do everything for themselves as a group and that seems to be the direction in which The Place is moving.

I'm not sure if this is a totally general feeling but my informants also described The Place as a giant educational institution into which people from all over the city could come to learn skills or at least to watch them in actual operation. The idea is to make it into a place where each of the artisans would encourage kids or adults to participate with him in his thing, so eventually there would be an incredible educational flow of people and ideas. This is their ideal picture and it is a long way from realization right now.

P.S. The Place has already agreed to allow a local private high school to use the premises as a resource facility. The dream is beginning to come true.

S.B.

THE HEAVENLY HOST

HISTORY. Found out about Heavenly Host from Carol Decatur. She crashed one night at their San Francisco aid center. Then again from Oz, who mentioned to me that the Host maintained a commune in the Sebastopol area. Got the exact location of the place along with directions from the lady who runs the occult bookstore on the main highway in Sebastopol.

ACCESS. Host is located in Sebastopol at the very end of a road that winds its way through rolling, tree-studded farmland. The last part of the road dips some and then rises into a grove where the commune is situated.

PHYSICAL LAYOUT. The commune occupies eight acres of farmland and pasture. It consists of one main house, a small, modestly-furnished pillbox and several still smaller cabins which house two adults each. There is also a chicken coop and a goat pen for the small herd maintained by the commune. There is a small vegetable garden not far from the main house.

PEOPLE. I drove up to the commune without warning and was invited inside without question or hesitation. Inside I saw a bunch of young kids running around and a few adults. A man dressed in priest's habit, blond, good-looking, in his mid-twenties, introduced himself as Reverend Bill and invited me into his room (combination bedroom and office). He seemed a bit nervous with me at first but I soon realized that it was not nervousness but a slightly stilted manner of speech that threw me.

Reverend Bill explained to me that the commune served two purposes. Its main reason for being was raising children of initiates into the order. Initiates into the Host move into instruction centers in big cities like San Francisco or Chicago. Since the order requires the full attention of the initiates, some parents prefer to send their kids to Sebastopol to be brought up by priests and priestesses of the order until they are prepared to take them back (usually in about a year's time). The second purpose of the Sebastopol operation is healing. Briefly, the Host believes that disease is 90 percent psychosomatic and that its cure is not the province of medicine but the province of spirit. They believe and have shown, according to Bill (whose own daughter, says he, was cured partially of mongolism by the same techniques) that they can in fact cure people of whatever ails them by helping them achieve spiritual fulfillment.

The Host philosophy is what is most interesting about the commune. Bill explained to me that it makes no distinction between religion and science and bases all of its religious beliefs on scientifically corroborable data. The Host considers Jesus to be the most important avatar ever to have descended to earth. They also believe that Moses, Buddha, and Mohammed were avatars, but not on JC's level. The reason they believe this is that there was a marked increase in what they call energy flow when Jesus appeared on earth (measured by something like the strength of the earth's magnetic field—who knows?), a flow which they claim is continuing to grow at such an amazing pace that they are sure we are on the verge of the Aquarian Age, just as Jesus ushered in the Piscean Age. Yes, that's right, they believe in astrology too. They also believe in some Tantric meditation and yoga practices, some concentration exercises (Bill keeps an orange on his windowsill), auras—in fact they believe in everything. Bill says that anything that will get you closer to Thyself, to spiritual attainment, is a good thing by definition. So Host preaches a whole megila's worth of Eastern and Western stuff aimed at Enlightening the initiate and ultimately helping him reach Spiritual Attainment.

The order was begun about two or three years ago by a Master Teacher named Peter who organized the first school in San Francisco. The purpose of Host was to do away with formal church services and bring Jesus to the people on the street, the people who needed him most. Peter instructed a small group of initiates in the Bible and Christian mysteries and sent them out on the street to help others in the same way.

Today, there are about a half dozen Master Teachers in major cities who were not instructed by Peter but who, in their own right as Master Teachers (high vibration count), joined the order of their own volition. Each Master Teacher runs a school for initiates, who are instructed in the Bible (just as it is, man, not as an allegory, but just what it says) and in the Christian mysteries ("as above, so below," for example, which means that the earth is just a microcosm of the heavens, and that every living thing on the earth is just a further microcosm of it . . . read concentric circles). In San Francisco, where the order is headquartered, there is also an Aid Center which serves meals and provides lodging to some 6,000 poor people per month without any obligation.

To become a priest or priestess (it is one of two religious orders in the world that allow women to take the vows of priesthood), one has to achieve spiritual enlightenment, which can take anywhere from a few months to a few years, depending upon the Karma (yes, Karma) of the individual and his plights in previous incarnations. Bill told me that a year ago he set out with his wife and mongoloid child for Hawaii, in search of the perfect wave. He was heavily into drugs and not at all into Christ. The drugs got worse and he happened to meet a Host priest in Hawaii who turned him on to the order. Bill was reluctant to even bother at first but stopped by once and the cat turned his head around. Bill joined the order and studied the Bible and Christian mysteries for a year before he was enlightened enough to go before an Esoteric Council, be tested ("I was asked questions impossible to answer except through spirit and what could be known by perceiving changes in auras"), and take priestly vows for this life and then for all lives. The vows included obedience, service, humility and poverty.

Bill was called to leave Hawaii after he took his vows and come to Sebastopol with wife and daughter to manage the commune there. He has been there for the last several months and is completely comfortable in that environment. He and his wife, who is a very attractive brunette priestess in a floor-length brown monk's robe tied around the waist with a length of cord, come originally from San Francisco. Neither of them misses city life and both appear to be above the mundane aspects of this existence and very much into the spiritual ones.

I stayed for dinner at Bill's request and got to see the commune in action. About twenty-four people live in the place, half kids and half adults, including the three clerics. The dinner was fish, zucchini, french fries, and everything was delicious. There were a few blacks among the adults and there was none of that usual tension at all. Everything was really smooth all over with good Christian feeling all around. As usual, I might add, with that religious thing in there.

S.B.

HIBISCUS

On our first weekend alone in the city, two hip publications, *Rags* and *The Organ,* came out with picture stories about The

Cockettes, a theatrical, transvestite commune in San Francisco composed mostly of hippie drag queens, and a few real girls as well. *Rags* quoted one member as saying, "We're not queer. We're just chicks with cocks." Given the iconoclastic drives of the hip community, nothing could more certainly merit the encomium "Far Out." Guys who are chicks who are guys—this was far in advance of the middle-class camp of female impersonation, in which for performer and audience, perfect illusion is everything. The joke would go sour if the imitation were not strictly imitative. But The Cockettes were not making jokes: they appeared in drag, yes, but also bearded; and their name derived from their tendency to flash their cocks at the audience. This kind of deliberate combination of maleness and femaleness in one package transcended camp and barged into sexual politics. Although, as one writer put it, "No one who hasn't seen a chunky youth attired in little more than a feather boa belting out 'Old Man River' in falsetto is even qualified to discuss camp," a local critic cut deeper when he remarked that The Cockettes "romp, bump, grind, kick, scream, flaunt, swish, stagger and writhe their way through the rooms behind your mind."

The articles said that The Cockettes shared a house in the city; Steve and I briefly considered whether we should go to visit. But we concluded that we were both too defensive and uptight about drag and drag queens to bring off a face-to-face confrontation. There was something so threatening to us about their on-and-off stage mixing of sexual roles that we decided to cool it. We did, however, decide that we would attend one of their two weekly performances. The Cockettes perform every Friday and Saturday night as part of an extravaganza called the Nocturnal Dream Show, a post-midnight spectacle of old cartoons and movies at a Chinese movie house in North Beach called the Palace. It was only a couple of blocks from David's apartment, so we agreed to drop around on Saturday night and take in the whole show.

That Saturday night the sidewalk under the marquee of the Palace was jammed with longhairs, as if Woodstock were taking place within. We joined a long line to buy tickets, then a great crowd surging through the doors of the theater. The place was so crowded, orchestra and balcony, that we thought we'd have to settle for squatting in the aisle but, as an ancient Tom &

Jerry cartoon absorbed the audience, we managed to find two seats down front and on the side. This was a poor position for viewing the cartoon, but a great spot for audience watching. I saw virtually no straights anywhere; it was entirely the sort of crowd that turns out for rock festivals, or evenings at the Fillmore. Stoned freaks, all of them, and the air was thick with the aroma of burning grass.

When the screen went white and ascended, there was a long delay, with muttering and gabble-gabble from the audience and a great deal of bumping and banging behind the curtain. Finally a voice came over the microphone in radio-announcer tones, saying: "Ladies and Gentlemen: The Cockettes!" The audience went wild, screaming and stomping, as the curtains parted and onto the stage swished about thirty incredible phantasms, radiant in every conceivable kind of drag from blackface pickaninny to South Seas femme fatale. The Cockettes assemble their own costumes out of junk stores and thrift shops, and their drag was unbelievably tatty and piecemeal, but it had a kind of mad genius about it, a make-do quality that combined wit and determination. The girls were doing a sort of opening number, but I couldn't make out what it was supposed to be—just that they seemed to be singing one thing, or maybe several things, while a combo in the corner was hammering out something else. They were terrible, all of them, appallingly bad and, as a consequence, funny as hell. And everybody was in on the joke, including the performers. The hall rang with laughter and applause.

They then embarked on some kind of musical fantasy that combined all the worst elements of *Blossom Time* and *South Pacific,* with techniques borrowed from Busby Berkeley, Cecil B. DeMille, the high school triumphs of Andy Hardy, and all the Esther Williams movies ever made. If there were a guiding spirit to the whole affair, it would have to be Carmen Miranda—or more specifically, Carmen Miranda played with the masculine intensity and muscular bravado of Charlton Heston. There was a Special Moment for each player to come forward and sing or dance off-key and out of step—everybody got a solo in which he bopped and twitched and flipped his gauzy skirts to show his cock, if indeed he was still wearing skirts. This was mad, crazy; I thought perhaps it was what Berlin had been like before the

Nazis. Every solo ended in some kind of Hollywood group tableau, the chorus spinning away into pyramids of specious pulchritude, trailing dusty wisps of tulle, wigs at angles, vermilion mouths frozen in the painful grins of 1940s movie stars. And there were even special effects, culminating in the explosion of a volcano while everybody struck Dorothy Lamour poses. This was more than stagy foolishness; it was a radical put-down of the whole society, and a violent parody of the narcotic, witless entertainments of our parents. It was political, all right; psycho-political. And far to the left of Andy Warhol and his Superstars.

Finally it was time for Hibiscus, the star of the show. He came on stage to thunderous applause, wearing a wild costume of fussy silver lamé, with wax apples and pears in a corona about his head, supporting a flowing veil. He pranced toward the apron, throwing kisses to his admirers, sequins dancing in his luxurious blond moustache and beard. His number that night was "It Takes Two to Tango," and to our surprise, he sang well, his voice in a middle range between tenor and baritone; what's more, he did the whole song in the key he started in. His delivery was salacious and grotesque, of course, accompanied by bumps and grinds, but he did not show his cock. And more than any other Cockette, his performance, his nightmare illusion, was successful. He *was* both handsome man and beautiful woman, both at the same time. His presence was more than amusing, it was affecting, persuasive of something . . . we weren't sure what. He seemed to be saying to all sexes—"Don't kid yourself . . . sweetie."

When we left the theater it was after four in the morning and we were bleary-eyed, dead tired. We walked home talking about how awful the show was, collapsed into our beds, and thought no more about the Cockettes or Hibiscus for a long time.

SETTLING (UNEASILY) IN

Sunday turned out to be a fine day; we spent the morning at the Glide Memorial Methodist Church, attending Sunday services.

This is an experience nothing like attendance upon ritual at, say, the First Methodist Church of Bristow, Oklahoma. No, sir. The Glide is a large church in downtown San Francisco that draws its congregation from among hippies and the black community, plus liberal Methodist families from all over the Bay area. Though the church sanctuary is old and conventional, nothing conventional happens within. The interior has been painted white, and a light show sends bands of color floating and congealing all over the walls and ceiling, pulsing with the rhythms of the evangelical hymns and rock songs sung by a vibrant congregation. Scripture is read from a tiny red book called *Quotations from Chairman Jesus;* the black preacher, Cecil Williams, combines the style of revivalist exhortation with the content of social and political reformation. The Glide takes the message of Christ on its toughest terms, as a directive to change the world, and on Sundays the church reverberates with shouts and applause on behalf of social justice and human love, in despite of the criminal impersonality of modern institutions, the cruel, sapping war in Vietnam, the slow but perhaps inevitable evolution of the country into a police state. The Glide is regularly attacked by the John Birch Society as a center for Communists and the drug trade in Northern California; that endorsement alone would draw me to it. I find there a kind of Christianity that makes no apology for Christian action, a tolerance and love and collective fervor that seems to have vanished, long before my time, from any quarter of the organized church. The kiss of peace at the end of a Glide service is the warm embrace of all your neighbors and linked arms for the singing of the final hymn. There is a great spirit in the air, and many people weep on their first exposure. They realize they have never been to church before. This is one reason why the lines of people waiting to get into the Glide on Sunday mornings stretch two and three blocks long. The word "relevance" has got to be a joking reference among critics of the New Left, enough so that I find myself wanting to avoid it, as somewhat compromised, in discussing the Glide. But I am stuck with it: here is religion that *is* relevant; here is a Christian church that takes itself seriously, as an extension of Christ's ministry; where else is that to be found? If cynicism is the true vice of our age—and I think it is—then in the passionate

Christianity of the Glide is a hint of the antidote. Ministers who gaze upon empty pews, Sunday after Sunday, might take some note.

Attendance at the Glide is, for people of radical persuasion, however discreet they are about it, like an immersion in the balm of fellowship—something you may have given up hoping for. We left elated, cheered up, hopeful. Steve's enthusiasm was buoying to me. "If religion could be like that," he said, leaving me to fill in the happy blanks.

After lunch we drove to Golden Gate Park to attend a free, open-air performance of the San Francisco Mime Troupe. But they were not playing that afternoon; instead, they had given their facilities over to a women's lib mime group, who with puppets, players, and special effects, told the old, depressing story of woman's subjection to man and society. The social crime, they pointed out, lay not in woman's weakness, but in man's ignorance and avoidance of his own dimensions. His insistence upon playing a uni-dimensional John Wayne role in every area of his life was the ruin of marriage, the tyranny of family, the death of love . . . and, not incidentally, the destruction of woman as a whole creature. But all this was changing; woman was no longer going to stand for it. The implication was that Lysistrata was once again on the move. We sat in a large group of people on an open park lawn; they seemed to endorse the performance by applauding loudly, but I don't know if the applause was for the ideas or the special techniques.

In the late afternoon we went to see some friends of mine at their apartment for drinks. When they learned that we were scrumming in sleeping bags at David's, they suggested that we come to stay at their place. They were about to leave town for their cottage in the country north of the city, would be gone ten days to two weeks, and would be glad to have somebody there to water the plants and answer the phone. We had been worried about intruding any longer on David and Lenore, but a search for sublets had not turned up anything we could afford, so we were grateful for their offer. It was set that we would move in on Tuesday afternoon, immediately after their departure.

That night David and Lenore returned from LA, and we broke the news to them of our good fortune. David was pleased for us, but urged us again not to feel under any compulsion to leave. His house was ours whenever we had need of it; in fact, he and Lenore were buying a big new bed for their bedroom and were installing the old double mattress in the back bedroom; there would be no more need for sleeping bags in the future. That same night, Steve and David discussed the question of Nora—Steve's desire to take her out, David's assumed prior claim to her. And they decided that all four of them, including Lenore, would meet at David's the next evening to have dinner and discuss the matter. Nora was called and readily accepted the invitation. Because this matter was nothing to do with me, I made plans to spend the night elsewhere, and caught up on events only second hand.

The evening turned out to be highly satisfactory to all parties. Nora professed herself more than ready to intensify her acquaintance with Steve, and admitted to no restraints on herself from David. David said, "But I felt this intense energy flow from you on the camping trip," and Nora said, unresponsively, "Really?" So negotiations concluded with the agreement that Steve and Nora were at liberty to get a thing together without wounding David's feelings; a larger ménage, possibly a foursome, would remain a possibility, David and Steve agreeing that they should consider whether they could respond to one another sexually, Lenore agreeing to consider whether she wanted to be a party to these speculations. In all these matters, Nora's position remained open; her responses would be entirely situational at all times.

Steve and Nora consummated their mutual enthusiasm that very night, right on the premises; in point of fact, on David's living room sofa, while David and Lenore audited the union from their adjoining bedroom, psychically urging them on. After the interpersonal festivities, Steve found that, in his ardor, something of a mess had been made on one of the sofa cushions, so he crept silently to the bathroom, washed out a large section of the cushion, and then set the wet side against a wall heater in the hall, to dry.

In the night he was awakened by thick, acrid fumes drifting through the apartment. He found the cushion, set ablaze by the heater, burning quietly away in the hall, cotton, kapok and all, sending forth an effluvium that, had he not woken up, would ultimately have asphyxiated them all in their beds. Steve extinguished the blaze, opened the windows, and disposed of the ruined cushion in the bathtub. He felt awful about the whole affair, but next morning David was entirely forgiving, and embraced him for saving their lives.

On Tuesday we moved to the new apartment—a big, old-fashioned flat on Russian Hill, above a grocery. There was no other apartment in the house and, since the grocery was being remodeled, we had the entire building to ourselves. I set to work at once, trying hurriedly to finish a backlog of *Holiday* pieces, and Steve undertook to start making contact with local communes. He would spend one day in the city, another in northern Marin, seeing what was up. I was torn in two: locked to my typewriter with *Holiday* work that could not go well because I was so desperately eager to get busy on communes research. It was an anxious time.

Effectively, Nora moved in with us, though she maintained her room at Connie's house in Pacific Heights. At the front of the apartment were double drawing rooms, divided by an archway and carved sliding doors. My friends had furnished the second parlor as a bedroom, and on a toss of the coin I got it. Steve and Nora used the hide-a-bed in the front room. It had the advantage of a gas stove set under a large and elegant Victorian wooden mantel with inset mirror; the fireplace was closed and the gas fire provided the only heat in the flat. For my work I used a study at the rear of the house; it was equipped with a desk and typewriter but was unheated, and in the midst of foggy San Francisco summer afternoons, I wore a couple of sweaters and wished for just one more gas stove.

Nora continued to go to her job in the bookstore during the day, but we three were always together in the evenings, when she and Steve would return from their day's chores and I would knock off my writing. We would spend hours talking about the dynamics of various communes, communal politics, communal personalities. We began to reflect that in some ways our little structure was not unlike incipient communality, since we depended almost entirely on one another for our amusements, and the very little we needed in subsistence money came out of a common pocket—mine. Also, the easy manners about dress and undress continued on the new premises, and every semblance of privacy dissipated. Steve and Nora had embarked on an explosive and passionate love life which I could not avoid being a silent partner to. With only double doors between me and them at night, I was a captive audience for their very noisy and un-inhibited love-making. It put me in mind of several things: (1) the raising of children in slum conditions, when the amours of parents are necessarily overheard by their offspring; (2) the plot of Calder Willingham's *Providence Island*—a man and two women marooned on a desert island work out a "marriage" of the man to one of the women, and their love-making ensues on one side of a strung-up blanket; on the other side the other woman lies sleepless, and the hero remarks that after a few days of listening, she would probably respond erotically if a fly landed on her shoulder; (3) how it really is in a commune where forty-seven Harvard and Radcliffe drop-outs live together in two rooms and any half of their number are making love in some combination or other at all times. This is pretty provocative, I would say to myself, sinking into another sensual dream with real-live sound effects; I sure am mature and grown-up and ter-rifically controlled not to let this bother me.

I was not entirely without sensual release—a kind and inter-ested lady painter had been very hospitable to me, and we met occasionally at her place. But I was trying to be earnest about my work, and so mostly chained myself to the apartment and did not go out at night. On a couple of occasions, Steve and Nora went with me to visit the lady painter; apart from being a charming lady, she had excellent dope and owned some records that Steve was particularly found of hearing. Unfortunately, every time he walked into her apartment, her stereo would go on the blink. We thought it was curious that, as soon as he left, the set played normally for the remainder of the evening.

AN EXTRAORDINARY CONVERSATION

One night David and Lenore invited us to come to dinner. There we met Tony and Bernadette Wolfe, a couple who had been nine-month Fellows at Esalen and had been leading joint encounter workshops, both in and out of Esalen, mostly for couples, ever since. They had just spent the weekend at the Oakland branch of the House of Plenty, a new Bay area commune, in a workshop on basic sexuality. Naturally we wanted to know all about it, and Bernadette, with some misgivings, told us, while Tony sat in the corner, looking wise and cunning.

Bernadette is one of the prettiest, sweetest-looking blond girls I have ever seen; she has the simple, innocent face of a freckled Nordic virgin and the lithe body of a teenager. She sat cross-legged on the sofa and held us spellbound with her account of their weekend.

"It was all just rap," she said, "straight rap. No demonstrations. And also they said we shouldn't say anything about it until at least Wednesday, because it takes time for everything to sink it. But I've been wondering how to use this stuff in our workshops so it's all right on the tip of my tongue.

"Well, you know that the House of Plenty philosophy is More —more everything. They really feel that you can have more of whatever you want, on the principle that everything you do, you do for yourself, to increase your own pleasure. You may call it something else—sacrifice, gratitude—but in fact you're incapable of being unselfish and you might as well face the real origin of all you do, and then do it right. So how do you get more of what you want? How do you maximize your own pleasure? By maximizing first the pleasure of everybody around you, everybody you're close to. In simpler words, do unto others. But not what *you* want, what *they* want. To the maximum. Take the concept of Strange Ass, for example."

"Whaaat?" we all cried, disbelieving our ears.

"Strange Ass," Bernadette repeated. "This is a tenet with them, an article of faith. You love your partner, of course, and you do everything in your power to make your partner happy. But one thing you cannot provide for your partner is Strange Ass. That has got to be somebody else. So when you feel your partner needs Strange Ass you don't throw a fit, you don't make it impossible for him to have it, you help. You associate yourself with his need for Strange Ass, go out and find it for him if necessary, join him in enjoying it if that's right for everybody.

But never cut yourself out of the fulfillment of his need. It only stands to reason that he has to love you more than ever for your understanding of his need, and that's more love, right? You give him what he needs, what*ever* he needs. You give everything to him, he gives everything to you. And it works.

"Or say he likes to fantasize in bed. I mean every time he's in bed with you he's not necessarily conscious of you personally, he may be doing a fantasy, he may be imagining you're some other chick, or a tiger or a monkey or anything. His mother, maybe. Well, you find out what his fantasy is and you try to validate it, like *be* the other chick or the tiger or whatever it is. And then you've got him absolutely, you are *with* him, you become what he wants. And he returns the favor, of course. But the important thing to me was the practical sexuality stuff. The stuff about plastic bottles and all."

"Plastic BOTTLES?" we chorused.

"Yeah," she said, "they have this method for increasing contractions in orgasm—what's the average, Tony, five to twelve contractions per orgasm? But they say that if you work on it you can do much better, you can have more, one hundred, two hundred contractions per orgasm. But it takes a whole program. Like first you start with what they call Receiving the Honored Guest—that's you, right? This is all auto-erotic. You're by yourself. You dedicate the evening to yourself, and for a couple of hours you do whatever turns you on. You play the right music, drink wine, light incense, smoke a joint, whatever puts you in a groovy mood. Then, when you're feeling very together, you undress yourself and stand in front of a mirror and dig your body, groove on it, look it all over, get with it. And caress it. You— how does it go, Tony?—the first night you just turn yourself on generally, do whatever you like, but noticing what you like, stroking certain parts of your body that really respond, your pleasure points. Like your tit, or the back of your knee. You key yourself up sexually—and you can carry on to orgasm if you like, or not. Next night, same again, only this time you take a little vaseline—they recommend vaseline because it has good tactile quality, it doesn't get absorbed into the skin—you stroke a particular pleasure point, then another, then two at the same time. And say you're working with your left hand on your left tit, and your right hand on your right knee—after a while you lift up your left hand from your tit and see if you can feel the caress of your knee in your tit, see if there's not some connection. Next night same as before, but this time with the vaseline you see if you can't enlarge two pleasure points, stroking them outward and toward each other, so that you awaken everything that lies in between. Get them together, enlarge the area of response, and night by night you tie all the pleasure points into one big bundle.

"By the fifth or sixth night you are just a tingling, sizzling *thing*. And then you come together with your partner, who's been doing the same number on himself all these nights—and you exchange all this information, and from there you're home free. I mean after that nobody can turn you on like you can each other, right?

"But there's still more—about the contractions in orgasm. They say there's a problem with the vergyner [I'm sorry; Bernadette is from Maine and that's how she pronounces it]. Because when the orgasm is approaching, the penis needs tighter contact with the vergyner, but the vergyner is lifting away from the penis, arching off it in a kind of ballooning action. So what you have to do is train yourself to do a push-out orgasm, that is, instead of ballooning inside, you must flow outward, from inside out, a long squeezing reflex. They say you should get a plastic bottle and practice this push-out orgasm. You can learn it, so that by sheer muscle control you can push this bottle out and bring it in again, in and out.

"Now also about this bottle, they say that men and women both limit their orgasms because they tighten their anal sphincters —toilet training or something, unconsciously they're afraid they're going to fart or leak or something, so they're very tight there and they cut off at least half the follow-through of the orgasm, prevent the deep, ongoing contractions. So male or female, you experiment with the plastic bottle, and vaseline, learning to allow the push-out orgasm to involve the anal sphincter until you open up completely."

We were writhing on the floor. We were thunderstruck. Not shocked—nothing was shocking us anymore—but delighted with the improbability of this virginal little girl talking so blithely about vergyners and anal sphincters and plastic bottles. It was a gas.

As the evening wore on, Tony behaved more and more peculiarly. Despite Bernadette's enthusiasm for the House of Plenty sexuality course, Tony had said next to nothing on the subject, preferring to sit and apparently listen, brooding. But as the conversation turned to more general subjects, he got up and began to prowl the room, almost in parody of a jungle animal. Nobody took much notice; we all assumed that he had been smoking some kind of powerful dope before he got there and was enjoying an interior trip he couldn't share. At one point he went over to Steve, and several times stroked his hair—but it was less a caress than a slap. Later he stalked me, like a cat, and looked in my eyes and said, "I like you. You *know,* don't you? You know."

I really didn't know, but it's always nice to be told I do, and I nodded at him and he nodded sagely back, and turned away to stalk somebody else. When Tony and Bernadette left, David said, "Gee, Tony was really strange tonight. Wonder what he's been smoking." And that's all that was said about it.

But later in the week I talked to David on the phone and he said things had been very bad with Tony and Bernadette. Apparently the sexuality rap at the House of Plenty had caused Tony to flip utterly. He was manic, as if stoned twenty-four hours a day, never sleeping, always grooving and freaking in this peculiar animalistic way. Little as she cared to, Bernadette took Tony to a straight psychiatrist who said he was schizoid, was in a profound homosexual panic, and ought to be sedated at once. Bernadette would have none of that. She got in touch with Julian Silverman, the Esalen-based shrink who runs the only Laing-oriented Blow-out Center in the country, in a wing of Agnews State Hospital near San Jose; Silverman agreed to accept Tony as a voluntary patient. Tony was rarely lucid during discussions leading to his arrival at Agnews, but he was able to agree to admittance and sign the right papers.

When I next saw Bernadette she was exhausted from dealing with Tony, sleeplessly, for four days, disturbed at what their families would conclude from all this, desperately eager that Tony be able to go through his psychosis quickly and come out, healed, on the other side. And she was fiercely angry with the House of Plenty, even if it *had* been a rap session only. Obviously, all this auto-erotic, plastic bottle stuff had got to Tony in secret places he didn't know about himself; his response had frightened him into the aforementioned homosexual panic. The House of Plenty people had asked Bernadette to bring Tony back to Oakland. They had seen this response occasionally in the past; perhaps they could help. But Bernadette was having none of that either: "The bastards should have warned us that that rap was dangerous! It's all their fault."

It wasn't, of course, but Bernadette was very tired and distressed, and at that moment I was not about to disagree with her.

The fault, if you want to call it that, *was* with the House of Plenty for assuming that everybody attending their basic sexuality seminar was sexually mature. The assumption would have seemed especially justified in Tony's case, on the evidence of his very considerable experience with Esalen and with group encounters of all kinds. But it seemed to us as laymen that the straight shrink's categorization of Tony's state as "homosexual panic" was correct. The suggestion of sticking a plastic bottle up his ass may have triggered in Tony long suppressed homosexual fantasies. And to have these suggestions delivered—much as Bernadette transmitted them to us—in wholesome, straightforward circumstances, set Tony on a cosmic giggle that we also thought was funny, but threatened with him to last a lifetime.

I admire the House of Plenty for approaching sexuality without embarrassment; time is long past due that we had a little honest talk about human sexuality, talk that deals with the dynamics of the subject without feinting and euphemism. No harm can come to those who are able to deal with sexuality maturely. Unhappily, those who are not sexually mature *do not know it,* have no means of signaling their inadequacies to their erstwhile instructors, and realize the extent of their hang-up only as they are freaking or passing out. This problem has to be laid at society's door, for society's meretricious drive to concealment and evasion. The House of Plenty assumes—quite innocently, I suppose—that married couples routinely share their intimate sexual fantasies. But the evidence (just informal observation of the lives of most married couples I know) would not seem to support the assumption. Many couples, in fact, would take such a suggestion as a bold, revolutionary idea. *"Tell* my wife that I sometimes fantasize in bed that she's another chick, or my mother? Why, I don't even dare tell it to myself!"

Clearly, the House of Plenty does not think that any part of human sexuality is "awful" or should be kept secret. And it may be, in the refusal to acknowledge social prudery in our times, that their assumption will one day become a reality. Meanwhile, I wonder how many Tony Wolfes are going to wind up in funny farms because of it.

LAST WORDS FROM THE MANAGEMENT CONSULTANT

HOUSE OF PLENTY

HISTORY. First read about the House of Plenty in a San Francisco *Chronicle* piece about an upcoming marriage of four Plenty couples. Then, heard of it from Bernadette and Tony Wolfe, who had just finished a weekend Plenty course in Basic Sexuality. Then went to talk to a woman named Joyce who managed the Esalen office in San Francisco and who was a Plenty family member. She told me whom to call and where to go.

ACCESS. There are seven Houses of Plenty, six in the Bay area an one in Oahu, Hawaii. The one I visited is one of two or three in Oakland. Plenty is a big, old Victorian mansion on a quiet, lower-middle-class residential street.

PHYSICAL LAYOUT. I didn't get to see the whole house, in fact I wasn't allowed to. I was sort of confined, because of the situation, to the combined dining and living room where I had been invited to breakfast with members of the family. The room itself was long and narrow with a long dining table standing along its spine. To the left, through a portal, was a living room with two overstuffed chairs, a record player and TV, and a sofa.

The room was covered with India hand-block prints which gave it a warm and cozy feeling. Music was played sporadically throughout the morning and early afternoon.

PEOPLE. About twenty-three adults live in the original Oakland House of Plenty. There are also about six kids. Not all of them are full family members. The way to join the Plenty family is to spend two weeks there in an Evaluate period, in which you get to know the people and they get a chance to know you. Then you have a meeting with the Housemother (whether man or woman, Housemother) and come to an agreement as to whether you will stay on as a Resident for six months, join the family, or drop the idea altogether.

Manfred Schultz is the founder of the commune. Schultz is a huge guy, bulging just so around the middle, dark-haired and goateed, with a flat rather tough-looking face but with a warm glow in his eyes. He speaks softly and kindly to all around him. He is probably in his mid-thirties. He dresses in San Francisco hip style, striped denim bell bottoms with an overhanging, boldly colored, bunched-sleeve shirt.

Manfred started out in life as a accountant or something, made a success of himself, and then, frustrated, dropped out altogether. With a friend of his named Buddy Vesp (supposedly, seven planets in Scorpio), Manfred established the Institute for Human Potential to preach a philosophy which he and Vesp had formulated to improve the quality of human life. Simply, the philosophy is called More and it states that any human being can have more, in fact he can have whatever he wants. But he has to give more to get more.

The purpose of the Institute was to teach this philosophy in as clear and concrete a way as possible to people who were out of touch with their feelings, with their wants. Manfred began a course in Basic Sexuality to dramatize his ideas. I know only a few parts of the course, information I ascertained from Bernadette Wolfe.

The Institute also offers courses in Jealousy, Money and Possessions, Communications, and others but the basic philosophy of the place is as I suggested before: if you have the right attitude, you can have everything you want.

I got a good example of this philosophy at work when I breakfasted with the members. One guy came jauntily into the dining room and, with a big smile on his face, declared that he had just gotten his Jaguar (auto, of course). I asked him how he did it (I thought communes were poor) and he replied that he just asked for it and got it. I inquired as to how this was possible and Tom Barrow, the man who entertained me most of the morning, explained that the House is organized as a hierarchy, a very tight hierarchy indeed. Manfred is the chief cat and Buddy Vesp number two. Then each of the seven houses has a Housemother and a descending order of authority involving all other members of the family. Members work either for the Institute or around the houses. None of them have time to hold outside jobs so they are completely supported by the commune. The commune earns its money primarily from the Institute courses ($35 to $45 per person for one weekend) and from the Residents, who put up about $200 per month for room and board. Each month, every family member is asked what he would like to buy (somehow no one ever asks for anything he doesn't want or deserve by commune standards; three of the members have already had Jaguars or Maseratis purchased for them) and the costs of these items are added to the general household expenses to determine the financial requirements for the month. Then, Manfred or somebody simply runs as many courses for as many people as are needed in order to fulfill the budgetary quota. The commune has been together for about a year and a half and it seems to work.

CONCLUSIONS. House of Plenty people appear to be very hip and their philosophy most attractive. They were extremely nice to me, invited me back, introduced me around, asked me questions about the book, about myself, invited me to a course, etc. The members are not a young group and I saw faces that had to be in their forties, maybe even fifties. The average, I'm sure however, is no more than twenty-five to thirty. They dress well, seem to live a nice life, speak not only articulately but enthusiastically about what they are into, a philosophy in which they really believe. For them, I think it works well.

S.B.

THAT OLD VON NEUMAN HAD US IN ITS SPELL

On most Sunday nights, Connie Grier opened her basement for the use of a local massage class in which she herself was a student. An Esalen-trained instructor and a class of twelve or so students would spend five hours naked in the basement, learning the techniques of massage and methods of concentration developed at Esalen to make the experience infinitely more than a brisk body rub. In the Orient, massage is an ancient method of preparing the body for meditation; Esalen aims for nothing less. Massage is also endorsed as a suitable prelude to love-making; the gentle, aware probing and caress of Esalen techniques is designed to bring the body erotically alive in all its parts; to relax the muscles into an easy, lazy sensuality. To achieve this, a sensitive psychic exchange must take place between masseur and subject, so that the masseur will know, as if instinctively, where tensions lie under the skin, and what parts are blocked and unresponsive. When the subject allows himself to give way to the control of the masseur, to open himself to the consulting hands (usually through the technique of concentrating his breathing in the area being massaged), a ravishing spiritual experience can result, after which orgasm can seem almost an anticlimax.

Connie had several times suggested that we three join the class one Sunday. "Any Sunday," she had said, cheerfully. But it turned out that, on the Sunday we came, the class had been called off. "Never mind," Connie said. "We'll do some massage anyway." She would demonstrate certain techniques she knew, and the rest of us would work on each other, patterning our strokes after hers. Oz, however, refused to join us. He said he had work to do. Connie tried to jolly him into coming down, but he would not be jollied and went off to a back bedroom. The four of us trooped down the stairs, helped Connie set up two massage tables, and then covered them with sheets while she went for the oil, a special lemon blend she had invented herself. Then we all undressed, and somehow arranged that I would be Connie's subject, and Nora would be Steve's. Nora and I lay down on our backs, side by side, and Connie started to work on my left foot and leg. Steve, picking up Nora's left foot, followed Connie's lead. We were not being at all solemn or meditative about it; this was just a practical session, and we chatted and laughed and kibbitzed as if we were learning how to knead dough or work with clay, except, of course, that two of us were being the clay.

Connie had an excellent touch, very intimate and confiding. In other circumstances, in a private session with proper concentration, I would have been hard put to know whether I wanted the culmination to be spiritual or erotic. But the atmosphere here was instructive, silly and completely playful; it was a grown-up game, but just a game nevertheless. By the time Connie had just about concluded work on my front, Steve steadily copying her on Nora, Oz suddenly came clumping down the stairs, saying that he had changed his mind and would like to get in on the massage after all. As we paused for a cigarette break, we discussed how we would manage five bodies at one time, since massage is usually arranged on a one-to-one basis.

"I know," said Connie. "Let's do a Von Neuman!"

"My God," somebody said. "What's a Von Whateveryousaid?"

"Von Neuman is some German professor who lived ages ago, who invented a massage where one person lies down to be the subject and everybody else works on him at the same time, in concert, all doing the same stroke at the same time somewhere on his body. Or it might not even be a massage technique—just something tactile. Like everybody scratching all over his back with their fingernails. Or everybody rubbing their hair all over him. Or whatever the group decides to do. One person is usually the leader and the whole thing is arranged with signals because you don't want the subject to know what's coming next." Connie smiled wickedly, as if daring us to play this daring new game.

All proclaiming that it was a wild idea, we finished our cigarettes and did One Potato-Two Potato to see who would go first.

Nora turned out to have the honor, and laid herself warily down on one of the massage tables, on her stomach. The rest of us gathered around her, Oz and Steve below the hips, Connie and I facing each other over her shoulders. At first Connie was the leader; she whispered that we should all place our hands firmly on Nora's back and do an Om, three times. Nora sighed and moaned under the concentrated vibrations. Then Connie signaled for general scratching, and Nora writhed deliciously. Then it was caressing with the hair, which all of us had a lot of. And it was Steve who signaled with his tongue that we should lick her all over; Nora's response was a half-strangled cry of sensual delight. Effects were alternated, hard and soft; the tongues, for example, were followed by firm tappings, the tapping by gentle rubbing with oil, the rubbing by vigorous hammering with the sides of both hands. Once Nora's body was slick with oil, we used deeper massage techniques, working deeply into the bone and muscle. When we ran out of ideas, we concluded with another set of Oms, and Nora lay silent for a long while on the table, as if sunken into the wood itself. Our work had prompted loud outbursts of laughter in the general excitement, but now we collapsed too, on all sides; had a glass of wine; rested.

Needless to say, I could hardly wait for my turn. It was good fun to be in on the doing, but fantastic to be the focus of it all. And first of all a little frightening, because when you have your face to the sheet and your friends whispering above your head, and you don't know what you're about to feel, even though you're sure it's going to be pleasurable, a slight anxiety stirs. I thought how predictable most of our experience tends to be; we always know exactly what we're going to get, and the limits of it, and somehow that makes us feel safe. Whereas the excitement lies precisely in not knowing.

The experience was remarkable; protean. With eight hands caressing and probing all over my body, I purely didn't know what to notice first, or how to assimilate the vastness of the input. Ooo-aaaa-eeee. I think that's the noise I mostly made. I spent a while trying to identify hands and textures; some techniques I couldn't identify at all but one stands out. Being rubbed all over with the hair of my friends. Oz and Steve, nodding into my legs and buttocks with their stiff, curly hair, came on like soft brushes. But Connie and Nora, both with long silken hair almost to their waists, were bringing me something I couldn't liken to anything but what it was. To be caressed with the long hair of women—you'll have to try it sometime, because I can't do it justice here.

After the hair I gave up trying to identify anything and just let everything come on, trying to take it as it came, for how it felt, not for what it was. I had been sort of looking forward to the tongues and realized, once the oil was on and the massage was deep, that I had failed to sort them out from the other applications. It was all delicious, sensually exciting and, in my experience, unprecedented. When it was over and I dragged myself up, I said, "Fantastic! Next time let's do fronts!" And everybody agreed, cheering for the good Doctor Von Neuman.

We continued until well into the night, ending with Steve, the last subject. As we moved about, picking up towels and sheets and clothes in the semi-darkness, Steve and Nora moved together on a mattress and embraced. Quietly, Connie, Oz, and I left the basement and went upstairs to shower. Much later, when we three were having tea and cake in the kitchen, the two emerged, showered and dressed, and then Steve, Nora, and I drove home together. While Nora was getting ready for bed, Steve reported that his love-making in Connie's basement had been extraordinary. "I guess it stands to reason," he said. "We'd all just done the right thing for each other. We were feeling sensual, all right. But this was different, cosmic. I felt as if Nora were in charge, as if I were discorporating, losing myself. It was beautiful."

Don't suppose, however, that I went to sleep that night without the usual sound effects. The happy result of open eroticism is that the more you get, the more you're capable of. Contrary to widely advertised fictions, there's no limit to what you can do if you allow yourself to do it. And it's one activity that never becomes boring, no matter what the savants say. The trouble with savants is that, on this subject at least, they really don't know whereof they speak. Unfortunately for savants, eroticism is not a subject that lends itself to intellectuality. Unfortunately for eroticism, savants have always tried to make it intellectual. In this case, three of us were right down out of our heads, and two of us, at least, were doing something about it.

THE SATANIC EVENT

So I reached the conclusion that we must search for and find something genuine and pure—something "raw" not only in our minds but in our history. I want to touch fire, but there is no fire in our present society. Who was the one in Greek myth who took fire from the mountain? Yes, Prometheus. I want to be Prometheus.

Of course, we already have fire—civilized gas fire; I want to use real fire. So I started to do body exercises, kendo, karate. I shouted, and when I shout I feel some fire and I feel some raw material of life. It was a new experience for me and something very difficult to find in modern life.

—YUKIO MISHIMA

I woke up very late the next morning, cursed myself for a slob, and staggered into the kitchen to find Nora at the stove, making coffee. That's funny, I thought; she's going to be very late for work. But what I said was, "Good morning," mustering such smiles and politeness as I could at the dawn of my day.

"Not so good," she said. "Didn't you hear anything last night?"

"Nothing but the usual," I replied, gamely.

"Go look in the living room," she said. "Just go look."

I looked. There was Steve, half asleep in a tangle of sheets. Nothing unusual about that. He saw me, covered his face with one hand and turned his head away in an overstated gesture of despair, his other hand pointing like the finger of doom toward the mantelpiece.

Goddam! There'd been a fire. Half the upper mantel was burnt to a black crust, the remainder seared and scorched, paint swollen and buckling. Anything that had been on the mantel was burnt to cinders as well, and as my eyes roved anxiously over the ruins, my mind's eye tried to reassemble those crisp black mounds into recognizable objects. The mantel was hooded, with a cornice and columns supporting it at either end, framing an inset mirror that was still, thank God, uncracked. But the interior of the cornice was blackened, and one of the little fluted columns seemed burnt through. Above the cornice was a blue glass vase holding a bouquet of what had been enormous pink paper chrysanthemums. The vase was seared and the flowers were reduced to black little balls, *fleurs du mal*. Miraculously, the upper wall and ceiling were unmarked.

I couldn't say anything but My God! and Jesus! and Ummmm as Steve began a slow and painful recapitulation of the night's excitements. A tall candle had been standing on the left side of the mantel; before bed, Steve had lighted it to make love by. He and Nora had fallen asleep, forgetting the guttering candle, forgetting also that it rested on a loose-leaf notebook and a few other papers. During the night the candle flame or the hot dripping wax had ignited the notebook and papers and they had burst into a lively blaze which, by the time Steve opened his eyes to it, had spread to the wooden mantel itself and the high pink chrysanthemums. Somehow, Steve had managed to beat out and smother the flames with wet towels; he and Nora had aired the house (except for my room), and not a whiff of char remained. But the furniture was adrift in wisps of blackened paper, the floor was spattered with hardened wax everywhere, and there was the great black smudge where once had been the pretty white Victorian mantel. Oh, poor trusting friends who so kindly lent us this flat, I thought. Oh God, how are we ever going to make up to you for this?

My thought was Steve's own. "I know, Dick," he said. "It's awful. Look, it's my responsibility because it was my foolishness. I'm going to fix it; by God, I'll fix it so you'll never know it happened." And his conversation drifted on into agonized reproaches of himself with which I could not but sympathize. Still, "No," I said, "I'll help you."

"No, Dick," he said. "You've got to finish the work for *Holiday*. I'll do all this, I'll buy white paint, I'll get brushes . . ." and feverishly he starting writing lists of all the stuff he was going to need to put the mantel right. Meanwhile, Nora and I started cleaning up the place, and found that nothing was irreparably harmed beyond the fireplace itself. The blue vase was okay; we could replace the paper flowers. By the time Nora left for work, she was already two and a half hours late.

While I tried to write my way through the afternoon, Steve was out shopping for paints and stuff, back to lay papers on the floor, out again to buy a scraper, back again to scrape, out again to buy sandpaper. He worked and sweated for hours, sanding and scraping, but by nightfall the mantel was still just a big black smudge. At seven a friend of my wife's from New York, who was vacationing just then in San Francisco, was to come around, have a drink, and then take me out to dinner; it was her vacation charity, since I was conserving money and rarely went out to restaurants. Before she came, I spent a while trying to calm Steve down, but he was determined to cover the black scar as soon as possible. "I just can't look at it," he said. "I can't bear to be in the same room with it. I'll never sleep if I don't get it covered up." There was a further reason for his antic behavior; Nora had announced that she would not be over tonight. "She's seeing an old boyfriend," he said, glumly. Nora had made it very clear from the start that while she loved Steve a lot, she was under no circumstances to be considered "his" chick; that she reserved the right to see other people, male and female as she pleased, to go out with them, to go to bed with them, whatever she felt was appropriate. She had told Steve that she expected the same independent behavior of him; she was not possessive, did not want to own him, in fact, refused to.

She had also startled him very much by stating that she had no respect for people who were incapable of bi-sexuality, and that she frankly did not believe him when he said he had no feeling for it. Poor Steve was now flanked by people he loved who deplored his claims to one-dimensional sexuality; a social situation he had never met before. Under the pressure of it, he finally admitted to occasional homosexual fantasies. When he had aired this news, he found himself under additional pressure from Nora to act on the fantasies, specifically, in fact, with me. In the intensity of our three-way involvement, a three-way sexual consummation had been exhaustively discussed, and Nora suggested that Steve and I ought to get it on as a prelude to a troika. It was the old David situation with new personnel and different dynamics. Now it was Nora who was pushing for action. I was temporizing; as Steve had often said, my open admission of bi-sexuality was heavy for others to handle, and he meant, pointedly, himself. I didn't want sex to screw up a very good friendship. Meanwhile, Steve was using all the ingenuity of a very agile brain to keep matters at the theoretical level. He still felt that he could maneuver Nora into an exclusive relationship. He never admitted this to Nora; if he blew his own strategy she would probably blow her stack and possibly would walk out. But he had told me about it on several occasions, and on this particular evening he was especially tormented; for the first time since Nora had met Steve, she was going out with another man.

While we were exploring all these tangents once again, my friend from New York showed up to take me to dinner. She is a very New York sort of lady. By that I mean that she goes straight to the point without any side trips. "You are never going to take the black out of that wood without bleach," she said. "Do you have any bleach?" No. "Okay then," she said to Steve. "Put down that sandpaper and go change your clothes. You're coming to dinner with us." In the face of this invincible logic, Steve did as he was told. It was nice to have a boss on the premises for a change.

We were literally walking out the door when the phone rang, and Steve ran back up the steps to answer it. When he returned he said it had been Nora. She was at Connie's, and she was upset. "The dude that was supposed to take her out never showed," he said, "but that's not what she's upset about. It's something else but I don't know what, and she wants me to come over. Will you drop me?"

As it happened, we dropped Steve in front of Connie's at approximately 9:14 P.M., a point that we would later consider very significant, inasmuch as a mild earthquake hit the city at exactly that time. It was not much felt in Pacific Heights, nor would we have noticed it anyway, sitting in our banging and rattling little car. And my New York friend and I continued on to Señor Pico's, a Mexican restaurant in Ghirardelli Square, and had fancy drinks and eats which she most kindly paid for and I most thoroughly enjoyed. I delivered my friend back to her hotel sometime after midnight, stopped off at a couple of bars on the way home, and arrived back at the apartment shortly before three to find Steve and Nora sitting up in the living room, very nervous and upset.

It took me a while to get any clear account of what was so agitating them. Nora had arrived at work hours late; when her boss reprimanded her, she quit, and though she stayed on until closing time, he refused to pay her for the hours she had worked. She went home to Connie's very angry, and decided that a hot bath and a joint would calm her down. But the bath had been unbearably hot, and the joint had only agitated her further. She lit a candle in her bedroom and its flame fluttered menacingly. She tried to read but her book, *Auto-da-Fe*, was a hideous choice under the circumstances. The old boyfriend never showed; if he had, she would not have been in a state to go out anyway. She was jangled, frightened, she didn't know why. Finally she had called Steve.

When he arrived he found her weeping in her bed. He comforted her for a while, as best he could, heard her story, and then confessed that he had been very upset all day himself. It was the fire. So many stupid things had been happening to him. It was as if he were under a spell or . . . A SPELL. Witchcraft! That was it. Nora was quick to respond; witchcraft had been on her mind all day. Somebody or something was sending bad vibrations onto them, making everything go wrong. Compiling evidence out of every coincidence of the past weeks, they hurried back to the apartment to share their anxieties with me. Not finding me back, they fed their theory further, until by the time I walked in, they were clutching each other in fear.

"Look," Steve said. "It's on the record. I have been setting fires every place I go—first at David's we almost asphyxiate, here I practically sent the whole house up in flames last night. And the stereo set—you know yourself every time I walk in over there the fucking thing breaks down. Nora and the candle flame freaking, she's reading *Auto-da-Fe*, for Christ's sake. Fire—I'm a Leo, it's a fire sign. Wherever I go, things burst into flames. It's not coincidental, Dick, somebody is hexing me, sending some bad shit onto me." Nora moaned in agreement.

I asked who would want to do that, and he named his Boston

girlfriend, who is very adept at astrology. "That's ridiculous, Steve," I said. "She isn't an evil person. She wouldn't wish you ill even if she could."

"I don't know about that," he said. "She's very angry with me because she knows I've been lying to her by long distance about Nora. I said I *might* go out here with *some* chicks but I haven't told her I'm seriously involved with Nora. And yet she knows. She knows it and she knows I'm lying to her. It could be her, no kidding."

I don't know much about the occult, but the whole subject was disturbing and frightening to me; anyway, I felt that Steve and Nora were off on an entirely wrong tack, and I tried to persuade them of it. I pointed out that they were both physically tired and still suffering somewhat from the shock of waking up to a room in flames. Many heavy emotional events had occurred, including Nora's having quit her job, which was traumatic for her even when she was telling herself she was in the right. She had not been a good employee and deep within herself she knew it, and was suppressing her guilt about it. What's more, Steve had a lot of guilt weighing heavily on himself. He was lying to his Boston girlfriend on the phone every other day and hating himself for it. He was not getting out to visit communes as he and I both felt he should (this was a source of some friction between us) and he was feeling guilty about that. And through carelessness he was damaging other people's property, which was an agony for him.

As for the occult, I pointed out that Steve had been toying with its fringes for months in almost a wishful way. His Boston girlfriend had involved him in the details of astrology, and we had been reading horoscopes with faltering disbelief ever since. He had mentioned Satanism as one of the things, along with acid and faggotry, that fascinated and frightened him. But that, more important than anything else, he and Nora and I had been breaking taboos right and left ever since we'd arrived in San Francisco, from the camping weekend onward. We had run around naked, we had talked .dlessly about expanded sexual scenes, we had lived in each other's armpits for weeks with sex always heavy in the air. We had only just spent an evening licking and rubbing each other's bodies, f'chrissake. And while we were telling ourselves how liberated and nifty and terrific we were, the old taboos had never entirely relinquished their hold. So Steve and Nora were doing to themselves what man has always traditionally done when he finds himself defying ancient traditions and everything that mommy and daddy and the Pope ever said. They were conjuring our old friend Satan, the androgynous fellow with horns and a long tail and the rutting lust of an animal—a symbolic figure for what they were, however unconsciously, contemplating. I said that Satan was simply an embodiment, a personification of the fear of pressing past taboos into sexual freedom, that what they were suffering was only the psycho-sexual anxiety of a carefully civilized, guilt-ridden society. That in fact nothing magical and scary was taking place; it was only a head trip.

This speech, which I delivered with utter conviction, was very well received. Steve and Nora had been really very scared, and they were enormously relieved to hear a calm and rational argument against irrationality. So they relaxed, and we hugged each other goodnight, and I went to the bathroom to brush my teeth, whistling a happy tune and thinking only happy thoughts.

Content with myself, pleasantly weary, my mind more or less a blank, I went into the bedroom, shut the door, took off my clothes, and was just in the act of setting the alarm when I glanced casually into the mirror above the bed. Strange, I thought; how unlike myself I look. In fact, I scarcely recognized myself at all. It was my face all right, but the light from the low lamp on the bed table seemed to emphasize the down-turn of my mouth, the darkness of my beard, the shiny glint of my steel-rimmed glasses. I looked closer; I seemed not to be in the mirror at all; somebody else seemed to be looking at me from the mirror.

I looked at my eyes and they weren't mine. I couldn't believe it—the eyes were glittery agate points, utterly heartless; not cruel, beyond cruelty or any ordinary wickedness into icy coldness. Cold is not even an adequate word; they were conscienceless, as if informed by some maniacally brilliant intelligence, some inhuman clarity. And I just simply panicked; I didn't know who was staring at me from the mirror and I felt all the hair on my body stand straight out in the air. Some reason still working,

I thought, my glasses, it's the effect of the glasses, and I snatched them off. No—still the same staring eyes, somebody, something else was in the mirror. And as I watched, the mirror face seemed to melt, dissolve into the features of a pig, snout and ears and all, and still the same agate eyes stared out.

At the same moment the air in the room seemed to change its quality, to become dense, palpable. It seemed to take on the texture of a vast grid, like the inside of an insect's eye. The air acquired character, a malevolent personality. I was ready to die. I had to get out of there.

Pausing—how could I have?—to pull on a pair of pants, I burst wildly through the double doors, blood draining from my face and the surface of my body humming, and stumbled to the foot of Steve and Nora's bed. "I know you'll think I'm crazy," I said, hardly able to talk. "But listen . . . there's a . . . there's somebody in the mirror."

Shrieks from Nora as I babbled my story, talking about the eyes, the eyes. "OmigodSteve," Nora whispered, "what were you just saying to me? You were staring at my eyes and you said, 'I'd like to eat your eyes.'" Aaaaarrrrgggghhhh. We freaked, we flipped, we writhed and shrieked in terror. "This is crazy," I kept saying aloud, my whole body shaking and rattling. "This is just insanity, this can't be happening, we're rational people, there's no such thing as the devil, this is absurd, this is nonsense, I don't believe it." On and on, it was like a litany, trying to argue against my senses, and it wasn't a goddam bit of good. Because I knew very well that there was a presence in the mirror, a personality, a *thing* in that room, and I most terribly feared that it was Satan himself.

Still I argued. "This is ridiculous, we're just panicking over nothing, I'm going back in there." But I couldn't. I'd get as far as the door and feel the personality in the air, the cold presense that seemed to hate and abominate me, and I'd be powerless to go further. Oh God, I groaned, and forced myself time after time into the doorway. But I couldn't enter. Steve said, "Let me try," and walked straight in; he stared at the mirror, remarked that he looked satanic himself with his beard illuminated by the bed lamp below, came out again.

"Oh, is it going to come in here?" Nora moaned. Steve and I

rushed to the mantel mirror, stared, searching. No eyes. Thank God. We clung together in a shivering little heap. "Oh, Steven, I'm frightened," Nora said. "It's going to come in here. Oh, what are we going to do?" We were falling into complete panic, teeth clattering, eyes rolling. From somewhere, Steve mustered control. "We've got to stop this," he said. "In half a minute we'll be running screaming in the streets. Now let's calm down; let's talk sensibly now; let's reconstruct what happened."

This was pretty good therapy; to talk about what had happened tended to force present events into the past tense, to take the terrifying onus of Right Now out of the room to some extent. We were telling a story, taking first steps in converting horror into myth. But we were still frightened; we considered that there might be more to come; we desperately feared—and at the same time were unbelievably excited by—an actual visitation by Satan in corporeal form. If there had been a knock on the door at that moment, or a creak in the hall, I think we would have all died on the spot. As it was, I tried to think of practical ways out. If only Bishop Pike were still alive and well in Pacific Heights; we could get him on the phone. What about priests and rabbis that do exorcisms? How do you get in touch with those guys at four in the morning? The Yellow Pages?

Then I turned to reasons, causes. Utterly credulous now, completely convinced of Steve's theory that somebody was Doing something to us, I started to rack my mind for who it might be. My friend Rodney in London? Very involved with the occult, he was. Could Rodney be doing this? Where was the silver cross he gave me? Omigod, I hadn't worn it in a couple of days, chain got tangled, I hadn't fixed it. "Put it on," Steve said. "It's probably protective." I put it on. And went on ransacking my memory. I had visited a wise man in Jokjakarta, had never sent him a gift later, which was customary. Could this be his revenge? Not two months before I had attended the voodoo ceremonies of candomblé outside Bahia in northern Brazil; I had two voodoo necklaces in my suitcase. Something emanating from them? Oh God, my house in New Jersey was crammed with other people's magic—talismans, sculptures, masks I'd bought in primitive places all over the world, with respect for their rumored power but disbelieving essentially in such things, liking them for their beauty only. I had never taken any of them as seriously as they obviously deserved to be taken. I thought of how I had toyed constantly with occult things—now it was all coming home to me.

We wondered who—either evil or possessed of evil—might have touched us. Nobody we knew in San Francisco seemed a candidate, except for poor Tony Wolfe. He had prowled the room that night like a beast. He was certainly possessed of something or other, and he had touched Steve many times. But it couldn't be him, it just didn't feel right. We looked suspiciously at each other: who started all this—Steve? Nora? Dick? In these endless speculations we sat up anxiously awaiting the dawn. When it came, just a hint of light at the windows, the blessed sound of jiggling milk bottles came with it from the street below. Daylight, day sounds—a reprieve. I found I could enter the bedroom now; the strange hostile presence had vanished. I assured Steve and Nora that I was all right, that I would sleep. I knew I would. I was desperately tired. But before I fell asleep I wrote a long letter to my friend Rodney in London, describing in detail everything that had just happened, and begging him, should he be responsible in any way, please to stop scaring us so much.

Then I put aside my notebook and pen, and fell at once into a deep sleep. Some time after noon I was ripped from my slumbers by the phone ringing, and fumbled on the bed table for the receiver. It was my very dear old friend Bob, a writer and professor of English from down the peninsula. He was in a nearby grocery store and he was—as he often was that summer—furious. "Where the hell are you?" he rasped. "I was supposed to be there at twelve and I was there at twelve and I have rung the goddam doorbell for hours. Are you going to let me in or what?" I mumbled apologies, ran down to the door, and was standing beside it when he came grouchily up the street. "Here's your mail," he said, thrusting a bundle of letters into my hand. Mail was coming to me at his address, Bob had kindly offered to bring it to me and, like many professional grouches, he was furious with himself for being caught in a charitable deed. He was also generally annoyed at me and everything about me that summer; in all, his visit wasn't shaping up to be very pleasant.

I brought him into the kitchen, made him a martini which he

accepted sourly, and asked him what he knew about the occult. "Something, a little something, in a literary context only," he said. I asked him to read something, he reluctantly agreed, and I fetched my letter to Rodney. By the time I'd made some coffee Bob was in a very different mood, elated and excited. By now too, Steve and Nora had stumbled into the kitchen and were filling him in on details and ornamental flourishes. And Bob began to lecture us on satanism in literature, with special reference to Mark Twain's "The Mysterious Stranger." Many authors, he said, had been fascinated with the concept. Twain's Satan was a particularly engaging fellow, equipped with pure logic; logic, indeed, seemed to be Satan's strong suit. Bob suggested that we had, the night before, passed through the Christian apprehension of occult events into a pre-Christian, pagan freedom. He said that an encounter with Satan brought the enormous power of wisdom—the real knowledge of good and evil, which was that they are polar opposites, therefore the same, therefore nonexistent.

He at once pulled out a pen and began to write out a list of supplementary reading, works he thought would increase our understanding of what had befallen us. He didn't have to itemize *Faust,* of course. But he drew up the following list, starring items according to his opinion of them:

**   *The Turn of the Screw*—Henry James
       The Haunting of Hill House—Shirley Jackson
**   *The Mysterious Stranger*—Mark Twain
*   *The Golden Bough*—James G. Frazer
       Songs of Innocence and Experience—William Blake
***   *Black Ship to Hell*—Brigid Brophy
***   *Apocrypha*—D. H. Lawrence
       (may be titled *The Apocryphal*)
**   *The Double*—F. M. Dostoievski
       The Possessed—   "

Just as we were having some badinage about *Faust* not being on the list, and he was wondering aloud whether we were smart enough to remember it, the phone rang in the bedroom. I went down the hall, answered it, and a voice said: "Mr. Atcheson, my name is Desmond Colpits. I am a friend of . . . [and he gave the names of several people I know in the magazine business.] Now, Mr. Atcheson, I am about to start a new magazine, to be located in the Bay area, on the subject of experimental education, and I'm looking for an editor. People in the business tell me you're my man. Now I have several million dollars . . ." I didn't faint, but I sure came close.

When I came back to the kitchen and broke my news, everybody else almost fainted. We broke out the booze, we broke out the mahreewhooahanah, we made up new dance steps, we flew. We made quick and easy plans to take over the world in twenty seconds. We wanted to PARTY. But first I made a few long-distance calls, inquiring into the bona fides of Mr. Desmond Colpits, and various people assured me he was for real. I called my wife in New York and we freaked together by long distance. This was what I had wanted for so long—an intelligent magazine, dedicated to a subject I could believe in and commit myself to, with an opportunity to build the kind of working community I believe can function without tyranny, in the Bay area, where I have longed to live ever since I first laid eyes upon it. Unbelievable! Miraculous! FAUSTIAN! Except that nobody had requisitioned my soul.

The four of us spun out of the house and hastened to a beautifully-silly restaurant on Union Street called the Café Cantata, where we were shown to the best table in the house without asking for it, a table that occupies its own balcony and rides high above the heads of merely mortal diners. We had more booze, we had fantastic eats, we were already thoroughly stoned, everything was beautiful, we were beautiful. And when I paid for our ambrosial meal with a fifty-dollar traveler's check, the waiter absentmindedly neglected to take out the cost of food and drink, and returned me fifty full dollars in change! I didn't walk out without paying, but I certainly could have—and it seemed to us that this was simply more evidence that, from now on, we could have anything we wanted, even when we weren't thinking of wanting it. We felt radiant with power, drunk with it, and transcendent of mortal flesh, as if when the sun's rays struck us, we would shine clear through.

Another couple of drinks back at the flat, and old Bob was

thoroughly drunk. We entreated him to stay that night with us, not to attempt the long drive south, but like all drunks he insisted that he was perfectly competent to drive supremely well, and we should fuck off. In the end, with many misgivings, we let him go. The three of us, exhausted, were taking things more slowly now; a kind of reverie set in as we lounged about in the living room. Though it was dark outside, we weren't frightened anymore. We now felt confident that the worst was over; or if it wasn't, strong enough finally to take what came. I was on the sofa, reading the August issue of *Rags* magazine, and was deeply involved with Barbara Birdfeather's astrology column, *signs*. August was my month, of course, being Leo; Steve's as well, and much of what Barbara Birdfeather said seemed to make magical sense to me. For example, under Particular Portents, by sign:

Leo (Steve and me) :	So together you see from the tower's heights, financial affluence, gentle epistles put forth to benefit self through others; yet career still hard to get moving (more discipline necessary).
Aquarius (Nora) :	Your ole man/lady looking deep into your eyes finds satisfaction; shifting small fears can be disturbing.
Gemini (David) :	Home feels so good you don't need to go out much, it comes to you . . . the traffic may cause logistical problems.
Capricorn (my wife Jean, hearing all my wild news by long distance) :	High friends seeming weird behind your accurate predictions, your philosophical consciousness knows what's happening and solves problems gracefully, bringing secret praise.

I wondered how Barbara Birdfeather could possibly be so right on.

Among "highest" days in the month, Miss Birdfeather had forecast the 2nd and the 4th. For the 2nd, she had written: "Run naked in breeze flowing ferns, laugh loudly as your head spins." Well, that seemed to make sense. On August 2 we had been Von Neumanizing one another naked in Connie's basement.

"Ferns" would be a reasonable analogy for all that long soft hair, and all the other good stuff. For the 4th, today, nothing about Satan at all. Just: "You catch special love completely open and willing." Hmmm, not even Barbara Birdfeather could be 100 percent accurate. Here it was ten o'clock at night and no sign of any special loves. Just then, the phone rang.

Nora came back from the phone to say that her friend Silvia, who was doing a summer course at Stanford, had come unexpectedly to town and was over at Connie's, hoping to see her. Could one of us run over and pick her up? I said I'd be glad to, put on my jacket, and drove the few blocks to Connie's house in a kind of amiable stupor, not thinking about much, really too tired to think. In Connie's living room was Silvia, a lovely, black-haired girl with almond eyes and a lush, opulent figure. We said hi, and not much else, and I drove her back to the flat. She and Nora retired to the kitchen for a while, presumably to gossip, and after a while they joined Steve and me in the living room. Steve proposed a little more dope, so we smoked a couple of joints, after which Steve and Nora began to engage in ever more serious amorous play. I was punchy for want of sleep, so I said goodnight, went off to brush my teeth, returned to the bedroom, and found almond-eyed Silvia naked under the sheets.

"You catch special love completely open and willing." Barbara Birdfeather, you know something.

THE BREAKTHROUGH

Time ponderously raced: a count-down of seconds passed at fever-speed and yet in the detail of slow-motion. This was an experience of time with enlarged pores.

in transit, BRIGID BROPHY

It seems in retrospect—indeed it seemed at the time—that over the next ten days, events telescoped with amazing rapidity. We began then to talk about a sort of psychic time machine. Hours seemed to elongate when necessary, shrink when that was desirable. It was not something we controlled, it just seemed to happen for our convenience. It was not unlike the period after the camping trip, at David's, when collectively we turned night into day. But it was not so exhausting; in fact, we were rarely tired.

We were conscious of extra energy, as if Satan had shot us full of adrenalin. Despite the fact that my friends were coming back from the country soon, and we had to vacate the apartment and return to David's, there was an abundance of time to get things done. I zipped through the remainder of my work for *Holiday* in no time; Steve restored the burned mantelpiece in a day. There were no more miracles and visions, and there were hard emotional times, but our lives were infused with a new confidence. We felt that nothing would go really wrong anymore, since everything that happened was right. And we had plenty of time for even faster rapid-fire discussion of what had happened and was happening to us. We were utterly self-absorbed.

We soon put together an explication of what we were now calling The Satanic Event. Obviously I had imagined that I could get through life—certainly through the pressure-cooker intimacies of my life with Steve and Nora—as dear old Gary Goodguy, friend to man, without a lascivious thought in his head. And when those lascivious thoughts couldn't break through my culture armor and my stunning vision of my own innocence, they pushed and probed until they found an outlet. Steve provided the weak spot by evoking Beelzebub, of whom I was less disbelieving than scared to death. And you are not scared of anything you *really* do not believe to exist. It was an easy one-two step from brushing my teeth to being propelled right back into a room where my lascivious thoughts wanted to be, i.e., Steve and Nora's room. So we now felt we understood one important dynamic of communes where people live, as we were living, cheek by jowl, without artificial barriers. It was true that I loved them both, and they me. And Nora was vaguely cross that I had culminated my day with the devil by going to bed—rather noisily as it turned out—with her friend Silvia.

It was not so much that she was herself an occasional lover of Silvia's; Nora was not a jealous person. But she argued that Silvia was essentially a frivolous, silly girl who, at the age of nineteen, was only just coming onto the sexual scene and was ready to go to bed with everybody. Nora argued that, though herself only nineteen, she was a much more sober and experienced nineteen than Silvia, who, she confided, had been a virgin until two months before. Silvia, she said, was going at sex as if it were push-ups. Nora was glad we had had a nice time, but she didn't feel that an important day should have been concluded with such a frivolous person. I was important; she was important; Steve was important. That was where my attention, and my sexual energy, ought to have been.

I had to agree with Nora that I felt kind of stupid about my night with Silvia, lovely partner though she had been. I had got almost no sleep—tiredness having vanished as if by magic when I saw how the land lay—it had been a delicious night—but early in the morning I dozed. When I woke, Silvia was dressed and sitting on the edge of the bed, nestled into the curve of my back. "Wha . . . whu . . . whu time izzt?" I asked. "It's seven," Silvia said. "My girlfriend is coming by to pick me up in five minutes to drive back to Palo Alto; I have a class at nine."

Ah, the vigor of youth, I thought, sinking deeper into my pillow. "Hey," said Silvia, "I just thought of a funny thing. I don't even know your name." Solemnly, we introduced ourselves to each other, shaking hands over the sheet. "How do you do?" "How do *you* do?" Surely, I thought, there was a movie out just recently about something like this—*John and Mary*. Dick and Silvia. Steve and Nora. Bob and Carol and Ted and Alice.

"Hey," said Silvia again, rubbing my back pleasantly. "That was really neat. I've never been to bed with an older man before. Gosh, I hope you're not as old as my mother."

"How old is your mother?" I asked, worried.

"Thirty-nine."

"Wow, what a break," I said. "Missed it by four years."

Silvia looked relieved, and just then there was the toot of a horn out on the street. "Whoops," said Silvia. "There she is." She bent down and kissed me very ardently. "Listen," she said, on her way out of the room, "maybe I'll see you next week . . . and maybe I won't. Bye." And she was gone.

I chuckled to myself about the winning ways of nineteen-year-old girls these days. They didn't make 'em like that in my time, I thought, but neither did they make the Pill. And I thought no more about it, and soon fell into a deep sleep. On waking, though, I felt sort of rueful. Here I was, a guy that had got zapped by Satan and was Faustian and altogether remarkable, falling into the sack with the first girl that happened to get there first. It seemed random, unplanned, unworthy somehow. I swore a private oath that I would not engage in cheap sex ever again (unless, of course, I really knew it was cheap sex and that was what I wanted at the time), and from then onward, fueled by Nora's disapproval of that scene, the Silvia incident came to be known as The Necessary Mistake.

Look, said I, finding out what I thought as I heard the sound of my own voice. Going to bed with Silvia was dumb and meaningless, but if I hadn't done it I wouldn't know now, so vividly, what "dumb and meaningless" really is. It was only after she left that I realized how shallow and despicable cheap sex is. I want all my human contacts to mean something; I want them to be important. You can't go around falling in bed with any old body, not if you have any respect for yourself; for you make yourself as cheap as the fleshy activity in which you are engaged. Steve and Nora nodded in complete agreement. In Steve's terminology, poor old Silvia wasn't heavy. You shouldn't have to do with people who aren't heavy. And who were the heaviest people we knew? Ourselves.

This mutual realization, however, cost Steve increased anxiety. If at the moment there were only three heavy people in ready access of one another, he was going to have to shit or get off the pot. And he didn't want to; oh, *how* he didn't want to. Theories were all very well and good, but realities were threatening. And not only to him; when it came to the mechanics, Nora and I both talked a fairly sophisticated line, but we admitted we didn't have the least idea how to get on with the thing. But the pressure was pumping up very fast, so fast that, once we returned to live at David's, life became incredibly difficult. One or the other of us was breaking into tears at the least provocation; once Steve spent hours in tearful collapse because he didn't know what to do and didn't feel he could relate his problems to anybody but us two. And all the hugging and comforting and back-patting we could do didn't alleviate the situation. We got to be awfully tired of weeping and hysterics all the time, yet beatified and saintly on their account. An emotional freak-out was an occasion for the safe display of affections; at the same time, it took some of the intense sexual pressure off.

Two things happened to save us from ourselves. First, dear old *Holiday* called. They wanted me to wing off to Fiji and Tahiti to get a couple of stories—right away, in a hurry. Second, when I called Jean to discuss this assignment with her and to tell the latest developments of our hot-house ménage, we had a most difficult phone conversation. She was terribly conflicted over what I ought to do. She thought I should leave Steve and Nora flat, get out of the whole situation, and most importantly, stop smoking dope. "How much are you smoking?" she would ask, fury in her tone, a Cary Nation of marijuana. On the other hand, she couldn't see abandoning the book research in the middle, to go off on toots for *Holiday*. "It's ridiculous," she said. "You've put aside this time to get that bloody book researched, and you should be doing it." There was also the pathetic situation that she was there and I was here, and she couldn't make an instant's sense of what was going on with us; she is a patient, long-suffering wife but the tales were getting too horrific to bear. In the end, I pleaded with her to come out to San Francisco. On the practical side there was an upcoming meeting with Mephistophe-lean Desmond Colpits, who was coming to town and would attend a joint birthday party, given by David and Lenore for Steve and me, on the 9th. If my future were going to be shaped at this summit, Jean should be there. And of course there was the whole matter of what kind of crazy freak she was married to, and what he was doing. I fervently felt that if I could just see her, I could explain everything. At the end of a torturous phone conversation, during which she made several allusions to the uselessness of Going On Like This, I persuaded her to drop everything and fly out the next day. "Never mind the goddam rent money," I said, "this is important." On the same day, I called *Holiday* back and said I would accept the two South Pacific assignments.

Steve was furious with me for accepting *Holiday*'s offer. "We're here for the book," he lectured me, "and the book needs your energy and your enthusiasm. If you're leaving to take the pressure off the threesome, don't. It would be wrong. We need you here. Don't leave if you're leaving because of us."

"Steve," I said, "I *may* be leaving because of you. But mostly

I'm leaving because we need the dough. We are near flat and we have to have an influx of money to support ourselves out here and keep the home fires burning. As it is, Jean is avoiding phone calls because it might be bill collectors. If I don't take these assignments we all starve to death, and there won't be any book anyway. And in fact, I really think you and Nora can get your thing together a whole lot easier if I'm not here. What's more, you might even do a little research while I'm gone."

Steve remained dead set against the plan, but I was adamant and had my way. Jean took emergency leave and flew straight out to San Francisco with nothing but her handbag. I took a room at the inexpensive but respectable Hotel Beresford in foggy downtown San Francisco and we embarked on The Four Days That Shook A Marriage. And on the Saturday night at our joint birthday party, Desmond Colpits showed up and turned out to be an unmitigated ass, never mind how many millions he had in his pocket. So much for deals with the devil.

The time with Jean was the happiest we've ever spent together. It was terrible at first—from the meeting at the airport onward, she couldn't stand the sight of me. But we worked it out, somehow. I was so glad to see her—it had been months—that she couldn't mistake my ardor for fraud. When she decided that I wasn't insane after all, or a complete psychic stranger, but just plain old fucked-up Dick—and maybe not so awfully bad at that—we embarked on a magical time, that doesn't even bear talking about. The failure of Desmond Colpits to be more than an obnoxious jerk was not even a bee sting to our happiness.

In the midst of the weekend, which we spent a good bit apart from Steve and Nora and David and Lenore, Steve called the hotel one afternoon in a state of agitation, saying that he needed to talk to me urgently. But when I suggested that he come around at once he refused, not wanting to intrude. We agreed that after Sunday services at the Glide, where we would all meet, he and I would find a way to have a little private conversation.

Outside the church on Sunday morning, we arranged that Jean and Nora would walk on ahead to David's, where we were to rendezvous for lunch, and Steve and I would take a slower, more circuitous route, and I would hear him out. Mostly, his subject was his agony of conscience over his lies to his Boston girlfriend. What was my advice? How could he extricate himself from cruelties upon her, not intended, but very real? I suggested that he write to her, not lying; that he lay out, as best he could, what was happening in his life. That it might be fatal to the relationship, but better than being twisted in a knot of prevarications he could not even recall accurately between phone calls. I don't know for sure that this was good advice, but I knew that even the truth was hard to convey, perhaps impossible to convey, by long distance. I thought that if Steve wrote what he felt, the result could only be right.

It was in the middle of Chinatown that he switched to a second, pressing subject. Nora felt most strongly that we ought to consummate our three-way relationship sexually. She and Steve were timid about proposing it, particularly with Jean on the scene and her sentiments not known, but whenever they came together sexually, they told each other, "Dick ought to be here." So they felt that it ought to happen and he was here to tell me so. I asked him what his own feelings were in this matter. "I think you know how I feel about you," he said. So I said yes, that it would be a handsome and fine thing, that it seemed that, at that moment in my life, many fine people loved me and wanted me—and I think I have never felt happier or more expansive and real as a human being than I did then. We reached David's long before Jean and Nora, and Steve and I sat on the steps, heads in hands, talking about how very good it is to move past the hurt of anxiety and doubt in human relationships into a kind of celebration of life. We were feeling that. And when Jean and Nora rounded the corner and saw us with our heads down, they thought we were weeping. For a pleasant change, we weren't.

A CURIOUS DREAM

I remember now, hazily, as if it were a particularly dear and romantic dream, the night of my send-off from San Francisco airport to Fiji. Our little band—David, Lenore, Steve, Nora,

Jean, and I—were together that night in an extravagant intensity of shared feeling that we had never equaled before and would never experience again. It was one of those rare moments of mutuality among people, an orgy of sentiment in common, when the physical fact of impending separation revivifies and glamorizes the pleasure of one another's company. It is ironic that moments of this kind are rarely allowed except when it is too late to act on the passions evoked—airports and bus terminals make a poor setting for love feasts. Still, we were so dazzled by each other that night that we did what we could.

Mine was a late-night flight to Fiji via Honolulu. Jean's plane was to leave for New York just thirty minutes later. We checked her in first, then me, and in the rush and hullabaloo still had a chance to dig the rather special quality of a special city's airport. San Franciscans don't just wear clothes; they costume themselves. Bells, beads, hair, mauve shades, trailing gowns surrounded us. A film production unit had set up lights in front of the Pan Am counter and were staging an airport scene with straight, conventional-looking, boringly dressed actors self-consciously playing the part of straight, conventional-looking, boringly dressed travelers, and we giggled at the fraud involved, since in constant ebb and flow around the phony scene moved a rainbow of humanity, infinitely more colorful and excited and tinkling than anything the camera was catching. There was even a white-bearded Indian guru and his band of WASP followers in saffron robes, chanting quietly and gazing reverently at their departing leader. Someday, David said, he would do a film documentary on San Francisco airport; it was better than the Ice Capades.

Shortly before flight time, we strolled arm-in-arm to the departure lounge and stood about, saying little but still holding each other. David proposed an Om, and we clustered together, hugging and auhmmmmmmming, feeling extremely corporate and deeply connected. I was intensely aware of the beauty of everybody—had there ever been such lovely women with such luminous, dancing eyes; ever men so lithe and electric, so warm in their smiling and touching? It was that glowing, emotional bath again, a state vibrating indecisively between laughter and tears; we laughed with damp eyes. Then they called my flight; reluctantly I began to pull away, then was embraced by each in turn, held and kissed deeply and passionately by each. It occurred to me that, in being kissed by David and Steve, another taboo was being, this time, publicly broken; I imagined the impact on the people around us, and entered proudly into those embraces, with a warmth as vital and free as I felt it. A final, burning embrace with Jean, and I was off and running, with backward glances, down the long retractable tunnel into the plane.

The aircraft was sealed, motors revving and thundering in a muted way, when suddenly the door was sprung open again, and there came over the intercom a message from the Passenger Representative, paging Mr. Atcheson. I wrestled out of my seat, spilling my complimentary champagne as I went, and found Jean frantic at the mouth of the tunnel. "Darling, I can't find my ticket in my bag," she said, rifling nervously through a thousand slips of paper, still searching. Except that in the next instant she produced her ticket; her suspicion that I had carried it with me evaporated before the eyes of the Passenger Representative, and Jean and I were sharply aware in that instant that we were retarding the progress of an aircraft worth millions of dollars, and 130 eager Hawaii-bound passengers, and in general the efficient operations of a giant, world-circling airline. It was terrific. So I accused her of just making the whole story up in order to provide us with one more embrace, and she was amused at the notion and half believed it, and we had one more fervent embrace, courtesy of the long-suffering Pan Am Passenger Representative. Then I was back aboard, the door was shut with a woosh of finality, and in no time, as the plane taxied for take-off, I was mopping my champagne-moistened seat with my handkerchief.

During the flight I felt so loving and benign that I found myself writing love letters to practically everybody I know; the passion of my language scarcely knew any bounds. I was the world's lover and that was perfectly okay with me; I was energized with passion, a sparkplug of love, and ready to embrace everybody who opened his arms to me. Time after time, I fondled the going-away card that Steve and Nora had given me. On the cover was the profile of a man, with a hibiscus springing from his eye. Inside, an art-nouveau pinnacle with stardust edges, the larger stars labeled Steve and Nora, and in Steve's hand the inscription: "It's all just beginning to blossom." I was moved by that. Maybe it was possible that we were all going to grow into such caring for one another that all the old barriers, all the psychic walls our society had taught us to erect, would come tumbling down; that we (and I knew no limits to that collective pronoun) would slowly begin to live together without designations, without secrets; would be just people, loving people, together. Romantic dreamer, en route to romantic Fiji.

The next ten days were pleasant work, the kind of work I love to do. It is really no hardship to see old friends on an exotic island halfway around the world, to bask in the expansive friendliness of a simple, demonstrative people. Tahiti, my next stop, was better yet; I stayed in Moorea, at a small resort which is, to my mind, the most perfectly placed pleasure dome on earth. My cottage stood on stilts out over the reef; I spent most of every day snorkeling off a raft in the middle of Cook's Bay, with the spiky, ascending peaks of "Bali Hai" looming above me. And I learned an object lesson from my rapport with the reef. One day I found a large coral formation beclouded with thousands of tiny, iridescent blue fish; entranced, I swam nearer, and at once they disappeared, as with a common intelligence, into the deep crevices of the coral. But when I would backtrack in the water, not very far, they would emerge again in the same blue cloud, and glitter for me. I got to be very precise about it; the school responded to the exact moment when I would push too near. They would vanish; then, as I returned to a respectable distance, they rematerialized. In, out, all afternoon, we danced in the water as I tutored myself (or did the fish tutor me?) in the understanding that you do not get washed in beauty by pushing for it, but by allowing beauty to come to you.

Late in the day, just before the raft was to set sail for the hotel again, I tipped off a vacationing Los Angeles housewife to my discovery. She snorkeled over, circled for a long time, then erupted from the water, spitting out her mouthpiece and shouting to her husband, "My God! My God! It's like a spiritual experience." So "like," I thought, that it is.

It was, when I thought about it, very good to be away from San Francisco for a while, away from the book that wasn't getting done, away from Steve and Nora, who were. The only troublesome, personal, pertinent moment of ten days came in a peculiar dream I had one night in Moorea. My dreaming consciousness was, as usual with me, audience to an elaborate charade in which the acting I, plus just about everybody I knew in the world, were working out very fiercely and laboriously at jobs and calisthenics, and we were sweating and puffing and heaving away, busy-busy-busy, work-work-work. Whew. When all of a sudden the perspective widened just slightly for my dreaming consciousness and I saw, off at the side, as if in the wings, a very tailored, businesslike sort of junior executive type, all trim and respectable, sitting in an armless office chair, a secretarial sort of chair. And the bastard was not only directing the work, he was conducting it, coolly and officiously, in what was clearly the only air-conditioned cubicle in my dream world that night. Son Of A Bitch. I popped out of my dream, sat straight up in bed, and very consciously addressed the slick dream image. "Who *are* you?" I spoke into the darkened room. And I smiled. Because I knew very well who the bastard was.

Now comes the part that is hardest to tell, the part that will not be reduced to a simple explanation because there was nothing simple about it, nothing logical either. There are no rational explanations of unreason; but that doesn't mean that unreason isn't real.

When I returned from the South Pacific, it was not to the colorful bohemia of Grant Street and Telegraph Hill, but to Connie's large and imposing townhouse on a tree-lined street in elegant Pacific Heights. She and her children had gone off on a long camping trip to the Sierras, leaving the premises to us. Her lover Oz was staying on to work on his novel, but otherwise the house was free, and Connie in her generosity had suggested that we move our little gpysy caravan into her shelter. It was a lovely house, warm and comfortable without being in the least overwhelming; the windows at the front were arched, and wore mauve plaster eyebrows of a discreet but amusing nature; the large rooms had high ceilings and white-painted Hershey Bar paneling, comfortable furniture and a casual jumble of art objects and paintings—pieces placed so that they could be enjoyed, looked at, touched; nothing consciously *displayed,* to

impress and intimidate. The sort of decor often evolved by people who have been to Esalen.

I was glad that Oz was there; during the evening of the Von
Neumanizing I had come to like him very much. He was a man
of radically shifting moods, but his touch in the massage had
been simultaneously firm and tender, and a force of goodwill
emanated from him, even when he sulked. I thought it would
be fine to know him better. Steve and Nora felt the same; and
all three of us were glad to have a fourth for whatever game it
was we were playing.

The game image is perhaps the best one to pursue in trying
to explain what happened at Connie's in the next two weeks.
Later I found myself referring to it as "the commune we had
for about an hour and a half." Actually, it lasted a good bit
longer than that, but as the world tends to measure time, it still
doesn't come to much. A few days, scarcely more, of intensive
interaction, inter-being. As linear time goes, not much; in spatial
depth, however, an eternity. As a communal friend of mine has
put it, "Experience of community can't be measured with a ruler
or a metronome—it's not how long it lasts but how intense it is."
And he's right. Just because a marriage lasts fifty years, and the
tottering couple get their pictures in the paper, does not mean
that fifty years of physical proximity have produced a good experience for them. It may signify only a certain milestone on a
lifelong endurance test.

At Connie's we experienced, in the beginning, a sort of "as-if"
game. It was a shared awareness that our situation now was not
unlike early communal experience; in terms of that reality, we
played house. At first we did it without commenting on it; later,
we talked of little else. When we talked at all. Because the first
thing to report is that we felt little need to verbalize. It became
apparent early on that we were feeling and thinking the same
things. It was a kind of telepathy brought on by proximity and
disposition, and it was instantly taken for granted. Oz prompted
our recognition of it by joining us in the living room one afternoon, where we were sitting around quite silently, and then after
a time breaking the silence by asking if we would like him to
read his account of a dream he had had the night before. We said

yes, he got his dream notebook (he was keeping a careful record
of all his dreams), and read an account of having found his
dream-self at a bi-sexual orgy, peopled largely by low-life, cycle-
riding types. The sexual configurations of the orgy were rendered in careful detail. Then Oz's dream-self is taken to another
room by one of the low-life characters. He is given a cigarette,
but a girl nearby signals that the cigarette is doped. Oz tries to
flee but the low-lifer pursues him, tries to lock him in. He breaks
out, runs through hills and valleys, and ends in the cottage of
an old woman who keeps a pig.

Oz's dream was electrifying for us; the dream imagery was, it
seemed to us, imagery with which we ourselves had been dealing,
but no one had described this to him in advance. He had apparently absorbed, the instant we came together in the house,
our concerns with the bi-sexual implications of our social troika.
The hills and valleys of the dream corresponded with an image
the three of us had been exchanging for some time, an image of
waves, specifically of "peaks and valleys," to describe the rhythm
of our relationship together. The introduction of the doped
cigarette related to our quite low-intensity fear that we might be
smoking too much grass—and we were, starting with breakfast
coffee. The old woman in the cottage seemed to us to be childhood's own witch symbol, connective with our witchcraft concerns. There was even a character to correspond to my Satan
symbol—the pig.

We decided that Oz had dreamed a dream that any one of us
might have had, but hadn't. Or anyway, hadn't remembered
having. How was it that the dream had come to him? "I don't
know," he said. "I guess I just picked it up by being with you.
Anyway, as soon as I woke up and wrote it down, I knew it was
connected with you all in some way."

Oz, never one to avoid issues when they were raised, went on
to explain that there were plenty of reasons in his own life why
he should have had such a dream. He was, he said, sexually
vitalized by the energy among us, and had turned on, particularly, to me. He said he had had bi-sexual orgy experiences in
the past, but in the last couple of years had suppressed them,
because they had been among what he called "low-riders," bike
freaks and their women. These scenes had been ugly and violent

and disagreeable to him. Now, with our arrival, he felt able to allow his homosexual drives to manifest without threat. Nevertheless, the old woman of his dream he felt to be Connie—an older woman, more settled and economically secure, with whom he had found temporary shelter in a wandering life. It was an old theme, as old as literature itself: a life with men is a life of adventure and risk; women are a port, a safe harbor longed for but, when found, binding.

Nora felt that she was suited to all the roles in Oz's dream—the girl who gave the warning about the doped cigarette, the old woman who provided shelter; but also one of the low-rider orgiasts. "I often feel like a boy," she said, "just as often as I feel like a girl. Sometimes I dream that I *am* a boy. A stud." Steve conceded that he too would have been suitable for any role, except, perhaps, that of the old woman.

There was a further observation to be made about Oz's dream, one with implications far larger than Oz's own apprehension of life. The drugged cigarette, it seemed to me, served well to symbolize the fear that all of us had of unleashing our bisexual drives, of falling into a well of open, fully rounded sexuality. To allow oneself to acknowledge the androgyne that is at the center of all of us is, as we see it, to become trapped, to lose control and identity. How terrifying to be no longer able to say, in resonant baritone, "I'm a *man*," or in trilling soprano, "I'm a *woman*," but only, in a quiet and natural voice, "I'm me."

And then I recited a dream *I* had had the night before. In it, Nora and I were carefully lifting a naked and recumbent Steve onto a gridlike pallet; then we were carrying him over to a large tub, where we were going to slowly immerse him in a warm bath. "That's *my* dream!" Steve shouted. "I should have had it, because that's how it's seemed to me—you and Nora nudging me into something I'm afraid of, so in the dream I have to be unconscious—drugged?—and handled like a baby. That's how I feel sometimes, like a baby, helpless."

From then on, there was no holding us. Everything, from the details of dreams to the slightest gesture, became significant, however banal it would have appeared to outsiders. We were having each other's dreams, we were sharing a common consciousness. What would happen next? An energy exchange, of course, that same stuff David had been talking about early in the summer. But now there was Oz to put a name to much of what had been sensed but nameless and therefore unacknowledged until now. Oz lived with a great store of myth, man's myth through recorded history; there was nothing happening to us, he said, that had not happened endlessly before, no acts of ours that did not correlate with complete accuracy throughout the entire cosmos. "As above, so below." And as on this plane, so on other, invisible but entirely real planes. We began to feel that there was much more happening in and around us than what we could label in a conscious, waking state, and perhaps more to see than we had been seeing.

It was felt first—a literal vibration that crackled between us like a charged wire. One night, we even saw it. Some girlfriends of Nora's were with us for dinner. The conversation was lighthearted, giddy, but the girls seemed to want to turn it in a sexual direction. Orgy was in the air, we all sensed it. Shortly after dinner, while we had coffee in the living room, Steve said something to me, I replied—and in that exchange, we *saw* the space between us ripple like a heat wave, much as the heated air forced from underground tunnels shimmers visibly as it rises through sidewalk grids. I was so startled I was speechless—it was not so much a flow in transit from him to me or vice versa; it was just there, vibrating in the air. I felt hot, flushed, slightly embarrassed.

The visiting girls seemed annoyed, only slightly, that orgy was not developing. Their conversation grew less pointed, more vapid. I had a terrible headache, the legacy of a hard day at the typewriter, and I asked Oz to lift my head—a massage technique whereby, if you can give your head into the hands of another, relax into the trust that he will not drop it, he can roll your head around on your neck as if it were a rubber ball; and when you abandon your head in that way, the tense muscles that brought on the headache in the first place loosen and relax too, and you are sure that if your head did drop, it would bounce harmlessly on the floor.

I lay on the floor on my back; Oz sat in the lotus above me and cupped my head in his palms, his fingers kneading the muscles at the base of my skull, his hands slowly turning and lifting my head. Between us, Oz and I achieved trust and relaxation; I was ready to give up control to him, he was ready to bring relief to me. But something else happened that I was not prepared for. I felt a surge of power rush from his hands into and through my head and on down into the rest of my body, relieving me of all tension, filling me with a soft, tingling glow. I saw the power, a bolt of fiery energy, a burning cable, extend from Oz to me to Steve to Nora and back again, and also in every other one-to-one connection between us, but excluding the gossiping girls. This was similar to the shimmer I had glimpsed between Steve and myself, but more intense and confined, like a shaft of light. This was a definable cable, and it was rippling and pulsing with a buzzing energy, waving and sizzling in the air, a gentle lightning bolt. The four of us exchanged glances; we knew.

The conversation of the visiting girls rasped and shrilled against the electric connection, and at some almost but not quite unconscious level, they knew they were not getting through. One girl had the instinctive good sense to leave; the other persisted, angrily, in an utterly dum-dum conversation with Nora. She was trying to get Nora to recall certain former Chicago boyfriends. "You remember Stanley Shapiro, Nora, of *course* you do. He was the cute, dark-haired one you went with just after you stopped going with Lester Goodman." Nora was saying yes and no and this and that, but nothing committal; the girl's voice drilled like a buzz saw against our connecting cables, and was completely blunted.

The girl did not know what was frustrating her, but we did because we could *see* the barrier upon which her insensitivity was breaking itself. And even when Oz finished working with my head, and laid it gently down on the floor again, the cable continued to hold. Now I understood the force of communal reality—we were in something together and it was no longer simply social or sexual or theoretical. It was utterly esoteric; it was magical.

Reviving somewhat from the languor brought on by Oz's touch, I asked him (while the girl chattered on ceaselessly about Benny and Tommy and Judy and Gloria) whether he was tired, whether the energy he had expended on me had cost him anything.

"No," he said. "I feel okay. Sometimes they send it to me a little fast, and if I don't filter it right, it can wear me out. But I handled it fine tonight, and you took it so openly, that there really wasn't any problem."

"You bet I took it openly," I said. "It was beautiful. But who are 'they?' "

"The Illuminati," he said, matter-of-factly. "The really evolved souls, that have been reincarnated so many times and grown so much that they're pure spirit now. They help sometimes, send power for healing when you need it. You have to be careful though. You have to be ready for it. Like if you hadn't been ready for it, I couldn't have passed it to you, and *I* might have got hurt."

Now the visiting girl was in a real state; angry with Nora for nothing we could figure out. There was no cause for conversational rancor—it had to be those cables, and a subtle message being sent to her by her unconscious that she was distinctly not in sync. But she couldn't receive that message in any conscious way; she could only fuss about "nothing." So finally Nora took her into an adjoining room and closed the door. Immediately Steve, Oz, and I came together in an embrace. The vibes were very powerful. We tried to send some of this goodstuff into the other room, literally attempting to consolidate our feelings and beam them through the door. No use—apparently our visitor was too insensitive to pick up anything. So we embraced some more, and kissed, and briefly considered (without discussing it) dropping neatly onto the level of physical orgy. It would validate the dream for all concerned and, if Nora ever concluded the big argument in the other room, we knew that she would drop into that scene without a moment's hesitation. But the time was not right for Steve—this also we knew without conversation—however lovingly he was then hugging and kissing. He was fervent; but it was also his way of forestalling, not provoking, the act of bisexuality. So in the end—the girl's voice still ringing angrily through the closed door—we parted with helpless smiles. Steve went to break the girls up; Oz and I had a shower together, embraced again, and went contentedly to our separate beds.

THE WALLS ARE SHIVERING!

If *you* are receptive, *everything* will be receptive—receptive and reactive to what is happening. On the other hand, nothing would be straining for it, or unduly exaggeratedly open for it: you would be like a healthy child or animal when it is interested—simply *there* for it. In the moment a person is really interested, it shoots into the very bones. The tissues would let it through, the whole organism would be a ground of resonance for whatever happens.

—CHARLOTTE SELVER

From then on we seemed to be into something very much over our heads, but too powerful to struggle against. And too wonderful to spark resistance. It was magic—magic of a rather inconsequential kind, perhaps, but fascinating. The sexuality of Steve and Nora intensified, and every time either of them experienced an orgasm, the phone would ring or a clock alarm would go off or fire engines would roar by. The same thing would happen if one of us wept—and since we were often weeping, the odds were fairly good for that particular phenomenon. More remarkably, it seemed that we had only to speak of somebody and the phone would ring and it would be that person, or the mail would come and there would be a letter from that person. One night I had a persistent fantasy that some party of Mansonesque freaks was going to break into the house and kill us all in our beds; it kept me awake and nervous for hours. Next morning it turned out that we had all had the same dread, in our separate rooms, all night.

That same morning we had a long conversation, exploring these phenomena and searching for their significance and relevance. Nora was saying that it would be nice if my book did not have to be square, but could be made in the shape of our experience, and we began to discuss what kind of shape that would be. She first thought a triangle would be nice, suggesting a mountain peak, because that was what life was like, a high peak. But Steve said it was not just peaks but valleys, ebb and flow, up and down, a wavy pattern throughout. And you can't very well make a wavy book.

Then Nora said, "Waves . . . curling waves . . . the problem is riding the crest of the wave. Maybe it should be shaped more like a . . ." And she formed a half-circle with her hands. "No," I said, "not just half." And I formed the underside to complete a circle in the air. "I see it as rounded," I said. "And not just flat, but three-dimensional. You suppose a printer could make a three-dimensional ball of a book? It would open like a flower . . ."

"What kind of flower?" Nora asked.

"I don't know," I said. "A chrysanthemum . . . a hibiscus . . ."

Together we shrieked HIBISCUS. Steve rushed into the other room and returned with a matchbox I had brought from Fiji. "What is on that matchbox?" he demanded, holding it before my eyes. It was a hibiscus, because match-making is a government monopoly in Fiji, the island of the hibiscus. I flashed the card they had given me when I left for Fiji, the one with a *hibiscus* springing from the eye of a man.

"Get that card!" Nora said, and I did.

"And listen, listen, you guys," said Steve, eyes gleaming. "What have we been talking about for weeks and weeks? Bi-sexuality, right? Accepting the androgynous nature of the self, right? And who is the most flagrant androgyne you ever saw? We saw him our first week in San Francisco? Star of the Cockettes?

"HIBISCUS!"

"A circle like a flower."

"Yin-yang!"

"What else is in a circle?" Steve demanded. "What else?

"The zodiac!

"And what's our image all the time, peaks and valleys, riding the crest of the wave. What's the waviest town you know? San Francisco! Peaks and valleys—and who lives here? Hibiscus! And the card . . . and the match box . . ."

Somebody, we decided, or some thing, had been trying to tell us something.

We discovered quite promptly that the significance of this conversation was lost on most other people, unless they were accustomed to smoking a lot of grass. Coincidence seems utterly idle to people who live in the severely practical world—but in the stoned world, as in the primitive world and the world of the occult—coincidence is enormously significant. Grass has the capacity to take the practical mind and put it in a more open, more childlike state—the state, perhaps, of primitivism. Puns spring readily to the tongue, word associations can absorb hours. What is dismissed as silly and banal in the straight world is taken to the bosom of the stoned freak, played with, toyed with, enjoyed. And valued. Grass prompts connections—and I need hardly add that, on the morning of this conversation, which continues months later to make perfect sense to me, we were completely stoned.

It seemed to us that we had found a larger purpose, a cosmic commonsense, to all that had happened. We felt that the universe was trying to open to us, to indicate that a mighty intelligence existed, of which we were an integral part. We had stumbled onto a wonderful secret—the world was us, we were the world; the "vibes," the electrical cables that we saw connecting us, were just one manifestation of an incredible, invisible energy. To the extent that we were open to it, it would course through us in our physical state and illuminate us with the wisdom, the very simple wisdom, of all times, all philosophies. The wisdom seemed to us ridiculously simple to have been overlooked for so long: we *were* one another; we weren't just imagining that; as yin to yang, we were composed, each of us, of male and female in equal force. The stifling of one source of energy was just the first of a long line of choked powers that wracked and contorted the human soul, and canceled its natural vision—that each of us is male and female, each of us is the other, a complete sharing is taking place unseen by mortal (blinded) eyes, we are, in fact, God.

Oz was the only one of us to take these phenomena calmly. "You all have to realize," he said, "that God is you and everything you touch or look at, that the world you see is just an illusion, the *maya* of Hindu philosophy. What's actually happening is what you haven't been able to see but are just beginning to get a glimpse of, the world as composed of raw energy, protons and electrons leaping around in space, a galactic force field. You've got yourselves open to each other and now you're ready to open to the universe. Down at the Fellowship they call it the Christ, this energy you're feeling. I wish you all would come down there with me."

For several months Oz had been spending a lot of time with the Fellowship, a religious order formed along monastic lines, peopled by adepts in the occult. They were all possessed with "the power," and they chose to channel it into service to others, particularly the down-and-out. So they were living together in small communities, and working together in operating soup kitchens and health services. Oz had not joined their company, but went regularly to their religious services.

"For me," he said, "the Fellowship is on the right track. I'm tired of all these so-called Holy Ones that get illumination and go floating up to heaven. They're so pure they're always painted from the waist up, as if they had no feet of clay, no contact with everybody else that's suffering down here, the children that are hungry and get rickets, the ones that have disease and die in agony, the ones that hurt each other and get hurt because of sex and jealousy and possessiveness. Damn 'em. People are in pain, and they're up there floating around, cut off from all that. The Fellowship is illuminated, they've got grace you can see and feel, but they don't cut themselves off. They don't just meditate on the One, they fight the symptoms of the evil that is in this world."

We were interested in the Fellowship, particularly because they seemed to promise some explanation of the energy we were filled with. But for the moment we were quite unable to go anywhere. What we were feeling together was too fascinating to interrupt, as was the ongoing dialogue, our intellectualization of the feeling. For our intense vibrations we credited our openness—we felt we were being entirely honest with each other about feeling, stripping away all secrets—and our discovery of the androgyne. By projection we concluded that everyone in the world was like us, and that the maintenance of masculine/feminine identity roles prevented others from tapping the enormous vitality, the energy flow, that now so animated us. We knew, also, that in our conviction that all things were the same—black and white, good and evil, animus and anima—we were expressing a classic symptom of schizophrenia, a refusal or inability to discriminate between what is self and what is other. But that didn't bother us because, at the metaphysical level, we felt, intellectually, that this was correct.

Interestingly, the sexual anxieties that had obsessed us so long seemed to recede as our divinity increased. Steve remarked on one occasion that we seemed to have advanced to a level of "meta-sex," in which the acting out of sexual relationship became unnecessary, even silly. Most of the time we played, much as children play: we went through peaks of experience when one or other of us was an animal or, in one remarkable instance, Nora was (felt herself to be) a sphinx. She was a sphinx all morning and Steve and I knew it and responded to it; not a word was exchanged. We did, however, begin to exchange roles —or, more specifically, to become (we felt) interchangeable. I recall going out on an errand one afternoon in a state of supreme divinity and elation and noticing suddenly, while visiting a friend, that I had inadvertently worn the wrong body that day—Steve's. Steve and Nora, too, frequently exchanged physical and psychic identities.

One evening, when we felt we were too trapped in our play, too remote from the world around us, Nora insisted that we should go visit friends, go dancing, have a Chinese meal, anything to overcome, however slightly, the indifference we increasingly felt toward the world outside. The problem, you see, was that nothing beyond our walls was a quarter so interesting to us as what was happening inside. The banality and insensitivity of life outside was appalling to us; we couldn't anymore relate to it. So when we did go out, and visited David and Lenore, we were no longer able to relate to them. Here we were God, and they were still having sex and chatting about friends and reading *Newsweek*—it was no longer interesting to us. Lenore picked up on it, though we were outwardly polite and relatively unchanged. She resented it (David was too kind to even think of resentment). And both of them concluded, after we'd left, that we must have run across some powerful dope. That same evening, we went to eat in a Chinese restaurant. I remember that we ate slowly, carefully, noticing every subtle taste and texture, speaking very little. Toward the end of the meal Nora looked up from her plate and her chopsticks, smiled conspiratorially, and said, "I have a wonderful idea. Let's go to the woods and fast for a couple of days."

It was as if, at some earlier, less illuminated point in our lives, a beautiful and fascinating girl had said, "Let's all take our clothes off and have an orgy." We were past all that fleshy stuff, that was too earthbound to move us now. It had to be something utterly wild and woolly—fasting, fasting in nature. A beautiful idea. Why had we never thought of it before? The very notion gave us a physical buzz. "Fantastic!" I said. "The minute you suggested it, my cock stirred." Meta-eroticism? Later we went to a unisex discotheque and quite naturally danced together, three of us, to the hard acid rock. At first separately, then with our arms joined, embracing. We moved slowly and closely together to fast and frenetic music, while the other dancers jiggled and rocked frenetically outside our charmed circle. We'd get inadvertent jabs in the ribs from the flailing arms of the other dancers—the floor was very crowded and wild with action—but in our little triangle we moved to a quiet, slow rhythm of our own.

Our last stop was at a homosexual leather bar down the street, where none of us had ever been. But we were stopped at the door by the bouncer. "Sorry," he said, "it's against our policy."

"What's against your policy?" Nora asked, sensing discrimination.

"Well . . . uh . . . you know this is a gay bar and . . . uh . . . you're a chick."

Nora was righteously indignant. "How can you say a thing like that?" she demanded. "That's being very, very uncool. I refuse to be discriminated against on the grounds that you think I'm a chick. I might just be a very feminine sort of boy, for all you know."

"Ah . . . I don't think so," said the bouncer, taking in Nora's undeniably female appearance.

"Anyway," said Nora, "it doesn't make any difference."

"Well," said the doorman, "to our clientele it *does* make a difference." He was very polite but quite adamant, and we went back to our car going tsk-tsk for the limitations of the gay world. "They're just as bad as the straight world," Nora said, indignantly. "Keeping us all out because I happen to be a female-type person. What's the *matter* with everybody, anyway?"

We concluded, on the drive home, that there was little use in trying to relate to society as we found it Out There. *Maya*, illusion, seemed to prevail everywhere.

So in the next days, the implosion of our energies became ever more intense. We felt full of life, capable of enormous tasks, but we had no idea how to channel the energy, where to take it, what to do with it. The house was literally jumping with vibrations, and so were we. And various interesting but utterly useless things happened—the walls would pulse and shake and tremble, the rooms we were in would glow with unearthly light, at one point I glanced idly at the retreating tail of one of the resident cats and she leaped three feet in the air, spun around while airborne, and landed facing the place where my eyes—or whatever was beaming out on the end of my gaze—had touched the sensitive tip of her tail. "Oh, shit," I thought. "Now I'm freaking out the cats. A nice parlor trick—maybe I can get on Ed Sullivan sometime. Big deal."

Through all of this Oz walked in safety, though he became increasingly concerned that one or the other of us might indeed be possessed of demons. There was no telling, he said, whether these phenomena had a good or an evil source, and it did make a difference. He urged us to stop smoking grass, which he felt increased our sensitivity to the vibes, and to come on down to the Fellowship with him. Still we resisted; I thought I had a better idea.

"Look," I argued. "If this energy, this power we're feeling, is, as Oz says, Christ, then we have got to settle down and receive it in a more orderly way. It's like, I guess, the apostles in the Upper Room; you know, sitting around waiting for Christ to return, and he came in the form of tongues of fire, the Holy Spirit descending on them. And you know what a hollering and shouting and pure-D sanctification went on at a time like that. I mean, there's a precedent for this, and I think we'd better ritualize our reception of this energy somehow or other. Just sit together in one room, quietly, and wait. Something like that. Steve has been telling me for days to stop calling it 'Goodstuff' because that's *Time*-style smart-mouth for something that is holier than that. Okay, so if it's holy, let's at least be respectful enough to organize and formalize our response."

And the moment I suggested ritual, this extraordinary period was over. Both Steve and Nora felt, most strongly, that what was upon us was happening only through the magic of coincidence, by our refusal to attempt to control or manipulate it in any way. Life by coincidence was our only key to the power, our only hope of riding the crest of the wave. Ritual would be ruinous— and as it turned out, the very mention of it was enough to short-circuit what had been happening. For the first time in two weeks, we were no longer in perfect sync. Steve later said that he felt that, for the first time, Nora was siding with him instead of with me on a question of joint importance. And it was true that Nora was fiercely opposed to the ritualizing of our experience. And Oz said later that what we didn't know was that he was at that moment down in the basement, using a variety of rituals taught him by the Fellowship, exorcizing the house. "I just felt I had to clean everything out," he later said. "You all wouldn't quit smoking dope, and the walls were vibrating and we weren't getting any sleep. We just had to have some rest."

So, as it turned out, I cannot report to you on Pentecost. With three of us not wanting it to happen, it didn't. The house began to settle down at once, and we descended from a mighty peak into a low valley. But not before we did, at last, go to the Fellowship.

FLIGHT TO THE FELLOWSHIP

Oz arranged for us to see Master Cyril of the Fellowship early on Sunday morning, before Sunday services. That morning Nora was feeling ill, and also reluctant to go on general principles. The Fellowship sounded to her more ritualized than anything that I had proposed. Instinctively, she felt it was not for her. So Steve and I drove over without her.

Following Oz's directions, we drove into a deprived and depressed neighborhood near the Mission, and found the Fellowship occupying a large brownstone across from a tatty park. My heart sank on sight of the place: it looked identical to the many rectories of my childhood, right down to the potted rubber plant in the bay window, and a bad reproduction of the Sacred Heart of Mary in a frame on the wall. "Oh, no," I said to Steve as we climbed the steps, and through a window saw several men and women sitting around in clerical garb. "I grew up with this shit. I don't think I can stand it now."

Inside, a polite, clean-cut young man in roman collar said we had been expected, but that Master Cyril had been detained. "He suggested that you come back for the services at eleven," said the young man, "and then afterwards have some breakfast with us. We'll be fasting until then." But breakfast was already in preparation, somewhere in the house; we could smell bacon frying, coffee perking. My stomach gurgled. That, too, reminded me unpleasantly of my childhood.

Steve and I went to a greasy spoon (a California greasy spoon, where everything is bright and fresh and the spoons are never greasy) for breakfast, then returned for the services. The clean-cut young man directed us around the side of the house and through a basement door. In a little corridor we saw piles of shoes, took ours off, and padded down the dark hall to a curtained door. From inside, we could hear a slight murmur.

Pushing aside the curtain, we entered a large, low-ceilinged chapel, crowded with people, illuminated only by the six candles on the altar at the far end of the room. Groping our way in the darkness, we found places in a side pew and settled ourselves just as the congregation stood to sing, most slowly and lugubriously, "Holy God, We Praise Thy Name." Oh my no, said I to myself, that terrible hymn. Why don't they just go down to the nearest Catholic Church and get it over with?

Disgruntled but fascinated, I took in as much as I could. Everything was depressingly familiar to me. The form of worship was the Mass, celebrated in English by a handsome young man in a dark blue habit. He was assisted by a lovely girl, dressed identically with him. They followed a pattern of the Mass that belongs to my childhood and youth, before liturgical reforms, with the celebrant facing away from the congregation. The only thing markedly different about it was the great deliberation of the young celebrant. Every movement was made with enormous slowness and concentration; every word of every prayer carefully and clearly enunciated, obviously meant. I had never seen this ceremony performed with such reverence in any Catholic church; how odd, I thought, to find such loving attention to it in a cold dark basement in a slum neighborhood, lavished by a guy who doesn't even look old enough to be ordained.

That thought in turn reminded me of a dear friend of my adolescence, a boy I often served Mass with at the cathedral in those days, a youth of conspicuous piety. He invited me over to his house one afternoon, and I supposed he wanted to get into mutual masturbation or something of that sort, which was how adolescent boys in Tulsa, Oklahoma, were passing Saturday afternoons in those days. But no—after pledging me to secrecy, he took me into his basement, where he had built an elaborate altar with all the fitments—altar cloths improvised out of his mother's old antimacassars and frayed napkins, rows of candles, banks of wildflowers. He had fashioned vestments from his mother's discarded sheets, decorating them in the Byzantine mode by means of crayons. He had done all this, he told me, at the suggestion of a priest who wanted to encourage his vocation to the priesthood. Every Saturday afternoon, he said, he celebrated solemn pontifical High Mass at this altar, but he was tired of having to sing the whole Mass himself. Would I, he wondered, care to celebrate Mass with him, as his deacon?

Pious as I was, I thought it was a pretty weird suggestion, and would really rather have enjoyed mutual masturbation. But he was a good friend and I did as he asked, and we celebrated our makeshift Mass all afternoon, taking it very slowly because we were constantly correcting each other about details of the ritual. And I have seen cardinals and apostolic delegates do no better, pushing each other around the high altar of St. Patrick's Cathedral, so I'm not embarrassed by our ineptitude. But the point is that we really tried to mean it, that afternoon, as no priest we knew ever had seemed to. And of course we had felt very secret and underground about it.

And that was what I felt at the Fellowship—transported back to adolescence, a time of caring about and intensely *meaning* things. I felt myself rejecting it on precisely those grounds. And yet grudgingly liking it because it evoked for me, to some extent, a sense of what the persecuted, hiding early Church must have been. When the time for Communion came, I was still in conflict. And though the entire congregation went to the altar rail, I could not. Partly it was a conviction I realized I had not rid myself of, that to accept the communion of any priest not "rightly" ordained was mortal sin (and how hung up I still was on those old taboos, though not believing them). And partly it was snobbish disbelief, and a disdain for the form and for all who would copy it. So I watched the others go to the altar rail; I watched *Steve* go to the altar rail. I could scarcely believe my eyes. He seemed to be swept up in the entire thing, and when he returned he fell to his knees, buried his face in his hands, and appeared to pray. I was stunned.

I continued in uncomfortable conflict until the end of the Mass, when the young celebrant turned to give the congregation the final blessing. As he lifted his hand I saw that he suddenly began to radiate the most intense golden light. It shone from his entire body, a vast golden aura that spread outward in irregular, connected beams. Beautiful. It's a trick, I thought, an illusion. Or some accident of my vision. But I knew that was not so. There were no tricks. There was just an aura. So okay, I said to myself. You've been seeing auras all your life and pretending that you don't see them. But you may as well give that up; it's a lie. The guy has an aura and that's that.

Out on the street again, people hung around much as they do outside any church on Sundays, lighting cigarettes and gossiping. Numbers of clerics, in blue capes and dark blue habits, hung about too, chatting with the faithful. Steve fished his pack of Camels out of his breast pocket, palmed the pack and stared at it a second, then tossed it straight into the nearest trash barrel. "Finished," he said, in very good cheer. I pulled out my Salems, stuck one in my face, and lighted it. "Yuk," I said. But I continued smoking. Steve went inside to see if Master Cyril was ready to talk with us, and quickly returned to say that we were put off again, and were to return at 2:30. It was okay; we decided that, in this way, we'd be able to bring Nora.

On the way home I asked Steve how he found the stomach for that service. "You seemed to fall right into it," I said. "Don't forget," he said, "that's not my tradition. It's not ruined for me as it is for you. And I just felt absolutely right about it, that it was a right thing, and no time for bullshit. I'm no Christian, and I've never taken communion in my life—but today, it was the right thing to do."

Later, however, Steve's fervor dissipated. Nora returned to the Fellowship with us, but she was terribly uncomfortable there, and complained and fussed as we waited endlessly in the parlor, under the annoying picture of the Sacred Heart of Mary. Steve, affected by her unease, finally announced that he felt that Master Cyril really didn't really want to talk to him. "I think this Master Cyril knows that I haven't got anything to say to a really holy man today," he said. "I feel I'd just be wasting his time, and I think he knows that and he's sort of waiting us out. I think Nora and I should split." And split they did, running across the street into the park, where I could see them wrestling and playing on the grass while I continued to wait. I was feeling stubborn about it —little as I liked the style of the Fellowship, it was obvious to me that they had something to tell me. Quite apart from Oz's endorsement, there was the undeniable business of the aura. And an undeniable rightness about the spirit of the place, no matter what I thought about the rituals and the decor.

Finally, a pretty young girl in clericals came in. "I'm Reverend Martha," she said, smiling. "Master Cyril is busy—he thought maybe I could help you." So I spilled the entire beans to Reverend Martha—who turned out to be a very nice girl from Oklahoma—about the Satan trip and the psychic phenomena and the whole spooky, improbable thing. She seemed to know exactly what I was talking about, excused herself a moment, and came back to say that Master Cyril would see me promptly at six P.M.

Between then and six, I smoked no cigarettes, and presented myself back at the Fellowship, alone, full of anticipation and barely suppressed excitement, at precisely the hour appointed. As

I stood in the hall, a trim young man in his early thirties, wearing a roman collar and black trousers and a gray wool cardigan, came up and asked if I were waiting for him. "Are you Master Cyril?" I asked, for somehow I had been expecting a patriarchal sort of figure. "Yeah," he said. "Hi. Why don't we go into the other room?" And he led me into an office, closing the door behind him. He gestured me to a seat, and took his own behind a mahogany desk. "Now," he said, "why don't you tell me what's happening?"

So I went through the whole thing again, from the inception of the book project onward, and I ended with the aura I had seen surrounding the celebrant of that day's Mass. "Yes," said Cyril. "He's a very powerful young man."

Then he looked at me penetratingly and said, "You're not taking any kind of drugs, are you?"

"No," I said. "We've smoked quite a lot of grass, but none of us has ever experienced anything stronger."

"I didn't think so," Cyril said. "This sort of thing often does happen on acid, but we tend to discount much of it as not genuine spiritual growth. I think you're going to have to face the fact that what seems to be happening to you *is* happening, and you are probably going to have to deal with it. This power you speak of is, as it were, from Christ, and you don't have to be afraid. You don't have to run from Him.

"As for seeing Satan in the mirror, I suggest that what actually happened is that you discorporated for the first time, actually saw yourself from outside your body, and of course it gave you a terrible fright. If anything like that should happen again, if you should find yourself confronting any frightening phenomenon, some demon or something of the sort, no matter how terrifying it is, you say to it, 'I command you to stand in the light of Christ.' Now if its origin is evil, it will flee, it will be unable to stay. But if it can stand in the light of Christ, it is *of* Christ, and you can embrace it. You'll *want* to embrace it."

Master Cyril gave me a mimeographed meditation exercise which he highly recommended to me. He also said that, on the strength of my reports and what he intuited about me, he would under ordinary circumstances suggest that I come to study with the Fellowship. However, inasmuch as our time in San Francisco was growing short, and we would have to return to the East Coast, such a procedure would be out of the question. Where, he wondered, would my friends and I be on Friday week. I explained that by then Nora would have flown back to Chicago, and that Steve and I would be in Los Angeles.

"A pity," he said. "Because on the second Friday of every month we meet for an Esoteric Council, which all of our masters and particularly enlightened adepts attend, together with some other very wise and powerful people. And if you are really worried about these phenomena, I think they'd be very glad to hear you out and make suggestions that might help you. So if you feel the need of it, don't hesitate to come back Friday week. You might find it pretty interesting. With all those people in the room the vibrations get to be really incredible. It's sort of a spiritual festival, the receptivity is so high that everybody gets quite giddy. I've seen very solemn adepts stumbling over their words when trying to read Scripture; we're sometimes reduced to giggles.

"Listen," he said. "Don't worry about this. Christ is a great joy. You should be very happy. Don't be afraid—and do come back, anytime."

But I have never been back. I will say, however, that for another three days, I did not smoke a cigarette.

Within those three days, all phenomena ceased. Nora made her plane reservations for home. And Steve and I began to prepare ourselves for a long car journey back to the East Coast, without her.

THE TOTAL MATERIAL TRIP

On our second-last day in San Francisco, Steve, Nora, and I made a visit to the Oakland House of Plenty. The commune possesses seven large houses in the bay area, another in Hawaii, and a ranch near Chico, but the Oakland branch is the central establishment, the mother house of their organization. And it is unlike any other commune in the country, because in Plenty terms, community is not synonymous with brown bread, pinto beans, and poverty. On the contrary, Plenty community is a technique for becoming very, very rich by beating the system at its own game.

Knowing all this by report, I was nevertheless surprised at the lavish comfort of the Oakland House of Plenty, a huge Victorian mansion on a quiet, residential street of similar homes. The carpet in the wide front hall is of so deep a pile that you can practically trip in it; there are vases of fresh flowers everywhere, even in the downstairs bathroom, where in addition to a bowl of yellow daisies, a newly scrubbed comb and brush and folded hand towels testified to a constant attention to detail. There is a comfortable living room nicely furnished with easy chairs and a stereo; the large dining room was set for the evening meal— ten or more tables laid with white napery, silverware, and stemmed crystal. A bowl of fresh flowers and an arrangement of candles provided the centerpiece on each.

We were met by an attractive young woman who said that Buddy Vesp, the number two man at Plenty, was expecting us but had been delayed; why didn't we make ourselves comfortable. And would we like anything while waiting? A cup of coffee, perhaps? A drink? Gin? Scotch? A glass of wine? I was overwhelmed. I had been in more than twenty-five communes by that point, and nobody had ever suggested that I make myself comfortable, much less offered me alcohol, that ruinous beverage of the middle classes. For the pure novelty of it, I said thanks-very-much to a light scotch and water.

While we waited for Buddy Vesp, several members came up to us to introduce themselves, to welcome us and to chat. Men and women, of all ages from early twenties to mid-forties, so far as I could tell, and a couple of little children as well, all taking trouble to be warmly polite. From these amiable people we put together a somewhat larger picture of the House of Plenty than had been formed by Bernadette Wolfe's mind-blowing talk of plastic bottles and Steve's initial social call.

The underpinning of the Plenty philosophy is the conviction that every human being is essentially selfish; Plenty takes it for granted that everything we do we do primarily to provide ourselves with more pleasure, less pain. Certainly, pleasure and happiness are the common twin goals in mankind; however, very few of us ever realize those goals because we deceive ourselves about our motives. Plenty takes a very straightforward, even simplistic view of how to proceed: the only sure way to get more pleasure and happiness is to give more pleasure and happiness to others. The argument is not that man is good, only that good actions bring good responses and good rewards, and what makes the House of Plenty a pleasant and happy place to be is a common conspiracy to improve everybody else's lot, thereby improving your own.

This is no halfway, casual program of "being nice." This is an all-pervading way of life which, for the hundred members of the House of Plenty, seems to be proving out. For "nice," substitute a Plenty concept called "safe-porting." Every member strives in all his relationships to remain intensely aware of what could be threatening to others; he would never, never force a relationship in such a direction, but always attempt to embody, in himself, the "ports" safest for those around him. This is another way of describing how any set of human beings *could* develop firm, mutual trust and rarely ever do. The point is that, at Plenty, everybody is really trying for that. And the trust thus generated creates among the members a uniquely warm and mellow atmosphere. It has the effect, first of all, of removing all the petty annoyances that grind and grate subliminally until they build to sources of conflict; because everybody is working to his fullest extent to make *you* comfortable and fulfilled, and because you are working with the same dedication on *their* behalf, there is a good deal less in the way of minor pain and a great deal more of everything else: more caring, more comfort, more kindness, more love. And out of this agreeable shared situation grows more energy in the group cause, which in turn generates more enterprise in community projects, which earns more money for the common pot, which makes more financial stability for the commune and more individual affluence for every member.

Picture yourself entering a free society to which you are required to pay no moral dues. You're fine and dandy just as you are—like everybody else, a perfect human being. In order to enter this society you endow it with all your wordly goods, and if that happens to be a set of burdensome debts, that's what you give. You are on trial for an indefinite period, until the inner councils of the society, in the fullness of time, decide that you are a member for life. Meanwhile, you study the philosophy of the society in a series of seminars on such subjects as sensuality, communications and hexing. (Hexing has to do with the way in which we speak to each other; on the grounds that everything you say to me is subtly or otherwise designed to advance me or demolish me, you can learn how to "hex" me in such a way that my response is always to my own advantage. You are manipulating me, of course, quite deliberately, for your own good. For as you allow me to "win," you are at the same time "winning" my perhaps unwitting gratitude and affection. You are, again, "safeporting" me. The same policy obtains in sex or in any other form of human congress, so that we find ourselves doing the right thing for each other, more and more and More.)

The same thing applies in the economic sphere. The few small businesses operated by Plenty always give more for the money than their competitors; clients, deriving more, place more orders, thereby bringing more business Plenty's way. On the other hand, "more" cannot always be read in a purely numerical sense. One new member of Plenty, a man who owned a small, retail electrical supply house, interpreted "more" in terms of openness, honesty, and trust. One payday he gathered his six employees together and explained that there would be no more wages. On paydays, everyone was simply to go to the bookkeeper and ask for what he needed. The employees were shocked and distrustful —one or two demanded far more than their usual wage, just to test their employer, and the sums were given to them. Others, certain that the poor man had lost his marbles, took their regular wage or even less. In the course of a few weeks, however, the employees fell into the habit of taking what they needed, which turned out to be not a great deal more than they had been earning in set wages. And within the space of a year, the retail store had doubled its business, simply because—in this new spirit of trust and sharing—everybody from sales to stockroom was working, most cheerfully, twice as hard. Or at least, that's the story that's told at Plenty.

If you were a member of this society, you would very probably go to live in one of the Plenty residences, where your growth in the philosophy would be, to some extent, the responsibility of the housemother, who might be male or female. You would have your own room, and to the extent possible, the room you preferred, and your privacy would be guaranteed by the Door Language of all Houses of Plenty, which is: door open, anybody welcome; door ajar, knock first; door shut, stay out and do not knock. Again depending on resources, you would decorate your room in any way you pleased, and if puce happened to be your favorite color, you could indulge it there all you liked. Every month you would present your housemother with a list of your cash and material needs for the next four weeks; if the needs of the membership exceeded resources, the inner council would take steps to increase business, or to add on additional seminars for weekend visitors, in order to generate the necessary funds. And if it turned out that you badly needed a Jaguar or a Maserati, this requirement would be taken very seriously, and you might well get your wish. It would be assumed, however, that you would not "need" a Maserati until you genuinely felt that such an acquisition would not take away from the welfare of any of the others.

Emotionally and sexually, you would be quite free to form any attachments which were not harmful to anyone else; typically, you would spend several weeks or months exploring your new freedom, changing, switching, running wild. But in practice, Plenty is almost entirely monogamous, except when occasional needs for Strange Ass temporarily enlarge established pairings. Because you and your partner (the one you came with, or some other) have experienced the Plenty sexuality seminar, and have worked out the minutest details of each other's sexual needs and fantasies, your partner enjoys an intimacy with you, and you with him or her, that really cannot be equaled by anybody else.

When Buddy Vesp arrived—a tall, handsome man, bursting with smiles and energy—he expanded on this theme by slightly altering the concept of "more." "Look at it this way," he said. "How many shirts can you wear at one time? How many cars can you have? We find that when your basic requirements are assured, your needs actually are reduced. Life gets simpler, not more complicated. At Plenty you can have everything you want.

But after a while you figure out that your actual wants are very few."

I asked him about neighbor relations, considering that Plenty was an unorthodox establishment on a street of very orthodox-looking homes. "We take trouble about it," he said. "If a neighbor has any complaint with us, we correct the problem right away. For example, a couple across the street complained that one of our dogs was going into their yard; we stopped it at once, and apologized. We're interested in appropriate communications, and what is appropriate for our neighbors is different from what is appropriate for us. So we respect their privacy, and do nothing to upset them, nothing. But we've had surprisingly little trouble anyway—I think it's the general vibrations here. Look, everybody's smiling, there's a sense of happiness here. And it spreads. If anybody on this street, no matter how grouchy, wants something from us in the way of behavior, or physical help, or whatever it is, they can have it. And they know that—so how could they stay grouchy?"

It beat me.

"Or take our other relations with people outside. Say, the milkman. He started out thinking we were pretty weird, so many people living in one house, eating together and all. But we're an important customer on his route, right? We order a lot of milk. And whenever he comes we're glad to see him, we ask him for coffee, we want him to hang around, visit. We feel good and we want him to feel good. He was pretty wary at first, thought we were a bunch of nuts—but he can see we're living good, lots of beautiful chicks, nice guys, nice house, good vibes. And despite himself maybe, he's got interested. We're last on his route now, so that he can take the time for that cup of coffee, maybe help out around the house. We're kind to him, and he's kind to us. He can't help himself. And that's true of all people, in their own time, on their own rhythm."

"Okay," I said. "That takes care of the outside. But what about inside; I really can't believe that everybody is content with being content, all the time. Sometimes people just have to see other places, meet other people."

"Of course," said Buddy. "When you're a member of the House of Plenty you're a member for life. That means that you could go off any day, come back fifty years later, to any house, and you'd be coming home. Meanwhile, if it's just change of scene you want, we have a couple of houses in Hawaii now. Sometimes people want to go over there for a while, and they do. But basically there is never any hassle because Plenty is your family, and Plenty wants you to have more, and that includes whatever you need.

"And maybe some things you don't *know* you need. Like tonight we're having an affect night; every two weeks we have one. It's like a big birthday party but it's not on your birthday necessarily, it's whenever your turn pops up. There's a committee that's been working for two weeks on this party for Tom, studying all his likes and needs and wants, and tonight we all go out of our way to celebrate him. Two weeks ago it was Cindy —somebody had checked out her 'goody list' (every house keeps a goody list on you so the things you like to eat are always in stock) and noticed her habits and everything for dinner that night was what she especially likes, done the way she likes it. And somebody else had noticed that she always smokes seven cigarettes in the course of a party evening, so in the cigarette holder just in front of her place were exactly seven cigarettes. And just before she was getting ready to leave, and reached for that last cigarette, it hit her. It just about wiped her out.

"In ways like this we are constantly reminding one another that this is home, this is where it is, this is where we care. This is where you really can have everything."

"I don't know, Buddy," I said. "Some people get mad when you tell them a thing like that, because they don't *want* it to be true."

"Oh, yeah," he said. "I know. Some people say we're witches, that only the devil can give you everything. People are really weird. Because you can have exactly what you want, anytime, if you're willing to face what that really is. And that means facing who you are —which is, I guess, the scary part."

As we drove back over the Bay Bridge, we enthused over the rightness of the Plenty philosophy, which all of us found more attractive (for our various reasons) than the overt religiosity of the Fellowship. Two groups of people, getting exactly what they want—one by hooking into the pecuniary culture in the biggest possible way, the other by subliminating material and fleshly needs to service, and the life of the spirit. Both groups wonderfully happy in their choices, both deeply suspected of witchcraft and evil. Both, so far as we could tell, essentially honest and essentially good. But it was clear that, in both cases, personal honesty had to come first, and, as Buddy Vesp had said, that was the scary part.

THE COSMIC JOKE

I've made an intellectual/theological breakthrough. I've come to believe that nothing matters—no thing is the most important nonthing in the world (or out of it, for that matter). The atheists are right when they say there's nothing out there. Precisely the point. No thing is responsible for anything. God is the negative space in art, the dreamless sleep state for humans that the Hindus metaphorically say is Brahma. The process of creation is Om (TUM or, more accurately to me, MUA) . What do you think?

—FRAGMENT OF A LETTER FROM A GI FRIEND IN VIETNAM

At this last minute, we began to consider earnestly whether we could have any real and lasting respect for the bizarre events of the last several weeks. We had spoken endlessly of being really honest with ourselves and each other, but we knew that the more ruthlessly we had peeled away illusion and self-deception, the more endless that task came to seem. We could not be sure that we had ever reached the heart of the artichoke; and at the same time we were reconciled to the rather bleak conviction that at the deep, dark, seemingly impenetrable center of each of us was nothing but a void. The void, we felt, was God.

Yet that seemed to us, if not precisely okay, unavoidably acceptable, and also very funny. Because if we were all One, and if (and this we accepted too) in the eternal scheme we had led many lives before and would lead many lives in "time" to come (time was not linear or progressive to us anymore) ; if we were just to go on and on in successive incarnations, then all our petty concern with such divisions as male and female, pain and pleasure, right and wrong, achievement and stagnation, success and failure, was a total absurdity. An enormous cosmic joke, funnier still because we knew we would never be able enti.ely to dissolve those petty illusions in our own hyperactive minds.

Our problem, then, was what to do with lives that had been emptied of meaning. Work forty-five hours a week for IBM? Hardly. Engage effectively in the system? It didn't seem possible. Mountaintops and meditation seemed possible; suicide also. Anything seemed as right as any other thing, since nothing was wrong, except in the most conventional sense. And the conventional world was all part of the joke.

At this point we realized that we had come, in philosophical terms anyway, to a stage where Charles Manson and his Family were reported to be. If everything that you do is right, then murder is right. Murder is easy, a cinch, and no more important than having a haircut or trimming your toenails. There's boring old Joe Doaks over there, a part of me that really does nothing to turn me on. I think I'll just recycle old Joe, join him up once again with the cosmic ecology. It's not murder and death, really, it's just an inevitable process of decay and rebirth. Maybe he'll come back in better shape; meanwhile, he won't be around to annoy me.

This realization enabled us finally to understand why, in some communes, members thought nothing of stealing from others. It wasn't only that they rejected conventional concepts of private property, but that for them, there was no such thing as property, no I-It division whatsoever, no more than an I-You. God's body hungers; God eats Himself. If "Himself" in this instance turns out to be, in your terms, *your* lunch, that is just *your* illusion.

But where did this leave us with respect to society's attitudes toward theft and murder? Societal, still—most decidedly. At any level of intensity we believed that all men were One, and One's obligation was certainly to fill One's collective stomach; but that did not seem to us to give parts of One license to dispense with other parts of One, to cut off One's arms and legs. That would be schizoid, unless all of One could be surveyed and agree to take a cosmic saw to One's toe. In short, what Charles Manson's family stood accused of, war-making governments all over the world stand accused of also.

Yet here and there in communes across the country, we had heard Manson referred to as a great avatar, seen his picture framed and honored. Did they suppose that, if we are all God, we may then decimate the race of men? In that event, we felt there was a vast misreading of the mystical illumination that so many people had been alluding to in their conversation with us, an illumination we had not understood until now. And we knew that this access to mysticism was extremely pervasive in the society, particularly among young people looking for meaning in their lives. And there were tens of thousands of them around, now believing that there is a great energy shooting through all things, that every action of any thing has its effect, however subtle, upon all other things. That we are not separate, as we seem to be in this illusory world of the senses, but joined—so intimately, in fact, that all our pretense to ego and individuality comes to seem a joke. If the joke extended, in all these people's minds, to some conviction of the cheapness of human life, the society was in most terrible peril.

How did all these people come to be on this mystic trip? Some, no doubt, through the kind of communal pressures we had experienced. Scrape off a facade of civilization, remove the rules, scramble the sets, abolish the taboos, dissolve all schedules and programs—and man looks for spirits in the trees and rocks, exactly as his primordial ancestors did. It may not be an unhappy regression; it may be that the spirits are there.

Some people got there through drugs that enabled them to see their connection with all things—and what is called a bad trip can often be no more than the realization of the joke, in the loss of identity that the drug is reported to bring. After all, if you see your corporeal, visual limits "disintegrating" into juncture with all other matter, conventional definitions for who you are become silly. This is also why the Zen student laughs; this is why a Christian ascetic sits on a pole for thirty years. In light of this awareness, life offers a rich spectrum of possibilities, and simultaneously becomes utterly impossible. So the Maharishi giggles.

And the Manson family kills. Damn. We didn't care for the

company. What, then, might be said to distinguish our revelation from theirs? It struck us that Charlie Manson is not the only guru in the world, and far from the only "avatar." The world is full of willing leaders, and the sheep are numberless. If people are afraid, reluctant to accept apotheosis, then they run to somebody who's not that scared. They may cope with their timidity on the political level, crying Sieg Heil to any bold Hitler. And at the spiritual level, where the problem really lies, they are only too quick to knuckle under to a spiritual Hitler, a charismatic figure who will thunder that he has been to the mountain, he has the truth. You can sit in his shadow, percolate quietly on his heat, but don't try to get up to his plateau or you will find that he has already leapt nimbly a level or two higher. "This is *my* trip," he'll say. "You can try and try, but you will never, never be as super-terrific as I am. I will, however, levitate for you occasionally, so long as you continue to cringe; and I will preach sometimes, too. But remember, my sermons are scored solely for Amens." The temptation to do that is enormous, because so many people are dying for you to do it. *Please* do it— dominate me, rule me, tell me what's right! And where else than in the subculture of American society, among the rootless young, are there more souls aware of the wilderness in which they dwell; what segment of the society is screaming more desperately for help, for salvation?

Donna Mae Marsh of Middletown, USA, flees from the emptiness of her suburban raising; she fetches up like floating garbage on the shore of the New Society, rootless, aimless, frightened. What little structure her upwardly mobile parents may have attempted to inculcate in her, she has long since rejected; she is an empty vessel. She may be only seventeen, but seventeen is a very healthy age in our country today; Donna Mae wants to celebrate her sexuality, but her parents said No. She wants to believe in something, but her parents said Don't be Ridiculous. She wants a family, but her parents were at work, or at the country club, or in the bottle, or anyway busy somewhere. So there she is, wandering night streets in a shapeless city, her head as hollow as a Ping-Pong ball. From the wings, not leering in the manner of old-fashioned villains, but smiling beatifically, enter Harry Guru, Jesus to his friends, God Incarnate. He collects Donna Detritus (for that is what he calls her) from the unpopulous roadside, delights her with a physical sexuality which is beyond her wildest imaginings (because unlike the men she's known before he is really interested), and invites her to dwell in his personal garbage heap, where there will be love and caress and caring forever. Never mind that it is a filthy sink; at least it exists, and it envelops her. Others has he, that he likes as well as she—but she loves him. And lo, what are these beams that from his brow emanate, and what are these vibrations in the air that connect all of them? I am You, says Harry Guru. Dig it. Donna digs it, extremely. She has no trouble with metaphysics, about which she knows even less than I do. She can cop to what *is,* and Harry is. And anything he wants her to do is simply dandy, because his head is her head is our heads—and after a while he doesn't have to say anything. She *knows.* She will be his breastplate, and his sword. Because we are God. Exeunt omnes, apotheosized, to meet Sharon Tate.

That's how it's done, if you interpret the God in you as a platform for a power trip. And if your route to apotheosis led through the tangle of sexual identity, and if you uncapped yourself for the androgyne you really are, then your avenue to women is especially smooth. Because while the studs are still strutting their stuff, and talking about how manly they are, you are soft and open and unspecific—more like a woman. What the studs can't realize is that their sexual assumptions about themselves have denigrated the female half of the race for eons; and "womanly" has become a metaphor for "less." What woman cannot respond to a man who really likes her? But when has she ever met one? That's where you come in.

It was later, much later, in long circular conversations together about what had happened, that Steve and I pinned our apotheosis to what we called "the discovery" of the androgyne. Both of us had fiercely and protectively suppressed the androgyne in our natures, because it made us "less." I had admitted to my life, a bit, the physical expression of bi-sexuality, but for me it had been like exercise, a novel experience, and never embraced because—in ways I was unable to express—it was submissive, therefore womanly, therefore intellectually unacceptable. And Steve had never allowed its flow at all, even in relations with women—

until now. And as we exchanged these findings with one another, consulting Kate Millett and other spokeswomen for women's lib on the side, we realized who had educated us and made us free of our particular sexual illusion. None other than Nora, the beautiful girl who was glad to be, now and then, a boy, the nineteen-year-old who had always, very calmly, accepted her whole self. She and—symbolically, anyway—bearded Hibiscus, he/she of the Cockettes.

This is something known to all avatars. And it may even be in apprehension of it that painters have persisted in representing a feminine Christ. It struck us that we could run out and become feminine avatars—big deal. Collect a few helpless, beautiful people in the manner of spiritual capitalists, and be saintly for them. But exploitation did not seem to be the right bag for either of us. It would have been not only wrong-headed but, in ways we continue to respect, sacrilegious.

As for our hour-and-a-half commune—we parted on a note of anticlimax. Oz, resistant to our departure, made an uncharacteristic speech to us. "Don't go," he pleaded. "Stay here. Send east for anybody you have to have with you, but don't leave San Francisco. San Francisco is where it's happening."

"No, Oz," I said, in a remarkable peak of hubris, "it's happening wherever we are."

But it wasn't, of course, as we knew on our last day. Nora flew off to Chicago with an efficiency and dispatch that were somehow appalling; and Steve and I, after a final, almost perfunctory embrace for Oz, roared away in our little car, and down the Bayshore Freeway, southbound. As we left the city of peaks and valleys well behind us, Steve asked me how I felt. I shouted back to him over the roar of the traffic: "I feel thirty-six years old, and I feel very tired, and very stupid."

"Well," he said, "I have to agree you're right about all that."

PART THREE: REVERBERATIONS

When we left San Francisco, Steve and I were still in a state of semi-divinity, tempered somewhat by doubt already, but still quietly assertive about it in perfectly polite ways. We were neither as innocent as we had been at the beginning of our researches, nor as gullible and credulous as we had been during the San Francisco period. Our attitude was not, I think, arrogant, but we felt we knew, finally, when we were in the presence of serious communards, and when we were not. An encounter with an old friend of Steve's, an attractive script girl in Hollywood, put some of our Godly posture in perspective. One night Steve portentously advised her of our Status. "Oh, I know all about that," she said. "I realized, after thirty-eight acid trips, that I'm God. We're all God. Listen, what's happening in New York?"

EVERYBODY'S IN ON THE ACT

On our way to Los Angeles, we stopped at Esalen to see Dick Price, the resident director. There had been talk in San Francisco of some plans to turn Esalen's Big Sur Hot Springs location into an intentional community, and we wanted to know if this was indeed taking place. It had been (it always is) impossible to make appointments in or out of San Francisco with Esalen people. You have to take your chances and the chances are always maddeningly slim. I remember a time at Esalen when Dick Price and I spent very nearly a full day caring for and trying to settle the arrangements of a man who was taking a long psychotic trip before our wondering eyes; on that occasion I had volunteered to drive the tormented man to Monterey to a hospital (Esalen is *not* a hospital), and Dick Price had been perfectly decent to me at that time. But that was three years ago; I could not expect him to remember my name, nor—knowing Esalen—was there any reason to suppose that he would have seen me, even if he did remember me.

It all played out pretty much as I feared. Dick Price was in a seminar. No, Dick Price was at lunch. No, Dick Price was working and couldn't be disturbed. The pretty girls who staff the office have a wonderfully attractive way of being utterly feckless and unhelpful. Our phone messages had not been received; nobody knew when Dick Price would be available; in short, buzz off. So I still don't know if Esalen on the Big Sur is moving toward intentional community, but I do know that I needn't expect to be invited to join.

We did, however, run into Bernadette Wolfe, who had brought Tony here after he failed to make any progress at Agnews State Hospital. They were living in a comfortable cabin, but Tony, she said, was still quite unbelievably manic and she was worn out from no sleep and constant coping. Bernadette sponsored us as guests for the day, so we were able to go to the hot springs baths and pass a very agreeable couple of hours. And then we trudged up the hill to see Tony, who professed dimly but enthusiastically to remember us. He was arguing with Bernadette at the time that he was perfectly capable of driving the car; it was in the parking lot, in fact, that we found them. And Bernadette and Tony's brother, who had flown from the East to help out, were arguing back again that it was out of the question. But Tony took time out to chat with us about anything and nothing whatever, all options his. His eyes glittered with mischief and amusement; it was clear that he was having a perfectly wonderful time.

For a late lunch, we retraced our steps the few miles to Nepenthe, that eagle's lair of a restaurant hung thrillingly out over a steep cliff above the Pacific, where martinis, ambrosia burgers, and the works of Carl Jung enjoy equal popularity. Nepenthe is a lovely place—I know no lovelier—and it was very special that day. The staff, who are never less than the prettiest people ever born, were doing their Wednesday fashion show. Crazy fashions, of course, as attractive to the chi-chi north as to the vulgar south, and I remember a lot of fringed leather and cloaks and copes of every kind, and booties laced from toe to thigh and who knows what insanity. But mostly, I remember the infectious cheerfulness of the models, pretty girls and boys who didn't really much care what they wore, because they knew they were beautiful in anything. It was a giddy afternoon—not because we were drunk but because we were stunned by the beautiful setting and the gorgeous people, and a couple of the models were always careful to linger at our rather remote table, flouncing and posing for our special benefit. The eye contact was constant and provocative; the girls knew it was themselves we were digging, and not the clothes they were wearing.

On her last outing, one of the girls stopped off at our table for quite a long while, and asked where we were from, and where going, and what doing. When we told her, she said, "Oh, we have a commune here, too. We're all in it, everybody who works here—but we don't call it that, and not all the kids actually live on the place. For instance, I live down the road, but I'm still *in* it.

"I don't think the owners want it known, especially, but this really is a family. We don't share economically, but if we need something we can have it—like, I need to go to Europe this fall, and they're going to help me to get there. Things like that." And with a toss of her dear little head, she went twinkling off to dazzle the next table, while Steve and I looked at each other and he said, "Wow. I guess everybody's doing it."

JUST A QUIET LITTLE SENSORIUM

Los Angeles is a very American city and a very crazy place—I have never been able to find its center, its limits, or its heart. The buzzing freeways scare me to death and make me lose all sense of direction, so that when I get where I'm going, I'm not sure where I am, and when I leave, I'm never sure where I came from. Most literally, I don't know which way to turn. I visualize myself racing forever along an interlocking network of jammed highways with no exits, always seconds from death at seventy miles per hour, unable to see the edge of the road because of the smog, while a voice on the car radio assures me that the weather in LA today is bright and sunny.

Still, I have been caught laughing while in precisely that condition; there is for me no more rational response to the sheer insanity of the city, where anything can happen and usually does, where everything that happens is contradictory to all that has happened before, and is itself instantly contradicted by what happens next. Picture, if you will, the route to Manhattan Beach. On one side of the road, row upon row of quaint plaster cottages in soft pastels; each a Spanish villa in miniature: minute arches, minute towers, minute battlements. Rose trellises, white picket fences, Andy Hardy throwing papers from a wobbly bicycle on the sidewalk. Fill in, from your imaginary vantage, the thousands of cars rushing past in both directions, sightless. Roar, vahrooom. And what else do these chaste cottages confront, apart from all creation rushing past? Why, nothing less than a prairie of immense proportions, whereon stand at least one hundred giant oil tanks and a towering crude-oil cracking plant, from the plain pipe towers of which there belches an inferno of smoke and brilliant flame, night and day. At right angles to this extends the main street of Manhattan Beach, an irregular jumble of motels, bars, hamburger stands, and benevolent loan societies, and just below it, parallel, the rich, sandy strand, encrusted with the crisping bodies of a populace all blond, all beautiful, all languid. And all fully occupied in scraping from their bare soles the thick, sticky tars that are the residue, under the surf, of whatever tanker collision has occurred most recently.

The whole thing makes you want to rush in from the wings, like some nameless Messenger in an Elizabethan drama, shouting Alack! and Alarum! Sounding the tocsins and all that stuff. Toot! This is crazy. You're sunbathing next to a cracking plant, f'crissake; you are drowning, asphyxiating in oil. And what's more, the sun *isn't* shining. And everything is ugly, and it doesn't go together, it's all wrong. If you did something like that you'd get a big crowd right away, all saying Wow! and Far Out! and Dig it. A new nut on the beach, really freaky. Fantastic. Just like everything else.

I could go on and on. I could take you to a ritzy development where an entire hillside has been bulldozed (they call it landscaping) for rows of Roman villas erected at enormous cost, interspersed with simulated Roman ruins—broken columns, shattered temples, faceless Dianas, that sort of thing—and spilling fountains over which colored lights play nightly, while from hidden speakers emanate endlessly the orchestral strains of "The Pines of Rome." Grown people did this. Or we could take a stroll down some of the major arteries of the city, where the acid rock boites and micro-boutiques abound, and ten thousand children shuffle barefoot up and down the sidewalks, twenty-four hours a day, going no place. I mention all this not to put down LA, which already has more articulate detractors than I; but to set the scene for a visit to The Garden of Delights, which is at once a nudist center, a growth center and a commune, an earthly pleasure dome which, even in Los Angeles, is remarkable, but nevertheless could have grown to maturity in no other place.

The Garden of Delights is in Topanga Canyon, a wild and lightly-populated woodsy area that, for all its country pretensions, is within the city limits. Yet it is genuinely rough country; its steep arroyos and deep woods provide a seclusion and sense of remoteness not available in Brentwood. Certain people, eccentric about privacy or prone to a more rugged life, like it very much. There are said to be many communes and other unorthodox establishments back in there. The Garden of Delights, the dream-come-true of a magazine publisher named Toby Mann, is one.

Toby Mann has been a successful businessman in Los Angeles for more than twenty-five years, and a dedicated nudist for at least that long. His firm, Delight Publications, published official nudist journals for many years, together with a variety of slick one-shots of a less official nature, the prominence and popularity of which never failed to disturb old-line nudists who usually die declaiming that they did it only for strength and health. Let Toby's unofficial magazines suggest that there could be some additional reasons for social nakedness and nudists would meet in little groups all over the country, gravely shake their heads, and solemnly consider whether they ought not take their business elsewhere.

Nowadays they have to. Toby is out of the nudist movement forever; it strikes him as a sadly antediluvian organization in a day of rampant sexual liberation. He is incorporating all his interests, including magazine and book publishing and the operation of The Garden, under one foundation umbrella, the foundation also titled Delight; and Topanga Canyon has become home to him, and nerve center as well, as he strives to integrate his work and his play into one condition of being. He has picked a nice place to be.

If you had very careful directions, you would know how many roadhouses to pass on the main drive through Topanga Canyon before turning off onto minor roads and lanes which would bring you finally to the gates of the Garden, cyclone-fencing sort of gates, embowered in eucalyptus, where you would get out of your car, stride to a rustic box alongside the gates, and press a buzzer. Directly a voice would come through perforations in the box, inquiring after your name and business. And if you had the right answers, the gates would go bzzzt and swing wide, and you could begin the drive up a steep road, through woods, to a hilltop clearing. Toward the top you would spy a collection of quaint redwood chalets, bordering a wide green meadow, and at the first of these you would stop to register, and pay $5 for the day, whether a member ($100 a year per person) or first-time guest. As you spun your car around a circular drive toward the road to a secluded parking lot, you would be able to see that the lawn was spotted with many sunbathers, adults and children, most naked.

Our arrival was entirely routine to that point, but Toby was expecting us, and we had special directions to his cottage which, after we parked, was our first destination. On the porch we found a bulky, muscular man in levis, pulling on a pair of boots. He wore a full gray beard, his gray hair flowed to his shoulders, and a great gray mat of hair covered his chest and generous belly. Seeing that he was in the act of dressing, I said, "I hope you're not doing that for us."

"Not a chance," he said. "A guy has come over with a jackhammer today and we have work to do up on the rise. It's a slightly exposed position and we can't go naked up there."

With a sweep of his hand, Toby indicated the widespread

features of his domain, where we *could* go naked. The pool—the mud wallow ("genuine elephant mud from New Jersey")—the hydropool—the tennis courts—the volleyball court—the dressing rooms and shower rooms—the sauna—the meadow. Toby said the best way to learn about the Garden was to relax and enjoy it all, just "let it roll over you." He said he would get his work done, and we would play. "And when it feels right, we'll talk." Thus agreed, he set out up the hill, and we went to the men's dressing room, stripped, and established a little bit of tufted turf on the meadow as our vantage point for the day.

There were about 150 people sunbathing in the meadow, grouped in clusters of family and/or friends, obviously all devoting the sunny day to laziness and relaxation. There was nothing to do but enjoy yourself, and very casually, that's what they were doing. And as the spirit moved, so did we. A little run down the meadow to the pool, everything jiggling and jouncing. A plunge into the deliciously cool water, a long, easy swim. A sunbathe, another swim. A trip to the sauna, lazing on stair-step redwood benches until the sweat popped. An icy shower. A cold plunge. A volleyball bout, leaping and falling. A wallow in mud, oozily. A tussle with the liquid eroticism of the hydropool, as jets of water press and prod, massage and stimulate. Cold plunge again, for discretion's sake. Lollygagging on a water bed beside the pool, feeling the bloop and billow beneath you with every movement, yours or someone else's. Pure hedonism—delightful. But like so many nudist parks, limited. You get yourself all turned on, and then what? As Steve grumpily observed, "We've been here ten minutes and haven't been laid yet."

And yet by midafternoon, we detected that this was not like other nudist parks. We saw in the throng on the meadow a curious, subtle shifting, a movement of people restlessly from one group to another. And more and more, flashes of exhibitionism, some not so subtle, because it isn't easy to be subtle when you're naked. And embracing and caressing, and pre-erotic horseplay at the pool and on the luxurious water beds. Finally, during a trip to the sauna, I got the message in full from two long-haired young men, who struck up a conversation when nobody else was in there. "Pretty dull today," said one. "I'm not coming here any more."

"What's missing?" I asked him. "What happened last time?"

"Oh, wow, last time was fantastic. They were having a group encounter for everybody that was here. About two hundred people. They had this exercise where you move around naked with your hands out, eyes shut, feeling the texture of other people's bodies. Lots of exercises with touching. And then they broke us up into groups of six or eight for verbal and nonverbal encounters. I wound up with a terrific chick who turned out to be a nude dancer from Covina, and then we wound up in the orgy rooms."

"Orgy rooms?"

"Yeah," he said. "Come on. I'll show you."

We showered, then strolled to a nearby chalet, which connected with still another, just beyond the pool. My new friend and informant pushed aside a sliding glass door, parted gauzy curtains, and we entered a large, cool, high-ceilinged room. Indian cotton prints hung like banners here and there from the ceiling, vaguely dividing the space, rippling lightly in a breeze that also made some several sets of wind chimes faintly play. Here and there around the room were low beds, single and double, draped in the same cotton prints. There was a heavy metal sculpture of two abstract human figures, abstractly united, and over the stone fireplace, a gigantic ankh, a symbol much used at the Garden, originally Egyptian, of a cross surmounted by a circle.

"Wow," I said. "If you're going to have an orgy, this is certainly a charming place to stage it."

"Oh, there's more," my friend said, and he led me through a series of floating banners, that caressed our bodies as we passed, up a flight of stairs into the adjoining chalet, and down a hallway to two small bedrooms. On each door a sign announced, "These rooms are reserved for meditation and the brief use of guests. You are not expected to stay overnight in them." With the artful use of drapes and mirrors, these little bedrooms had been transformed into exotic bowers. Indian prints suspended from the center of the ceiling suggested the interior of a tent; mirrored brilliants sewn into the fabrics set light dancing all over the room. Large mirrors leaned against the walls; on low tables around the double bed were incense pots and fat candles, and vases bursting with fresh field flowers. "Last time I was here," said my friend, "there were thirty people in here, and at least twenty over there."

My, my, thought I, we appear to be in line for an orgy. But I hadn't seen very many people with whom I'd fantasize such an activity; most of the couples were substantially older than I, in their fifties and sixties. It was also a problem for the two long-haired young men. "This is all very nice," said my informant's companion, "but I don't dig the people that much. They're not very hip." And that was Steve's objection too, when I met him to tell my news. He had some news of his own. "They're trying to work up a sex scene in the sauna," he told me. "But these sixty-five-year-old satyrs turn me off. They're trying to pick up on the young chicks, and the young chicks are sort of into it, but the style is terrible. It's all 1940s bullshit. You know, giggles and 'That's a very nice necklace you're wearing,' and 'Where'd you get such beautiful red hair.' Stuff like that. It's sort of pathetic."

I posted off to the sauna, meanwhile studying my feelings about sixty-five-year-old satyrs. God willing, someday I'd be one myself; meanwhile I disliked the extent to which I shared Steve's snobbishness about them. Here I was in the first place I'd ever hit where an older man could be frankly horny without being thought "dirty." I should be cheering, especially as this man's freedom held portents of my own. But I couldn't help myself; all those cigar-smoking grand-daddies with flaccid white shanks, tongues in cheeks and bony elbows suggestively in other people's ribs turned me off. Obviously, what good taste grants, indeed goads in a young stud, it denies in his daddy. Harsh realities for a thirty-six-year-old man who is en route to sixty-five, not twenty-three.

Only two men were in the sauna when I got there, both well over forty-five, both businessmen to their very pores, but both in pretty good shape. They were chatting noncommittally, but finally one stretched his hand out to the other, saying, "By the way, my name's Sid. I don't think we've met here before. Have you been a member long?"

"Harry's my name, Sid," said Harry. "Yes, the wife and I joined over two years ago. We like it very much. But we've been abroad the last year, just got back to LA."

"Well, I thought it was funny," said Sid. "Not knowing you by sight anyway. My wife and I come out at least once a week. But we've only belonged for a couple of months. Tell me, Harry, is . . . uh . . . did you bring the little woman along with you today?"

"Yes, Sid," said Harry, "yes, indeed I did. She's right here with me. We're sitting up near the top of the hill, under an umbrella. I wish you'd come up; I'm sure she'd like to meet you."

"Well," said Sid, "I'm sure I'd like to meet *her*. And I'd like to bring my wife with me, because I'm sure she'd like to meet you. Yes, sir, I'm sure of it. I think that would be very nice, Harry."

"Well, then, I think you both ought to come up."

"Well, I think we will then. I'll just go get her."

"Yes, well, I'll go straight on up the hill. We'll see you pretty soon, Sid."

"Yes, sir, Harry, you betcha, ha-ha-ha."

And they went.

For me, the light slowly dawned. She'd like to meet him. He'd like to meet her. This room is for the brief use of guests. A-HA. And my education continued.

The sauna began filling up again with a very mixed crowd, men and women, and though it was very slick and sweaty in there, it was very pleasant except for the appalling banter, as if everybody was at a slightly crude picnic or particularly disheveled bar. And somebody produced a bottle of rose oil, and proposed that we all massage one another with it. At that point I was tucked up in a corner of the room and did not get into the rubbing, but pretty quick it became quite general; the scent in the air was pleasant, the squish of rubbed bodies continued apace, and the conversation dropped away to light sighs and heavy breathing. Just about then a lady of about fifty, with a very nice body still, entered the sauna and greeted a man who was sitting on the shelf just above me. "Oh, Tom, HI!" she cried, and undertook to climb up to where he was. This meant that she had to slither over me, and soon we were all arms and leg and thighs together, with her toe in my crotch and her pudenda in my left ear.

"Oh, my goodness," she said, "I do beg your pardon." But

there was something about the way she said it—*and* the way she did it—that made me understand that she wasn't sorry at all. "Oh, that's okay," I said, helping with my right palm to boost her left buttock onto the shelf above. "Help yourself." So she did. She first settled herself directly behind Tom, scrunching in spoon fashion in order to take his torso on her breasts. And as his head lolled on her shoulder, she commenced to massage his chest and belly with one hand. The other snaked down off the shelf onto my shoulder and neck, and began an exploration which couldn't really go far enough to interest me. Her leg and foot dropped before my nose, and I understood that I was to fondle it, but that didn't get me very far either. However, the lady's progress with Tom was more central and successful, and pretty soon he displayed signs of sensual excitation. "Ooooo, I'm getting pretty hot," said Tom, as if referring to the sauna heat. Well, that really broke everybody up. "Tom's getting hot! Did you hear that, Sadie? Tom says he's hot. Ha-ha-ha-he-he-he." Slap, tickle, belch, and giggle. "Well," said the massaging lady, laughing away, "You may be too hot to leave. You're not in any shape to leave now, are you?" Tee-hee. But I was in a shape to leave, so I stirred to go, displacing the lady's hand from my collarbone. "Oh," she and Tom cried, "you're not leaving?"

"I'll be back," I said.

"Yes, you come right on back," said the lady. "Don't be long."

But when I came back, Tom and the lady were long gone, and a whole new set of middle-aged swingers were at it with the rose oil. Why can't I get into this, I wondered. It's lovely to be massaged in this heat. It is indescribably delicious. And then to go plunge into the pool, like streaking through liquid velvet. Why am I such an age snob? Yet when a younger man remarked to me that some girl was trying to get up a Von Neuman group, I lacked any interest in joining the cause. Later, Steve and I talked about it, the subtle turn-off that had affected us both, and decided that the problem was one not so much of age— because many of the people were physically attractive—but of the gap in generation styles. I imagine—I have to use my imagination because I've never been in this situation with my precise generation—that my age group would be a little more direct about taking sensual pleasures in the group. If they ever worked up to it, they wouldn't converse as if they were *not* doing what they *were* visibly doing. And Steve, at twenty-seven, was sure that his contemporaries would be more straightforward about group eroticism. So was I. Because people under thirty simply don't rely on metaphors for their behavior, as older persons do. Generally, if the mood is sensual it's called sensual, and lies and evasions are a lot less necessary.

We discussed this finally with Toby, who in late afternoon gave up the jackhammer, took a shower and a swim, and came over to join us, bringing with him a beautiful woman of about thirty-five whom he introduced as Helen. They sat in the grass with us—Toby naked, Helen in a transparent pants suit— and I found conversation with Toby very difficult whenever I looked into Helen's eyes. I'm not in the habit of gazing directly into people's eyes, but with Helen it was impossible not to, and they were the loveliest, most confiding and seductive eyes I've ever drowned in. I had to fight to avoid glancing in her direction. "Scorpio," Steve whispered. There had been some talk around the pool that day of Toby and Helen getting married, this very day in fact, but I eliminated the possibility. Anybody who'd spent the entire day with a jackhammer would not be likely to marry when he finished.

I asked Toby if he didn't find the style of his membership a little square. He countered with a question. "Have you ever been to a nudist park?" I said I had. "Times are changing," he said, "but not at the speed of light. Not very many years ago, a kid would go to a nudist park and that would be pretty boring to him. But a kid coming here couldn't even *conceive* of a no-touch, no-sensuality nudist situation. This will be where he'll start, slightly in advance of what *I* had to face. And the next stage will be a lot better, a lot franker.

"But we're pretty proud to have come this far. We have endless problems with the LA City Council. They've sent helicopters over here to prove our violation of a city ordinance that forbids public nudity, and we've fought that pretty successfully in the courts. But now they're drawing up a set of impossible standards for growth centers, which is what the Garden is, the only growth center in the world with optional nudity, and we have to fight that through. And meanwhile don't forget that we have several hundred members who can come here and enjoy themselves and their eroticism without apologies for the first time in their lives. That's no small thing."

I said I knew that, and theoretically I thought it was nifty. On the other hand, one of the bored and disappointed young guys who had shown me the lay of the land had complained that, this being for sure his last visit to the Garden, he'd been trying to think of something outrageous to do, some crudester act like a Gotcha or what was also, in my time, called Mooning, but had realized that nothing properly outrageous was possible in a setting like this; that there was no way to break the trance of banality that everybody was conversationally and behaviorally in.

The thought amused Toby. "We do have rules," he said. "No open sexuality on the lawn or in public. No oppression of other members, no embarrassing pressure. Ladies and gentlemen. That's what the Ankh rooms are for. He shouldn't have come on a day like this, with no program. We do naked group encounters on the first and third Sundays of the month—and usually we have other seminars going, and sometimes people can join them. But today is quiet. I can see how he'd be bored."

I asked Toby what the communal set-up of the Garden was. "Well, there are only about twenty of us who are actually living here," he explained. "Everybody else is on a membership basis, welcome every day but Monday. And Wednesday afternoons are set aside specially for married couples only. Other than that, the place is available every day to all members. Those of us who built this place live here full-time. We tried living together in one building, but it was unsuccessful. There were people who liked children, and people who didn't. There were people who sought more privacy, and people who wanted less. We found we were spending too much time settling disputes. So finally we broke up into smaller family units, about six different house-holds right here on the premises. Sets of twos, threes, fours. It varies. With and without children. We're very liquid. But we remain communal, and scattered simply to accommodate indi-vidual preferences. And we find it works a lot better."

Toby's mood abruptly changed, just as Helen's hand took his. "Look," he said, "I'd like to continue this another time. We have an activity we've got to get into right now, so we'll have to leave you. Stay as long as you like, and come back when you can, okay?" We said okay, and thanked and shook hands with Toby; then the incredible Helen moved toward us and embraced and warmly kissed each of us in turn. Then the pair moved down the meadow, stopping here and there to chat with other groups of people. It was nearing twilight; Steve and I decided to get ready to leave. We went again to the men's dressing room, showered, dressed, and came outside again to confront a remarkable sight.

The "activity" Toby and Helen had to get into was marriage; it was just about to take place, halfway up the meadow. Toby and Helen were standing up there, holding hands; he wearing a long, richly patterned gown, looking very much like an Old Testament patriarch, she in a diaphanous white lace gown that rippled in the breeze. With them was a tall, deeply bronzed naked man, the minister, holding a black prayer book. The membership, pleased and excited, had momentarily abandoned their pursuit of bodily pleasures to cluster near the edge of the pool area, gazing upward, forming a distant but empathetic congregation. The wedding couple was just beginning to exchange vows as we slipped away to the parking lot and drove down from the hillside.

"What a great idea," said Steve of the sudden and nearly spontaneous wedding. "Get up in the morning, dig a trench all day, get married before supper. Do it when it feels right. If I knew I was going to ritualize my wedding, schedule it for April 26, I'd probably get so freaked I'd split from the country. But this way, doing it when you both feel like doing it, makes sense of the ritual. Not ritual for ritual's sake, but for your own sake."

We agreed that Toby was the only man we'd ever met who had, since Kubla Khan, decreed and actually built his own pleasure dome; probably a fantasy lurking in every man's mind. A fleshy paradise, of course—and since we were still feeling slightly divine, it had occurred to both of us to be patronizing about The Garden of Delights because we hadn't seen anybody sitting in the lotus or doing other ostentatiously religious sorts of things. But how absurd to strike such a superior posture. Here were people who were, at whatever primitive, fleshy level, breaking through sexual hang-ups that had inhibited and retarded their growth for who knows how many narrow and arid years; now, in middle age or later, what a pleasure and release it must be for them to be frankly sexual beings together in openness, to have available a playpen for grown-ups, to rediscover the excitement of joint physical eroticism. An acceptance of natural eroticism is, after all, an early step in all growth center programs; the distinguishing feature of the Garden is the deliberate indulgence of the joys of the flesh—an institutional approach which, by some miracle, the younger generation never needed. Maybe these people, once past the barriers of puritanism and politeness, would be freed for more cosmic pursuits. And after all, chanting and meditating are not of themselves certain signs of spiritual superiority.

The games at the Garden had seemed sophomoric to us, adolescent, childish. But of course: these people were at last working out erotic and hedonistic fantasies that had first intruded upon their consciousness in childhood and adolescence. They were hardly to be blamed for only just now gaining the freedom to act out what their children had always taken completely for granted. First missionaries of the post-Christian era, Steve called them—but I am not sure that "post-Christian" is the correct designation. I seem to remember hearing that a little child shall lead them; with respect to the Garden, it would seem obvious that a generation of parents is being led out of puritanism by a generation of children—their own.

Toby's success with his vision led us to speculate on our own futures. Steve wondered whether he would wind up back in Boston and New York, trying to persuade people into the new craziness, as he called it. He felt sure that, on account of my conviction that love is, like the universe, infinitely expanding, it was doubtless in my karma to wind up with a dome of pleasure not unlike Toby's. And I guess I am fairly earth-bound in my fantasies, unlikely to respond to heavy rituals with wafers and incense, equally unresponsive to the strong materialism of a place like the House of Plenty or the ecclesiasticism of the Fellowship. My fantasy, my dream perhaps, is a eucharist of joined spirit and flesh, with the good things of the flesh in rich abundance: hot baths and massage, excellent wines, handsome sex— a hedonist's prayer. Meanwhile, I thought what a boon the

Garden of Delights could be to every suburban marriage. Wednesdays were for married couples only—and what couple beset by work and children couldn't profit by one afternoon a week at the local sensorium, an erotic playground with only the pool and the incense and the mirrored draperies . . . and each other . . . to think about.

THE GOD(S) THAT FAILED

Steve and I had decided that, from Palm Springs, where we were resting briefly after the luxurious rigors of The Garden of Delights, we could make the long run across the desert to someplace in New Mexico in one long day of driving. Accordingly, we arose with the sun one morning, loaded the little MGB—which even just after dawn was already sizzling under the desert sun— and headed optimistically out of town. We were not as far as the outskirts when the dashboard gauge signaled that the engine was overheating. Some dumb gauge, we thought, and stopped to fill the radiator, just to be sure. Steve lifted the hood and the radiator cap blew off in his face. How strange, we thought; then we filled the radiator with water, and set out into the desert.

I would estimate that at least every hour in the course of a grueling, baking day, we had to stop to put water in the radiator. This is not easy in the desert, where gas stations are few and far between, but we had a gallon bottle of water with us and would use that when far from the sight of any watering places. Invariably, our arrival at any oasis was a colorful event, the car sputtering and smoking, the attendant rushing forward to bathe the engine and us with a continuous spray of blessed water. Halfway across the desert, the heat gauge gave out altogether; the car climbed the slightest hill only with great effort, knocking and banging, while we worried and fretted inside, the sweat running in rivers into our eyes and streaming down our chests.

By dusk, conditions seemed to improve, but at Flagstaff the radiator cap blew again, this time burning Steve painfully on his forehead and bare chest. Still, we pressed on toward New Mexico. It was night and finally the air was cool, but the radiator seemed to go dry just as quickly as in the heat of the day.

Somewhere past Gallup the poor old car simply gave up the ghost in a choking cloud of smoke, and we came to full stop by the side of the road in the middle of nowhere. It was about two o'clock in the morning, it was cold, all we had with us was a little water tasting by now of the plastic container it was in, and very few cars were passing. Every time we tried to start the motor again, it would wheeze and clank and subside, and more clouds of smoke would huff into the air and fill the passenger area. We didn't know what else to do but sit there in the dark until sunrise, when perhaps we could hitch a ride to the nearest garage. We considered the possibility that some samaritan might stop in the night, and the further possibility that he who stopped might be no samaritan. So we were not entirely tickled when a car hurtled past, braked, and began to back up toward us. As it backed nearer our vision, we saw it was a little Simca; and when four guys climbed out and started to approach, I said to Steve, "Oh, Jesus. I hope they're not planning to knock us in the head."

"I sorta wish they would," he said.

But it turned out that they had no such intentions. Maybe that's because we swaggered around the car in a method effort to simulate bulk, muscles and meanness, depending on the cover of darkness to obscure the truth; or maybe it was actually never in their heads at all to mug us. In any case, after taking a long survey of our plight, the driver of the Simca told us a long story of his need to reach Wisconsin in a great hurry, and his shortage of money. Here it comes, I thought—but all he proposed was that he push us into Alburquerque in exchange for a five dollar honorarium. Alburquerque was forty miles away over hill and dale, and the hills were the hard part. The little Simca huffed and puffed but could never get us up an incline at any speed greater than five miles an hour. We kept fearing that our benefactors would give up the effort in disgust, but they held on, and by five-thirty or so in the morning, we crested a rise and saw all Alburquerque spread out below us, a network of twinkling green lights, like a flattened Emerald City.

We made the last long downward slope into town at something like seventy miles an hour, whizzing silently through out-lying streets and watching frantically for traffic which never came, and the Simca pushed us the last blocks into the center of town, where we came to rest finally in the parking lot of the Hilton Hotel. In the thinning darkness, we gratefully paid our samaritans a double fee, and they set out again on their inter-rupted trek to Wisconsin. We then called the AAA, and saw our MGB hauled off to the only foreign-car dealership in town.

Standing by later in the garage, like anxious relations of the ailing patient, we got a lecture from the mechanic on what we had done to the poor old car, which had been signaling to us from dawn of the previous day that it was too ill to travel. We had very nearly burnt the little motor to a cinder; the mechanic showed us the ravages, the scoring of the pistons and rings, the melted bits and parts. All because we didn't know that desert heat alone could not cause such overheating; all because we couldn't recognize that the thermostat was faulty; all because we were stupid, idiotic, criminally ignorant of the internal-com-bustion engine; all because we wanted to be where we wanted to be When We Wanted To Be There, and too bad for the ma-chines charged with carrying out our will.

As the mechanic disassembled the remains, I grimly faced the fact that I did not know a piston from a lollypop; I was deeply ashamed, and horror-stricken at the estimates of what it would cost us to put the MGB back into working order, and the time it would take—five days, at least. We'd have to send home for money, like delinquent boys; what's more, we'd have to rent a car in order to visit the Taos communes. More money down the drain. At the emergency ward of a local hospital, an intern took a quick look at Steve's burns, prescribed an ointment, and charged us twenty dollars. Still more dues we had to pay for our foolishness. We began to face the fact that at least a degree of Steve's strange affinity for heat, fire, and flames had to be blamed on the fact that, in practical matters, he was often a clod.

When we went back to the Hilton, and before we fell into a restless mid-day sleep, we agreed that Princeton and MIT had been very mistaken to give us degrees. What sort of society is it, we wondered, that turns out imbeciles like us from the nation's finest institutions, alleging that we are educated, when we don't know the first thing about how to operate and care for the most ubiquitous machine in our lives? A pretty dumb society, we decided—very nearly as dumb as we were. We could not see our misuse of the MGB as anything but wicked, ignorance being no excuse whatever but indeed the cause of the loss. There we are, millions of us, zooming all over the country every day in cars that might as well be magic carpets for all we understand of their mysteries. We thought of the two or three communes we'd heard of, where no one is permitted to possess any machine he cannot take apart and put together again. A damn good policy, we concluded; we'd been getting a free ride and glorifying our ignorance for too long. We determined to sign up for courses in auto mechanics at our earliest opportunity. Stupidity like ours was intolerable in any sensible man; for God, it was nothing short of sacrilege.

GOING TO THE MOUNTAIN

Steve stuck his head out the window as we approached Taos in our rented Volkswagen. "There's nothing to breathe," he exclaimed, inhaling dramatically through flared nostrils. "The air is so thin there's no air in it. No wonder people go up on mountains to meditate; they're probably half stoned on lack of oxygen to start with."

We agreed that the feeling of slight lightheadedness was a pleasant trip, and that the altitude of nearly 8,000 feet must have a great deal to do with the evolution of Taos as the "spiritual center" of the communal movement. What a place for contemplation—closer by far to the infinite than anywhere on the dank, smoggy plain. The town had rich associations with the avant-garde; from every demi-generation since D. H. Lawrence, they had come here for retreat, renewal, and rejuvenation. The Indians of the Taos pueblo were legendary for their faith and mysticism. It was undoubtedly something in the air.

Yet the town itself was so ugly, with supermarkets in simulated adobe, and CONOCO stations in pressed plastic—one of them lodged smack on the corner of the central plaza, which might otherwise have passed for a genuine Mexican zocalo. Here an A & W Rootbeer stand, there a MacDonald's Hamburger Drive-in—thus has American culture served a remarkable landscape and an ancient architecture. See Taos, and you cannot escape the realization of what pigs we tend to be. The Indians lived here for centuries at a very high level of civilization, and never scarred nature; we swagger in and in a matter of minutes can cheapen and demean and prostitute anything naturally beautiful.

The center of town seemed peaceful enough in early evening, and we were somewhat surprised. After reading so many alarming reports in underground papers of violence in Taos, outrages done by chicanos against hippie types, I guess we expected fistfights and head-bashings to erupt the minute we got to town. Instead, the main plaza was practically deserted, very quiet, and at first glance, quite charming. The fanciest restaurant in town served us our dinner without demur, despite our hair and beards, and as I sipped my after-dinner coffee, feeling content and well-fed, I put forward the theory that all these alarmist articles in the underground papers were part of a conspiracy between the locals and the hippies to discourage further emigration. It turned out later that, in some ways, I was right; but it was by no means an amicable conspiracy.

From the restaurant we called Channing Brewer, a local rancher, the friend of a friend, and begged a corner of his garden for the night. Our idea was to throw our sleeping bags under a tree, but he turned out to be much more hospitable than that. After we had driven far out of town and past the little community of San Cristobal, we came to his spread and found him waiting with coffee on the stove, and beds made up in his bunkhouse for us. Channing's wife Mary had gone to bed, but he said they'd agreed that we should make ourselves at home that night in the bunkhouse, and were welcome to move up to their mountain ranch the next day, and stay there as long as we liked. He was a thorny fellow; he seemed not to want to give us the idea we were welcome or anything like that. But he was infected with Western hospitality and, as if he couldn't help himself, he made us feel very much at home.

I don't know if you've ever visited ranches in the Southwest; for me, it's part of my childhood, and it was such a nostalgic pleasure to stretch out between clean sheets on that chill night in midsummer, in a ranch building redolent of the good smells of leather and woodsmoke, the air crisp and clean and, nearby, the sound of a mountain stream gurgling. There was moonshine flooding bright through the windows, a slight stir of wind in the willows by the water, and in the black sky every star picked out like a diamond winking on velvet. I'm a sucker for that kind of stuff, and I said to Steve before I fell asleep that, for the first time in days, I could honestly say that I was having a good time.

The next morning, over a breakfast of bacon and eggs that Mary cheerfully cooked for us, she and Channing started to bring us up to date on what had been happening that summer in Taos. I repeated my frivolous theory of a conspiracy between resident communards and local chicanos, and Channing allowed as how there had certainly been a conspiracy to keep hippies out of town, but purely as an effort to decrease bloodshed. "Some terrible things have happened here," he said. "Terrible. There have been at least two killings, innumerable rapes, countless acts of violence against the hippie kids. The more responsible newcomers have tried to discourage any more kids from coming here because they stand a good chance of getting killed."

Channing and Mary told us a whole string of horror stories— of communes invaded by bands of drunks, boys shot and girls raped; of gunshots fired through the windows of local hip establishments; of hitchhiking kids side-swiped and run down on the highways by speeding cars. "It's no accident," he said. "The largest complaint of patients who show up at La Clinica, the local free clinic, is from kids knocked down deliberately on the highways." What, we demanded to know, had prompted this orgy of blood-letting?

"It's not really a question of hair," Channing said, "although that's part of it. You have to understand that the local Mexican-American population—now they call themselves chicanos, although that used to be a forbidden word around here, like nigger—are very poor people who work very hard, who have very high standards of cleanliness and order. Their houses are absolutely scrupuloso, you know? They may be poor, but they are determined that they can be clean. They have very middle-class values if they have nothing else. And then for these kids to wander in here. Look, we had over four thousand long-haired kids in this town in the spring, strolling around, sitting on the sidewalks, doing as they pleased, from God knows where and going God knows where. There aren't two thousand people in the whole town, you know? We were overrun—or anyway, that's how a lot of local people looked at it.

"Then too, in some of the communes, the kids showed no respect for the ecology around here, pissing and shitting right in a stream that went down the mountain and was the sole water supply for a whole community, like San Cristobal here. They couldn't seem to understand that you dip water out of a stream for washing and bathing in country like this, arid country. Water is precious here. You share water with a neighbor and it means you are very good neighbors indeed. These kids don't understand how to use the water. I'd say the biggest source of violence here was how they misused the water. That, and the nudity.

"There was an incident, I say it was one incident, of some kid wandering into a little Mexican village near here wearing nothing but a penis sheath. God knows where he got it, it seemed to him okay to wear nothing else. But you have to re-member that these people have very rigid standards about that sort of thing, and this is a spread-out but small community, and in about fifteen minutes the story had grown until you heard tales of a naked orgy in the town square. I don't think for a minute that there was a fraction of the incidents that were finally reported and gossiped about, but one way and another, quite a climate of ill will got built up here. Until finally, the hotter young bloods started breaking heads. And that's when the local underground newspaper, the *Fountain of Light,* started warning hippies to stay away from here. One of the editors drove into the A & W Rootbeer Stand and, according to his story, he got hit right in the face while he was still sitting in his truck. So you could call it all a conspiracy if you like, because that is in a way what it was. But it was all in one direction; it was like a conspiracy between a saloon-keeper and the Mafia."

Later that day, through Channing, we met some of the communards who had been longest on the scene, and instrumental in founding such hip institutions as the General Store, the Information Center, and La Clinica. They had disbanded their communal groups, had got short haircuts, were wearing Western un-hip clothing; in short, as they admitted, they were in disguise. They were also in the process of liquidating their hip businesses and services. Said one: "I came to Taos because this is the community where I want to spend my life. I love this place. My hope now is to infiltrate the local artsy-craftsy scene, take a low profile, and exist. I've closed down my commune because my head's not there anymore. I may go back to it someday, but right now I'm in the process of legally moving people off my land. When I came here from San Francisco six years ago, I had a lot of hopes and dreams and enough money to make some dreams come true. It sounds corny to say it, but the dreams came out as nightmares and I just want to retreat for a while and think things out." The *Fountain of Light,* which had at times been a sprightly and interesting paper, was defunct. The General Store was in its last days of closing out its stocks of blue jeans, sunflower seeds, and astrology books. The Information Center was boarded up. Only La Clinica remained open for the sick and the maimed, operating with volunteer doctors and nurses from state hospitals, and drugs and medicines begged from local physicians. "All the aspirin and stomach powders the chemical firms send for free," said one attendant, "but it sure is tough to try to get any penicillin." This despite the fact that, during and after the enormous hippie influx of the spring and early summer, the hepatitis and VD rates in Taos had zoomed astronomically.

These hip entrepreneurs, living now in single-family dwellings in a small community just outside the town, confirmed all Channing's reports of the misuse of land and water. "Water is precious in this country," said one. "So few of the new people understood that. They were absolute dreamers. There's only one way to live on the land, and that's the right way. Anything else is irresponsible. And yet we had people come here, try to drum up trade for the big Earth People's Park. You probably read about it. Their idea was for a huge rock festival, another Woodstock. They were going to raise a million ·dollars on it, and buy an

incredible amount of acreage, and open it as free land to anybody who wanted to live on it. Groovy. But when local people
pointed out some root truths to them, they didn't like it. Such
as, to have a festival with some 300,000 cars coming in on New
Mexico roads, it would take three days for the cars to get
parked. For that many people, you'd need three and a half miles
of latrines. But that wasn't the worst part. Somebody stood up in
the meeting and said it's terrific what you say about free land,
but what about the chicanos and Indians that live here and
have been living here for hundreds of years? How do they fit
into your program? And do you know what those dudes said?
They said, Oh, too bad for them. It'll take us good heads easy
fifteen years to get our thing together, and maybe then we'll
worry about whether those like Indians you talked about could
fit it.

"Fifteen years! What the hell were they talking about? Dudes
like that want to blow in here from LA and New York and tell
us about ecology, about the green revolution, about *people*, for
God's sake? The Indians aren't people? The chicanos aren't
people? Really, those dudes are crazies, they're completely out of
touch. They talk bullshit so fine they don't even smell it anymore."

TAPPING THE POWER

After our first orientation talks, we were unable to pass up
hitchhikers while driving around Taos. And I do mean "around";
the town itself is very small in area, and most people who say
they live there really ought to explain that they live eighteen
miles west, ten miles south—long drives through rugged, open
country, far from such amenities as supermarkets and rootbeer
stands. Sometimes we would become so enamored of the handsome country that we would chug past hitchhikers without re-
membering to pick them up—digging a bowl-like sky so big and

so huge, clouds moving in such massive armadas, endless views out over Dalmatian plains toward monumental blue mountains in the distance. It seemed that Taos and all its surround were part of some vast mesa, broken by arroyos and valleys into a dipping, sweeping geography, a giant mountain plateau. Even from a vantage no higher than the highway, we could sometimes see a hundred miles straight ahead, and rarely fewer than twenty. In this open magnificence, the sky was always changing, the light always different; it was hard to concentrate on refugees beside the road.

But when we noticed in time, we always did pick up people, though we could never take them very far. They were always cheerful, always grateful, always called us "brother." I remember one very hairy boy who beguiled our ride by raving about the natural foods trip he was on in his commune. It was near Santa Fe, he told us, and he dug into his knapsack to offer us fresh apples and peaches and plums that he had helped to raise in the communal orchard. He pushed them to us in the front seat as if he had personally invented fruit. But he had a sad story to tell. "You may have read about us in *Rolling Stone*," he said. "Dudes from *Stone* came along and brought wine and stuff and wanted to write us up as psychedelic cowboys living on a macrobiotic diet; it was all bullshit but we got drunk so we went along and made everything up and had a ball. It was in the magazine, too. And the part about the vegetarian trip, the natural grains and fruit was true, we were doing that. Until just lately one of the guys went out and shot a deer and skinned it, and a lot of our people were tempted, and ate the meat. I didn't know where my family was *at*! I couldn't cut it, man, I couldn't see that; we made a pledge we weren't into eating flesh, you know? I could not dig that, it blew my mind that everybody would eat that shit. So I'm hitching out to Fort Collins, Colorado, where I've got a couple of buddies. I want to lay out with them for a while, and try to get my head straight about that flesh shit, dig it? That was really heavy, man. Hey, have a plum."

One night at dusk, heading toward San Cristobal, we saw two lovely young girls hitchhiking, and stopped to pick them up. We couldn't take them far; our purpose was to warn them against being on the roads at all after dark. But we just couldn't get our message over to them. They were high school students from Denver, nice girls from nice families, pretty and blond and sweet and stupid, and they would not believe us that they were in any danger from side-swiping and worse. "Oh, brother, thank you for being worried, but really, we're perfectly okay. Nobody would want to hurt us." I hit my head with the heel of my hand in frustration. "It's true," I said. "You *are* in danger. People will hate the very sight of you. *Please* be careful."

"We will," they said, like two cheerleaders leaving home for the Big Game, and jumped out of the car gaily, disbelieving. I hope they got to Denver all right.

Then there was the case of the mother and children—this one really made me angry. While visiting communes we'd often give a lift when leaving to people who wanted to go to town for some reason or other; this time we were staying the night, high on a mountaintop, and planned to leave the next morning. Wandering around the edges of the commune was a young woman with two small boys. She asked if, when we left, she could come along with us. She'd come from Santa Cruz, she said; just threw over her whole life there, spent most of her money on bus fare, and came straight to Taos. Her children, about five and four years old, were obviously at home anywhere, playing with the odd old dog, chatting up anybody who'd pause to talk to them. She and the boys had hitched and walked eighteen miles to this particular commune, having to climb a mountain to get there, only to find that the commune would not accept stragglers and itinerants. So there was nothing to do but tramp back to town again, and wander up some other mountain.

The communards offered her and the children a shelter for the night, but she refused, and instead camped in our car, the three of them sleeping in their clothes, curled up tight against the mountain chill. Next morning when we drove them toward town again, the woman said she still had forty-five dollars left, and thought maybe she'd better use it to buy some old car; obviously these communes were hard to get to. Both the kids had noisy respiratory complaints, with lots of wheezing and coughing—no life for children, I thought, knowing it was none of my business but deploring the dim-bulb woman for trekking like this, cross-country, with so little regard for the kids. What was she looking for, we asked. She didn't know, she said, but whatever it was, it would be better than Santa Cruz.

Steve and I had not yet been to Our Thing, a large commune occupying a substantial residence very near the center of town. We asked if she'd like us to take her there, and listlessly she shrugged and said it was as good as the next place. So we drove through the streets of the town and came at length to the large gray house that had been pointed out to us as the new home of Our Thing.

I knew a little bit about them from times past. They had been shown on ABC-TV in a documentary on communes, and I knew from the film that they numbered more than fifty people, considered themselves all married to one another, and lived very much cheek by jowl in cramped quarters. I knew from a former *Time* correspondent, who had dropped out to join them for a time, that they were almost all very highly educated young people, and that they believed in free sexuality to such an extent that if a new girl brought gonorrhea into the commune, twelve to fifteen guys would have the drip within three days. He'd also told me that they had spent much of the previous winter making a film about their own life, expecting that proceeds from it would be sufficient to enable them to buy land and settle permanently in the Taos area. "But the film sucked," he said. "They couldn't even get a distributor for it, it was so bad. And it *was* bad. It took them a long time to face that fact—they wanted success so bad that they couldn't believe in failure, and they were so stunned by their own perfection that they lost all their critical faculties. They had no perspective. There are a lot of good people there but I couldn't stand it. I had to split." And I knew from local advice that they were given over to what Channing Brewer called "the lord and lady business," addressing each other by those titles, and changing their names as they pleased. "Their leader is a rather impressive young black named, at the moment, Lord Cronos," Channing told us. "For a while he was Lord Alfred, but the fashion seems to have shifted to the archaic."

When we drove up into Our Thing's front yard, we saw three young men working on the engine of a car parked in front of the porch. Our passenger and her children zeroed in on one of them. we concentrated on another, and for a while we lost track of the woman's fortunes. We told the young man we'd like to meet Lord Cronos, and he invited us into the living room to wait while he inquired.

In the living room, which was reasonably spacious, Our Thing was having breakfast. But as we pushed our way through the throng, it occurred to me that breakfast with the commune seemed a lot more like the evacuation of Singapore, as portrayed by the occupants of Dempster House with assistance of girls from Radcliffe, after the manner of Shakespeare. The room was carpeted in young men and women eating eggs and bacon; there were few children, but many babes in arms, and a great riot of noise and energy, all in a cheerful mode. "Has Lady Jane had her eggs?" one long-haired girl inquired of another, in my hearing. "Ask Lord Filbert if he wants some coffee," said another.

Directly the young man returned and said that Lord Cronos would see us in his office down the hall. This turned out to be a small bedroom with a crowded desk, a few chairs, and a bunk in the corner. Several young men were sitting around in apparent attendance upon Lord Cronos, a tall black man who stood, shaving with an electric razor, in the center of the room. He received us very civilly, reaching out his hand to be shaken and saying, "Hi! I'm Lord Cronos." It occurred to us only later that the proper response would have been something like, "Hi! I'm Peanut Butter, and this is Jelly." But at the time we dully gave our legal names, and shook hands like nice boys.

It is perhaps ill-mannered of us to have been, and to remain, a little scornful of Our Thing. They were very hospitable, offering us breakfast and/or coffee, and in conversation they very quickly spoke to us of The Power, an energy that had been on them forcefully for several months, and had recently inexplicably vanished. It was Lord Achilles, an attractive, blond young man, who spoke most candidly about the situation. "We had the power strongly, we felt it and saw it," he said. "There was nothing we couldn't do; our only problem was in deciding how to channel it.

So we directed all our efforts into the making of a film about ourselves."

We asked if they would release the film soon.

"No," said Achilles. "We've shelved the film for the time being."

"May we see it?" we asked.

"No," said Achilles. "We think it's better to let it rest right now."

One down, I thought. They have the power, or had it, but they're not prepared to admit that they made a rotten film.

"I understand," I said, "that for a long while you were staffing the general store."

"Yes, we were," said Achilles. "But we decided to withdraw our energies from that, and direct them elsewhere."

Two down, by God. We knew they had been fired from the operation of the general store, and for cause. But once again, lies and evasions. No wonder they had lost the power.

"We feel," said Achilles, Cronos nodding, "that the power comes in waves, hills and valleys. Right now we're in a valley, but we know that a hill has to come."

Not, I thought, as long as you aren't playing straight with yourselves. I've known many a middle-class worker to be fired from a job and say something very different about his situation, such as that he'd decided to direct his energies elsewhere. I'd expected a lot better of Our Thing. Steve and I did not have to communicate verbally to know that Our Thing was going to be in this particular valley for a long time. Politely but without lolling, we said we'd better go, and took ourselves off, through the throng of lords and leaders, to the front door.

As we drove away, we saw the woman and two children walking down the road. "I'm going to get my stuff," she said, "down at the bus station. They said they didn't have any room for us to stay there, but I could leave my junk until I find a room someplace. And they'll give us meals." We drove off, feeling a little bleak about the woman, and Our Thing, and communes in general, and spent the drive back to the ranch making up names for ourselves. But we never did come up with anything better than Peanut Butter and Jelly. Just about right for us, we thought.

PREPARING FOR THE PEYOTE FEAST

One morning while we were having breakfast with Mary and Channing, an old van pulled up in front of the ranch house and six girls, some with small children, piled out and stood around in the yard. "Oh," said Mary, "it's the Hesperus girls. We told them they could come over and take the apples from the orchard."

Mary went out to chat with the girls, who made a very pretty if peculiar grouping in their long, flowing print dresses. While directing the girls toward the orchard, she cut one of them out of the herd and brought her back into the kitchen. As they came in Channing said, "That's Mary Louise Ballard. We've known her parents for years; her father used to be in the state legislature."

Mary Louise was a lovely young girl with huge blue eyes and a soft, hesitant manner of speech. She had her baby with her, an infant of three months, in a deerskin pouch hung from her shoulder. Mary took the baby and Mary Louise sat down to have a cup of coffee. Channing asked after Homer, Mary Louise's ole man.

"Oh, he's fine," she said. "He's so happy with the baby. He just loves it."

"How are things up on the mesa?" Channing asked.

"Oh, fine," said Mary Louise. "We have about fifty people up there now, real nice people. We're having a big peyote feast on the weekend—that's why we wanted to get the apples today, because we want to make some pies and things for the feast."

Mary volunteered that Mary Louise had given birth to her baby up on the mesa. "How are you feeling, Mary Louise?" Mary asked.

For the third time Mary Louise said, "Oh, fine," and I decided that I had never encountered a more limited vocabulary in my life. But Mary Louise perked up a bit then, and began a monologue on the joys of childbirth on the mesa. "It was a beautiful birth," she said, looking dreamy. "All our friends came and we had just a wonderful time. I'd been practicing the LaMaze method, all the breathing exercises and all, and there were about thirty people there helping me with the panting during labor. And you know, thinking with me, and being with me. When the baby finally came I didn't have any pain, and everybody cried. Everybody held the baby, and then when the placenta came, everybody held that too. We had a big party, so much fun. It was just fine. Homer took a lot of pictures. Next time I come, I'll bring them and show you.

"After this I'd never have a baby any other way except with my friends. I was a little worried before—you know, I'd never had a baby, and my parents wanted me to go to a hospital and all. But I'll never go to a hospital to have a baby—it's so cold, like a factory. This was just a wonderful experience for everybody."

I said I thought it was maybe a little chancy to have a baby up on the mountain without at least a doctor in attendance. "Oh, I never went to a doctor," she said, as if it were the silliest notion in the world. "There's this girl in the commune who's real experienced at birthing babies; she's helped with about eleven births already, she's a real pro. She was there the whole time and she was wonderful.

"Well," she said, "I guess I better go out and help pick the apples. It's really nice of you all to let us have them." And then, to Steve and me, "If you're going to be here awhile, why don't you come up and see us?" We said we'd like to; that we had hoped to visit Hesperus because we were doing a book on communes. "Far out," said Mary Louise, hefting her baby and setting out for the orchard.

By chance we ran into Mary Louise and the baby, and her ole man Homer, the very next afternoon. They had come to town to do some food shopping for the peyote feast, were burdened with a load of groceries, and were glad to have a lift back up to the mountaintop. Homer was a tall, sallow young man with a Fu Manchu moustache, a Ho Chi Minh beard, Western clothes and a persistent giggle. "Freaky," Steve whispered to me. "Drug-freaky." He offered us a limp hand, a blank stare, a wide smile, and absolutely no conversation.

Following Mary Louise's directions, we drove about eighteen or so miles out of town, across the broad, stunning plateau, and turned off by a Standard Station onto a winding gravel road. A few miles up and then down, and through a deep gulch, and we came to an open gate, a rutty, muddy road, and very hard going. Lucky, we thought, that we had not tried to bring the MG into this country; we'd never have had a chance of making it. But the VW, so highly sprung, was just able to clear the large rocks and boulders that would have raked the bottom from any car built closer to the road. Power, however, had we none, and the last couple of vertical miles were climbed at a snail's pace.

Finally we got to the top of the mesa—mostly flat terrain of about two square miles in area, covered in scrub and cactus, with a small grove of trees near one corner. There was a parking area where a few old cars and vans were parked; we pulled in beside them, and Mary Louise and Homer invited us to their pueblo for crackers and cheese. We trudged through the low scrub and over a slight rise, and there before us was a clumsy but creditable simulacrum of an Indian pueblo, in miniature. Just as the Indians had done in these parts for centuries, the members of Hesperus were making bricks of mud and straw and building an ever-expanding apartment house—finished parts of the structure enclosed a central kitchen and some seven rooms; walls in process extended in several directions. "This is free land," Mary Louise explained. "Some people want to build rooms for themselves in the pueblo, but others are living in teepees in the grove, or in tents down the far side of the mesa, or whatever they want to do. It's all completely free and open here; you can live any way you want to."

We followed her to the pueblo, where alongside a mattress, shaded by the adobe wall and a square of canvas, Mary Louise pushed aside a hanging Indian blanket and stepped through a hole low in the wall. "We dug our room out," Homer volunteered. "Didn't feel like building up to the height of the rest of the pueblo. Anyway, it's cooler to be half underground and takes half the bricks, so we didn't mind digging." I slipped down through the hole and found myself in a cool, dim room, illuminated by a skylight in the ceiling. In the room were a mattress covered with another Indian blanket, a pile of cushions gathered into a bed for the baby, a set of shelves containing groceries and a few books, and in one corner what appeared to be clothes, folded and stacked. Homer knocked on the skylight and invited me to come up and test the sturdiness of the roof. I went outside, climbed a ladder onto the roof, and together we jumped up and down on the mud surface without dislodging so much as a pebble. Homer looked at me and grinned as if to say, "See!" Steve had wandered off to chat with some of the people standing about in the yard of the pueblo, and Homer and I climbed down from the roof, took places cross-legged on the mattress, and commenced silently to admire the fine landscape. Mary Louise's hand reached out of the hole, pushing a gladbag of marijuana and some papers toward Homer; without comment he took the stuff and set about rolling a joint.

Pretty soon Mary Louise wrestled her way out of the hole with a large round tray, filled with sliced cheeses, Triscuits, and taco chips. Then she returned to collect the baby and settled down with us to nurse. The sight of food and dope was sufficient to signal a party, and pretty soon ten or more young people were sitting with us, chatting, smoking, and munching cheese. At Hesperus people are not neighbors but family—what anybody has is everybody's, and it wasn't necessary to issue invitations to the party. People simply ambled over, rapped and partook, and ambled off again if they had some other place to be.

It was a very amiable crowd. One blond young man in khaki shirt and shorts ("They have the next room," said Mary Louise of him and the girl with him.) said he was AWOL from the army, and had been for over three months. He was very cheerful about it, not a bit worried. "I just can't do the army thing," he said. "For that matter, I couldn't do the Amherst thing either—but I can do this thing." There was Fred, an effulgently bearded, balding, and bespectacled man of about my age, very genial and well-spoken, who told funny stories about what it was like to be an assistant professor in the University of California system, shaking his head intermittently with disbelief that he had ever been in such a fix. There was a pretty girl named Kathy, accompanied by a toddler, who engaged in rough-house banter with the guys and talked about her straight, air force husband in Colorado Springs. A couple of the girls sat up on the mattress alongside Mary Louise, passing a joint three ways and discussing what they were going to fix for the feast. Mary Louise said she had a neat idea for a bean pot, and discussed the spices she would use. "My mother used to have this wonderful recipe for rice casserole," said another girl. "You take sliced mushrooms and mushroom gravy . . ." And it was then that I realized that, while the mothers of America are worried to death about what their daughters are doing up on those awful mountaintops, their daughters are up there gossiping about their mothers' casseroles. It struck me that we had fallen into a scene precisely as middle class as if we had gone to visit family friends in Wichita. The only difference, really, was that the social ice-breaker wasn't booze but marijuana. And the girl went on, ". . . and then you dice the pimiento and sprinkle it over the melted cheese . . ."

Well, there *was* one other difference. As we sat chatting in a little circle, I saw on a path in the far distance a strange procession advancing toward us. In the lead was a very tall young man wearing a blond crewcut and a blanket and that's all. Behind him straggled two girls, similarly covered. As they came along Indian-fashion, they walked very strangely, more in a shuffle and dip than a stride; and as they grew near, I saw that they seemed to be entranced, eyes tightly shut. And they were chanting. Navajo sorts of sounds, low, open-voweled, and repetitive. They approached, heads bobbing, to the very edge of our dope-smoking circle, and somebody was just saying, "Please pass the Triscuits" when the blond leader cut sharply and bowed to enter a room in the pueblo. The girls followed. Soon, from inside the room, I heard sounds of a drum being rhythmically beaten; the chant quickened, and was louder, and seemed to go on and on.

Meanwhile, the light was slowly fading, and at a point Fred looked up from the quiet high we were all, at that moment, enjoying, and said, "Oh-oh. It's about time." Abruptly everybody got up and started to move around the corner of the pueblo. I glanced questioningly at Homer. "Sunset," he whispered. And I followed the group around the corner. On the far side of the building, we were very near the edge of the mesa; the view of fields and valleys stretched some 150 miles to the horizon, where the sun burned like an orange ball, already half-obscured in low cloud.

Some of my new friends had taken up yogic postures facing

the sun; others simply stood quite still, watching. People had fallen at once into prayer, meditation, or simply intense concentration. I stood quite still myself, simply drinking in all there was to notice of the spectacle, and there was plenty. As the sun sank, spilling horizontal shafts of yellow, purple, and green into the low cloud formation, the blue of the sky deepened toward inky blue, and the golden light flooding our faces and the whole scene began to fade, passing through a whole spectrum of subtlest change. A young man knelt in tall grass just ahead of me, his arms raised and stretched before him, casting a light shadow which deepened steadily as the gold paled. The reverberations from that sunset were profound, and it was some while before I realized that standing very near me was a tall, red-haired young man, wearing buckskins and a head band, whom I hadn't met before. He was gazing at me intently when I turned to look at him.

"My name is Jason," he said, fixing me with bright, wide blue eyes. "Dick," I replied, holding out my hand to shake his.

"No, Dick," he said, taking my hand in both of his. "Let's not shake hands like that. Let's shake hands like this." And he grasped my wrist with his palm and fingers, so that our hands and arms were intertwined. Then he stood with me a long time like that, staring directly into my eyes. "Isn't this better?" he whispered. "Because this way, I feel that more of me is touching you, and more of you is touching me. I want more of you to touch me. Do you feel the same?"

"Uh . . . sure," I said, a little bit disturbed.

"I knew you'd feel that," he said. "You seem to me to be a very beautiful person."

"Thank you," I said, interested now in detaching and looking elsewhere, but still held by his eyes. "You're . . . ah . . . a very beautiful person too."

"Tell me, Dick," he said, still gripping and staring, "don't you feel that we're the *same* beautiful person?"

"Well . . . uh . . . duh." I couldn't produce a coherent answer before he said, "Dick, have you accepted Jesus Christ into your heart and soul as your only lord and savior?"

More gutturals and aspirants from me.

"You have, Dick, I can feel that you have. And this is what

makes us one in the spirit and one in the flesh. We are one mind and one body, the mind and body of Jesus. It's a wonderful thing, isn't it, to be cradled in Jesus?"

"Oh, yes," I said, "yes, indeed."

The boy released my hand, wrapped his arms around my shoulders and held my head tight against his chest.

"I have to go now," I said with some difficulty, my mouth squashed sideways.

"Go with Jesus, Dick," he said, releasing me. And I did.

HINTS OF THE REAL HIT

Stan Coleman, the founder and leader of Lyra Foundation in Taos, is the single most impressive communard I met in two years of wandering the field. He has spent nine years in the communal movement, and is now absolutely sure that he knows exactly what he wants from community and how to achieve it. If clarity of purpose and confidence in method are admirable characteristics, then Stan Coleman demands a great deal of admiration. He has but one principle, which serves him over all the levels of his relationships in the world, from the proper method for preserving the purity of a stream to the best way to deal with other human beings: "Don't pass your load on."

I suppose that everybody in Taos stops in now and then to visit Channing and Mary Brewer; it was perhaps inevitable that Stan Coleman would show up there one morning while Steve and I were once again free-loading breakfast at Mary's table. "Here comes Stan Coleman," said Channing, almost reverently, as a tall and handsome man in work clothes, with a leonine mane of golden hair, dismounted from a sputtering jeep and approached the kitchen door. "This is just a social call," he announced to Mary and Channing. "I have no business to be down off the mountain this morning, except to get the mail, and I'll have to do chores all afternoon to pay for the indulgence, but I wanted to see you." He smiled warmly, and it was clear that they were flattered to be honored with a visit.

After introductions and explanations, Stan settled at the kitchen table with a cup of coffee in his hand and told us a little bit about his commune, which he calls an ashram—Lyra. "I'm thirty-two," he said. "So's my wife Kim. We've been living in one kind of community or another for nine years, and now we think we know what we're doing. People always ask me what's happening at Lyra. And the thing is that nothing is happening, nothing at all. That's the way we want it.

"You may remember USCO, our first commune. We were into light shows and lighting environments in New York. Now that's a pretty good example of what we didn't want here. People at USCO were always running down personal scenes and making extraneous scenes and putting things together and getting up projects and Lyra is definitely not like that. Because at Lyra we don't have time for personal trips of any kind. We lead a very disciplined life—we wake up at four in the morning, we're at meditation by four-thirty, we eat breakfast together at six-thirty, and then we work together in the fields until two-thirty in the afternoon, which is when we have our major meal. Then we're free to do personal chores, that we sign up for by the week, and everybody's got at least six a day, before the evening meal at six. Then at eight-thirty we meet again for meditation until ten, and it's time for bed. Every week one person is named to be the hawk, the policeman, who's supposed to be sure that everybody does his regular work and the chores he signed up for; this is so everybody gets a chance to understand every job, including the job of pig, which is a legitimate job that everybody should be on the inside of.

"In the summers we have a series of seminars that help us to pay our way. We invite all kinds of teachers, older people, because we want to be responsive to other people's trips, and we have a lot to learn from older people, and we ask them in to lay their trips on us. And a lot of the people who sign up to attend these seminars want to play their games with us and run their numbers down with Lyra people. They often accuse us of being unresponsive and unkind. So when somebody goes into that too much we put him in a corner and all bow down to him and ask him if that's what he wants. We are not interested in these personal little trips, these ego feeds. We have very simple needs—we need to get our hands into the soil, we need to be in touch with what we're doing. Did you know that in Sanskrit, the word for 'mud' and the word for 'the divine will of God' are the same word? It's all the same with us too. Once you finally get down to doing what you want to do, it comes to doing what you need to do, and as human beings we need to grow our food and live. It's as simple as that.

"We are free, completely free, but within certain bounds. We believe in complete sexual freedom, with the proviso that nothing and nobody be destroyed. We're absolutely against destruction— no firearms is one of our rules, because firearms destroy. We don't hunt; we're vegetarians. Same with sex; we believe in the complete elimination of violence in interpersonal relations. So there isn't really very much sexual exploration. We had a hard time last year because a true love affair just about tore the community apart; we won't have that. We want to eliminate all negative vibes, and these intense personal emotions put other people in negative places.

"Two years ago, when we were just a year old, just getting going, we did a lot of gestalt therapy, used all those encounter techniques, stuff like that. But now we feel we've passed through that stage, into leaving each other alone. You give people a chance and they'll all work out their own scenes on you. Husbands and wives will try to do that in front of other people, because those scenes are interesting to the people who are making them, and they want to bring in an audience and involve them. And that's interesting for you too; you incline to want to get into those people and their scene, but usually not enough to stop the bad vibes or get control of their heads and put them in a better place. So the net result is that everybody is brought down, the level of the whole community is lowered. It's counter-productive to the extent that we just don't have that anymore. We try to leave people alone, not put them on other trips. We, each of us, leave all the others alone, in order to leave the community alone to develop in whatever directions it wants to go in. Like in the winter months, except for the regular farm chores, there really isn't much to do, and we don't even see each other very much. Everybody sort of hibernates, everybody retreats to his own little things.

"We believe in privacy, everybody to his own cottage in the woods, no living closely. We have a fine communal kitchen but you know how, especially during her menstrual cycle, a woman would rather not see any other women; well, for that, every woman has her own burner in her own kitchen and can do her own cooking in that time. We want everybody to have a door he can shut until he doesn't *have* to shut it anymore. Meanwhile, architecturally we're very together; we work on building doors too. And we look for the day when we'll rise above the necessity to be alone, the necessity for solitude, but meanwhile that's a concrete necessity. When it's not, the doors will disappear.

"Most of us have lived in a lot of communes; we're veterans. No more myths and fantasies. We've been through plenty of drug trips, drug communes, arts-oriented communes. That's all in the past. We're on a hard-facts trip now. Like, if you're admitted to Lyra, it's on a trial basis. You stay six months and then you're kicked out. You have to go back to your old scene, old street, old job, old college, and run all the old numbers down again. For another six months. Then—if you come back, it's because you really want to, because you've rejected the other trips. That's when Lyra becomes central. And don't forget what you're taking on—a system with a lot of rules, an absolute prohibition against any kind of drugs, including tobacco and drugs, very detailed work responsibilities, hours of rising, working, eating, sleeping, hours for prayer and chanting. And you have an enormous personal responsibility not to fuck up the community itself by fucking yourself up. You have to follow the rule."

I said he made Lyra sound like a monastic order. "We've had advice from many monastics," he said readily. "We've had Benedictines with us; we've had Indian gurus of a variety of religious disciplines. We've had Bishop Shannon, who was recently bounced from the Catholic Church. All the religious people who have come have not liked our thing, have thought we were too scrupulous, but they've all admitted that we at least have integrity.

"Our trip is simply a very highly structured soil and spirit trip. And we feel there's such a clear connection between those two things that there is no possibility for anything more basic. That's where we want to be; so as I say, nothing is happening, nothing is going on. We get up, we pray, we eat, we work, we go to bed. We do the very basic things because we want to do them, because we've learned that these are the things that fulfill us. To other people our life seems terribly dull. They're quick to say nothing is happening. But to us, everything is happening.

"On the larger scale, we see how we can be economically self-supporting before too long. In three years we've managed not only to keep ourselves together but we have gone from an almost wholly subsidized effort to about fifty percent self-sufficiency. We're entering the fourth year of our first five-year plan (we do *not* try to imprison ourselves exclusively in the Now) and in a year and a half I expect we'll be one hundred percent self-sufficient. We're looking for sideline profit-making activities— like we expect to begin a cottage industry in leather-working, because a couple of our members are trained in that. We're practical Marxists but, apart from our own operation, we're apolitical. And when we are economically sound ourselves, then we'll be in a position to deal on a wholesome basis with the remainder of the community—I mean the global community, the community of the world.

"Of course, we have our problems—life goes along in a kind of wavy line, just like ordinary energy, rise and fall, hills and valleys. And we've been studying how we can stay up when we're up, or at least minimize the down when we head down. The trick is to try to ride the peaks of those waves the way a surfer does, to try to make a general flow out of those wavy lines. And so far as cooperative living is concerned, we think the way to do it is really deep down to allow everybody and accept everybody doing his own thing. In other words, if you have a number that you want to do on other people, Lyra won't necessarily pay any attention to that, because it's counter-productive for them to be brought down on your bad trip. What we're into is supporting you right up front, but supporting you by our own strengths of personality, not being touched by your bad trip, giving example, in other words. So that you can follow our example and *not* lay your trip on other people, good or bad. Just do your thing contained in yourself.

"Like I say, people call us cold. It's true we don't do a lot of hugging and kissing and carrying on. We're into much more serious stuff than that. We take our responsibilities to each other as a kind of trust which is not verbalized, it's demonstrated. If I'm cutting wood fifteen miles from home with a Lyra member, and the truck breaks down, and in these woods the only thing to do is walk back; and if that member has his two-year-old child with him, I take it for granted that I share in the job of carrying that baby. That's just assumed. We don't have to talk about it or do a whole verbal thing about please and thank you. Or it's more basic than that. We're into architecture; we're doing very hard, complicated construction. So, say I'm dangling from a rope thirty feet off the ground, setting a beam in place, and a ninety-pound girl is holding the other end of that rope to keep me airborne. Well, if she fails, if she drops the rope, I'm dead. And we don't need to hug and kiss each other to know how important we are to each other.

"Look—when strong people come together, they generate a lot of extra-psychic energy, and it has to be channeled into exterior projects. This is one of the reasons we are doing so much architecture. First of all, I think that when you are doing a new thing, you have to have new spaces to do it in. You can't do new things in old rooms, you have to revise everything, start fresh. And what's more, it's a very good way to absorb all that energy, that would tear you apart if you just sat there vibrating. And in turn the architecture provides you with an outside face, an orientation to the rest of the world, an image they can deal with. We share a conviction that we are a part of God, but at the moment only an infinitesimal part, a baby part. We're only learning. Meanwhile, we need a worldly orientation, not only for others but for ourselves. And we feel that, in doing the old, the ancient things—the growing and the building—we are participating in God as directly as we can."

Stan stood up, stretched, and began to stride about the room.

"As for riding the crest of the wave—what's the usual experience? A bunch of people get together and they develop a com-

mon consciousness and exert an enormous amount of energy
toward one another, the sum total of which seems to be greater
than all the parts. They then have this incredible extra psychic
energy at which they're all amazed. So let's call that reality for
a moment, and reality insists that they *do* something. And there
are communes around Taos that have run half-cocked into all
kinds of crazy schemes, filming the communal life, that sort of
thing, projecting the thousands of dollars they're going to make.
Anyway, figures far in excess of what their capabilities actually
are. So in the grip of this thing the outside world comes to seem
trivial by contrast, and their fantasies spiral and inflate. And
then the film or whatever turns out to be a bust, *not* the realization of the fantasy outstripping reality, but reality itself. Which
is hard to face. So it seems that there is, after the creation of
this synergy, a down, a valley. You don't know what to do with
yourself, you're confused, you suffer an IDR—an identity diffu-
sion reaction—a breaking down into pieces, in which all the little
separately held fantasies fail to connect into any major sur-
reality. And the power falls off, dissipates.

"Some communes still manage to hold together, on remem-
brance of things past, in reflection on the utopia they briefly
had and confidently hope will rise again. But at Lyra we don't
press so hard anymore. There, we never did. IDR is counter-
productive, fantasy is counter-productive. We tend the soil. The
soil does not fail. We build our houses; we build them well.
There is no fantasy in that, no bullshit—just basic reality.

"I'd like you to come up and see what we're doing, but we
don't have any guests during the week. The earliest I can invite
you is for Saturday afternoon; after Saturday morning we rest
until Monday. Saturday would be best. There are only seventeen
of us up there right now, and on Sundays we're open to the
public so everybody hides, goes off in the woods or to town or
someplace, because it is so heavy to talk to people who just don't
know where you are. But if you come on Saturday I think you'd
find people around and it would be good."

After Stan took his leave, ruing the many chores he would
have to do once he got back, Channing and Mary, who had been
as silent as we had through his long monologue, looked at us
with amazement. "Well," said Channing. "That's about ten

times as much as I've ever heard Stan Coleman say in all the
many times we've met. And I never heard him on the subject of
Lyra. Remarkable about the discipline . . . but what does he
mean about the waves, and the surfboard, and all that God
business?"

Steve and I swore we didn't have the least idea.

We were delighted to have met Stan Coleman. We thought
that he had made Lyra sound almost unnecessarily severe in its
discipline; surely it couldn't be that stiff. But it was hard to
doubt him in anything, and we were struck almost speechless to
find that his metaphors were ours, even though applied to what
was clearly the most substantial and impressive communal establishment in Taos, and not to some fly-by-night foursome in
Pacific Heights.

THE MOUNTAIN THAT MELTED

Early on Saturday afternoon, Steve and I eagerly set forth on
our visit to Lyra. We had to drive north more than twenty-five
miles—once more across the endlessly exciting, empty plateau—to
find the turn-off for Lyra. And then we were on a grisly gravel
road that passed through rocky country and desolate pine woods,
and it was a long time before we spotted the first sign that we
were on the right road—the palm of a hand, etched in a piece of
wood with a hot knife, secured to the trunk of a tree.

Many miles onward, we saw the hand again, and an arrow
pointing to a vertical clay road to the left. We climbed the steep
road slowly but steadily for another several miles before finally
coming upon a large sign advertising sunbursts, peace, freedom, and love, and the suggestion that visitors stay out except
on Sundays. Here we parked the car and continued on foot,
counting on Stan Coleman to remember his invitation to us and
not throw us down the mountain on our ears.

A light, cold rain was falling as we trudged up the dirt road
for about a half-mile, through heavy pine woods. Directly, we

spotted an unfinished geodesic dome through heavy cover on our right, and shortly after emerged into a vast clearing, where a field of high, pale-yellow grasses rippled for many acres up a slope. At the crest of this open field stood a most magnificent building—a startling sight at 9,000 feet in the wilderness, but somehow exactly right, as if raised up in that place by nature itself. Fantasies of Shangri-La danced in my head as I studied its huge, towering central dome, a complex of triangles faceted with panels of glass that took blazing light from a very uncertain sun and the rushing clouds that sped across is. The building was of mudded adobe, tan in color, and filled with octagonal windows of every size, these too winking and flashing with reflections of the fast-moving sky. Looking out in the direction the windows faced, I had an incredible view out over mesas and valleys far below, a vista of some 250 miles, alive with ripe color and the purple shadows of the racing clouds.

Behind this main building was a smaller, taller, octagonal building—not really taller, as we looked more carefully, but higher on the crest, so that its two stories towered over the dome in front. Its walls were a series of small panes of glass, so that the whole of it flashed and twinkled like a jewel. Steve, a few yards ahead of me on the path, looked around with a wide grin, as if to say that this is the place, this is what we've been looking for. There was a distant drumroll of thunder from the mountains, and the rain came on harder against our faces. We interpreted this natural orchestration as a good omen. I thought to myself, well maybe, maybe this *is* the place that's really together. It looked so very fine.

Through the waist-high grasses we approached the front of the vast building, and searched for an entrance, but we couldn't seem to find one. Clearly, the structure wasn't finished yet—we located a small oaken door to one side, but no steps up to it. By placing a board as a bridge, we were able to climb up and enter what was, at first glance, a raw and unfinished room. But we saw that, viewed liberally, it was perhaps the most complete room ever invented. There was a huge Navajo-style adobe fireplace, shelves and shelves of books rising to a ceiling of over twenty-five feet, low, comfortable furniture, a mass of shaggy rugs—a sort of Jules Verne library flooded with the riot of purple, blue and gold lights from the roiling sky outside. We passed from there into the huge dome room itself. It was a magical space, perhaps seventy-five feet across, unfinished, filled with light from the glass facets in the arching ceiling. There was in the air the smell of raw lumber and sawdust; it was a fresh and glamorous space. As we crossed it, the woman and two boys I mentioned earlier emerged from a room on the far side. We greeted them but they said nothing; passing through the door they had exited from, we entered a room similar to the library, containing another arched Navajo fireplace, a large loom, some odd pieces of furniture and various pieces of art—Our Lady of Guadaloupe, some Navajo work, a crucifix or two—mostly religious art and very handsome. Leaning on the loom was a lovely blond girl wearing ski clothes. She said her name was Wanda.

We explained Stan Coleman's invitation; Wanda said she didn't know about it, but was prepared to believe it. Stan and his wife Kim were, she said, on a shopping trip to town, but she'd be glad to show us around. She said that the woman and children had arrived on foot just before us, and that she'd like to feed the kids, who seemed hungry. The woman said she had come to Lyra because she'd heard it was a good place. Wanda told her it was against Lyra's policy to take in strangers; but her heart was moved by the little kids, so she suggested that the mother take the children up to the octagonal house, which was the communal kitchen, and she would briefly show us the rest of the main building and be along in a moment.

Wanda said the room we were in was called the "only" room, because for a long time it had been the only room completed. She took us into an adjacent washroom, where seventeen washbasins stood in a row, with seventeen hooks and seventeen towels above them. Beyond that was a most magnificent room with a big, deep, sunken blue tub, suitable for at least twenty people at a time. A conventional, one-person tub was set beside it in the floor, presumably for loners. Casement windows on three sides gave a beautiful view of the outdoors, and everywhere there were fresh green vines hanging, and the lovely fresh smell of ferns and flowers. Wanda explained that a mountain spring had been piped into the bath, and she showed us a hidden heating system for warming the water.

Out the back door of the "only" room, we climbed a flagstone path through a meadow of colorful wild flowers, upward toward the octagonal kitchen, which turned out to be the most beautiful room I've ever seen in my life. Through heavy wooden doors, we entered an octagonal space supported in the center by four rough-hewn beams, the floor a sunburst of tiled strips radiating from the core, walls on all sides of casement windows, and counters and recessed refrigerators on all eight sides. There was hot and cold running water, there were bunches of fresh herbs tacked to the center posts to dry, and hanging from the beams. It was a fairy-tale kitchen—smelled good and was lovely to see.

Wanda got out some food for the children. She had fresh-baked loaves of stone-ground bread, honey from Lyra's own bees, goat cheese. While she made a meal for the children, Steve and I had a few crusts of the bread. It was delicious. Wary of waste, a little pan on the counter held all the crumbled crusts of other people's sandwiches, for anyone who wanted a bite.

A young man with a moustache entered the kitchen, introduced himself as Bruce, and turned to check the list of chores posted on the door. Bruce explained that he just wanted to be sure he'd done all his voluntary chores, because it was getting on toward time to milk the cow, and that was his steady, daily occupation. He invited me to join him, and we strode diagonally through the field of wildflowers again, into a grove of pines, where we came on a lovely weathered barn. Inside were several goats in three pens, and one pen empty. "This is Emmie's pen," Bruce told me, gathering up feed and buckets and other farmerly sorts of things. "Emmie is the cow."

While Bruce prepared the stanchions for his milking, he told me that he was a graduate of Antioch, class of 1957, and that until a year ago he had been an assistant professor of history at Hofstra College. He said he and his wife had started to do yoga quite seriously, that he had given up his teaching job to live in New Paltz all the previous year, working with a yogi, and had come out to spend the summer on the West Coast. Baba Ram Dass, formerly Richard Alpert, was a friend; he'd been to Lyra, and suggested they stop in on their way back to the East. "We came here on our way through," he said. "It took us just that one Sunday to fall in love with the idea of living here. We talked to all the members, waited for three days for them to decide whether we could come, and then we rushed back to New Paltz, sold everything we couldn't load in the car, and rushed right back. It was right for me. I wanted a place with a religious orientation, I wanted a community, and I wanted to work with basic questions, like the care of animals. I want to know how to care for them well. When I looked around for things to do here, I decided that the steady, invariable demands of a cow to be fed and milked interested me more than anything else. So now Wanda and I share the job. Wanda is a farm girl, raised on a New Mexico ranch. She knows all about animals; but I'm from New York City, I'm a greenhorn with no experience. I love doing this. I want to make it with this cow. If I can't make it with her, who *can* I make it with?"

We walked into the field and collected Emmie, a large black Hereford mix, from her tether. As the three of us walked back to the barn, Emmie made it clear that she had a distinct personality, and was most emphatically *the* cow around there. After Bruce secured Emmie's neck and began milking, Steve and Wanda wandered in from the kitchen. Wanda had noticed a hole in Steve's shoe, had assembled tape and cardboard, and had fashioned a reasonably serviceable temporary hold—serviceable so long as the rain let up, which it seemed to be doing. The four of us talked farming while Bruce and Wanda took turns milking. I haven't watched a milking since I was a small child, and Bruce enjoyed an audience. He went into some detail about what milking does to your hands, how they ache and hurt something awful until you're used to the job, how you learn to pull a teat, how much milk they get. Emmie is generous at two milkings daily, and with the goats giving milk as well, Lyra is flooded with good stuff, some of which they give away regularly to an Indian school nearby.

We could see daylight through chinks in the barn walls, and Bruce and Wanda said that one of their jobs for the fall would be to seal the barn as best they could. "But it'll be warmer in here this winter than you think" Wanda said. "The animals give off a very good body heat but the best source of heat is the shit; it steams a lot, you know. I don't expect the temperature in here ever to drop below zero."

Wanda led us out past the chicken coop, where a pretty girl in a long dress called to her for help in gathering some eggs. Then we wandered on to Lyra's "grow hole," a trench greenhouse, dug into a hillside, covered with plastic panels. The "grow hole" is planted year-round with tomatoes, beans, chard, and other vegetables, which provides the community with fresh green things in every season. We ate a ripe red tomato off the vine—it was ambrosial, and strictly organic.

Nearby was the sauna—a low, rounded hogan of canvas and skins—adjacent to two large ponds that absorb the overflow from the mountain spring. "We use the water in these ponds to water the vegetables," said Wanda, "and for cold plunges after the sauna. Except in winter; then, we can just run out and roll in the snow."

Wanda led us ever upward, into a thick pine woods, and we padded over soft needles while the tall trees kept the rain off our heads. Suddenly we came on a little A-frame tucked almost out of sight in the side of the hill, perfumed with pine, surrounded by forest. "All the A-frames are set like this," Wanda said, "ought of sight of all the others. Some of them are for couples, others for singles, depending on what your situation is." We knocked at the door of this one, got no response, and Wanda led us in. The main room was sparsely furnished; the balcony made up with a mattress. We gazed at the woods through the open end of the frame, which instead of containing a sheet of plate glass was filled with a fanciful art nouveau window, all dips and curliques. And as we wandered, we saw more, and every time a new pattern of windows—round ones, triangular ones, mandalas, all very trippy, like the fairy-tale houses in the fairy-tale illustrations of my childhood.

Farther into the pines we came to a small, shingled octagonal house set aside for any visiting guru. Simply furnished with minimal furniture and tatami, it was a lovely little button of a dwelling place. Beyond it was an aspen grove; beyond that, the spring, surrounded by myriads of mountain flowers, and strange ferns and vines. One low, light weed particularly struck us. It rose from the woodland floor like a pale tan cloud. As we stroked it with our palms, Steve remarked that it looked and felt very much like pubic hair—soft but springy. Wanda and I agreed.

And then after a brief pause to admire the community two-holer—in another A-frame—we returned to the kitchen again.

There we found Stan and Kim, back from the travels, peeling wet clothes from their three children. Neither Stan nor Kim took any notice of us, Stan scarcely seeming to recognize us and Kim saying only a brusque "hello" when introduced. But by now we were quite accustomed to the vagrant moods of communards, and didn't take their manner as an insult. Hadn't Coleman himself told us that Lyra people were wary of visitors who laid personal trips on residents? We kept our counsel and tried to look pleasant and ingenuous.

The rain was now starting to pelt down quite fiercely. The girl with the two children was lurking in the kitchen, and asked us if we were leaving soon, and would we take her down the mountain. We said we would, but Wanda proposed that first we come to have a look at the "truth room," the place where the community did its meditation. As we sprinted out of the kitchen and downhill again, the dark girl said she would take the children to the parking lot and wait for us.

Wanda led us to a half-buried adobe building adjoining the main dome. We had to remove our shoes and enter the room by crouching down and slithering through a low slotted entrance. We found ourselves in a vast, dark space, a cavelike arena built in two concentric circles around a center platform where a low oil flame guttered. In the ceiling were skylights cut in incredibly ornate patterns, but there was no light outside for them to admit; from an angry black cloud, rain was pounding down on us, and we could see flashes of lightning crackle across the sky. Little cushions were laid on the earthen circles, and we each picked a cushion and settled into the half-lotus to be quiet and meditate; against the flickering center candle, our bodies made giant shadows on the walls behind us, and I felt as if we had sunk almost to the center of the earth. It was a nice place for meditation; I found myself taking the full lotus finally, very easily, and I had a lovely trip, especially after Wanda said she was leaving to settle the hash of that poor woman and her children. Wanda thought we should not try to get off the mountain in the downpour; she said it would be worth our lives to negotiate the melting mud road in the lashing rain. Her idea is that we should all somehow be put up for the night. Such hospitality was strictly against Lyra policy, but—Wanda said—to hell with it.

After she left, I continued in a very pleasant, unmeasured state for a long time, until she returned to announce that in a scratch meeting of the community, it had been decided to put up the mother and children in a building called the double A-frame, and that we could sleep in the "only" room, the proviso being that Wanda do all the work and take all the trouble. All this being her idea, she would have to carry it out. In one respect, though, she would have cooperation; the mother and children having gone to the parking lot, one of the men would brave the downpour to go there, locate them, and bring them back.

The trip between "truth" room and "only" room got us soaked to the skin, and we were grateful to find a crackling fire in the adobe fireplace. Wanda made us some tea, got down a guitar, and played a bit. We were being very quiet and contemplative when the would-be rescurer of women and children appeared at the door, swathed in soaking blankets, and addressed Wanda angrily. "They won't come up," he announced. "They've got into a Volkswagen down there and she says they'll stay there until morning." I wondered aloud if they had somehow got into our car. "Did you bring those people up here?" he demanded to know, very unpleasantly. I denied it, and he stomped testily out into the storm again.

By now it was quite black outside, and still pouring—but when the rain let up a bit, we ran barefoot to the kitchen, towels wrapped fruitlessly around our heads. Wanda explained that no meals are served in community on Saturdays, but that she would rustle up some supper for us, and by poking about the kitchen she produced goat cheese for hors d'oeuvres, followed by cheddar cheese sandwiches on home-made bread with fresh home-churned butter, plus a salad of fresh greens, dressed with olive oil, lemon, and soya sauce. We had a choice of cow's milk or goat's milk, and I couldn't resist my first invitation to the milk of the goat. It turned out to be more raw, more gamy than the milk from a cow, and therefore more substantial somehow.

I had three bowls full, and thought again of fairy tales I'd read, of funky kitchens like that one, deep in the woods, and goat's milk in bowls. It was nice.

The rain never let up. All night the walls and windows streamed with water; the skylights thundered with it. Back in the "only" room, Steve and I again huddled by the fire. Just before ten, there was traffic in and out to the washroom, but after that hour, not a creature stirred on the mountain. Wanda sat with us a long while, chatting, and even gave us leave to smoke cigarettes. She said that with everybody else in bed, it would be all right, and we could blow the smoke up the chimney. So wicked was she, in fact, that she even smoked half a Camel herself.

Steve and I said we couldn't understand the strangely alienated behavior of everyone we'd been adjacent to ("met" would hardly be the word) during the day except for herself and Bruce. "Why are people so cold?" we asked. "Why was that guy so rude and accusatory? You would have thought the rain was our fault." Wanda explained that Stan Coleman was not interested in letting people get too close together. "He thinks it's a danger to the community," she said. "People get close, they work up love relationships, friendship relationships, spooky things happen. It's not healthy for community. Anyway, Lyra is not really a commune or a family, it's an ashram." I said yes, but an ashram without the leavening warmth of a resident guru, a benevolent personality. Stan Coleman, I suggested, was hardly a benevolent figure.

"I think," said Wanda, "that Stan uses his coldness as a technique for cooling people out. For example, Bruce, who is new, said at the community meeting last night that he thought people ought to be more friendly and together here, and Stan and everybody else really sat on him. Stan says we don't want individual trips laid on us here."

"But Wanda," Steve said, "If there's no friendship, and no love, isn't it awfully empty here?"

"Well," she said, "it is lonely. In fact, I think that everybody here is a little lonely, and sort of wishing they had somebody to talk to. But personal relationships are not easy, especially with the day very busy, from four in the morning, with work and everything. There just isn't any time to conduct a social life or a sexual life or anything like that. People are into cows or corn and that rules their lives.

"This is something I can handle right now. I've made the drug scene, I've made the marriage scene. Now I want to make the simplicity scene, and get high on the work and the meditation. Sometimes I feel low, sure; sometimes I'd love to just have a silly conversation, do some silly thing. But then you guys have come, haven't you? This has been nice for me; I'm glad you had to stay."

When Wanda left, we both kissed her goodnight on the cheek before she went out the door. The kisses really seemed to upset her; such things are not supposed to happen at Lyra. We wondered how long it had been since anybody had kissed that very kissable girl.

That night we slept on the floor in a welter of dusty blankets pulled from a deep window seat, our toes pressed firmly against the fender of the fireplace. Sleep is perhaps the wrong word to use in this case—the rain continued to batter the skylights, through which we could see nothing; the kerosene lamps were turned low and the fire faded, and the atmosphere was warm and cavelike—still, our rest was spotty. For company we had the communal German shepherd, a sweet great bitch named Aye, or Ai or perhaps initial I, and she filled the night with the deep sighs of dozing big dogs, and got up and lay down again, thumpily, about a thousand times. At about four in the morning, I woke to the sensation of a huge wet tongue laving my face from chin to eyelids, and it was Aye, wanting to go out. In a few minutes she was back with her babies—two boisterous roly-poly puppies—but who can sleep with puppies? They wanted to wrestle in our armpits, eat our shoes, nibble our ears. So we threw all the livestock out again, just as we heard a great bonging and gonging just outside the door. We stared into the murk and dimly made out the figure of a man in a cape, striking the gong. Presumably he was summoning the membership to meditation—but it being Sunday, and a day of rest, we assumed that most people would skip it.

After that I must have slept for a while, because Steve said later that a great parade of people had been through to brush their teeth. I missed all that, but awoke to hear a young man telling Steve that the room would be wanted soon, and it would be good if we would get up and get ourselves together. We were tired and punchy and cross with Lyra for turning out to be such a lonely place, so far from our hopes for it, so thoroughly on Some Other Trip, and we wasted no time restoring the blankets, adjusting our clothes and washing our faces. We strode to the kitchen, where we found several people making breakfast and ignoring us rather studiedly. However, when I announced that we wanted to say goodbye and thank you, everybody cheered up considerably. Wanda was nowhere in sight, and we asked to be remembered to her.

As we strode down the path again toward the parking lot—rain finished now and a pearly mountain light striking the dew in the tall grass—here came Kim and some male member of Lyra, bouncing down the hill in a van. We begged a ride as far as the parking lot, and Kim said, very disagreeably, "Oh, all right. But hurry up and get in. We have places to be." As we jounced along in the back of the van, Kim delivered herself of scorn for the feckless woman who had spent the night with her children in our car. "Somebody like that comes along and thinks she's going to find magical people on top of the mountain," said Kim. "And then when she finds out we're not any more magical than anybody else, we're just like the people she left behind in Santa Cruz, she goes down and sulks in your car.

"Well . . . I think we're nice enough." By then we'd reached the car, and Kim broke off her address. We asked if they'd wait for us just a minute so we could go down the mountain with them, because we didn't know what condition the road would be in. "Oh, all right," said Kim once again. "But hurry up." And I stalled the car twice trying to get it started fast enough to suit her. The back seat was all muddy but there was no sign of the refugees; we found them, however, on foot halfway down the mountain. They knew we'd be coming along, sooner or later.

And by then, for all the architectural beauty of Lyra, we were glad it was sooner.

THE END OF THE PARTY

Having been marooned on Lyra's mountaintop all Saturday night, we had missed the Hesperus midnight peyote feast. But since it was to be an extended affair, we decided to go along at about midday on Sunday, to see what was happening.

We didn't think it would be right to arrive at the feast empty-handed, and decided that the gift of a bottle of wine would be appropriate. But on a Sunday in that godforsaken country, where do you buy a bottle of wine? Near the turn-off to the Hesperus mesa, we saw a roadhouse, clearly a chicano watering hole. Do we dare go in, we asked ourselves; Steve dared, while I sat in the parking lot outside, revving the engine of our little VW, glancing nervously from left to right into the cars full of drunken, roistering chicanos. It was a Sunday afternoon—but outside a cantina, there was nothing peaceful about it. Steve was gone a long time, but returned nothing the worse for wear, bearing a half-gallon of Tokay wine, of a brand I'd never heard of. We opened and took a taste of it, and agreed that it was the most despicable swill that had ever passed the lips of either of us; still, it was all there was, and we were sure that the denizens of Hesperus would accept it in the spirit given.

We drove across the main highway, passed a Standard station on the corner, and headed up the side road toward Hesperus. We hadn't gone very far on the muddy country road before we came to an impasse. At a narrow turn ahead, two sedans confronted one another; a late-model Buick, bearing New York plates, was stymied in its course by a beat-up Chevvy facing the other way. In the Buick were a man and woman of middle age; in the Chevvy were three drunken chicanos. Steve got out, consulted briefly with Mr. and Mrs. Buick, then approached the Chevverino brothers. He came back to report that the Chevverino brothers were completely fried, that their car had broken down, and that even if it were in perfect running order, they would never be able to run it. One of the chicanos, he said, was covered with what appeared to be dried blood, and might well have been injured some time past in a family or friendly knife fight. All occupants were now, however, so drunk as to have forgotten what had precipitated their journey, including the bleeding man. He suggested that we could inch around the two cars without falling into the ditch, and this we did, the chicanos taking no notice of our little VW as we passed.

Mr. and Mrs. Buick followed our example; once past, we leapt out and guided and signaled them through the narrow passage. Then they asked us if we were by chance going to Hesperus, and when we said we were, asked if they could have a ride with us up the mountain. "We already failed to make it once," said Mr. Buick. "Tore a hole in the gas tank last time around. We'd appreciate a lift." Mr. and Mrs. Buick were hefty people, and the rear end of the VW sagged ominously when they came aboard. But we made pretty good progress, steady but slow, almost halfway up the mountain. Finally, however, the VW just couldn't do another rise, and we four agreed that we'd make better and surer time on foot. So we left the Volks off the road by a fence post, and set out along the rutted, muddy tracks, a curious party for a peyote feast if I ever saw one.

The Buicks seemed a very congenial couple, both in their late fifties, both as cheerful as could be. Their daughter Patricia was a member of Hesperus, they said; they weren't climbing the mountain to eat peyote but in aid of a family reunion. What, we asked, did they think of Patricia living in a commune?

"Well," said Mrs. Buick, huffing and puffing, "I don't think anybody's living right these days. I don't think it would necessarily be better if Patricia were living at home on Long Island in her own room. I don't think the older generation has any better solution than what she's after up here."

Mr. Buick chimed in. "I like the fact that young people are searching for better ways to live," he said. "I don't particularly like Hesperus; I think Pat has been in better communes. But she's twenty-one and she can do as she pleases, and this is what she wants."

"We tried to see that all of our children would make their own choices," said Mrs. Buick. "We have a son in the Zen

Center in Rochester, and we don't entirely understand that, either, but we respect his choice."

"We tried to raise them to be honest with themselves," said Mr. Buick. "You plant the seed . . ." He raised his hands in an eternal gesture of acceptance. "It isn't that we approve," he said, "but we stay open. If we took some other attitude, we'd lose our children. And we don't intend to lose our children."

What nice people, I thought. And also, what slow people. They just weren't making it up the mountain as fast as my younger lungs wanted me to. With apologies to the Buicks, and polite encouragement from them, Steve and I stepped up our pace and moved very rapidly away and out of sight of them.

We had pretty well conquered the mountain and were just coming up a low rise onto the top of the mesa when we saw in front of us on the road one of those classic Western images—two horsemen silhouetted in the sun. Except that they weren't quite as classic as they ought to have been; one shaggy gunman was firmly astride his mount, and a rifle was slung casually over the saddle, but the other fellow, his companion, seemed unable to heft himself into place. He was as befuddled as W. C. Fields, flinging his boot-shod foot up toward the stirrup, missing every time. He and his buddy were giggling about it. They broke up their hilarity just briefly to advise us that the feast was still going on, and if we would cross a rough, mesquite-strewn area, and go past the pueblo, we would find a path that would take us around an arroyo and onto another portion of the mesa. "Just walk on past the corn," one boy said, "and you'll see a big teepee. That's the place."

As we approached the pueblo, which at that moment seemed abandoned, a wild-haired youth popped through a skylight and, hoisting himself onto the first-floor roof, began to address the mesquite, the cactus, the endless valley, and the limitless blue sky. Also, perhaps, us—though I'm not sure he spotted us coming along. "I know that Jesus Christ is my Lord and Savior," he shouted, flailing the air. "Now I want you to come out here, I want you to come out here in the open, and apologize."

Steve and I glanced at each other in alarm. What to do about this? Did he mean us? Was somebody else in danger? Should we hide? We went skulking off into cover of the mesquite.

"You heard me," the boy cried. "You apologize or I will have your eyes. Your eyes, you hear me? You will no longer consort with the devil."

I won't, I won't, I silently pledged, and wondered what poor Mr. and Mrs. Buick would make of this, as we crawled along, staying low to keep out of the raving boy's sight, trying to find the right path. Suddenly we ran right up against a bearded youth who was hoeing the earth at the base of a tree. Jesus, I said to myself, what's this?

"Hi," said the boy, setting his hoe briefly aside. "You coming to the feast?" We said we were, and also remarked that somebody seemed to be flipping over at the pueblo. "Oh, don't mind him," said the boy. "That's just our resident madman. He's harmless if you don't get too close. Anyway, everybody's over at the feast right now. You stay right along the edge of this grove of pines and you'll find your way without any trouble." Wherewith he hitched up his buckskins and started hoeing again. It crossed my mind to ask him what on earth he was doing, but I knew that if I asked a stupid question, I would get a stupid answer.

By now well out of sight and nearly out of hearing of the maniacal shrieker, we made our way around the edge of the arroyo and found ourselves on a new plateau, with a huge cornfield on our right and a path stretching clearly straight ahead. Far in the distance we saw a huge teepee, and knew we were in sight of the feast.

We also saw we were within sight of a couple coming toward us; as distance closed, we realized it was Mary Louise and Homer, with the baby. They were in party clothes—Mary Louise in a long print gown, her black hair loose and flowing; Homer in beaded buckskins and a black sombrero. The baby in baby clothes. In their quiet and gentle way, Mary Louise and Homer said they were sorry we were so late, that there was plenty of food, and they began to escort us back to the scene of the feast. In a clearing by the teepee, several trestle tables had been set up and laid with bowls and dishes, now pretty thoroughly scoured of their contents, but Mary Louise set about filling a couple of plates for us while I wandered toward the teepee, from which I could hear drumming and a faint chanting.

Homer came along with me, gestured that we should stoop and enter, and escorted me inside to a place where we could sit. People were sitting cross-legged all around the interior; others were laid out, utterly laid out flat, presumably under the influence of the peyote. The people sitting or squatting around the edges of the teepee were all very wide-eyed, very wet-eyed, as if they'd recently been weeping. And on the ground beside several of them were small bowls—I assumed they were there for vomiting into.

Homer whispered that the ceremonial peyote button rested in a heap of ashes in the center of the teepee; I was not to pass between it and anybody who was playing a drum or singing or in any way obviously praying. Small twigs of fir were occasionally placed in the ashes and they would smoke slightly and give a pleasant scent. To one side were a drummer and singer. The drummer did a steady bomp-bomp-bomp, but even within that he could do some interesting sounds by varying the angle and tautness of a fairly shallow drum. He could even make it go woooooeeeeeee, and a lot more than a simple thunk. Although there were some Indians present, it was not they who were making the music and chanting.

Around the edges of the teepee, on thin pallets, some people were lying or sitting in stupors. We sat cross-legged listening to the music and looking around. The air inside was cool but a little dense. At one point I felt rather hot and flushed, but I blamed that condition on the couple of swallows of that disgusting Tokay we'd brought. In the dim light I studied the circle of people sitting or lying close to the inside rim of the teepee. There were many infants and small children among them, some unnaturally quiet and still, and it crossed my mind that they had perhaps been turned on to the peyote. Adults, when not gazing sightlessly forward, would smoke cigarettes, smoke dope, eat bread and plates of beans. The scene was semi-social and semi-religious—nothing overtly worshipful in the Christian tradition, just a general mix of chatting over here and chanting over there.

At one point a young man came to the mouth of the teepee, stood there stock-still for about ten minutes, presumably absorbing the scene, then entered and went forward to the ashes, knelt, brought the smoke from a flaring twig toward his face, and brushed the smoke toward his eyes with his palms, rubbed it around his face and head, and then went out again, shuffling backward. Occasionally someone else would perform this ritual. Otherwise, apart from these vaguely ceremonial gestures, the mood continued to be extremely casual. I spotted Fred, the older fellow we'd met on the mesa some days before, stretched out flat on the far side of the ashes. A girl was massaging his head, chest, and arms, working his fingers, constantly touching and kneading him. It occurred to me that an effect of the drug may be to make one physically stiff.

On the whole I found the scene agreeable—primitive but unthreatening. I had to keep reminding myself that I was not in some distant country, but on my home ground among people who had been raised very much like myself. These were not historically primitive people at all, but Archie, Betty, and Veronica, dropped out of Michigan State and having visions on a mountaintop. And very satisfactory visions, too, from the feel of things. Bizarre vibrations, it's true, but gentle ones.

After a spate of quite vigorous drumming and rattle-shaking and chanting by a tall, thin young man, he got up to leave. People came up to thank him, kissing and embracing him, holding his hand, while two replacements took over. Some of the chants were unintelligible to me, rendered in Navajo, I presume, but there was one number I understood at least part of. The drummer would sing, "Jesus is my lord and savior," and then follow that up with Indian chanting familiar from Indian pow-wows, the Lone Ranger radio show, and the like—hoodeee-haya-hoowah—that sort of thing. And then repeat. I much regretted that we had been able to arrive only for the closing hours of this feast, and told Homer that if it had not been for the rain, we would have participated in the entire event. Homer looked at me waveringly and alleged, "Oh, it rains every time we have a peyote feast. Never fails." I didn't argue with him—maybe that's true. But I couldn't see how; if there's a peyote meeting practically every weekend somewhere around Taos, and if it rains every time, every pueblo up there would have slid down to Santa Fe by this time.

After an hour and a half in the teepee, however comfortable

I kept telling myself I was in the half-lotus, my legs were numb from the knees down, so I signaled Homer that I wanted to go. We backed, crouched, out of the teepee, straightened, and found ourselves standing between a young man and woman who were staring fiercely at one another. We stepped quickly aside, but I stood for a time to see what they were doing. The girl wore a long green dress and a green shawl, and had deep green eyes; she stood staring as if transfixed into the young man's eyes. He, standing just as stiffly and dramatically, staring just as intensely back again, was making signs at her with his hands in the air. Neither of them blinked at all for minutes and minutes, nothing broke the connection—until Mary Louise stepped out of the tee-pee with her baby in her arms, directly into the path of eyeballs. The young man reached out, took the baby from her, and caressed it very lovingly, staring still at the green-eyed girl. Then Steve emerged, behind Mary Louise, and the girl broke her former connection to stare briefly into Steve's eyes. He nodded; her eyes flicked away, and back into sync with those of the young man.

Many people were sitting or standing about in the cleared area surrounding the teepee, but there was no conversation—just a lot of wet, staring eyes. There seemed nothing to say, and in common unspoken ascent, we and Homer and Mary Louise began to stroll slowly away from the scene. We walked in silence the entire way back to the pueblo again, noticing the corn, the trees, the scrub, the sky. There was only one person in the mud yard of the pueblo—a plain-faced blond girl wearing an enor-mous patchwork coat, sitting in a rocker alongside an adobe stove, holding a flute. I was still carrying the execrable Tokay, so I put it down beside the girl and she smiled a little smile at me. Then we thanked Homer and Mary Louise, wished them well and they us, and we set out to walk down the mountain again. As I looked back to wave, Mary Louise was hefting a bucket, and Homer was smiling more or less in our direction.

Down in the parking lot, where our car was not, we noticed a young man and woman about to get into a large van. We begged a ride and were allowed to climb into the back, where a mattress and bedding fully covered the floorboards. In the jouncing downward ride, the girl was quite talkative, praising Hesperus for its free-land policy. When we reached our Volkswagen, the man had to get out to open the rear doors of the van, and he and I had a brief conversation while Steve walked forward to chat more with the girl. The young man was another of those neatly dressed drop-outs we'd started to identify with the Harvard and prep-school image, in which work clothes and climbing boots do little to obscure a classy background. This young man was very articulate. He said he had spent all the preceding year at Tassahara, the Zen Buddhist monastery on the California coast, and had found that he was not suited to monastic life. So he had set out to wander in his van—another one of what must now be thousands. "I've visited a lot of communes," he said, "and I'm beginning to get the picture. People always try it awhile, and then split, and pick it up some other place, and then break up again. They don't seem to go backward, but they don't seem to go far enough ahead either, to bring things off. They get into weird shit—the devil, parapsychology, all that—and they get scared. They run . . . and I guess I don't blame them."

"Neither do I," I said.

As we drove away, I asked Steve what the girl's conversation had been. "Aw, she just wanted to tell me that she's coming East in the fall," he said. "So she wanted my phone number, so she could look me up in New York." And he put his head back and dozed as I drove down still another mountain.

SUMMING UP TAOS

Soon after we left Taos, Steve and I spent many hours attempting to sort out a bewildering complex of conflicting feelings about the town and its communes. While we were deeply affected by the plight of resident and transient longhairs—indeed, as hairy strangers, tarred by the same brush—we knew that it wouldn't have required a degree-bearing sociologist to have forecast the murders, rapes, and beatings that began in the spring of 1970. The townspeople of any tiny community, however liberal and accepting their reputation and disposition, would be bound to react in fear and hostility if overrun by twice their number of transients. In this instance, four thousand longhaired hippies in confrontation with two thousand locals fractured into three distinct ethnic groups was the perfect formula for violence. The situation would not have been very much eased if the transients had been wearing Brooks Brothers suits and clumsy, broad-toed cordovans—the imbalance would have reeked of take-over, whatever the costumes. But it is important to point out that the throngs of arriving hippies did not have a sociologist in their employ, and that they were not in any recognizable manner "organized." They came independently, separately galvanized by the same romantic dream—a dream of peace, love, and freedom that was wafted like pollen from one end of the country to the other. The question for Taos, however, was: peace, love, and freedom for whom, exactly? When one man's freedom transgresses upon another's, peace and love turn with breathtaking suddenness to discord and hate. It is always best to place human considerations well in front of anybody's dreams, theories, and romantic designs.

No single member of the counterculture still remaining in Taos—in or out of a commune—is less than fully sensitized to local conditions today; they know, at last, what is happening around them, and in that knowledge remain dedicated to their alternative way of life. In 1971 in Taos, nobody could doubt the seriousness of their commitment. Those who remain understand, with some empathy, at least, why their way of life is so out-rageous to the chicanos, the resentful have-nots of centuries, a poor ethnic minority who now so desperately seek the bourgeois comforts and advantages that communards have possessed and rejected. And in sustained confrontation with a barren soil which yields crops only with the greatest reluctance, they have learned a respect for water that only hard-scrabble farmers can have, a respect that is not learned in the middle-class suburban homes they come from. They seem to understand now that, in that arid country, to share water has a significance that cannot be derived from science-fiction novels and is not represented by city reservoirs. In short, they have learned, as Stan Coleman so clearly and inelegantly put it, not to pass their load on.

What the Taos communards had to learn the hard way, Steve and I were able to absorb less painfully. We had come to Taos with a few romantic delusions about communality still clinging to us, and the tatters, at least, of a semi-divinity that made us feel we knew all there was to know about how communes are born, and why they live and die. Yet we found half a hundred people at Our Thing, paralyzed into inaction and frank foolishness by psychic phenomena they could deal with no better than we could. Perhaps The Power would come to them again—but if it addled their ability to judge the value of their own work, was that, in fact, a condition to be longed for? There were Stan Coleman and his folk at Lyra, stripped of passion and emotion, rejecting even friendship, abominating human tenderness, into work and meditation and institutional loneliness. Androgyny had come to all of these—and so what? Then there was Hesperus. If anybody on that particular mesa had penetrated to the duality of sexual identity, if any had even inquired into, much less pressed past women's lib or men's lib to human lib, we had seen no sign of it. We had seen, on the contrary, a perfect hip mirror to middle-class life, an unconscious parody of the traditional sex roles as played out every day and night in all the suburbs of America. In the face of this, we could fall back only on Stan Coleman's cautionary comment about passing your load on. There's no point in trying to impose one's own theories on other people's experience; as members of the counterculture are wont to say, "Different strokes for different folks."

Our observations of Hesperus were, in that spirit, at least, the ones most educational for us. I've edited the tapes of our dialogue about Hesperus, removing much of what is extraneous, but retaining the conflict we felt between the way of life they have worked out and theories of ours which we continue to hold. I pass them on to you here—not as a load, I hope, but as a set of reflections which you can value or not as you please. In questions of communality, it remains the province of each man to decide for himself which fences he prefers to straddle.

DICK: At Hesperus, a lot of good things seem to be happening. These people have learned to survive; they have learned about living on and from the earth and about living with one another.

Certainly the general toleration level for eccentricities is very high, and if you can have a resident crazy, screaming from the roof when he feels like it, and still everybody lives without fear, then that's very fine. Maybe the crazy kid at Hesperus will be better able to work his way through his psychosis if he can sit on top of the pueblo among people who love and tolerate him, who will let him blow it all out. I think there are possibilities that, in such a community of nonstructured others, he could come through psychosis into a more stable state. Certainly all the people up there are willing to deal with that kind of reality —psychological instability—much more so than the straight society is. They do not run away from aberrations that the straight society fears and incarcerates. They face all varieties of human behavior pretty well head on. That sort of thing could, I concede, be disastrous, but it is also humane and admirable.

I wonder whether Homer and Mary Louise will ever come down from the mountain. Unless they're driven down, of course, which could sometime happen. They seem to be perfectly happy there, though I marvel that Mary Louise doesn't express any of the popular resentment against male sexism. I guess since she lives on the mountain she can't very well keep up with the press, which means she's probably never heard of women's lib. It fascinated me that, very sweetly and matter-of-factly, Mary Louise does all the work for her little unit up there. She bears the baby, carries the water, cooks the meals, sees to the hygiene. And meanwhile Homer sits on his duff, stoned, smiling, on a very floaty trip. Kind, gentle, vacant eyes. Well, not vacant exactly, but as if he's viewing everything from afar. Is that the dope, or the peyote, or just a softness in the head? He's very calm and cooled out and gentle and useless, so far as I can tell. I suppose that if Mary Louise were to die or get hepatitis or something, Homer would function in a practical manner to care for the baby and so on, but I don't really have any confidence in that. It's Mary Louise and the other women who do all the work, look after all the practical matters, keep things together. My last sight of her was with the baby on her hip and a water bucket in her hand.

STEVE: I've been thinking all evening about community—about hippie communes versus serious intentional communities versus anything I could evolve on my own. And it blows my mind that I can be in a situation from which I pick up very good vibes— and from Hesperus I did pick up not only good but weird vibes, and as you know I'm into the weirdness of the Hesperus trip— yet I'm not into it enough. I'm holding back. I find it small-time on the dope level, small-time on the maturity level. I don't know what, if anything, they've evolved, and I walk away from the experience unfulfilled. And yet it's very clear to me that communality, the Hesperus variety, is highly satisfactory for all kinds of people, including the ones who never want to go down the mountain *and*—like the one guy we met—the ones who are AWOL and don't dare go down the mountain, and spend every single day of three months right up there on top. These kids are living full-time with one another in a completely isolated spot with no stimulation other than from one another, and so com- munity is a full-time riff with them. We can't stand it on a three- and four-hour basis—maybe that's partly because we're in there as observers rather than as full-time participants, but neverthe- less I don't know that I'm capable of doing anything for twenty- four consecutive hours, day after day after day.

DICK: Well, we talked this afternoon about liking to go to the movies, to go dancing, to read, to meet people, looking for cer- tain areas of excitement in our lives, needing and seeking enter- tainment and stimulation. I don't think I could ever fit into life on a mesa in a mud hut, however enthusiastic I was about the community or the act itself, without wanting occasional change. But I feel that there ought to be a great spectrum of communes —for conservatives, for radical people, for all. And by no means is everyone expected to go and live in a commune forever. I'm beginning to think that communes might function as retreats for some people who could never get behind them as a full way of life.

STEVE: It occurs to me that the experience is educational—it's an education for living. Kids who are spending even one year at Hesperus are spending a very incredible year. First of all, they're learning a lot of outdoor skills they'd never learn elsewhere; secondly, they're learning lots of indoor skills they'd never learn elsewhere. You can't beat it—it's a much more relevant, powerful, durable experience than a year of college would be, or a year working for Bloomingdale's. It's clear to me that they're spending this year in a very useful and effective way as far as their own lives are concerned, regardless of how long the commune lasts. Every communard that we've met has learned more indelible lessons about life on top of the mesa than he could have acquired in a year of classroom study. On *any* subject. And every time a commune fails, or is bulldozed by some police chief, fifteen new ones spring up in different places. What it means to me is that, like anything else in the world, mistake or not, if it gives you an interesting enough experience for you to want to continue that experience, then it was educational, valuable, productive, and constructive. Hesperus, even if it lasts a day and a half, will have put a number of people through some important changes and—even if later regretted—will also be seen in retrospect as a very educational place, because it involved those people with their real selves in a very meaningful way.

I'm into communes now as a form of life university experiment —I really do think that people get a lot out of living together in a group. Now that may not be the way they end up for the rest of their lives. I couldn't *conceive* of those kids—eighteen, nineteen, twenty-one, thirty, whatever—living for the remainder of their lives in those mud huts on top of a New Mexico mesa. It just doesn't make any sense to me, which may be my limitation. But for one thing they're just not going to be able to raise enough food to sustain themselves indefinitely, because the land sucks. So in three or five or ten years, when their wildest dreams aren't really fulfilled, what's going to happen? I suspect they'll fall apart, people will go in their own separate directions. Maybe they'll start other communes with more interesting concepts or communes with the same concepts but more limited goals. Who knows? But I can see lots of possibilities for social forms going through major changes because of the communal reality.

I don't think communes are the answer for all America. I don't think everybody can get into communes. And I don't think communes are going to take over the country; I don't think they're a super-Communist plot. I *do* think they're a very interesting plot, because there's no question that when these kids drop out of the system and spend a year in a commune, they'll find it very hard, maybe impossible, to go back to regular jobs. What they're doing now is just so much more valuable in so many different ways, in learning how to live on their own and be responsible for themselves, that they won't ever willingly participate in the straight routines again.

DICK: Well, one thing we know is that *we* wouldn't know how to live for sustained periods of time with other people in that situation. We have talked a lot about what we had for an hour and ten minutes in San Francisco—we were all turned on to thinking that we had something going, but we haven't worked it out in the long haul. These guys are working it out on a day-to-day basis. They're up on the mountain and they are deeply committed to being there. They can come down anytime, and they are *not* coming down. After all, some of these people have been there for three and four years and they know something we don't know: they know how to live together. They're not organized at Hesperus, they're completely anarchic. Anybody can go there and live. It's free land dedicated to the principle of No Energy Blocks for anybody. Do your thing. So anybody can go up there, and dig a hole, and he's at home.

You would think this would be unworkable. Certainly, we have ways in straight society to deal with such potential problems; we keep one another at a distance, out of our own needs for safety and privacy. I admit I don't want a lot of people coming into my place and pitching tents and digging holes in the yard because I'm property- and privacy-oriented. I feel possessive about my privacy. We don't live out in the middle of the countryside for nothing. And I realize that, though I talk a lot about community, I notice that I don't want to get that close to my neighbors. Now if I could pick my neighbors and they pick me, that would be a step in a very pleasant direction. It would be very nice. But I've never been in a situation of that sort and I think that, outside the communal system, I'll never have it. And if I did, I don't know what it takes to sustain it for a long period. In the Taos communes, it seems to take a certain amount of peyote.

STEVE: One objective remark about peyote. If you become a member of the Native American Church (and to do so you do *not* have to be a southwest American Indian) then peyote becomes instantly legal for you. It's not an illegal drug and you can take it so long as it's part of a religious ceremony. So these kids who are using it are doing a perfectly legal thing; they are not fugitives from justice. They smoke marijuana too—no question about that—but that's small-time compared to their peyote meetings, which seem to me to be the heaviest thing that's happing to them. And they have evolved a kind of peyote culture which it will take us some time to understand, if ever. We will obviously have to take the drug, but even taking the drug may not get us where they are—enjoying a kind of looseness with one another, making very few demands on one another. Their life is very loosely structured. They seem to get along very well because they are all willing to do whatever has to be done. And if it doesn't get done, I think they'll all accept that too. It could be a groovy group of people, if you wanted to look at it very simply. On the other hand, if one is applying stringent communal criteria for success and economic self-sufficiency, one wonders whether Hesperus will survive. On short term, it's an interesting idea for kids who want to lay out for a year or for two weeks or for ten minutes. They're open to everybody and they smoke a lot of dope and they feel content and together—so that's fine.

DICK: Yeah, that's fine, but I can't see myself in it. I can see myself doing . . . a creative unit. I can see myself doing a good living thing with good people. But for myself I see a lot more structure than Hesperus represents. I've never taken peyote; maybe I'd feel very differently if I had. It's hard to say—I had no objection to the people we met there, except that the sexual quotient seemed remarkably low, and for revolutionaries they seemed extraordinarily bourgeois, very sexist in the dreariest sense.

STEVE: You're objecting to the male chauvinism, right? The overall chauvinism, the men laying out and the women doing all the work? And in conversation the couple of times we brought up the androgynous qualities that we thought were really at the heart of a successful communal living effort, it turns out not to be the case with Hesperus. I'm not sure they pay any attention to their androgynous qualities, socially, emotionally, sexually, or otherwise.

DICK: *Right*. And I find it weird, in light of the fact that *we* are responsive, finally, after an hour and ten minutes, to an androgynous reality in ourselves. It's a general response that you and I make to our little instant commune, through Nora's acceptance of herself more than anything else; okay, we plus a few other males are responding to the women's lib argument, which has fallen into place for us at last. We've both read the story by the woman who lived many months in a rural commune with supposedly revolutionary guys who on this point were not in the least revolutionary, who expected her and the rest of the women to go cook and wash and clean and so on, while they were in the fields in their tractors, doing *man's* work. So the group finally erupted in male-female hassles about whether the women had a right to work in the fields, which led at last to a conspiracy by the women to dump the guys and form a commune of women only, to get rid of male chauvinism altogether. I can see how it really wears women down. And it does seem to be past time for men to realize the inequity of present arrangements—especially in the communal movement—if only because it wears the men down, even more so. Long past time—and good luck to women's lib and their shrillest advocates. Were it not for Kate Millett and all her works and pomps, I wouldn't have known what to do with this androgyne thing, wouldn't have recognized the aptness of it in working out a truly egalitarian set of relationships in my life. I was content to consider the androgyne in myself to be a purely sexual thing, never noticing that in every other respect I was a thorough male chauvinist vis-à-vis the women in my life, which is a lotta crap. So I'm advanced by our experiences and by women's lib to that uncomfortable realization, and I'm motivated now to go home and make the anyrogynous reality an integral part of my life, relating to women as equal human beings, something I've never done before.

STEVE: I think the conscious attempt to become egalitarian is going to be dependent on women's ability to earn that respect. It's got to be a fifty-fifty deal; freedom doesn't come easy, you have to earn it. By that I don't mean that women have to prove anything to men, except their independence. I mean, to the extent that women refuse to pay attention to your chauvinism, to the extent that they make it very clear that they are worth as much as you are, you are going to find yourself, consciously or unconsciously, having to deal with the fact of your chauvinism—because it will no longer work. Women will have to learn to say, "Fuck you."

DICK: Yeah, I appreciate that it's not up to me alone. But I have a lot of reparations to make. I have eight years of chauvinism to make up for in the one marriage, for example, plus whatever other relationships I've had with women, that I don't think I've been especially sparkling about. I've been shutting off a lot of possibilities in the exchange of ideas and the flow of excitement generally because of these unconscious attitudes of superiority and machismo—the tacit assumption that male means more and female means less. I'd like to get straight with that shit. Which means that me and mine have got to be open and honest with one another as we've never been before, in important areas, to the degree that we have been open with ourselves this summer. It seems to be a first requirement to get anything together—friendship, marriage, community—because we found at Connie's house that every time we thought we were being ultimately open and honest, there were still layers and layers of the artichoke to unpeel; that there was always masses more going on than we were recognizing in ourselves or in other people. Of course nobody finds this procedure easy, peeling and peeling back until you discover what's really at the core, because of the very human fear that by the time you are rid of social mannerisms and learned response, there will be nothing down there, nothing at all. But it's an invaluable experience, however painful, because it delineates the real from the unreal, prompts the recognition that the nothing is the central core in which we all participate, the God-reality, and enables us to throw out the junk, the non-us, and build with real substance. I feel there's no logical life to be led unless you open all the closets of your mind and let the air in. Unless you unburden yourself of all the garbage, as Reich calls it, you can never live in such a way that your life is more exciting than *Time* magazine. And anybody who enters into any relationship—especially into a commune or a group marriage or anything of the sort—with those closets still shut, that garbage still intact, is not going to make it.

So, whatever I do—if any commune were to become a potential reality for me ever—then there can be no lies and evasions, no secret pockets. Everything has to be up front, nothing buried, and it's got to be absolutely mutual. Unload the whole ego issue first off—and live honestly with it, or walk away from it.

STEVE: One comment on our findings with respect to the Hesperus communal consciousness—it doesn't seem that that upfrontness exists; they're not really there. I don't think these guys are facing the ultimate questions of their own sexuality. At Hesperus I didn't pick up on any of the truth vibrations that we went through this summer. I did, obliquely, from Stan Coleman, who claimed that all that was part of his past, that he'd gone through that in previous communal experiences, that he's over that now and into productivity, into working with his hands, into self-sufficiency. You know, five-year plans and all that shit—and that's a very different place from where we are now. It doesn't mean we will never be where Stan Coleman is. Stan Coleman seems to be back in the real world in a very serious way, while we're still operating in this isolated psychic area where we're still exploring our own sexuality, our own realities with respect to the women and other men we know, our friendships and our loves. So we're in the very early stage of communal living—and I presume that I would not want to spend the rest of my life arguing out these questions; they would become at some point consummately boring. So I speculate that what happens is that, after a couple of months of this self-examination, you probably get into some new phase, and I have a feeling that what we simulated in our hour and a half or one week of commune was just that first stage. In other words, we had a little bit of everything, and we had it very quickly. And we intellectualized a lot, even though we were feeling a lot. The symbolism business is totally intellectual, it was our heads working out the problem. While our hearts were telling us, now here's how we feel, our heads were saying at the same time, now this is what it means.

DICK: Yeah—and we do bring an awful load of intellectual apparatus into everything we experience; clearly everybody doesn't have to do that. We are constantly, willy-nilly, demanding that our visceral and spiritual experience meet certain intellectual criteria already established to cope with all phenomena, as if we had a built-in filter. The communards at Hesperus are, by and large, not taxed with intellectuality. And it's possible that they haven't been troubled by a recognition of two sexual realities in each life because they haven't even *thought* about it, haven't copped to that duality at all. It's hard to imagine, given that in peyote, as in acid, a revelation of that sort is given. Because I'd suppose that you cannot watch your body atomize without realizing that you are unspecific sexually, as in so many other ways; that you are joined to other atoms in a very general way and that your sexual identity is not all that much of a key to your existence. Reportedly, when people feel themselves atomizing in this way, they sometimes panic for fear of the loss of self, of ego. But if you go through that into a reconciliation of self with all things, then you are certainly, even if unstated, androgynous. How can you be something else—because you're part of the One, and both sexual identities, plus everything else in which you participate, are working for you, of you. And yet, perhaps because the Hesperus people are operating quite deliberately *below* their minds, there seems to be no sign of this kind of recognition.

STEVE: The thing that puts me off about Hesperus with respect to the principle of the androgyne is that it appears that they haven't arrived there and they haven't gone through any of the processes that one goes through to arrive there, and that makes me wonder about them. I really believe in androgyny as a natural state: I believe that it's true not only for me but for every other human being, that we are both male and female, and if you want to work that out behaviorly in bi-sexuality, that's cool. I don't know where I am personally on that, but I do know that I have an androgynous reality and I've always had it. To the extent that I was not interested in being nelly or swish, I decided to suppress it. But the point is that I have all the submissive qualities that are usually associated with the feminine, I have all the dominant qualities that are usually associated with the masculine, and I have them in conjunction with one another every single moment of my day. The problem, then, is to find a lover or lovers who, acknowledging the same duality, can complement me and whom I can complement—at every level from the sexual to the psychic.

And maybe one of the reasons it's difficult for two men to sustain an emotional relationship is that both are suppressing their female qualities to some extent, so they don't form a whole. Just as we know many heterosexual couples where the guy is all stud and the woman is afraid and guilty about her own urges toward aggressiveness and domination and he is afraid of submissiveness and they're not together—well, we know at least one homosexual couple who are playing out that same stubborn imbalance, as if they were acting in a bad TV serial, and one is utterly masculine and dominant, and the other is utterly feminine and submissive, and it's a parody of a parody, it's all pretence, in both cases—heterosexual couple, homosexual couple, they're carrying an enormous load of lies into their relationship.

DICK: Okay, given that neither of us can accept the naturalness of a totally homosexual relationship, neither can we, logically, accept the naturalness of a totally heterosexual relationship, if the sex roles are going to be so rigidly adhered to that there is no androgynous dimension, no flexibility. Because I don't dig that anybody is *totally* animated in a single sexual expression, it's just not so. What I don't accept in the avowed homosexual is that he does not allow himself access to women, cannot appreciate women. It is appalling to be locked into a limitation of that sort; and it's equally appalling in a heterosexual who just as determinedly denies himself access to his own sex, saying Nossir, I'm Stanley Stud, I'm Popeye the Sailor Man. Nothing soft or giving or androgynous about me, buster. It's so dumb.

STEVE: Okay—as we used to look at it, probably as most people look at it, what is "natural"? You have one woman and she's supposed to be the woman, and one man and he's supposed to be the man, and it's never more complicated than that. Except that we've found that it *is* more complicated than that. You crave to be submissive sometimes, she craves to be aggressive— okay, you might foray into the homosexual world to play out the opposite role. But if you can find a partner of the opposite sex, and we know you can, who will be flexible with you—maybe everybody can have everything in heterosexual pairs. I don't know how to deal with this, but it comes out that both of us understand existentially that the androgyne is real. I am an androgyne, you are an androgyne, everybody is an androgyne. If we are honest with one another and we live together, that can't help but come out. There's just no question about it. And I guess the source of my confusion at Hesperus is that the people there, who have lived there, some of them, for four years now, have not got to that recognition. So I don't know what level of honesty they are on with one another, but it doesn't seem to be coming out in terms of pan-sexuality—so where are they?

DICK: I suppose, though it's not a very attractive thought, that they do with their androgyny what the straight society does; they put it in the closet, sublimate it, suppress it. Anyway, don't forget that a lot of these people are very young, eighteen years old and thereabouts. And when I think back to when I was twenty-seven, twenty-eight, for God's sake; oh, man, I didn't know half of what they know ten years before that age. So there's an awful lot of chronological time for these kids to get through before they come to any greater clarity about who they are, what's happening in terms of their sexual dimension. Not, of course, that the realization is dependent on chronological age, in that we met many communards at Hesperus who appear to be at least my age, or older. And I am thirty-six, and you are twenty-seven, and yet we're coming to this realization at the same calendar date. So it doesn't have only to do with how old you are; it has to do with the moment at which you're ready to look at yourself, and with how intellectual you are prepared to be about your emotional realities, how thoroughly you want to examine them. And vast numbers of people—I dare say the vast majority —go through life without ever looking at any of these questions. They act out various problems and solutions but if you asked them what they were doing I'm sure they wouldn't be able to tell you, or have any *interest* in telling you or telling themselves. They have no intellectual fix on their own behavior, they're just lurching clumsily through life any which way, actively but not consciously suppressing information they do not want to examine, because it's inconvenient or troublesome or deeply threatening to long-held fictions. Clumsy but comfortable fictions.

needed to express freely—I wouldn't have dared to go because I was too much a creature of society.

STEVE: You mentioned before about being able to pick your neighbors, and they pick you.

DICK: Yeah, they're doing that on the mountaintop. Even at my present age I have no real access to that, unless I want to play God/guru and get a commune together. But by this point the sort of commune I would have to be in is far different from anything at Hesperus, in that I am stuck with intellectual compulsions that would just put me once again through the kind of wringer we went through this summer. It is So Hard to deal honestly with other people, such a searing experience, that it becomes at my age a question of energy. Listen, a lot of things get harder as you get older. When you're eighteen you have energy enough for everything in the world. You haven't begun to think of slowing down, or of protecting yourself, of being cautious, of husbanding strength. But by the time you get to be thirty-six, you get tired, you know.

STEVE: Not only that, Dick. The fact is that you've grown used to certain comforts and elegances; you're used to stemware, for example. You've grown accustomed to privacy and possessions—your own car, your own house, your own library. These kids haven't. They're not even aspiring to that, that's not even part of their reality or fantasy or aspirations. They don't want it. Middle class as their origins are, what they want to have together is a good rap, some dope, some sex—the women taking care of the kids and the food and they take care of the garden—and that is all they really need. They have been having that as a way of life for four years, which is very heavy. I've never had a consistent way of life of any kind for four years running. So I have a lot of respect for nineteen-year-olds who are able to go up the mountain. I think what they're producing for themselves is a very good scene, a much better scene than they would ever have in the city, or in any conventional environment. And for that reason alone they deserve what they have. It makes good sense.

DICK: When it comes to the root requirements, the basic needs of mankind, it makes perfect sense. They have what they need and what everybody else wants, at least in some part of their minds. But I can hear the objections of the mass of people, who do not have what they want and somehow find virtue in their deprivations. Life on the mountaintop is irresponsible, life of that sort doesn't build a progressive society. It's the end of the society. Stuff like that. If young people at Hesperus are living precisely as they please, I can hear their elders shouting, We're ruined, it's the end. And I have to agree—for society as we have long known it—it is the end. It is.

BEYOND

After a summer that by any standards would have to qualify as heavy (colloquially, heh-VEEE), we came home. My own home-coming was not propitious: Jean could not stand the sight of me, unfolding hairily from the MGB, my unruly, wind-tossed locks held only slightly in check by a yellow, long-billed golf cap from the Bing Crosby Open, in which I acknowledge that I looked absolutely ridiculous. But the children thought I looked cool, and once I took the golf cap off, Jean recovered from her initial withdrawal.

I was glad to be home—but I was not glad to be back in the general ambiance of the East, or in snagging distance of New York, where, as Janis Joplin had suggested, people are all too eager to tear you to pieces. The New York I know is, at any level of relationship—from hiring a taxi to negotiating a con-tract—combative; not a place where community has any real pertinence. People are contentious as a reflex action merely; survival demands that attack be a life style. In New York, you score points against the other guy, best him or be bested—this *is* human contact. Strangers are offended and horrified when other people crash into them on the streets, as if they were not there; in fact, in the minds of those who walk over and through them, they're not. They can't be. In a life already swarming with too many bodies, the man who hopes to survive must eliminate, mentally rub out, the very existence of pedestrians who block his path. We see in New York the prototype of the world to come. It is not pretty.

This is why everybody you meet in New York wants to get out. Everybody has an escape plan; meanwhile, he searches his unresponsive brain cells for some clues to survival. And despite the most entrenched distrust of other people, New Yorkers are coming, in increasing numbers, to consider, to toy with, the idea of the commune. The fact is that many people are at their wit's end to know how to live decently anymore in urban environments, and are beginning to advance some purely practical arguments for communality, as a solution to personal crises that are both economic and social.

Consider the thousands and thousands of young single people who hit the city every year—bright, well-educated, eager to take a big bite out of the Big Apple. It turns out, of course, always, that it is the Apple itself that does the biting, the chewing, and the digesting. One girl I know, a research assistant on the staff of a large magazine, is getting desperate about the conditions in which she lives. She earns $130 a week—scarcely a dazzling wage in any city but, in New York, a poverty pay packet—and in a city where the price of every service and commodity has sky-rocketed and continues an upward spiral, she is unable to survive at all without occasional transfusions of financial aid from her parents. She can afford a tiny one-room apartment in the East Village, formerly Hell's Kitchen, section of the city; it has a pullman kitchen, a minuscule bath, and one window with a view of an excavation site. She is never late for work because the construction workers start blasting at seven in the morning. When they have finished their building, she will have a view of a brick wall.

Though she buys just enough in the way of new clothes to show her face without embarrassment in the rather smart office where she works, and though she has taken up a vegetarian diet, more for economy than for purity, and though she spends most Saturdays at the laundromat and in front of the ironing board and avoids dry cleaning like the plague, she is constantly oppressed by the notion that she spends profligately. She never goes out to drinks, dinner, the movies, or the theater unless invited by an admirer; fortunately, she has several, because she is young, pretty, bright—delightful company. But what if she weren't? What if she were not *quite* so bright and pretty? When do those girls get to go to the movies?

"It isn't the movies," she says. "I don't care, really, if I never see another movie. And not having money isn't so bad except for the constant guilt. It's the lack of personal dimension that bothers me."

"What do you mean?" I asked, bluntly. "Are you lonely?"

"Lonely, yes, lonely," she said, a little annoyed to have to admit it. "I have my own writing to do, you know. I work hard at it, several nights a week. But then I'm finished and I look up, I'd like to see a friend, talk to people, be in human contact. But how can I? I live on a shelf on East 10th Street. My friends live on shelves in places like West End Avenue, like Barrow Street, like Washington Heights. And even if I dared to step one foot onto my street at night alone, and if I dared to go into the subway at night, I'm still at least an hour from my friends, any of them.

"I don't expect to have to live the rest of my life this way, thank God. I really do not think it is a God-given part of human destiny to have to spend every Saturday afternoon for the rest of my life in a broken-down laundromat on First Avenue. I really do not think that a nice, Midwestern girl like me should accept dates with men more because I am stir-crazy and really would like to see a movie, than because I like the man. I don't enjoy feeling like a whore, but how can I explain it to myself any other way?

"So some of us have been talking about getting together—not a commune, exactly, maybe a cooperative. Pool our money for a large apartment, for groceries . . . *be* there for each other, experience a little human caring, be in touch . . . you know?"

I knew. Since I've been back, several people—most of them women—have made similar arguments to me. A professional woman, in her late fifties and at the top of her particular heap, is desperate to get out of the city and/or take some giant innovative step to change her life style. She has a lovely apartment on the upper East Side and she's afraid to sleep in it alone any more. It takes two double bolts and a police lock on her front door, plus four martinis and two Demerol, for her to get any sleep at all. "This is a crazy way to live," she says. "Crazy. I've been single and independent and more-or-less happy all my life. I've had my family, my nieces and nephews, a couple of long-term indiscretions, my work. I wasn't so scared until the last last few years—I was busy, I was content. But now—there's nobody in my life, nobody, really. And the work doesn't sustain me anymore; it's not enough, and I guess it never was. Where is the commune for me? An old folks' home? God forbid, it's the gas oven first, even if I am a life-long Catholic. I'm scared and I'm tired and I need people in my life. What in God's name am I going to do? Where *are* my people?"

Where, indeed, are any and all of us? Where are our people? Mostly, I suppose, hiding from each other. Though I must admit that, these days, the barriers seem to be down just a little bit. A year ago, the two women I've quoted would not have been talking communes. And at a party I went to in New York, soon after my return, I was agreeably surprised to observe a certain subtle softening of the old, brittle ways, among people not formerly noted for softness. "Don't you notice," said a friend of mine, as we stood with drinks in our hands coping with the kiss-kiss and "darling" mannerisms of the literary cocktail party, "that people seem a little nicer to each other than they used to?" I said I guessed I didn't feel quite so alienated that evening as I usually do at such affairs; for example, a couple of extremely plastic people had just actually said to me things they seemed to feel; they had seemed genuinely to listen to what I said in reply. "That's what I mean," my friend said. "There just isn't quite as much nastiness tonight as there used to be. I think it's because of the so-called recession. Listen, half the people here are out of work, and the other half expect to be. There's nothing like trouble for making people behave decently to each other."

I suppose that trouble, however and whenever perceived, is a great unifier. We felt it, certainly, after the lewdness bust at Pyramid Lake. The disciples of Morty Wells feel it all the time. Perhaps, as the cosmic trumpets herald the final corruption of the city, the breakdown of systems, the ecological doomsday conditions of right now, humankind are rediscovering a taste for one another, a tolerance and a mutual dependency and, in some cases, a love. I don't count on it much to save us from ourselves, but it's better than nothing. Some of us, at any rate, may be able to do a little living before it's too late.

Very probably, most of us in this country have been waiting a long time—without much hope, admittedly—for permission to live our lives more freely and openly. At last, permission has been granted, by sheer force of numbers. There is no doubt that our children tutored us in this, that their wholesale departure from the standards of a mendacious society pointed out our way to us. Community, communality, cooperative, sharing—however you phrase it, these impulses away from a competitive, acquisitive system do not come to us courtesy of capitalism, except if viewed as a reaction against it. Our children, glutted to bursting on too much Crest toothpaste, have in overwhelming numbers rejected the product-oriented society as a sick, death-seeking system. Gradually, in part, perhaps, as a sympathetic response to the revulsion of youth, in part as a result of their own apprehension of their engorgement, many people—some older than I—are feeling a little bilious. I don't think there's any doubt that we are going to see more getting together in this country—communally, cooperatively, familially—than ever before. We are going to see many changes, and they will come fast, as everything does these days.

I don't think we need to fear that everybody is going to go off to mountaintops to eat peyote, or that everybody is going to smoke dope and sight the devil and freak; we don't even need to fear any decisive end to the nuclear family. Communality is not for everybody—and even for those disposed to it, it shapes up in many disparate ways. The value of the national mood for change lies in the possibility of creating more options and greater diversity of style; anything can happen, and probably will, and I'm sure that all of it will happen right away. It is, after all, not three years since I returned from Esalen on the West Coast with good news about encounter, and breaking through, and touching, and all that stuff. My New York friends and the readers of *Holiday* magazine scorned me for a shameless sybarite and lubricious loudmouth. Yet what do we find at the end of 1970? In the travel section of *The New York Times,* the Concord Hotel, that Catskills palace, advertising across entire pages: INFORMAL SINGLES ENCOUNTER GROUP WEEKENDS involving such confrontations as ASKING FOR LOVE—ACCEPTING AFFECTION—SAYING NO—ENJOYING PHYSICAL CLOSENESS—COPING WITH REJECTION. Not to mention potato latkes and indoor and outdoor pools. It seems that the message has so overshot the messenger as to have become a borscht belt entertainment.

Jean has suggested that I may be a little bitter about it, bypassed as guru of the world in favor of Jennie Grossinger. But it's not so; I'm not on a guru trip, if you believe the preceding contents. I do feel, however, that it won't take three years for the House of Plenty's weekend seminar in Basic Sexuality to reach the Catskills. Can't you see it now? Eight thousand hotel guests fervidly going after all those pleasure points, hotly grasping those plastic bottles, triumphantly achieving pushout orgasm for all. My God, the mountains will ring with the thunder of it. And maybe, come to think of it, I *am* a little bitter.

But never mind—I wish good luck to them, and all the orgasms they can manage in a society still largely reluctant to enjoy the pleasures of the body. If I had the dough I would open a Garden of Delights on the edge of every suburb in the country. Don't you fret, Mr. and Mrs. Grundy; I'm just about as poor as churchmice used to be, when there were still churchmice. Too bad, though; in a society where a genuinely inadequate book like *Everything You Always Wanted to Know About Sex But Were Afraid to Ask* can sell hundreds of thousands of copies, a Garden of Delights—perhaps with a House of Plenty Basic Sexuality seminar thrown in as a prerequisite—would be a godsend.

I should perhaps acknowledge here that the politics of sexual sharing in community is far from the only kind of sharing in this context that is important and pivotal; yet I have explored that subject almost to the exclusion of other equally pressing considerations. This is, in part, because of my belief that, short of the religious experience, there is nothing that Americans of my generation are more afraid of or handle more awkwardly than sex. In my age group, happy and companionable marriages are practically unknown; it is not coincidental that, specifically in these times of domestic misery, women's liberation and communal movements should have emerged in search of antidotes to the common poisons generated by conventional nuclear marriage. The male-female relationship is, generally, up for review, and about time, too. The sexual role-playing that we do within the marital contract results in the demeaning of the wife's human worth; she turns out to be physically isolated, sexually neglected, and intellectually deadened. The husband maintains, at the least, business and social contacts with the outside world, but the cost is that he is a visitor in his own house, a stranger to his children and inert matter to his wife. Intimacy with his wife is a matter not available even for discussion; there is no place where he feels more threatened and impotent than in his own bedroom, where candor about who he is and what he needs would destroy his myth of perfect machismo. He cannot be the Last Great Swordsman of the Pampas and a sentient human being at the same time; typically, the Swordsman wins, and everybody else loses. So even though sex is not the *only* thing to talk about with respect to communes, I don't apologize for talking about it.

Richard Fairfield, the editor of *The Modern Utopian,* has proposed the founding of a practice commune, for people who rather like the idea but want to experience the politics of sharing on a trial basis before committing themselves fully. I think that's not a bad idea, purely as a workout. Anybody energized by hopes of an expanded circle of caring fellowmen, where candor is the rule and free sexuality an open option, should pause for a good long while before leaping permanently into anything with anybody. Depending, to some extent, on the intensity and intimacy hoped for in a projected communal union, at least as much care and caution ought to be exercised in advance as would once have been expended on legal marriage. This is less the rule for young people, who appear to be able to handle all kinds of sharing with less anxiety than their elders, probably because they are less rigidly conditioned to possessions. Those of us who are older have become accustomed, often without realizing it, to concepts of privacy and personal ownership that make it always painful, sometimes impossible, to share. Our many decades of personal capitalism have, inevitably, cramped our capacity to loosen our grip on ourselves, on other people, and on things; after so many years of emotional negotiation—I do this for you and then you do that for me—many of us are ill equipped to share so much as the time of day. We tend to put an emotional price on everything we do, and if we are not paid off in the specie of our choosing, we feel cheated, hurt, ruined.

Consider the anxieties of the traditional husband whose wife has been radicalized by the arguments of women's lib. She suggests that their domestic arrangement is not fair, that she has personal and professional aims in life and needs equal time outside to take a shot at them, that house cleaning and child care and cookery are as much his business as hers, that this old business of pipe, slippers, and a nice martini by the hearthside has got to go. What does he do—leap up, tie on an apron, and get dinner? Don't you believe it. He may deck her. He may go out and get drunk. He will certainly rant and rave that he works hard all day, and he *deserves* certain rewards for it, namely an unchallenged authoritarian role to play at home. This is his quid pro quo and no wonder he feels threatened when his comfortable *role* is threatened. Why should he divvy up jobs and responsibilities in the home when his *deal* is so much better than hers? A businessman would have to be crazy to fall for an equal sharing of jobs and obligations—but life is not a business, as more and more couples are lately finding out. Keep in mind that in a commune or expanded family, traditional male privilege is under ultimate attack. Even in conventional arrangements— under Morty Wells, or at Hesperus—everybody does his share of work on the domestic front. With few exceptions, the men are not keeping exclusive access to the tractors, and the women are relinquishing the exclusive proprietorship of the pots.

Or consider another kind of drama expressive of communal sharing. Say that you stay up late in the communal kitchen, baking bread. When you come to the kitchen next morning, all the fresh loaves have been eaten. Will you be glad that people have enjoyed the food you prepared? Or will you resent the fact that you were *cheated* of your just rewards: adulation, gratitude, adoring looks, lip-smacking appreciation, personal control over your product? The question is whether you work for the joy of the work and the pleasure of providing food to all and sundry, or because you expect a big pay-off. Most of us make deals and call it living with others; in communes, this sort of negotiation has to be unlearned, and it's not easy, especially for those who are older and subject to ten thousand commercials in which mommy wins big plaudits for opening a certain kind of cereal box or unfreezing a certain kind of stringbean or infusing the family wash with a certain kind of groovy whitener. "It smells so fresh," trills daughter, sniffing eagerly at her own blouse, while mommy looks wise and fulfilled in the laundry. The young people in communes are not prey to any of that stuff.

Say that you have a healthy enthusiasm for freedom in sexual relationship; theoretically at least, you extend the same rights to your partner. But what if, in the commune, she exercises these rights? It's all out front; no lies, no evasions; you are not preserved in protective ignorance. At the very least you will, perhaps for the first time, experience a sense of personal loss which she, as a female in our kind of society, probably has experienced or at least fantasized many times. This may be deeply painful, however liberal your theories are. The conviction that you cannot own another person is of no great consolation when the fact that you do not own "your woman" is demonstrated to you by "your woman." This kind of thing has disrupted more than one theoretically liberal commune in the past, because what we say and think sometimes fails to be what we feel. After all, we cannot really know much about possessiveness, jealousy, and the rage of loss until we experience them. In brief, we can't entirely know how we will react in certain challenges until we are challenged; we can't perceive how thoroughly we exploit other human beings for purposes of our own security until they refuse to be exploited any more.

There is a vignette in Part One of this book that speaks directly to the subject of possessiveness. It's the one about Ruthie and the mayonnaise. A commune is not the place for private stashes of mayonnaise, caviar, or dope. A commune is not the place where a private attachment to a book or a chair or a piece of jewelry or, for that matter, a pair of coveralls, can take precedence over attachments to people. All parents learn that this is true, even in nuclear families. The beloved child breaks the treasured vase, loses the valued ring, destroys the irreplaceable list of names—and, not without some effort, those losses are borne. After all, the child is infinitely more precious than any mere *thing*. In a commune, the silliest and most feckless yo-yo on the premises (face it, you cannot love everybody equally, in or out of communes) is more precious than any treasures in your store. Before you undertake community in any form, you have to wonder whether any thing, or any concept of possession, comes before other people.

Authoritarian communes take a slightly different view. At Lyra, among Morty Wells's disciples, even at the House of Plenty, possessions are irrelevant but Hard Work is essential, and more important than individual preference. This greatly reduces the number of yo-yos in the first place; but it also greatly reduces the option of members to do as they please when communal needs make demands on their time.

There are other, outside losses too. Whether a commune goes the whole route into vivid parapsychological phenomena or not, there is, even at a relatively unterrifying level, a tremendous amount of energy generated by the fact that several people are gathered together in common cause. The self-generating excitement and élan of the group define a new and unfamiliar exclusivity, an us-ness from which old friends will necessarily be estranged. You do not wish to cut them off, they don't want to lose you—but so much good stuff is happening within the group that all exterior events lose glamor and even significance. Your collective chemistry gathers and demands focus; life outside blurs, and old friends don't seem anymore to know what's happening. How can they, if all that is happening happens only at your house? But that's the way it is—communes are a full-time, life commitment; they take most if not all the interest and energy you've got.

If a certain amount of dope is being smoked on a regular basis, the sense of exclusivity will certainly be heightened. Marijuana is a mild euphoric agent, productive of quiet good times and plenty of good cheer. It is also effective in softening the hard resistant edges of the psyche, in reducing the acuteness of critical judgment. Just as people who are stoned delight in verbal play, in word jokes and puns, they love to let their minds range widely and wildly, free of the parental voice, free of the censor. People become more credulous, more accepting, more charmed by one another, and before they know it they are conscious and willing members of a magic circle, and that circle is the effective center of the universe. Certainly it was the use of marijuana that spurred our little hour-and-a-half commune on its way; nothing would have happened quite so fast without it, though we undervalued its significance at the time.*

The fact is that, unless you are in a hell of a hurry, as I suppose we were in San Francisco, you don't need any kind of dope to have a commune, or to get stoned. You get high on each other. Morty Wells and his disciples take no drugs—they find it sufficient to give themselves wholly to Morty, and thereby reach and remain in a state of religious euphoria that drugs can only simulate. Basically, it is the shared human energy that binds, lifts, and delights. Intimately shared work and play are, when you catch yourself at it, thrilling, sometimes intoxicating. Particularly in our times, when freedom really is a condition of having nothing left to lose, of having cast off ownership of things and people, of having jettisoned the jealous vanities of the ego, the shock of having done that, of being totally at liberty, comes with a powerful, dizzying rush of elation. And since that condition is experienced by very few people, a sense of exclusivity, of remoteness from the mundane concerns of people outside, is inevitable.

To break sexual taboos in common is another act that identifies and binds the group—brave iconoclasts together. Even among the very young, sexual freedom is not taken lightly in groups; however, the young come much more readily to it than older people, people of my generation, say, who have no history of it even though they may, in theory at least, acknowledge a universal need for sexual variety. Preceded by a generation which practiced serial monogamy—first wife, second wife, third wife— so enthusiastically that today one American marriage in four

---

* This is, perhaps, the only way in which marijuana is similar to booze; a drunk always denies that he is drunk; somebody who is stoned always reports delightedly that he is, but he assures you that it doesn't make a bit of difference.

ends in divorce; and having found that practice destructive of all parties, especially of children, we tend to hope that variety can be achieved within the family context. Thus we get the expanded families proposed by Robert Rimmer—a bold step certainly, but confined in numbers and confirmed in strict familial configurations—a far cry from calling the world your bedroom, and everybody in it your roommate. The young people do not, on the whole, consider that free sexuality is a problem; it is an accepted way of life for most of a generation. And very possibly a young communard would consider my interest in the sexual arrangements of the commune to be irrelevant, uncool, and old-fashioned. But I come of a generation that worries about these things, the generation Robert Rimmer has been addressing.

At least two authoritarian communal leaders, met in the course of this work, take the position that free sexuality or any sort of sexual sharing is destructive of community. Jason Cripps and Stan Coleman, who are separated by generations in time and light-years in attitude, nevertheless hold this view in common. But Cripps's generation of communards—intellectual, idealistic, agrarian reformers of a very old, near-Fabian school— never seriously considered sexual sharing. Coleman, who has been through all that, confirms Cripps's suspicions. On the other hand, people at places like the House of Plenty would, of *their* experience, entirely disagree. While they find that members tend to group in units of two, it is a tenet of community health, in their view, that free sexuality always remain an available option.

Of course, the kids think the whole question of sex is so self-evident as to require no discussion—and it must be said, in all fairness to them, that they are much too busy doing it to sit down and make rules about it. The rest of us were never able to take the matter so naturally.

It is interesting to speculate on what the children of the communes will be. Most groups I visited are themselves quite young, so most of the children I saw were under the age of six. Every communal child I met looked healthy and happy and bright— secure in the love of many adults, often hugged and held, much cherished. If you believe the proponents of the cyclical theory of generations, all those kids will grow up to be John Birchers. At this point, we can't do more than wonder, but I like to think that a child's rejection of his parents' values is not inevitable—not, at least, if the parents believe what they say and practice what they preach. It is always hard to reject parents, if you love them at all, but hypocrisy doesn't build love. And this is the experience of so many contemporary communards with their parents as to appear to be a general rule. The children of the dream will face many problems as they grow up, but one of those problems is unlikely to be a pair of lying parents. The natural mother and father, removed from the hot-house pressures and secrets of the nuclear marriage and unaffected by mendaciousness and the drive for productivity, have no pretences to maintain. They live simply, doing their work in full view of the child, taking their simple pleasures in the same fashion, together with many other adults who take an equally lively interest in the child and his raising. Were the natural parents by some fluke inclined to do a number on the child, their fellow communards would spot it at once, and be quick to comment. The authoritarian family structure that has so faithfully served the industrial, product-oriented society will fade as more family units within the society become people-oriented and serve themselves. If a child can grow up free of the tyranny of expectations, cherished because he is himself rather than for what he represents or what he can do—if he is in no sense a product but just a free man—I suspect that he will be in a position to thank his parents for having been free enough, themselves, to let him be.

I persist in the belief that all men are natural allies, and that human beings must learn to live and love together, in any of the thousands of ways they may select, or perish from this planet like the biological pestilence we sometimes seem to be. I don't believe for a minute that simply coming together in community is sufficient to answer the profound questions that each of us harbors deep in his consciousness, about the meaning of life; but I do think that a life lived intimately with others can provide the catalyst to provoke the introspection necessary to embark on a search, perhaps a collective search, for answers to those root questions. Ultimately, of course, each of us must cultivate his own garden, and one's own garden is very small. It does not extend beyond the limits of one's own person. But until one's own garden is in order, there is no hope of pulling down the fences that separate your garden from those of your neighbors. If community is ever to mean anything, each of us involved in it must meet the ultimate test of friendship; and that test is, simultaneously, the test of love—to want, for the one you love, what *he* wants for himself, more than what you want for and/or with him. It is possible to live freely with others only if you live independently, without conditions, without bondage. To come together for an idea, even if it is a good idea, is not to come together at all. Put the people first; the idea, if any, will flow from the dynamics of what they want and do, singly and collectively. Life is a process of individual loss, and the process cannot be reversed by making rules and counting betrayals of them. As the House of Plenty holds, the only way to get is to give, and what must be given is absolute freedom, unconditionally, devoid of blackmail, emotional or sexual. A tall order, selflessness—and that is why, perhaps, there is so little community in our lives.

We try to bind others to us, of course, because we are afraid to be alone. Indisputably, however, we are born alone and die alone—and in between it behooves us to have such adventures as are sufficient to keep the mind and imagination lubricated. Real community, real human sharing, based on equality and in a context of complete personal freedom, beyond providing indispensable warmth and security, is the only life that provides the slimmest measure of self-respect or self-fulfillment, in an atmosphere which is, unavoidably, richly adventurous. Proximity, intimacy, and sharing may not of themselves touch on man's ultimate questions; but, like sand-lot baseball, high school football, all the play of children, community is probably a pretty good place to work out for the big leagues.

Naturally, when I say "community" I am not talking about the BPOE or the Volunteer Fire Department, though even those groups go some tiny part of the way toward alleviating human alienation. Let us not knock anything that helps. But I believe it is self-evident that there is more community, more sharing in the counterculture as a rather formless entity than there is in the isolated institutions that seek to bind elements of the established culture. It is not simply a question of long hair and peace symbols. It is an acceptance of basic shared humanity—amorphous at best, but a much more specific acknowledgment that we human beings are all in the same boat than anything that emanates from the institutions of present society. Take, for example, an incident that occurred, somewhat to our embarrassment, after Steve and I were back in the East, attacking a stack of books by Reich, Laing, Goodman, Perls, Brown, Jung—all those people we should have read before we left. Steve had been going through a lot of the pamphlets and magazines laid on us, in the course of our travels, by activists in the counter-culture, and one day, rather sheepishly, he came to me with a small pamphlet entitled "Directory for Personal Growth." He directed me to an interior page, where I read the following:

REPRESSIVE	CREATIVE
FRAGMENTED ROLES	INTEGRATED
A mask for every occasion; parent, lover, employee, boss, friend. People who slip from assigned or expected roles make other people uncomfortable and uptight. Rigid role definitions: girls don't climb trees, the boss doesn't sit on the floor in his office, a twenty-five-year-old shouldn't enjoy the company of a fifteen-year-old. Fragmented types have continuous "identity crises" (I don't know who I am) but continue to define people in terms of what they do (banker, lawyer) or what they are to others (housewife, boss) .	A mask only when necessary (in the presence of hostile or possibly hostile people such as cops) , but awareness that the mask is a con. A refusal to play "roles" or social games. Same behavior with a state senator as with a Bowery bum. People are defined by what they are, as people, right now.

"Okay," I said to Steve. "No need to cringe."
"Ah," he said. "But read on, read on."
So I read:

REPRESSIVE		CREATIVE
SADO-MASOCHISTIC	SEX	ANDROGYNOUS

Mrs. X hates her husband. She hates him because she hates being a woman because, the way sex roles are defined in our glorious Western civilization, a woman is a pretty lousy thing to have to be. If she is old-fashioned, she gets even with her husband by not wanting to fuck very much; if she is new-fashioned, she lets him know in a million little ways that he's not "man enough" to make her come. Mr. X isn't interested in sex, he's interested in rape, a device to prove to himself over and over again that he's really not a powerless little boy. In his fantasies (which scare the shit out of him) he's either an axe murderer or the axe murderer's victim. Mr. and Mrs. don't see their kids as people but as tools to be used in the continuing war against each other. Their kids will be fucked up.

When you see John and Mary coming down the street, it might take you a long time to figure out which is the boy, which the girl. They wear each other's clothes. When things have to get done, nobody gives a shit what is "woman's work" and what is "man's work." When they go to bed, John reacts to Mary as a person, not to stockings, high heels, or eye shadow. Mary doesn't have to be punished before she can come. When one of them wants to fuck somebody else, that's cool, and nobody gets uptight. Sometimes they take a friend to bed with them. Sometimes they take a whole horde of friends to bed. Nobody fucks because of an obligation to do so or to "prove something." As long as they don't manipulate or use people, other's sexual trips are regarded as pretty much unimportant: "Yeah, man, he's a drag queen. That's his thing." John and Mary aren't perfect; when John comes on with heavy masculine bullshit, Mary lets him have it right between the eyes. John and Mary see their children as people (not as property or game objects). Their kids will be even freer, less "masculine" or "feminine" and more "human" than they are.

And then I stopped reading, and toppled slowly out of my chair, pantomiming the performance of an adult male upon receipt of heart-stopping news. "Do you mean to tell me," I gasped, "do you mean to come to me *now* and tell me, that all our rigors of the summer, and all we hoped to tell in this goddam book, were already encapsuled and in print in this tiny, pestilential pamphlet?"

"Ah . . . yeah," said Steve.

This chastening incident was followed, soon after, by one much more startling. I offer it to you now only in confirmation of my claim that communality is popping up in unexpected places, but indirectly, at least, in support of the theory of androgyny. If you have already read more than you care to on this distressing subject, you have my leave to skip. Different strokes for different folks, of course; but this is *my* book.

You know, one place I never thought to look for communality or (as in this case) group marriage was among my own generation, particularly among the people I knew in college. We were popularly known as the Silent Generation—not because we were sulking, mind you, but mostly because we really didn't have anything to say. Our kind will be remembered, if at all, as the last generation of young Americans who did exactly as we were told and didn't even think about it much. Thinking, you may remember, particularly on the part of the young, was not at that time encouraged; we were, with such perfection as no plots could have achieved, the children of Eisenhower. And with such startling rare exceptions as Ralph Nader to prove the rule, most of us remain the children of Eisenhower to this day.

So I was very surprised, toward the end of the year, to have a call from an old college friend who knew I was writing this book and wanted to assure me that—whatever many of my contemporaries might say to or of me—I was not on a wrong track. My old friend Ted was excited and ecstatic; in fact, he sounded slightly drunk or slightly crazy. Ted had always been a rather cautious and conservative person—I could scarcely credit my ears when I heard his news. But after a visit to him and his wife, and the other couple involved, I wrote the following (I swear it) very true story.

TWO NICE COUPLES

Bob and Carol and Ted and Alice (obviously not their real names) are slowly exploring possibilities for a group marriage. In no particular do these two couples resemble the characters in a movie of the same name. There is nothing unusual or flamboyant about them; by no stretch of the term could they qualify as "swingers." They are, respectively, graduates of Harvard, Wellesley, Princeton, and Vassar; all four attended single-sex private schools before college. Each comes from a conservative New England family tradition—in each case, there is a history of rocklike stability through several generations, and high standards of thrift, education, and service which are reflected in the present life styles of the two marriages. Each couple has three children under ten years of age. Bob and Ted are modestly salaried executives ($15,000 to $20,000 range); Carol and Alice supplement family income by part-time work. They have all been friends since college years; now in their middle-thirties, they have met irregularly, with and without their children, for weekends and holidays, two or three times a year; because they live in two different cities in the northeastern United States, they have never lived as neighbors, and have often wished that they could.

All four have attached great importance to their occasional meetings. As Carol says, "Every time all four of us are together, Bob and I carry home so much more understanding of ourselves and our marriage; we always feel much richer for the experience." In their long friendship, the two couples have eliminated almost all evasion and indirection from their conversation; they relate, with remarkable candor, both individually and as two separate entities. In the last three years, both couples have been influenced in their thinking by the works of Robert Rimmer, B. F. Skinner, and others; also, at different times, they have attended encounter workshops for couples, and have taken seminars in sensitivity and massage. Two years ago they spent a long weekend together in an open-ended marathon encounter which brought them to a shared emotional peak, the intensity of which surprised everybody. Individual flaws, faults, guilts, and suppressed hostilities were exhaustively dealt with; everybody did more than his share of screaming, shouting, weeping, and recriminating. Also laughing, dancing, and embracing. Exposed and examined during this session—among many other characteristics of themselves as a group—was the high sexual quotient which obtained whenever the four were together. It was not, they confirmed, anybody's intent to switch partners—nothing so simple and (to them) tawdry as that. It was a feeling generated by all four together. None of them had any idea where to go from that admission, and all possibilities, from living together to the complete suppression of the feeling, were seriously considered.

On that occasion, no conclusions were drawn. During the following month, however, Ted devoted a great deal of free time to considerations of how the four could create one large family, and he finally produced the following document (which, by the way, he no longer endorses as a sensible plan):

HOW IT COULD WORK

Presumably, Bob and Carol should stay where they are. Bob's professional situation is more binding than mine; I am flexible. So it would seem easier for Alice and the children and me to move in your direction, rather than vice versa. And I still think we ought to explore a self-sustaining enterprise in which we can all share as equal partners. I am distressed because my work life and my family life are not really integrated. Bob feels something of the same. Could we not *all* do *everything*? An educational consultancy, perhaps? We are all qualified. With ongoing family responsibilities, we could not always all work in exactly equal roles, but according to ability, inclination, guided by what is fair, I think we could work out professional and domestic sharing that would be right and good for all of us. Surely the four of us would bring a lot of strength both to our enterprise and to our family, shared tasks lightening everybody's individual load.

Where? Bob and Carol have mentioned the necessity for discretion in the community, Bob having suggested a duplex arrangement. This would answer the constantly raised question of two women in one kitchen. But I think we should look more imaginatively into that question. We're really talking about four people in the kitchen, if, as I hope, we really mean to share, and to free Carol and Alice from the drudgery of certain traditional responsibilities. (I would like not to be a complacent incompetent about the house; I would like to learn to do things at something like Carol's and Alice's level of competence.) So we should consider the possibility of a large shared house—for purposes of discretion probably in the country, probably secluded. Even so, in course of time the unorthodox arrangement would be bound to become known, at least to a few friends and observers. We could lie, if questioned, or we could tell it straight. I would prefer it straight, but I don't think Robert Rimmer exaggerates possible community hostility. Still—the lure of a shared house, apart from its personal appeal, is economic. By sharing price and upkeep, we would save dough.

If we used the duplex arrangement, our lives would remain essentially separate. There would be institutional barriers to be crossed again and again. Maybe that's a good thing—I worry about privacy myself—but it's a pretty limiting concept. Still, two families with two living rooms for living, two dining rooms for dining, two bedrooms for whathaveyou—and whose bedroom is whose? It could *create* problems that might otherwise be demolished if confronted head on.

In a shared house—it would have to be large—there ought to be privacy for all, personal nooks inviolate except by invitation. Two and two, or single? I would hate to go to bed by myself after all these years of double-bedded comfort with Alice. Perhaps each of us should have a province of his own *and* a double bed in it.

Arrangements for the children could be made on an availability basis, plus their own inclination. We have noticed that the children have always loved to share, but just lately Emily [Ted and Alice's eldest child] is hankering seriously for her own room. A big, shared space for children is a happy thought in grown-up heads, but it might not suit the children. However, if sharing is the family rule, without exception, the children might go for it.

Certainly the children would enjoy the larger spectrum—always having playmates, always having friends. There would no doubt also be terrible scenes—*mine mine mine*. And some efforts at establishing a pecking order. Here the sharing will probably be limited—Alice is Emily's mother, Carol is Bonny's mother, and nothing is going to change those basic affiliations. But as Carol has often said, all our children are nice people. They are all delightful people to be with. Could we not be open and generous enough to spread the love pretty equally around the whole brood? I know I like the small Smiths, and I think the large Smiths like the small Joneses. We could work it out.

Benefits for the children seem enormous. Beyond the pleasure of having each other, they also have all of us, and we are sufficiently different to make quite an intriguing full-time show for them. If, as we hope, they see quite a lot of each of us, individually and together, it will be a happy experience for all. The premise is, of course, that when they see us we will be seeing them, and neither too tired nor too distracted by other chores to give them fullest attention. They deserve that, for God's sake, and so far as I know, none of us has ever been able to give it.

As for us—I hope that we can be freely together or freely apart, when and as we will, but always joined in the dedication to Ourselves as a unit. I think this can be achieved through honesty with each other. It ought to be absolute and it ought to start long before we ever try to get this thing off the ground. Hesitations, resistances, dislikes, and hates ought to be thoroughly discussed. In the doing, we might conclude that the whole idea is crazy, that we're actually unsuited to a larger family together, and drop the idea. I hope this won't happen, but the relationship must be open-ended and free to go where we all want it to go. And if that's in different directions, we have to accept that. But I reserve my conviction that we can work it out.

If we do it, we ought to have regular encounters, and a lot of them at first. Certainly we should meet in conscious honesty at least once a week. To talk out everything that may be standing in our way. I don't only think that's hard, I almost rue it. But I think it's absolutely necessary. I know I have ways of hiding myself from myself so as to behave negatively. I need to be told—and so does everybody else. The rule, of course, would be that we would tell each other What, in the trust of shared love. That way, each of us can handle it. We've already come so amazingly far on that course; we can go so much farther.

Politics of sexual sharing—I've been trying to avoid this issue. After all, we've never shared so far, and I'm nervous about exposing my own needs and fantasies here. I also don't know anything about procedural matters and we don't have much to go on; there aren't any how-to books on the subject. But I do think there's a danger in being too goddam solemn about our mutual sexuality. I feel that sex is a means to ecstatic physical pleasure and an expression of love. I have experienced it in both forms and I like it both ways, but prefer the two to be joined. When that happens, real communication takes place, and that makes me joyful. I have felt freer to search for intense physical pleasure apart from Alice rather than with her, because I am still shy with Alice, insanely, still afraid to express what I want. With others, whose approach to sexual experimentation seems closer to my own, I am more open and frank, and the physical rewards have been fantastic. There seems to be no limit to what you can feel if you're open to feeling. Yet with Alice I have experienced such intensities of emotion that I have wept for joy of that. I love sex—I think it is the most fun available to us, and I like fun without apology. I have sought it in both the physical and romantic spheres and I don't apologize for that either. I think that a whole lifetime of delightful entertainment is literally sitting in our laps and I don't want to ignore it, let it wither, unexperienced. Yet a set of unexamined taboos keeps most of us (including me) from being free and spontaneous in our sexuality. We somewhere learned to suppress the beast—at least, among people to whom we've been properly introduced, like our wives. This is silly. It's only in sex that the beast, so certainly a part of us, can freely roam and flourish, and bring us into full contact with our animal nature. We need that contact. If everyone had it, the drug industry would be out of business.

So okay, why not break through on this level with Alice, and do all my beast-contact at home? One, because Alice and I have yet to overcome this absurd politeness problem. And two, because even if there were no politeness problem, and we could fuck on a trampoline whenever we felt like it, there is still more. Everybody *knows* there is more—men and women—but few dare to do anything about it. And the heightened sexuality that we four have experienced over the past couple of years is proof of that. I am proposing, of course, that we abandon our timidity and press on toward what might be—a four-way sexual and emotional union that is open to growth in any and all directions. I think that basically we come in pairs—that is surely incontrovertible in nature—and I have no quarrel with that. I would like to explore that still more deeply, and at the same time pursue as much else as there can be among us, in a spirit of play, trust, and love. For I do love you all—each specially, jointly, in all the configurations we take together—and if I love Alice more than anybody else in the world, it must not be a love excluding all others, but a bond to build on.

I have talked about what *I* want—and that is important because you all accuse me of being the pushy one, the one in active search, and you have to know what I'm searching for before you can say whether we seek the same things. I would limit my search, if out-voted, for the advantages I think would exist even in a limited union —but I feel that our emotional union is already advanced beyond conventional limitations. Some stiff set of rules—"Thus far, no farther"—would be harmful to what is already possible.

We would be so dumb to reject such a tough, complicated, dangerous, *glittering* future. Surely as sentient and open human beings we should try. I do not believe in the literal perfectibility of man. I don't think we would turn into new and lovely beings without problems and hangups. But I do believe in the process of becoming, and feel we could go some long way along a new path (not so new, really, but bold). I don't say we should do this for some outside reasons; I don't want to prove anything in general about man, or verify a theory. I say we should do this because we're us, and we want to.

Ted signed this document, gave a copy to his wife, Alice, and sent the other in the mail to Bob and Carol. Bob and Carol did not write a reply, but called to arrange a subsequent meeting. A month later, they flew to Ted and Alice's town for a long week-end, and Ted and Alice had taken the trouble to arrange a weekend away for the children. The two couples had privacy and time to work out their various responses to Ted's tentative proposal, and at first it was very heavy going. Bob was in a wait-and-see mood, committing himself to nothing. Carol was highly wrought up, sensitive to the implicit group demand that she "come across," as she put it. She resented being pinned to any expectations, and made Ted pay for his provocative letter by precipitating two or three difficult social contretemps on the first evening. Yet, on the Saturday, it was Carol who suggested a massage session in the living room before a roaring fire, and it was the nakedness and sensuality of the massage that precipi-tated, finally a shared sexual experience among the four.

By report, it was a lovely time for everybody. All four re-mained at least slightly astonished at what they were doing. The common contemporary term for it was "orgy," but given them-selves, their past, and their intents, the word simply didn't suit. The culture had infused in them an almost automatic rejection of this behavior, but once they were in it, the culture seemed to be mistaken. Their long weekend was given over, night and day, to a sexual banquet, and yet they themselves were unchanged, still enjoying each other's company at the same level as before, still as conventional in their mutual esteem as ever. It seemed only that they had dropped a useless pretense, and were exploring their mutual sexuality in a way that they had, in the past, explored their mutual interest in skiing, in sailing, in books, in behavior. They were even surprised that, when it was over and Bob and Carol had to get a plane back to their home, there was no sense of degeneracy, or profligacy in their estimation of selves. They'd all had a delightful, remarkable, wonderful time, but were precisely the same people who had begun the weekend as old friends and sexual strangers. Nobody found any grounds for self-hatred; nobody was appalled. A barrier had been breached, no doubt about that. And they were all glad that that barrier had fallen.

At Monday lunch, Bob and Ted talked of how they felt. This remarkable event in their lives did not mean, for either of them, that they should implement the program sketched in Ted's letter. The extent of their joint feeling was that, most certainly, it would be nicer to be neighbors than to be so far apart. But they found themselves cherishing the experience in caution, unwilling, either of them, to say more than that there was much more to learn, and many miles to go, before they would be ready —if ever—to change the routines of their lives.

Subsequently, Carol wrote to Ted and Alice that she and Bob felt humanized in a new way, that she "could never see a roaring fire in the fireplace, or friends visiting, without seeing how naked and how dear they really were, and how much tender sharing might really be possible." Alice felt equally cosmic about the experience. "I'd be interested to do it again," she said, "if we all wanted to. It was like an affirmation of being a human being. That was what was so terribly exciting about it, that we were all God's creatures, all part of an elemental existence, and that things were simpler. You could just enjoy these good people who cared for each other. We weren't doing it in some idle, fanciful way—that might be all right for nineteen-year-olds, the whole, experimental, hippy thing. For us, this answered both the fanciful and the meaningful at once. It was special. It was impossible to tell whose hands and bodies were whose. That's what made it so special—human beings together. It was a web of human caring, of valuing the body as a body but also for soul, for who it was that occupied it. It was joyous on all fronts at once—which very few experiences are. It was probably the most fulfilling experience I've ever had. It was astonishing. Astonishing."

These are people who are not, nor have ever been (except perhaps for Ted) sexual adventurers. A long puritan past demands that everything they do be important, significant, and measurably valuable. And their excursion into sexual sharing has—in several important ways—changed their lives. The sexual relationship between Ted and Alice is now openly experimental; politeness and its barriers are a thing of the past. In his personal and business life, Bob is galvanized—the animal vitality he displayed to such enthusiastic applause in that extraordinary, temporary, suburban bagnio has been allowed full flow; he is a changed man. This has created problems for Carol. The quiet, conservative businessman she married is now behaving like a tiger; however urgently she had once complained that he should allow the tiger in himself to flourish, she now finds that real tigers make new and unexpected demands, and she is having to cope with those.

Bob and Carol and Ted and Alice do not know where they are going. Ted is embarrassed by the adolescent inadequacies of his provocative letter, which he feels is not a substantial plan for a group marriage. But nobody is sorry that the four of them have come this far. And in a very good spirit of open inquiry, they all confidently expect to go much farther.

I think what pleased me most about Bob and Carol and Ted and Alice is that all four of them were so excited, so turned on about their lives. That is a good thing to see in old friends, and we see it rarely. There is no question that, for them, a shared sexual adventure had been thrilling, and erotically very fulfilling. Yet their sexuality was only an extension of the concern and tenderness they felt for one another as fellow human beings —outside of roles, outside of labels, they celebrated an interrelatedness much more deeply felt than seen. All things that are so cannot necessarily be seen—the psychic phenomena shared by Steve and Nora and Oz and me; the "web of human caring" described by Alice; alike invisible, but no less real therefore.

Of course, Bob and Carol and Ted and Alice are much more conservative and cautious people than Steve and Nora and Oz and Dick. And when I am not riding the crest of the wave, when I am down in a valley, I incline strongly toward caution, re-trenchment, no-risk, low-profile living. But the pulse is the pulse, the wave always comes again—and then I find myself straining up and outward, confidently hoping to ride the crest as long as it lasts. Out of our experience this summer I bring no counsel, no advice; it was a crazy time in many ways and I do not pretend to understand it. Least of all would I advise a similar course to anyone else—but I am certainly not sorry for anything; not even my idiocy.

When I got back from the West, one of our first visitors to welcome me was an old friend of ours, a professional woman in her fifties and one of the most attractive women I know. She wanted to know what had happened in my travels, and I set out on a rather detailed, somewhat cautious account. She inter-rupted at a particularly crucial moment to say, "Why, Richard, Atcheson! Do you mean to say you did X and Y and Z? Don't you realize you're a middle-aged man?"

And I confessed that until that moment I truly had not thought so—I mean, I had never walked around town saying to myself, "Atcheson, you're a middle-aged man"—and it was clear that she was saying to me that I had not been acting my age. And I guess that's true, if you have some notion of exactly how people who are thirty-six are supposed to behave. But then I figure that Stan Coleman is not acting his age. And my friend Ted is not acting his age. Nor is Oz. Nor is Master Cyril. Nor is Toby Mann. Nor are a whole hell of a lot of people I met in my travels. And they're all having a *wonderful* time.

I was reminded of a conversation Steve and I often had—a rather circular one, I guess—toward the end of our travels. He called it my three-day self-pity riff, in which, he charged, I would get to feeling very morose and sorry for myself and say that I regretted all we had been through, and was down on communes forever. "After all," I'd say, "a child doesn't put his hand on a hot stove twice." And then Steve would crash back with a reminder that we had spent, unquestionably, the most vivid, exciting, eventful days of our lives in this pursuit, and he'd dare say that if any child could say that about putting his hand on a stove, he damn well would do it again.

And I would knuckle under to that, and admit at Steve's urging that the experience had certainly been the most educational and exciting of my life, in which at no moment could I take the trouble to read *Newsweek,* because my life was infinitely more eventful than what was in its pages. It was, I admitted in those conversations, like living on the edge—a very dangerous exercise, like on the edge of a sharp knife. But thrilling, incomparably rich in the sense of being alive.

As I think I mentioned before, neither of us has any regrets.

I don't much mind that some other people will think I have been a jerk. It would profit me not at all, I think, to live my life for some other people. I have to live it for myself, or I will not have a life at all; and I leave it to other people to make their own conclusions for themselves. If it suits them not to be present for what can be, no shouts and screams and exhortations from me will alter that. In which respect, I am reminded of something Charlotte Selver, a woman I much admire, has said in quite another context, about the childlike capacity to be present.

"The most thrilling experience I had as a child," she has recalled, "was when I went to the circus. The meadow where the circus was held belonged to my grandparents, and we children had a seat for all afternoon performances. At first the arena was empty. Suddenly the clown would rush in, stop abruptly, stand perplexed for a moment, look around and listen, then would call out, 'Are you all there?' and all of us children would shout back, 'Yes!' (In German it rhymes: *'Seid Ihr alle da?'* . . . *'Ja-a-a!'*) Each time we went to the circus, no matter how often, we waited for that great moment. Today it still comes back to me. Whatever we happen to do asks us, 'Are you all there?' How wonderful when we can shout back, 'Yes!' "

When *I* was a child, I had a recurrent dream in which many arms and hands reached out blindly through a dense fog in search of contact, but always missed each other by a fraction of an inch. It seems to me marvelous that, now I am grown, some of those arms are touching, some hands clasping. And I do not have to be asleep to see it.